Chinese Discourses
on the Peasant, 1900–1949

SUNY series in Chinese Philosophy and Culture
Roger T. Ames, editor

Chinese Discourses
on the Peasant, 1900–1949

Xiaorong Han

State University of New York Press

Published by
State University of New York Press, Albany

For information, contact State University of New York Press, Albany
www.sunypress.edu

Production by Michael Haggett
Marketing by Anne M. Valentine

Library of Congress Cataloging in Publication Data

Han, Xiaorong, 1963–
  Chinese discourses on the peasant, 1900–1949 / Xiaorong Han.
    p. cm. — (SUNY series in Chinese philosophy and culture)
  Includes bibliographical references and index.
  ISBN 978-0-7914-6319-2 (hc. alk. paper)—978-0-7914-6320-8 (pb. alk. paper)
  1. Peasantry—China. 2. Peasant uprisings—China. I. Title. II. Series

HD1537.C5H38 2005
305.5′633′095109041—dc22

                                                                      2004042992

10   9   8   7   6   5   4   3   2

To the memory of my late grandfather Han Pu'en and all the Chinese villagers who perished in the famine between 1959 and 1961

Contents

List of Tables

Acknowledgments

This book is a revised doctoral dissertation. For his advice and assistance during my dissertation research, I owe great thanks to my adviser Daniel Kwok. Frank Tang (Deng Yanchang), whom I was fortunate to meet through Walter Chang's kind introduction, generously offered many hours of academic advice and editorial assistance; Cho-yun Hsu discussed extensively with me about my research plan during and after his stay in Hawaii in spring 1996; The other members of my dissertation committee—Jerry Bentley, Ned Davis, Truong Buu Lam, Alvin So, and Kate Zhou, and three other members of the history department—Hugh Kang, Harry Lamley, and Robert McGlone—all helped in different ways; Wilma Wilkie and Melvin Yee of the Hamilton Library helped obtain many books and articles; David Kenley read and commented on the last chapter. They all have my profound gratitude. I also want to thank the history department of the University of Hawaii-Manoa for granting me the Hung Family Fellowship and the Hung family for their generous donation.

In transforming the dissertation into this book, I have benefited greatly from thoughtful comments of Roger Ames, Guo Qitao, and Steve Uhalley Jr. Steve Uhalley has been very supportive since the beginning. Chen Zhongping read chapter four and offered insightful remarks. Diane Moroff provided editorial assistance during the last phase of the revision. My editors at SUNY, Nancy Ellegate and Michael Haggett have been very patient and professional in guiding me through the revision and production process.

For their unfailing support, I would like to thank Wu Wenhua of Xiamen, Li Yifu of Beijing, and Dan Boylan and Ned Shultz of Hawaii. My wife Liu Meng and son Boning deserve all my gratitude for sharing weal and woe throughout the years.

1

Introduction

Rural China and the Chinese peasantry in the first half of the twentieth century have attracted much academic attention since the Communist takeover of Mainland China in 1949. There have been heated debates on such issues as the living standards of the peasantry, the performance of the rural economy, the influence of imperialism and capitalism on the rural economy, social stratification of the rural population, the relationship between the revolutionary intellectuals and the peasantry, and so on. In the process of such debates, various theories have been created or tested.

These are not the earliest debates about rural China and the Chinese peasantry of the revolutionary era. The earliest ones were conducted during the revolutionary years among the Chinese intellectuals themselves. One crucial difference between the theories offered by contemporary scholars and those created by the Chinese intellectuals during the revolutionary years is that the latter were much more politically motivated and politically oriented. The intellectuals' theoretical works formed an important part of their political agenda aimed at solving China's then acute national crisis. To the Chinese intellectuals of the revolutionary era, purely academic interests, if there were any, were subordinate to political needs. As leaders and direct participants of the peasant movements, the Chinese intellectuals in the revolutionary period were deeply concerned about rural China and the Chinese peasantry because they believed that villages and peasants were at the heart of their political programs for changing both rural China and China as a whole. In other words, if academic works on rural China and the Chinese peasantry created by outsiders were for understanding the ideas and actions of the peasants and intellectuals of the revolutionary era, the writings of Chinese intellectuals during the revolutionary period were produced to justify their own plans and actions.

This study intends to reveal Chinese intellectuals' perceptions of rural China, of the Chinese peasantry, and of the intellectuals' relationship with the peasantry during the first half of the twentieth century, as well as how such perceptions were politicized. It intends to be a history of theories rather than a theory of history or a history of movements. It covers not only the works of Communist intellectuals, but also those of the non-Communist and anti-Communist intellectuals. While both Communist and non-Communist intellectuals seemed to agree on one basic point—that is, in order to save and rebuild the Chinese nation, the peasants needed to be utilized and transformed—beyond that they had little in common, maintaining widely differing views about how to utilize and transform the peasants.

Analysis will begin with the encounters between the intellectuals and the peasants in modern China, which were made possible by the birth and growth of the Chinese intelligentsia and the rise and expansion of the Chinese national movement in the first few decades of the twentieth century. These encounters were inevitable, predetermined by the logic of a national movement. One outcome of such encounters was the images of the peasant created by the intellectuals. Ignorance, innocence, poverty, and powerfulness were the four characteristics of the peasantry that figured prominently in the works of all groups of intellectuals, yet different groups of intellectuals attached different importance to these characteristics and offered different interpretations of them, in order to suit and justify their own political programs. However, even though the images of the peasant created by the various intellectual groups differed, the general tendency was to transform the peasant from someone seen as useless, despicable, and negative to someone considered useful, admirable, and positive.

In addition to developing images of the peasant, the intellectuals also endeavored to discover and define the nature of Chinese rural society. This concern caused a protracted debate among different groups of intellectuals about the nature of Chinese society in general and Chinese rural society in particular. The debate formed part of their effort to justify their respective political strategies. The first stage of the debate, which occurred in the early 1920s between the early Chinese Marxists and the reform-minded intellectuals, was centered on whether China had already become a capitalist country and whether revolutionary socialism was applicable to China. The second stage of the debate took place in the Soviet Union during the First United Front of 1924 to 1927. The participants of the debate included Stalinists, Trotskyites, and supporters of the theory of the Asiatic Mode of Production. The debate was about whether China was a capitalist society or a semifeudal and semicolonial society and, in turn, what kind of revolution China should undergo. After the Northern Expedition, the Chinese intellectuals launched the third phase of the debate, which became more and more focused on rural China and continued until the Japanese invasion and after.

Their encounter with the peasant finally made the intellectuals ponder their relations with the peasant. Though the majority of intellectuals who went to the countryside were originally from rural areas, they found it hard to merge with the peasants after they returned, mainly because of their education and urban experience. As a result, intellectuals felt the need to search for suitable patterns for their relations with the peasants. Different intellectual groups developed different patterns relevant primarily to the specific aims and political programs of those groups. The creation of the peasant's images, the debate on the nature of rural society, and the search for a suitable pattern of intellectual–peasant relations are all related in one way or another to the political strategies of these intellectual groups. There are close connections between the intellectuals' perceptions of the Chinese peasantry and rural China and their perceptions of and plans for the Chinese nation.

The major source materials for this research are the works of the leading intellectuals who were involved in the various peasant movements of the revolutionary era. Since the early 1980s, the writings of many of these leading figures have been republished in the form of collected works. Important journals published during the revolutionary period by the various groups of intellectuals involved in the peasant movement have also been useful. A special note should be made about the use of literary and artistic works. John Fitzgerald, in his recent book *Awakening China*, allows that "fiction and fashion, architecture and autobiography, take their places alongside politics and history," and he asks his readers to "move about among writers, artists, philosophers, ethnographers, revolutionaries, and soldiers who have little in common apart from their appearance in the book itself."[1] The readers of this book are asked, on occasion, to do the same. The use of literary and artistic works in this research is justifiable for two main reasons. First, Chinese writers and artists of the revolutionary era belonged to different political groups; they were not just writers and artists as such, but were writers and artists with political affiliations and positions. Many writers and artists were direct participants in the peasant movements and their works were very much politicized. They endeavored to provide justifications for their political course through fiction or paintings, as the political leaders, theoreticians, and scholars at the time tried to do through their political and academic essays. The literary and artistic works I consulted can all be classified as social, or social science, novels and paintings. As Lee Ou-fan observes, this type of novel formed the major literary genre of the 1920s and 1930s, especially the 1930s.

Lee attributed the rise of this genre to China's national crises, which urged the writers to shift from the personal to the societal and to write about the cities and villages.[2]

The second justification for using literary and artistic works is that those I consulted are not used to reconstruct the social realities of revolutionary China, but to demonstrate what the writers and artists of that period believed the social reality to be like. In commenting on the writings about peasants in twentieth-century Chinese literature, Helen Siu remarks that "Most of these images of peasants should not be treated as 'real'...but they do reveal the author's sense of outrage toward an entire social order. The works illumine how the underlying political assumptions of these writers guided their efforts to participate in a new political culture, a significant historical narrative in its own right."[3] It is these underlying political assumptions rather than the social-economic reality that form the focus of this study. After all, this is a study of social-intellectual history rather than social-economic history.

The term "peasant" itself has caused much debate among Chinese intellectuals in revolutionary China as well as among contemporary scholars. The problem has been whether to translate the Chinese word *nongmin* into the English word peasant or farmer. The issue is keenly germane to the debate about the nature of Chinese rural society during the revolutionary era and the evaluation of the modernization process of China. Generally speaking, those intellectuals who believed that rural China had already entered the capitalist stage in the first half of the twentieth century would use the word farmer, while those who argued that rural China was still a feudal or semifeudal society in the revolutionary period preferred the word peasant. As Kathleen Hartford remarks, "The problem is that there is no term for cultivators enmeshed in the Chinese rural economy that does not imply some assumptions about their relationship with the economy; 'farmer' casts a vote for the maximizer-marketeers as much as 'peasant' does for the Chayanovians or others."[4] Scholars are still debating the issue today, and some have argued that the word "peasant" was invented by Chinese intellectuals for political purpose.[5] This book will use the word "peasant" to mean those freeholders, part-owners, tenants, and hired laborers who worked on the land for a living. This definition is neutral and close to the meaning of the Chinese word *nongmin*. It has a wider meaning than that provided by Eric Wolf, who viewed the peasant as someone standing midway between the primitive tribe and industrial society.[6] Wolf's definition is based on the assumption that the peasants lived and operated in a unique system of economy, which is defined by Karl Polanyi as the distributional mode of trade and elaborated by A. V. Chayanov as a system that aims at providing subsistence rather than maximizing profit.[7]

Determining which year the modern Chinese intelligentsia was born and which year they began to write about the peasantry is difficult. I have chosen the year 1900 as a starting point, not entirely arbitrarily, but because it was that year's Boxer Rebellion that first drew the attention of a number of modern Chinese intellectuals to the peasant rebels, which led to some initial writings about the Chinese peasantry. The intellectuals' interest in the peasantry continued to grow after the Boxer Rebellion. In 1902, the Mi family in Dingxian County of Hebei started their reform program aimed at modernizing traditional village life. Five years after the Boxer Rebellion, Dr. Sun Yat-sen proposed the equalizing of land ownership as one of the four cardinal objectives of his revolution. He also began to exploit the power of the secret societies, which were mainly composed of peasants. At the same time, the Chinese anarchist group in Tokyo led by Liu Shipei began to write about the peasantry. In the late 1910s, Yan Xishan began to implement his rural program in Shanxi, and Chen Jiongming started to reform rural education in Guangdong. Meanwhile, in Beijing, Professor Li Dazhao made the first call to students to go to the village. The early 1920s saw the emergence of the first modern peasant movements led by Shen Dingyi and Peng Pai. During the Northern Expedition of 1925 to 1927, more and more intellectuals returned or relocated to the village. After the end of the Northern Expedition in 1927, all kinds of peasant movements began to thrive in rural China. Though the focus of this study is on the 1920s and after, its coverage includes the first two decades of the twentieth century because encounters between intellectuals and peasants were already under way during that period.

2

The Intelligentsia, the Peasantry, and the Chinese Nation

THE RISE OF THE MODERN CHINESE INTELLIGENTSIA

In an article written shortly before his death in 1948, the famous Chinese writer Zhu Ziqing described how the May Fourth Movement, in which he was an active participant, divided the new educated Chinese from the old:

> The May Fourth Movement marks the beginning of a totally new era. Liberalism became firmly established upon the foundation of autonomous employment for intellectuals. Those of us in the world of education were pursuing independent careers, not serving as officials or waiting to become officials. As students, we were able to choose among many different careers, and were thus freed from having to make the one path of becoming a bureaucrat. Thus we became emancipated from the ruling elites. No longer acting as the effete nobles and bookworms of earlier times, we became members of a new intelligentsia.[1]

The difference between the old literati and the new intellectuals described by Zhu Ziqing was perhaps most clearly manifested in the change of attitude in the university professors and students around the May Fourth period. According to Zhang Guotao, a student of Beijing University at that time, before Cai Yuanpei took over the presidency of the university in late 1916, Beijing University was still a stronghold of the old-style literati, who likened themselves to the successful candidates of the imperial examinations of the previous period. After the arrival of Cai Yuanpei and the new professors he recruited, however, the atmosphere changed dramatically. The new

7

students began to believe that they should study for knowledge, for the purpose of application of knowledge, and for the sake of rescuing the nation, rather than in pursuit of positions as government officials.[2] Li Dazhao, one of the professors recruited by Cai Yuanpei, argued in 1919 that the traditional family system had destroyed many educated men because the relatives of a knowledgeable and wise man would always want him to become a "bureaucratized bandit," so that the rest of them could enjoy a life of luxury on the basis of his sacrifice. "If they treat you that way, then what they have for you is the utmost enmity, not a bit of love!"[3] Li warned the intellectuals.

Zhu Ziqing, Zhang Guotao, and Li Dazhao touched upon one of the most crucial features of the modern Chinese intelligentsia: their emotional and physical alienation from the bureaucratic system of the state. On the one hand, this feature differentiated the modern Chinese intelligentsia from the Chinese traditional literati and, on the other, made the modern Chinese intelligentsia comparable to the intelligentsia of Russia and some other East European countries. The traditional Chinese literati, while very much alienated from the peasant masses,[4] were closely tied up with the state. The modern Chinese intelligentsia, however, were alienated not only from the peasant masses, but also from the state.[5] In the words of another member of this group, these new intellectuals were considered "aliens" by their own people and were "exiled" by all other members of their own society.[6]

While both Zhu Ziqing and Zhang Guotao believed that alienation first took place during the period of the May Fourth Movement, many others have suggested that it actually occurred some time earlier. Lu Xun, for example, described four generations of Chinese intellectuals, although he argued that a true intelligentsia like that of Russia did not exist in China at his time.[7] According to Lu Xun, the first generation of modern Chinese intelligentsia is represented by people like Zhang Taiyan, who was once Lu Xun's mentor and whose generation matured around the turn of the century; the second generation by people like himself, who launched the New Culture Movement in the mid-1910s; the third generation by people like the Communist leader Qu Qiubai, who came of age during the May Fourth Movement; and the fourth generation by the young intellectuals who emerged during and after the Northern Expedition between 1925 and 1927.[8] This genealogy has been widely supported by Chinese intellectuals as well as foreign scholars. Zhou Enlai, for example, discussed the differences between the second and third generations in 1941 by comparing Lu Xun and Guo Muoruo. According to Zhou, Lu Xun lived in the transitional period between the Qing and the Republic. He was educated at a school set up by the Qing government and later became a teacher at a state school; he also served as a bureaucrat for the warlord government in Beijing. He did not break with the old tradition until the period of the New Culture Movement, when he was already middle-aged. Guo Muoruo, however, became a free and independent intellectual immediately after he left his home in Sichuan when he was only about twenty years old. He served neither the Qing dynasty nor the warlord government. He wholly belonged to the new era, that of the May Fourth Movement and the New Culture Movement.[9]

In America, Benjamin Schwartz supported Lu Xun's genealogy. His "three generations" basically conform to the first three of Lu Xun's four generations, and he noted these differences between those generations:

> There is the transitional generation of the late nineteenth and early twentieth century—men whose roots lie deep in the old culture, who have undergone the regimen of a traditional education, but who are already deeply shaken by the desperate plight of their state and society. They are already prepared to consider new institutions and foreign ideas, and yet are in many ways still part of the older literati. The crucial break comes with the student generation of the beginning of the twentieth century, many of whose members must be considered as the first truly "alienated" intellectuals of modern China. The third significant generation is the student generation of the May 4th period, men now in their fifties and sixties. It is in this generation that the basic intellectual tendencies of recent decades crystallize.[10]

Schwartz lists Kang Youwei, Liang Qichao, Yan Fu, and Zhang Taiyan as representatives of his first generation; his second generation probably includes men like Lu Xun, Li Dazhao, and Chen Duxiu; and his third generation is obviously the generation of Mao Zedong, Qu Qiubai, Guo Muoruo, and Zhou Enlai. Schwartz argues that the first generation was still not yet truly a modern intelligentsia because it was not yet alienated from the state. "It still yearns to be 'used,' and still hopes to save the state from ruin," he wrote, while the second generation was surely a modern intelligentsia because of "the emergence of the mystique of revolution" among them.[11] Schwartz's "three-generation" theory was adopted and elaborated by Yip Kache in his study of the Chinese student movement in the 1920s.[12]

The Chinese philosopher and historian Li Zehou and the American historian Vera Schwarcz also fully support Lu Xun's genealogy. Li pays special attention to the relations between the intellectuals and rural China. In his opinion, the first two generations described by Lu Xun and Schwartz still lived in a time when the "feudal" society had not fully disintegrated, therefore the intellectuals were either directly from the countryside or maintained wide connections with that society. The outstanding members of the third generation made the greatest contribution to the Chinese revolution, while typical petty bourgeois intellectuals who gathered in the cities and were disconnected from the countryside formed the fourth generation.[13] Schwarcz, on the other hand, focuses more on the differences among the first three generations of Chinese intellectuals in their political attitudes.[14]

The difference between the new independent intellectuals—university professors and journalists, for example, and the bureaucrats or the ruling elites described by Zhu Ziqing, Zhang Guotao, and others—roughly conforms to the difference between what Antonio Gramsci calls the organic intellectuals and traditional intellectuals. The former are the result of new social and economic development, while the latter emerged in response to previous economic and social development and continue to exist in the new environment as representatives of historical continuity.[15] In China, the new social-economic development that created the modern Chinese intelligentsia was largely the result of Sino-Western contact, which brought about the disintegration of Chinese traditional society, the establishment of new institutions, and the spread of new ideas. Of special importance to the rise of the modern Chinese intelligentsia were the abandonment of the imperial examination system, the creation of a modern educational system, the development of modern industry and commerce, the rise of the institutions associated with a civil society or a quasi civil society, and the emergence of modern professional groups affiliated with these institutions. The Chinese intelligentsia thus created, like the intelligentsias of many other third world countries, was neither the product of pure indigenous culture nor something wholly imported from the West, but the result of the mixture of Western culture and indigenous traditions.

THE RADICALIZATION AND EXPANSION OF THE CHINESE NATIONAL MOVEMENT

It is somewhat ironic that from the first day of its birth, the modern Chinese intelligentsia had to engage in a fierce and protracted fight against the very force that had helped create it: imperialism. One striking feature that links the modern Chinese intelligentsia to both nineteenth-century East European intelligentsias and the traditional Chinese literati is its strong sense of responsibility for the fate of the nation and its claim to national leadership. This is not surprising because, according to Aleksander Gella, national crisis is actually a precondition for the development of a true intelligentsia. "The intelligentsia stratum develops in a given nation when the educated members of the establishment are unable to face and solve the nation's growing problems. In response," he argues, "the intelligentsia appears as a new element of the social structure, as a stratum placed between the 'power establishment' on the one hand, and all other classes on the other."[16] The growth of the modern Chinese intelligentsia was accompanied by a process of the deepening of the Chinese national crisis and the radicalization of the Chinese national movement, which was in turn indicated by the radicalization of the Chinese intelligentsia itself. In fact, the most striking difference among the first three generations of modern Chinese intellectuals was the progressive increase of the degree of radicalization: on the whole, the second generation was more radical than the first, and the third more radical than the second.

The process of the radicalization of the Chinese national movement was understandably accompanied by a process of the expansion of the social base of that movement, since the shift from peaceful reform to violent revolution was at the same time also a shift from imposing change from above to fomenting change from below. From the late nineteenth century to the 1920s, the Chinese national movement underwent various stages of development: from an intellectuals' movement, to a student movement, to an urban mass movement, and finally, to a peasant movement. The first generation of modern Chinese intellectuals was mainly engaged in an intellectuals' movement. The 1898 Reform was carried out by a small group of scholars. The 1911 Revolution, although supported by some soldiers and secret societies, remained a revolution of a small group of revolutionary intellectuals without a truly mass base. The May Fourth Movement represented the turning point from the intellectuals' movement to the student movement. Although workers, merchants, and other strata of the urban society took part in the May Fourth Movement, it was not until the Beijing–Hankou Railway Workers Strike (1923), the Canton–Hong Kong Workers' Strike (1925), and the May Thirtieth Movement (1925) that the urban masses truly demonstrated their power and political consciousness. Then, in the latter phase of the Northern Expedition between 1925 and 1927, the peasants were drawn into the movement, thus realizing the ideal of incorporating all the major classes of China in a common effort to fight the imperialists and their Chinese followers.[17] Hence there were clearly two tendencies taking place simultaneously in the development of the Chinese national movement: the expansion of the social base of the national movement, not by one group replacing another, but by one group incorporating another; and the diffusion of the intellectuals, who were the leaders of the national movement throughout the period, into the lower strata of the society.

The course of the Chinese national movement indicates that the intellectuals' "discovery" of the peasants was not an accident, but something predetermined in the nature of a national movement. In fact, the "discovery of the people" or "to the people" is almost a universal phenomenon and has occurred in the modern national movements of many countries, including early modern European countries, nineteenth-century Russia, and many colonial countries during the early twentieth-century. Eric Wolf's survey of the twentieth- century peasant wars in six countries—Mexico, Russia, China, Vietnam, Algeria, and Cuba—indicates that the fusion between the intellectuals and the peasants occurred in all six cases.[18] Hans Kohn finds that "the growth of nationalism is the process of integration of the masses of the people into a common political form."[19] Tom Nairn observes, "The arrival of nationalism in a distinctively modern sense was tied to the political baptism of the lower classes. . . . Although sometimes hostile to democracy, nationalist movements have been invariably populist in outlook and sought to induct lower classes into political life."[20]

In his thorough work on early modern European popular culture, Peter Burke argues that European intellectuals went to the people, or peasants and craftsmen, in the early modern period, mainly because they were attracted by the culture of the "people."[21] In early twentieth-century China, though some were indeed attracted to the culture of the "people," most intellectuals went to the peasants for their potential political power.[22] In this the Chinese intellectuals were closer to their counterparts in nineteenth-century Russia and early twentieth-century colonial countries than to the early modern European intellectuals.

It is true in any national movement that the more acute the national crisis, the more urgent it is for the leaders of the movement to draw ever more compatriots into the movement, since the wider the social base of a national movement, the stronger its power and the better its chances of success. Joseph Stalin once remarked, "The strength of the national movement is determined by the degree to which the wide strata of the nation, the proletariat and peasantry, participate in it."[23] Peter Alter agrees. According to him, "the national movements in all countries earned a body of support whose social origin was more variegated than and went far beyond the narrow stratum of the educated middle classes."[24]

This process of the expansion of the national movement led by the intellectuals represents a great transformation of the traditional relationships between those in China who work with their brains and those who work with their hands. When the country was at peace and the traditional order prevailed, educated people normally belonged to the ruling class and the uneducated to the ruled. But now that the peace of the country had been lost and the traditional order had been destroyed, the educated class had to persuade the uneducated that they actually belonged to the same group and that they should unite to fight against their common enemies—in China, the foreigners and their Chinese followers. The one had the understanding but not the physical strength, the other had the physical strength but not the understanding; by uniting they could complement each other and form a powerful force.

THE INTELLECTUALS MEET THE PEASANTS

There has been much debate about whether the Taiping Rebellion was a modern peasant revolution or a traditional peasant rebellion. At the time of the rebellion, Karl Marx called it a revolution.[25] The Chinese Communist Li Dazhao defined it as "the first Chinese national revolutionary movement."[26] Both Sun Yat-sen and Mao Zedong emphasized the anti-Manchu and antiforeign spirit of the Taiping Rebellion and viewed its leader Hong Xiuquan as their predecessor. Moreover, according to Chinese Communist historians, who take the Opium War as the beginning of China's modern history, the Taiping Rebellion surely fell into the modern period. Further, Hong Xiuquan was undeniably somewhat influenced by Western culture, and his cousin Hong Rengan, who was one of the most important leaders during the latter phase of the rebellion, was even more familiar with Western culture and institutions than Hong Xiuquan. Despite all this, the leaders of the Taiping Rebellion shared more similarities with traditional peasant rebels than with modern revolutionary intellectuals: a modern Chinese intelligentsia did not exist at the time of the Taiping Rebellion.

Peasant rebellions led by traditional peasant leaders continued to break out even after the birth of the modern Chinese intelligentsia and the rise of the modern national movement led by the modern intellectuals. As foreign penetration became more frequent and more intense after the Opium War, the peasant rebellions turned more and more nationalistic, to the extent that one could conceivably talk about two separate national movements going on at the same time around the turn of the century: one carried out by the intellectuals, the other by the peasants. Since the visions of the two groups were quite different, the two movements went separate ways. This becomes apparent through a comparison of the 1898 Reform masterminded by the intellectuals and the Boxer Rebellion of 1900 led by the peasants. The purpose of both movements was to regain the strength and dignity of the Chinese nation, yet the intellectuals wanted to achieve that through a well-planned peaceful modernization program, while the peasants preferred violent and nativistic means. Moreover, the two groups, although sharing a common purpose, had no connections with each other. The peasants did not show any enthusiasm toward the reforms advocated by the intellectuals; in fact, they had reasons to abhor these reforms because it would be none other than the peasants who would have to pay their heavy costs. Likewise, the intellectuals stood by idly while the peasants shed their blood fighting the invading foreigners during the Boxer Rebellion. Mocking the ignorance and stupidity of the peasant rebels was not at all uncommon among the intellectuals at the time of the Boxer Rebellion.

However, despite this, compared with the period of the Taiping Rebellion, the period of the Boxer Rebellion did show some progress in the relations between the intellectuals and peasants. During the Taiping Rebellion, there simply were no independent intellectuals. During the Boxer Rebellion, however, while on the whole the intellectuals' comments on the Boxers were quite negative, a few intellectuals did perceive the latent power of the peasantry and foresaw it as an immense reservoir that could be tapped in future national movements. In this sense, the Boxer Rebellion represents the first contact enjoining the traditional Chinese peasant rebels and the modern Chinese revolutionary intellectuals. After that, attachment between the intellectuals and peasants increased, which finally led to the rise of a new type of peasant movement.

It was a small group of Chinese anarchists who first paid serious attention to the living conditions and the revolutionary potential of the peasants shortly after the Boxer Rebellion. They also strove to portray the peasants in a positive light. Meanwhile, Sun Yat-sen's collaboration with the secret societies, whose members were mostly peasants, escalated after the turn of the century. Sun Yat-sen's followers also infiltrated into regional peasant rebellions, such as the Bailang Rebellion in the 1910s in northern China, and they tried to use the peasants to carry out Sun Yat-sen's programs.[27] However, before the 1920s, there had not yet been any significant modern peasant movement in China: the anarchists' interest in the peasants was very short-lived; and Sun Yat-sen's involvement with the peasants was quite shallow. Although there have been arguments that the peasants were more than inert onlookers and were influenced by and even actively involved in the political activities during the 1911 Revolution, it is basically true that that revolution had little to do with the peasants. Many scholars, as well as Chinese revolutionaries, and especially the Communists, take that as the main reason for the failure of the 1911 Revolution. In fact, as Robert Marks argued, in places like Guangdong, it was in the interest of the reformist gentry that emerged from the 1911 Revolution to keep the countryside in peace and order. To avoid rural disturbance and rebellion, and to make sure that they could squeeze more from the peasants without causing upheaval, these new landlords did not hesitate to use the police and the courts to deal with any rebellious peasants.[28]

It was mainly through the efforts of the third generation of modern Chinese intellectuals—the generation of the May Fourth students, such as Peng Pai, Mao Zedong, Fang Zhimin, Li Lisan, Deng Zhongxia, Liu Shaoqi, and others—that the workers and peasants of China were drawn into the national movement, although some of the second generation of the Chinese intellectuals, such as Liu Shipei, Zhang Ji, Li Dazhao, Lu Xun, and Shen Dingyi had already begun to pay attention to the workers and peasants. Shen Dingyi was even directly involved in the peasant movement. Before the establishment of the First United Front in 1924, there had already been some successful cases of modern peasant movements, the most famous of which were the Yaqian peasant movement led by Shen Dingyi and the Haifeng peasant movement led by Peng Pai. After the creation of the United Front in 1924, especially after the May thirtieth Movement of 1925, the peasant movement became one of the hottest topics among the intellectuals. It became a cliche among the intellectuals at that time that "the national revolution is the peasant revolution" because the peasants formed the great majority of the population of China. More and more intellectuals, mostly Communists, went to the villages to help with the peasant movement. The peasants rose up everywhere, and those in southern China were especially rebellious and powerful. For a while, it seemed that Chinese intellectuals, especially the revolutionaries among them, had reached a consensus about the peasant movement. Because of that, it seemed that the social base of the national movement was appreciably extended and the national movement reached its greatest momentum.

Unfortunately, the moment the national movement reached its most critical period and achieved its widest social base was often also the moment of its split from one national movement into several national movements. The reason is that the more social classes a national movement incorporated, the greater the possibility for clashes of interests. In China, the incorporation of the peasantry into the national movement, while vastly increasing the social base and power of the movement, also posed new questions for the intellectual revolutionaries because the interests of the peasants were not completely compatible with the interests of some other classes also represented in the national movement. The radicalization of the national movement required the expansion of the movement to incorporate the peasantry, but the incorporation of the peasantry also further radicalized the national movement because, as William Hinton observes, the Chinese peasants, although generally subservient and passive, have been prone to radical actions once aroused.[29] In order to draw the peasants into the national movement, some concessions had to be made to them, which would inevitably damage the interests of the landholding classes in the national movement. As Barrington Moore observes, "The Kuomintang's partial success brought to the surface latent conflicts among the disparate elements that a program of nationalist unification had temporarily brought together."[30] Clashes thus ensued.

The split of the national movement often occurred first within the stratum of the intelligentsia, which would lead to the various groups of intellectuals striving to portray themselves as the true nationalists and all other groups as imposters. One explanation for this division within the intelligentsia is that since members of the modern Chinese intelligentsia had been exposed to different trends of Western thought, it was inevitable for them to embrace different Western ideals: democracy, socialism, or Communism.[31] In other words, the division within the Chinese intelligentsia was actually an extension of the division within Western intelligentsia. Another explanation views the division within the intelligentsia from the perspective of class struggle. The Communist intellectuals tended to believe that the split was actually inevitable. According to their class analysis, intellectuals do not form an independent and unified class. Instead, they are affiliated with different classes, depending on their positions and consciousness. Therefore, the "intelligentsia" was in fact formed by educated people representing the interests of different, sometimes antagonistic classes. This view is supported by Aleksander Gella, who maintains that the leaders of the intelligentsia never fought for their own group interest and never formulated an ideology of their own stratum, but, instead, produced leaders for all other class movements, parties, and ideologies.[32] This view is also partially endorsed by the Marxist scholars of the Soviet Union, who found in the developing countries of Asia and Africa three different groups within the so-called national intelligentsias. These three groups were, first, the elite group, which was closely related to the privileged class and was composed of important ideologues and publicists, the organizers of scientific research, the leading artists, and so on; second, the lower group, which was linked to the working class and the nonproletarian laborers and was formed by the so-called semiintelligentsia or proletarian intellectual workers, including lower-level administrators, village teachers, clerks, nurses, and all those involved in publicizing and disseminating rather than creating cultural traditions; and, third, the middle group, whose social status was between the previous two and was unusually influential. The third group included engineers, technicians, medical doctors, agronomists, middle-level government officials, functionaries of political parties, college professors, students, some army officers, and servicemen of religious groups. They were people like Sun Yat-sen, Mahatma Gandhi, Sukarno, Ang San, Francis Fanon, Kwame Nkrumah, Patrice Lumumba, and Gamel Abdel Nasser. The Soviet scholars believe that despite all these differences, the "national intelligentsias" still formed a more or less independent and unified social group because all these countries were still in transitional periods, hence social stratification in these countries was not yet very distinct, and the intelligentsia could still act like an intermediary class. It is only when society became more and more stratified that there would appear different classes of intelligentsia, such as bourgeois intelligentsia, gentry intelligentsia, and proletarian intelligentsia.[33]

In China, it seems that the unity of the intelligentsia had always been more apparent than real. Before the breakdown of the United Front in 1927, there had already been many controversies and fissures within the intelligentsia, which were manifested by debates on revolution or reform, issues or "isms," socialism and philosophies of life. The peasantry had never been a hot topic for debate before that point, partly because the peasantry had been basically outside of the national movement. By 1926 and 1927, however, the peasantry had become one of the most controversial issues within the national movement. The peasant question loomed so large in the minds of the revolutionaries that the attitude toward the peasant movement was regarded by many as the sole criterion for differentiating the leftists from the rightists, or revolutionary intellectuals from counterrevolutionary intellectuals.[34] After a short period of passion between the intellectuals and peasants, during which the rightists, leftists, and the middle elements all pledged their loyalty to the peasants, the intellectuals realized that they actually had quite different ideas about the peasant question. The heart of the issue was not whether the peasants should be incorporated into the national movement, or whether a way should be found to solve the peasant question, but how. There were drastic differences between the various groups of intellectuals in their national programs, their views of the peasants, and their solutions to the peasant question. It is these differences that the following chapters will address.

3

The Image of the Peasant

From the beginning of the twentieth century, Chinese intellectuals began to pay more and more attention to the peasants. This was a result of their increasing awareness of the peasantry's importance to the rebuilding of the Chinese nation, and their ensuing strong desire to incorporate the peasants into their nation-rescuing programs. Such interest in the peasantry grew so fast that in the 1920s and after, there was a tremendous outpouring of writing about them. Peasants became the subjects of political and academic works, heroes of novels, plays, and poems, and figures of paintings. Never before in Chinese history had the educated class been so enchanted with those who had toiled in the fields for untold generations.

Various images of the peasant began to emerge from the multitude of works. The images were diverse and at times the prototypical image created by one individual or group would be transformed. However, while there were such differences, some constant and common elements can be discerned in the images of the peasant created by various individuals and groups throughout that period. This chapter will describe and interpret such common elements as well as the differences in the images of the peasant and attempt to demonstrate the general transformational tendencies of the peasant image through time.

THE IGNORANT

On May 17, 1903, indignant at Russia's new demand for unequal rights in Northeast China, the young radical Chen Duxiu called for a mass assembly to discuss the matter in Anqing, capital of Anhui Province. To his dismay, only about 200 people showed up. His speech at the meeting denounced those who were apathetic to national affairs. He targeted four types of people, defining the first three as the traitorous ruling court, the shortsighted gentry and merchants, and the literati who only pretended to be open-minded. "The fourth type," he said, "are the wild stupid people who are ignorant of both the unequal treaty that is being imposed on China by Russia and the dismemberment of China that is going on. How could such people develop patriotism? Peasants in villages all over China belong to this type."[1] Obviously, in Chen Duxiu's mind, the other three groups of people knew the situation well but did not care, whereas the peasants did not care because they knew nothing of the nation's perilous condition.

Nine years later, at a meeting held in Hangzhou of Zhejiang, Sun Yat-sen called on every Chinese person to stand up and assume the duties of a citizen. He then castigated "the wild peasants who had no understanding of the true meaning [of the revolution]" because they believed that after the revolution the only thing left was freedom with no need to pay taxes either in cash or grain.[2]

Both Chen Duxiu, later a co-founder of the Chinese Communist Party, and Sun Yat-sen, founder of the Chinese Nationalist Party, were critical of the peasants for their ignorance and indifference. Their portrayal of the Chinese peasant was not very different from what Karl Marx wrote about the peasant of India, who cared about nothing but some miserable patch of land and who lived an "undignified, stagnatory, and vegetative life."[3] It is interesting to note that at one point Chen Duxiu and Sun Yat-sen shared the same view about the Boxer Rebellion. Chen attributed the humiliation China suffered after the rebellion to the Boxers in a 1918 article about the demolition in Beijing of the Von Ketteler Monument, built immediately after the Boxer Rebellion to commemorate the German minister killed by the Boxers. Patriotic Chinese viewed this monument as an extremely humiliating symbol. "How shameful China is! What a curse the Boxers are!" Chen wrote. He warned that the Boxer Rebellion might happen again because the superstition and ignorance behind it still prevailed in China.[4] Sun Yat-sen, although praising the Boxers for their spirit of resistance, called the Boxers "bandits," as many educated Chinese of his generation did,[5] and described the Boxer Rebellion as "a widely arrogant and presumptuous action."[6]

Intellectuals were critical of the peasants for whatever it was that they did. The peasants were blamed for not acting and not assuming their duties as citizens, such as participating in the anti-imperialist mass assembly and paying taxes to the republic. However, if they rose and acted to show their concern for the nation, as the Boxers did, they were condemned as well. In the minds of the intellectuals, ignorance explained both the indifference and unwanted actions of the peasants. Ignorance was believed to be the root cause of other weaknesses; for example, it was thought to be one of the most important factors contributing to the peasants' superstition and subservience, as well as to their lack of the spirit of cooperation.

For some time, this image of the ignorant, unruly, indifferent, and superstitious peasant was to persist in the minds of Chinese intellectuals. Even those who truly sympathized with the peasants would not argue against it. For example, almost all educated Chinese who supported the Boxers during the Boxer Rebellion admitted that the Boxers were indeed ignorant. Chen Shaobai, the editor-in-chief of the *Zhongguo ribao*, the mouthpiece of the Xingzhonghui, although refusing to call the Boxers "bandits," nevertheless believed that they had no political consciousness.[7] The editor of the *Guominbao*, a newspaper run by Chinese students in Japan, held that the Boxer Rebellion reflected the xenophobia of the ignorant and stubborn people of the interior areas, adding as a side note that such xenophobia could be transformed into a moving force for independence.[8] An essay in the *Zhongguo xunbao*, a supplement to the *Zhongguo ribao,* stated that the Boxer Rebellion demonstrated that the Chinese people had spirit, but no wisdom.[9] Even the author of the most famous editorial defending the Boxers called the Boxers "ignorant people" with a "low level of thinking."[10] These Boxer sympathizers agreed that the Boxers were brave and righteous, but also ignorant and superstitious.[11]

In the early 1920s, both Chen Duxiu and Sun Yat-sen still adhered to their earlier evaluations of the peasants. In 1923, Chen Duxiu, who was general secretary of the Communist Party, acquiesced to help expand the influence of the Nationalist Party among the workers and peasants, especially the latter. At the same time, however, he was troubled by the fact that the Chinese peasants, although large in number, would not be able to contribute much to the revolution because they were too backward to be mobilized.[12] In 1924, Sun Yat-sen still held to the notion that the peasants were generally indifferent to national affairs because of their lack of knowledge.[13]

This view was to a large degree shared by the leftist Li Dazhao, co-founder of the Chinese Communist Party. In a 1917 article calling the young intellectuals to go to the villages, Li described the countryside as a dark and uneducated world and the peasants as ignorant people.[14] In a short article written two years later, he compared rural life in America with that in China, and found that "there are three things that are indispensable to American rural life: the library, the post office and the church. There are also three things that are indispensable to the rural life in my native place: the old-style school, the opium house, and the temple."[15] Zhang Guotao, Li Dazhao's disciple in Beijing University, had similar views about the ignorance of the peasant. He declared in 1922 that the peasants had no interest in politics, and that all they wanted was a true Son of Heaven to rule them and a peaceful, bumper year.[16]

Even the famous peasant movement pioneer Peng Pai agreed that the peasant was ignorant. When Peng started his work among the peasants in his native Haifeng County of Guangdong, his close friends told him that peasants were incapable of organization and ignorant, and that to conduct propaganda work among them would be a waste of time.[17] Although Peng Pai ignored their objections, he agreed with them to some extent that the peasants were indeed ignorant. In 1923, Peng Pai wrote that "we common people, especially the peasants in the village," had to be blamed for China's miserable position for "our lack of self-consciousness and laissez-faire attitude."[18] After he had successfully organized peasant associations in several counties in Guangdong, he proudly told his friend that he had gradually become "a member of the ignorant class."[19]

Yan Yangchu, a Western-trained liberal who became a champion of the mass education movement in China, offered his personal experiences to illustrate the ignorance of the peasants. Yan worked among the Chinese Labor Corps in France for the YMCA in 1918 and was shocked by the behavior of his compatriots, most of whom were peasants from northern China.[20] As he later recalled, ninety percent of the 200,000 Chinese people working in France were illiterate. "They did many things there that harmed our national prestige. They ate peanuts in the train and threw the shells on the floor; they spat in the train; it is the French custom that man and woman walk hand in hand, our people would point at the couple and laugh at them....It was in France that I got to know the real China," he said.[21] Nearly a decade later, he still held the belief that the peasants were truly ignorant. "The brains of the peasants in the villages are just like a piece of blank paper. You [the intellectual] may paint it red, but you may also paint it black," he argued.[22] Yan's perception of the peasant might have been largely shared by his followers in the Mass Education Movement. One article in the *Nongmin* published by Yan's mass education association claimed that the peasants had strong points, as well as three distinct weak points: they were ignorant, conservative, and superstitious.[23] In the 1930s, Yan's view about the ignorance of the peasant was also shared by Liang Shuming, Yan's famous colleague in the rural reconstruction movement. Liang repeatedly argued that the peasants were simpleminded. They could intuitively feel their own sufferings, but they were unable to understand the causes of their problems, not to mention find their solutions. Only intellectuals could help them with that.[24] In fact, during the 1920s and 1930s and later, the intellectuals' emphasis on mass education was mainly based on the idea that the peasants were ignorant.

Lu Xun argued in 1908 that the gentry scholars accused the common people of being superstitious in order to ascribe this as the cause of China's humiliation. To Lu Xun, this was a pretext for the scholars for shirking their own responsibility.[25] However, it was none other than Lun Xun who created the most vivid literary images of the ignorant, indifferent, and superstitious peasants about a decade later. The gullible Sister Xianglin in "New Year's Sacrifice" (1924), who was in constant fear of being cut into two pieces by her two dead husbands in her afterlife; the comical, ignorant, and tragic Ah Q who lived on psychological victories and forgetfulness; the callous and indifferent people who watched Ah Q's execution as no more than a game in "The True Story of Ah Q" (1921–1922)—all are peasant creations of Lu Xun. As late as 1923, Lu Xun still called the Boxers "boxer bandits," and denounced the masses for their indifference.[26] From 1923 to 1925, he continually mocked the Boxers for their belief that canned meat was made of Chinese children killed by "foreign devils,"[27] and the belief that if their martial arts had reached a certain level of perfection, their bodies would be impervious to the bullets and shells of the foreigners.[28] He also blamed the villagers around Hangzhou for destroying the historical Leifeng Pagoda out of superstitious beliefs.[29]

Like the friendly critics of the Boxers at the time of the Boxer Rebellion, the great majority of the intellectuals who talked and wrote about the ignorance of the peasant in the late 1910s, 1920s, and after, took it as the reason for their sympathy rather than contempt toward the peasant, and they usually faulted society or others rather than the peasants themselves for such ignorance. Yan Yangchu, for example, argued repeatedly that the peasants were not innately stupid, but had been deprived of opportunities. Li Dazhao and Peng Pai also attributed the ignorance of the peasants to social problems and urged the intellectuals to go to the village to help them.[30] Immediately after Shen Dingyi helped the peasants in his native village form peasant associations and carry out a rent reduction campaign in 1921, the local elite in Zhejiang began to denounce the peasant associations and called the peasants ignorant country bumpkins, attributing their "ugly crimes" to their ignorance. Shen Dingyi commented in a 1922 newspaper article, "About this word 'ignorant'—I don't know how many wrongs coming out of the blood, sweat, bitterness, and tears of life are contained in this word."[31] Shen did not explicitly deny that the peasants were ignorant, but he certainly believed that the peasants themselves should not be blamed for their lack of knowledge and understanding and that people should feel sorry about this state rather than resort to condemnation. In fact, three years earlier, Shen had already suggested education as a means to overcome the ignorance and narrow-mindedness of the peasants so that "the wasteland and mineral resources in their minds" could be exploited to benefit the nation.[32] Like Shen Dingyi, Lu Xun was also a sympathizer with the peasants. It is widely believed that Lu Xun had deep but critical sympathy for Ah Q.[33] His sympathy for Run Tu

("Hometown"), Ai Gu ("Divorce"), and Sister Xianglin is even more obvious. In Lu Xun's own words, he wrote these stories to describe "the corruption of the upper class and the sufferings of the lower class."[34] It is even suggested that Lu Xun's thought reflected the demands and desires of the peasants and that he saw society through the eyes of the peasants.[35]

THE INNOCENT

The peasant sympathizers also did not believe that all aspects of peasant life and peasant character were negative. True, the peasants were ignorant, the reasoning went, but they were also innocent, uncorrupt, uncontaminated, pristine, and pure; and, it was often implied, they were innocent and pristine *because* they were ignorant and unsophisticated. Frequent comparisons were made between the peasants and city folks, and between the lower class and upper class by the peasant sympathizers, to show that actually the peasants, not the city folks or the upper-class people, were better human beings. Sometimes this made the sympathizers' views appear somewhat self-contradictory. For example, to prove that it was rewarding for young intellectuals to go to the village, in a 1919 article Li Dazhao offered the following sharp and vivid contrast between life in the city and that in the village, which seemed to counter his criticism of the darkness of the countryside and the weak points of the peasant: "There is much evil in the city and much happiness in the village; urban life is mainly dark, rural life is mainly bright; urban life is almost the life of the ghost, rural activities are all activities for human beings; the air in the city is filthy, and the air in the village is clean."[36] Li's remarks were echoed by Yan Yangchu fifteen years later, who argued that "the bad and weak points of the Chinese people are almost all carried by the 'city folks,' or at least we can say the city folks have more serious bad points than the 'country bumpkins.'" He reasoned, "In the villages, you can still see some survivals of the virtues of the Chinese people permeating the life of the country bumpkins, which are very difficult to find in the cities."[37]

Liang Shuming and many others agreed with Li Dazhao and Yan Yangchu. Liang argued in 1928 that the spirit of Chinese culture no longer existed in the cities because the city people had been strongly influenced by foreign cultures and the good traditional customs could only be found in the villages.[38] Peng Pai praised the peasants for their spirit of honesty and righteousness and their loyalty to their own class.[39] Deng Zhongxia, leader of the Chinese Communist labor movement, commented in 1923 that even imperial rulers such as Zeng Guofan and warlords such as Feng Yuxiang were aware that the peasants had pure hearts, honest character, were brave and hardworking, and much more loyal than the unemployed hooligans of the port cities.[40] An author of the *Nongmin* compared the peasants with the urban businessmen and found the peasants hardworking, simple, and honest, while most businessmen liked the comfortable and luxurious life and were excessively cunning.[41] The leaders and participants of the folk literature movement in the late 1910s and early 1920s believed that the folk literature of the peasants was fresh, simple, natural, and sincere, while the elite literature was exactly the opposite. Many of them argued that the city dwellers were so polluted and hypocritical that they not only lacked the ability to create folk literature, but also lacked the ability to appreciate the folk literature created by the peasants. Some of them, notably Gu Jiegang, tended to believe that folk culture represented the genuine pristine Chinese heritage. In Gu's view, the common people were innocent and sincere by nature.[42] Even sympathetic foreigners found that the Chinese peasants were more attractive than the urban dwellers because of their native purity.[43]

Underlying all these discourses is the assumption that the peasants are innocent and pristine because they are primitive, natural, simple, and hardworking, and because their lives had not been penetrated and contaminated by modern foreign civilization. Innocence, simplicity, and honesty are also the attractive elements Lu Xun found in the character of the peasant. Critics have suggested that among the peasant characters Lu Xun created in his stories, Run Tu ("Hometown") represents tenacity, Ai Gu ("Divorce") is unbending, and Sister Xianglin ("New Year's Sacrifice") displays the peasant's ability to endure humiliation. Furthermore, these critics note, it is precisely on these qualities that Lu Xun laid his hopes for the future.[44] Therefore, Lu Xun's characters are usually formed of mixed and contradictory features: they are uncultured, superstitious, and subservient, but they are also hardworking, honest, simple, and innocent.

The peasant characters created by other writers engaged in the so-called regional literature movement are even more innocent than those created by Lu Xun. In the 1920s and 1930s, writers such as Feng Wenbing (Fei Ming), Shen Congwen, Yang Zhengsheng, and Li Jingming devoted themselves wholly to the creation of the image of poetic rural life and the innocent peasant. Fei Ming's stories are filled with moving and innocent village people. In reviewing one of his stories, one of his contemporaries remarks that "What he writes about are ideal characters and an ideal realm. The writer closes his eyes to reality and creates an illusory Utopia."[45] In "Snow" (1927), "Aboard and on Shore" (1927), "Husband," and other stories and essays, Shen Congwen, who claimed to belong to the "country folk," portrays the corrupt urban life in contrast to the simple and pristine rural life; he also attempts to expose the hypocrisy of the urban upper class in the mirror of the actions of the innocent rural lower class. In "Aboard and on Shore," an old Hunanese woman selling pears and peanuts by the river, who would never cheat her customers, reminds the writer of the hypocritical "philanthropists" in the cities who smuggled rice and kept as their private property clothes that had been donated for the poor. A Chinese scholar researching Shen Congwen finds that Shen possessed a villager's sense of moral superiority over the city folks,[46] while an American authority on Shen Congwen remarks that "in urban China, Shen Congwen had a negative mirror image of the life he would celebrate in his regional literature."[47] Shen blamed the urban centers for destroying the pristine world of the rural frontier. This theme also appears in Ye Shengtao's 1921 story "The Sorrowful Heavy Burden," in which the writer is saddened to see women from the villages leave their hard but upright lifestyle for the dissolute lifestyle of the cities.[48] Similarly, there is Lao She's story about Camel Xiangzi, a rickshaw driver who was born and raised as a simple, good-natured village boy, but was later gradually destroyed by the depraved and inhuman urban life of Beijing.[49]

The emergence of this group of writers who devoted themselves to portraying the innocence and purity of the peasants led Pearl S. Buck to describe, in 1935, a transition in themes in China's literature in the 1920s and 1930s:

> The subject of modern Chinese novels of a few years ago, for instance, dealt chiefly with modern love situations, with semi-foreign liaisons, with rebellions against home and parents, and the whole tone was somewhat sickly and certainly totally unrooted in the country. There is still more than enough of this in both art and literature, but health is beginning to creep in, the health of life from plain people living plain and sturdy lives upon their earth. The young intellectuals are beginning to discover their own masses. They are beginning to find that life in the countryside, in small towns and villages is the real and native life of China, fortunately still fairly untouched with the mixed modernism which has made their own lives unhealthy.[50]

This new trend was reflected not only in literature, but also in art. Hence, "One sometimes sees these days a peasant woman upon a canvas instead of a bird upon a bamboo twig, and the straining figure of a man pushing a wheelbarrow instead of goldfish flashing in a lotus pool." Buck attributed this new trend to Western influence, namely, the Western interest in all proletarian movements, particularly the influence of Communism.[51]

This image of the innocent and pristine peasant fit in perfectly with the slogan of "the sanctity of labor" [*laogong shensheng*], which was then very popular in China and the world, especially among left-wing intellectuals. One researcher has argued that before the May Fourth Movement, when Li Dazhao talked about the laborers' class [*lao gong jie ji*], he meant both the factory workers and the peasants, but most of the time he meant the peasants only, because at that time there were not many factory workers in China.[52] This holds true for many other intellectuals who talked about the laborers' class around the May Fourth period.[53] The word "*laonong*," which literally means the working peasant, was created, and it was interchangeable with the word "*laogong*," which means working worker. The slogan of "noble laborer" argues that those who work with their hands are more honorable than those who work with their brains, and those who work with their brains are in turn nobler than those who do not work at all but reap without sowing. Firmly believing in that slogan, Li Dazhao made repeated calls to young intellectuals, not only to go to the village, but also to till the land personally.[54] Li declared that "anyone who does not do any labor has no right to talk about the 'noble laborer'"[55] and that "whoever labors is noble and sacred, hence better than you gentry, sages, and politicians who are vampires disengaged from human affairs."[56] Li also told an interesting story about an artist in Beijing, who would stand on the city wall every morning to observe what was happening around him, but would stay home and refuse to go out in the afternoon. When asked to explain, the artist said that in the morning, he could see the laborers who carried vegetables to the city, school students with their school bags on their way to schools, and the sanitation workers with their night-soil carts: all these people were laborers, illustrating the beauty of human life through their work. They were innocent and pure people. By midday, those "devils and robbers" who only consumed but never produced would appear one after another. Their noisy cars and ferocious guards would turn the world of human beings into a world of ghosts. Therefore, to the artist, midday was the dividing line between the world of brightness and the world of darkness, and between purity and immorality.[57]

The catchphrase of the "noble laborer" was so influential at that time that even the warlords Chen Jiongming and Wu Peifu declared at one time that they would support and protect the laborers. Although not many students went to work with the peasants, as Li Dazhao had wished, many short-lived work–study mutual-aid groups were formed by the students in the cities, with the purpose of bridging the gap between laborers and intellectuals. If, since Confucius's time, those who worked with their brawn had always been ruled and looked down upon by those who worked with their brains, now the order seemed to be reversed in the minds of some intellectuals. The peasants might be ignorant, but they were also innocent and noble, and the intellectuals had something to learn from them.

THE POOR

Besides their ignorance and innocence, the peasants had something else to attract the attention of the intellectuals: their poverty. Among the modern

Chinese intellectuals, the small anarchist group in Tokyo led by Liu Shipei was the first to pay serious attention to the living conditions of the peasants and they were very likely also the first to conduct organized research about and among the peasants. Liu Shipei organized the Association for Investigating the Sufferings of the Peasants in 1907 "to expose directly the cruelties of the officials and the rich people, to seek remedies, and to help the common people."[58]

The association conducted surveys of the living conditions of the peasants in various provinces and published the results in their journals, *Tianyi* and *Hengbao*. Their concerns were shared by many other nonanarchist revolutionaries at that time.[59] However, like the anarchist movement itself, the anarchists' concern about the living conditions of the peasant was short-lived. In the 1910s, Sun Yat-sen and other Nationalists began to talk about the poverty of the peasant and they paid special attention to the land problem. By the 1920s and 1930s, the Chinese intellectuals of most schools had reached an agreement on two points: first, although all social classes in China suffered from the social-political disorder of that period, it was the peasants who bore the heaviest blow; second, the damage on rural areas had become ever more severe after the beginning of the twentieth century because of the further deterioration of the general situation of the country.

Causes of Poverty

Before the 1911 Revolution, the intellectuals usually attributed the poverty of the peasantry to the exploitation of the landlords and the Manchu government. Zou Rong, Liu Shipei, and Huang Kan all denounced the Manchus and the landlords for their mistreatment of the peasants.[60] A sympathizer of the peasant participants of the famous Laiyang Rebellion of 1910 also blamed the local gentry and the Manchu government for the insufferable conditions that forced the peasants to rebel.[61] Starting in the early 1920s, however, more and more Chinese intellectuals began to take imperialism as the most important factor behind the bankruptcy of the Chinese rural economy and the poverty of the peasant.

The specific causes of the peasantry's poverty were believed to include the following: the bankruptcy of the rural household handicraft industry due to the import of cheap industrial goods from Western countries; the indemnities demanded by foreign countries that were mostly paid by the peasants in the form of taxes exacted by the government; the rise of the cost of living as a consequence of foreign invasions; internal political disorder, especially warlord politics, which was also often blamed on the imperialists; and the frequent natural disasters and banditry that often ensued. Though left-wing intellectuals still maintained that the exploitation of the landlord class was also an important factor, the new trend was to view the internal factors such as warlord politics and landlord exploitation as by-products of foreign invasion or independent factors of only secondary importance. However, there were also some intellectuals who argued that foreign and domestic factors were equally important, as well as a small group of intellectuals who held that the decline of China's rural economy had nothing to do with imperialism and was caused entirely by China's internal problems.

In 1923, Chen Duxiu divided the sufferings of the peasants into general sufferings of the whole peasantry and particular sufferings of the landholding peasants and the landless peasants. According to Chen, the general sufferings of the peasantry had three major causes: the import of foreign products; the unhealthy politics; and, finally, the peasants' ignorance and their lack of organization, which made it easy for the landlords and gentry to exploit them. In explaining the particular sufferings of the landholding and landless peasants, Chen paid more attention to class difference and class exploitation.[62]

Chen listed imperialism as the prime but not the sole cause of the sufferings of Chinese peasants. The manifesto of a Communist-led peasant association in Hunan, written in the early 1920s, put more blame on imperialism than Chen Duxiu did by linking foreigners with Chinese warlords. The manifesto attributes the sufferings of the peasants to "foreigners who increased the price of cotton and hence monopolized the cotton market, leaving us with nothing to weave," who also "made the warlords fight each other... and sent their products to China and made our handicrafts worthless."[63]

The Nationalists shared this view of imperialism with the Communists in the 1920s. Dr. Sun Yat-sen agreed that imperialism was the biggest problem of China, and when the first United Front was established in early 1924, both the Nationalists and Communists agreed that the targets of the national revolution would be imperialists and warlords. Mao Zedong remarked in 1949 that "Sun Yat-sen had a world outlook different from ours and started from a different class standpoint in studying and tackling problems; yet, in the 1920s he reached a conclusion basically the same as ours on the question of how to struggle against imperialism."[64] In its "First Manifesto about the Peasant Movement," released in July 1924, the Nationalist government told the peasants that the penetration of foreign goods and the control of Chinese customs by foreigners were responsible for China's rural bankruptcy. The imperialists were also responsible for the protracted warlord wars because it was in their interests to keep the warlords fighting each other.[65] In another declaration to the peasants released a month after the First Manifesto, the Nationalist government argued that the ultimate source of all the sufferings of the peasantry was the foreigners. These "red-haired, green-eyed 'tough guys,'" "namely, the foreign capitalists who encroached upon the Chinese people," were believed to be "crueler and more savage than the [Chinese] officials and warlords."[66] Liao Zhongkai, a leading left-wing Nationalist, argued in mid-1924 that "the invasion of the imperial-capitalists is the source of all evils [in rural China]." He also supported the idea that the warlords could exist only because they were supported by the imperialists.[67] The Guangdong Provincial Peasant Association took the same stand. The political report passed at its first congress clearly states that the Chinese warlords and capitalists were the tools of imperialists.[68]

After 1925, largely because of even stronger antiforeign sentiment aroused by the May Thirtieth Movement, more and more Chinese intellectuals began to accept the view that imperialism was the sole cause of China's rural problems, and they usually supported their argument by grouping all evil Chinese as the lackeys of foreigners. Chen Duxiu had changed his position by now. In 1923, he listed imperialists, warlords, and landlords as three independent factors, but in 1926 he linked them all by arguing that "Warlords, compradores, and landlords and gentry are the three means by which the imperialists exploit and oppress the Chinese people."[69]

The popular view that imperialism was the chief culprit for China's rural crisis was supported by Peng Pai,[70] Fang Zhimin,[71] Zhang Wentian,[72] and other Communist intellectuals. Deng Yanda, founder of the Third Party, also repeatedly accused the imperialists and their Chinese collaborators of oppressing and exploiting the Chinese people in general and the Chinese peasants in particular.[73] The leaders of the short-lived Fujian government in the early 1930s, who were very much influenced by the Third Party, held a position very close to that of the Communists.[74]

The view that imperialism was the chief or even sole factor behind China's rural bankruptcy was fully supported by the United Front government of 1924 to 1927. After the breakdown of the United Front, that view continued to be held not only by Communists and the Third Party, but also by the Nationalists. After 1927, the Nationalist government led by Chiang Kai-shek and Wang Jingwei did not argue against listing imperialism as the leading enemy of China, but only rejected the Communist idea of lumping the right-wing leaders of the Nationalist Party among those traitorous Chinese who served the imperialists. In fact, the threat of imperialism provided the Nationalists with a pretext for opposing social revolution and the Communists. They argued that since the chief enemy of China was imperialism, all Chinese should therefore unite to carry out a national revolution against the imperialists and a few colluding warlords, and that social revolution and class struggle would result in Chinese fighting among themselves and hence would be detrimental to the national revolution. Wang Jingwei, for example, argued right after his break-up with the Communists in July 1927 that the land problem was not as important as the Communists believed because "the strongest oppressors are the imperialists, and so what China needs is unification and cooperation of the different classes of people against imperialism. A class conflict...would therefore be detrimental to China."[75]

Most Chinese scholars supported the political leaders' assessment of the general situation of rural China and its causes by providing data and academic theory. Immediately after the outbreak of the May Thirtieth Movement in 1925, Qi Shufen, a left-wing economist trained in Japan under the famous Japanese Marxist economist Kawakami Hajime, published a book entitled *China under Economic Invasion* to denounce the foreign powers for plundering China. While not paying special attention to rural China, he argued that foreigners had tightly controlled the whole of China and China had become poorer and poorer because of this. He focused on the unequal treaties and their resulting evils, including the concessions, the foreign control of the Chinese transportation system, and foreign investment. "It is capital-imperialism that has weakened China and it is the unequal treaties coming with capital-imperialism that threatens our existence," he concluded.[76] Warlord politics, he argued, is also caused by the unequal treaties.[77] He cited many works in English and Japanese and provided statistics as well as tables to support his charges. The book included prefaces written by prominent figures such as Wu Jingheng, Xu Qian, Tang Shaoyi, and Guo Muoruo, who were from very different backgrounds and would later lead very different political lives. The fact that they all praised the book indicates the existence of a consensus among different groups of Chinese intellectuals about the negative evaluation and total rejection of imperialism at that time.

Qi was later gunned down by the Sichuan warlord Yang Sen, but his research was carried on by other scholars, Communist and non-Communist. In the 1930s, left-wing rural economists led by Chen Hansheng and Qian Junrui were very active in collecting and presenting the facts about the causes of China's rural bankruptcy. In reviewing a report written by a joint team of Chinese and foreign scholars about China's economic development and foreign economic cooperation with China, one left-wing scholar argued that "the imperialist invasion is the most fundamental cause of the decline of China's rural economy."[78] Independent sociologist Li Jinghan, whose several years of rural investigation in northern China convinced him that "although there are various complicated factors behind the abrupt collapse of China's rural economy and the gradual deterioration of the living conditions of the peasant, the penetration of international capital might be the central element,"[79] supported this view. He provided a vivid description of how international capital destroyed rural China step-by-step, which resonated with the Communist theory.[80]

Besides political leaders and scholars, writers, and especially the leftists among them, also joined to denounce those who exploited and oppressed the

peasants. The difference is that while the political leaders and scholars usually expressed their ideas directly, the writers often expressed theirs indirectly
through the mouths of the characters they created. Hong Shen, the Harvard-
trained left-wing playwright, wrote *The Bridge of Five Degree Holders* in 1930
and *The Fragrant Rice* in 1931, the first two plays of his village trilogy, in
which he accused the landlords, gentry, officials, and capitalist usurers of
exploiting the peasants on behalf of the imperialists. He vividly described
how drought, wandering soldiers, and the unpredictable market affected the
peasants' lives. In *The Fragrant Rice* a village scholar suggested that the peasants became poor because they could no longer sell their handicrafts to the
cities; instead, they had to buy everything from the cities, and the people in
the cities in turn bought everything from foreigners.[81] Commentators remark
that the trilogy demonstrates "the anti-imperialist and anti-feudal spirit of
the author."[82]

In Mao Dun's story "The Spring Silkworm," written in 1932, the old
peasant Lao Tongbao feels that since the appearance of foreign yarn, foreign
cloth, and foreign oil in town, and foreign steamships on the river, the commodities in town have become more and more expensive, while the products
of his field, silkworm cocoon and grain, are increasingly worth less and less.
He also feels that he has to pay more and more taxes and levies because the
officials have begun to collaborate with "the foreign devils." As a result, he
loses all his land and becomes a landless peasant. He frequently curses "the
foreign devils" for "cheating the Chinese out of our money," although he has
never seen any of them.[83] A contemporary critic remarked that Mao Dun's
story proved "the firm and unshakable theory of social science," which
claimed that the penetration of the commodities of international imperialism
would cause the collapse of the rural economy.[84]

Through the words of a character in his story "Young Master Gets His
Tonic," the left-wing writer Wu Zuxiang said in 1932, "Everything around
here going downhill from one day to the next has nothing to do with fate. If
you ask me, it's because we've been cheated out of all our money by the foreigners."[85] Ye Shengtao, in his "A Year of Good Harvest," published in
1933, describes how a harvest turned into a disaster for the peasants due to
the drop of the price of rice caused by the import of foreign grains and the
monopoly of the merchants.[86] In fact, "how and why a harvest turned into a
disaster for the peasant" became a very popular theme at that time among
both writers and social scientists. The control of the market by foreign capitalists and the exploitation of native feudal forces were usually taken as the
two most important factors for the creation of the strange phenomenon.

In Wang Tongzhao's 1933 novel *The Mountain Rain,* which is about
peasant life in Shandong, an old peasant asks an old village man of letters to
explain to him why things have gone so bad in the last twenty to thirty years.

His reply: "All those things have been done to us by the foreign devils!" The old peasant and a dozen or so other peasants all agree that this is the right answer. The old peasant then remembers the local peasants' resistance to a railway built by the Germans and the antiforeigner rebellion launched by the Eight Trigrams sect. All these failed. The railway was built, and "the strange locomotives, foreigners with swollen bellies and thick fingers, electric poles, guns and small black tablets" all arrived. All evil things came with the railway. Foreigners not only destroyed the rural economy, the old peasant argues, they have also destroyed the people's morality. Since the coming of the churches and modern schools, the character implies, more and more people have turned evil.[87]

This is how the writers imagined the peasants would explain their miserable conditions. Needless to say, the writers' imaginations might have been strongly influenced by the intellectuals' own explanations of the rural bankruptcy, to the extent that what the peasants in the stories say are intellectuals' words put in peasant mouths. Obviously, foreign invasion and the internal turmoil that was usually linked to foreign invasion were widely believed to be the major causes of rural poverty. Intellectuals of all groups, from Communists to Nationalists, agreed that imperialists and warlords supported by imperialists were the major enemies of the Chinese nation and the Chinese peasantry. Qi Shufen remarked in 1925 that "the word 'imperialism' is constantly in our mouth and ear, and it is engraved in our hearts and on our minds."[88] The veteran Communist Zheng Chaolin describes how the Chinese revolutionaries were preoccupied with the issue of imperialism during the Northern Expedition and after:

> Of the two main slogans, "down with the warlords" was subordinated to "down with imperialism." People viewed the warlords as no more than tools through which the imperialists controlled China. What's more, every disaster, every potential cause of disquiet, was blamed on imperialism. The compradors were the tools of imperialism, the right-wingers of the Guomindang were running dogs of imperialism, agricultural bankruptcy was the result of imperialist aggression, and so on. In a nutshell, people diverted the workers' and peasants' hatred for their Chinese oppressors onto the imperialists and the foreign oppressors.[89]

To some extent, it may be said that in the real world the chief enemy of the Chinese intellectuals were the imperialists, whereas the chief enemy of the Chinese peasants were the landlords and gentry. Therefore, to link the imperialists with the landlords was to link the intellectuals to the peasants. Chinese disciples discarded Marx's teaching about the dual role of imperialism—namely, that imperialism was both a destructive force and a constructive force in the colonies. Among Chinese Communists, only a small group of Trotskyites held the idea that foreign and Chinese capitalists were equally exploitative, and, in turn, that imperialists should not be singled out as the target of revolution. Among the non-Communist intellectuals, the sociologist Fei Hsiao-tung was among a few Chinese intellectuals who argued that internal and external factors played an equal role in causing China's rural problems. In 1939, he agreed that rural poverty was the biggest problem of China: "It is the hunger of the people that is the real issue in China."[90] He found that in the village he investigated, economic depression was caused by the decline of domestic industry, which can in turn be attributed to the larger problems of relations between the village industries and the world market.[91] Fei viewed the issue from the perspective of the process of modernization and social change in the context of traditional-modern and native-foreign contact and conflict. In his opinion, the traditional society was able to maintain subsistence and peace because the traditional rural industry provided an important supplement to agricultural production. Rural problems arose when the traditional rural industry was destroyed by foreign machine-made products or the modern factory system. The method of reviving rural economy was to develop modern rural industry. He elaborated this theory in an essay written in the late 1940s.[92] Although one scholar argues that Fei "saw the inroads of Western imperialism as responsible for most of contemporary China's rural economic and social problems,"[93] Fei's criticism of imperialism was much milder than that of many other Chinese intellectuals.

The liberal Hu Shi was one of the very few Chinese intellectuals who held that his so-called five great national enemies of China—namely, poverty, disease, ignorance, corruption, and disorder—were all China's internal problems and that they had nothing to do with imperialists because "imperialism cannot injure a country that is not first devastated by those five devils." He asked: "Why has imperialism done no injury to the U.S.A. or Japan? Why has it chosen China for exploitation? Is it not because we have been so greatly weakened by the five devils that we no longer possess the power of resistance?"[94] Hu's argument was supported by a small group of scholars surrounding him and a rural economist named Gu Mei, who agreed that rural economy had declined and the peasants were poor but attributed all these to internal factors rather than foreign inroads.[95]

If Hu's article had been published before the May Fourth Movement, he would have been supported by many iconoclastic intellectuals who blamed Chinese tradition rather than foreign invasion for China's problems. But the social context had totally changed by the 1930s and the target of the Chinese intellectuals was no longer native tradition, but the imperialists. It was therefore small wonder that most people felt offended by Hu Shi's view. These included not only the radicals, but also conservatives such as Liang Shuming, who wrote an article to criticize Hu immediately after Hu publicized his views in 1930. According to Liang, Hu's five enemies could be reduced to two: poverty and disorder, because ignorance and disease are linked to poverty and corruption to disorder. He then argued, "poverty is caused by the direct economic penetration of imperialism, and social disorder is caused by the indirect manipulation of warlords by imperialism, therefore, imperialism is the chief culprit."[96] Hu responded by pointing out that both poverty and disorder existed in China long before the imperialists arrived. He once again cited the modernization of Japan to show that China should blame itself for its problems.[97] Liang, however, would not change his views about imperialism. In a book published in 1936, Liang continued to argue that "the rural destruction that has occurred in China in the last several decades is totally the outcome of foreign influence."[98]

The Longing for the Lost Golden Age

Most Chinese intellectuals supported Liang Shuming rather than Hu Shi. They not only argued that imperialism was the most important contributant to China's rural problems, but also held that the process of pauperization in rural China was accelerated around the turn of the century due to intensified foreign invasion following the Sino-Japanese War and the Boxer Rebellion, the rise of warlord politics, and the expansion of commodity economy, among other factors. As a result of all these, many Chinese intellectuals argued, more and more small landholding peasants lost their land, and the life of the Chinese peasant became harder and harder. It thus became very popular among the Chinese intellectuals to compare the good old days with the unpleasant present, and to focus on depicting the process of bankruptcy, collapse, and decadence of rural China in the first few decades of the twentieth century.

According to Peng Pai, in the 1920s, of the 56,000 peasant households in Haifeng of Guangdong, twenty-five percent were semilandholding peasants, and fifty-five percent were landless peasants. Some villages had ten landholding households twenty years before, but now only two to three (or three to four) households still maintained that status. Consequently, there were many village people who had worn shoes twenty years before, but now could afford them no more. The peasants no longer had decent clothes. Twenty years before, many peasants could still afford to get married. They would use sedan chairs to carry their brides and beat gongs and drums to make the wedding ceremony boisterous and exciting; now very few peasants could afford a wife.[99] One of the reasons for the deterioration of the peasant conditions, according to Peng Pai, was a change of the landlords' attitude.

Before the 1911 revolution, the landlords were kept within certain bounds because there were still certain rules they had to obey, but after the revolution, the landlords became offensive and overbearing.[100]

It seems that the process of land accumulation started somewhat later in northern China than in southern China.[101] The percentage of small landholding peasants, semilandholding peasants, and landless peasants varied between the north and the south, and between coastal and interior areas. Compared to the statistics of Haifeng and other places in the south, during the same period, landless peasants constituted a smaller percentage in the north.[102] However, according to Chinese intellectuals, this did not mean the peasants in northern China were not poor. For example, estimates made in the 1930s show that in Shanxi Province in northern China, full tenants formed less than twenty percent of the population and hence tenantry was not a big problem there,[103] yet Chen Hansheng argued that the peasants in Shanxi were living in the utmost poverty and that, in 1930, a peasant in Shanxi received an annual income considerably smaller than that enjoyed by most peasants in impoverished lands like India and the Philippines.[104] The British economist R. H. Tawney offered an explanation. According to him, in the northern provinces, owner-peasants still formed two-thirds of the peasantry, not because they were rich but because the yield of the soil was too low to make it an attractive investment to the capitalists. In addition, the peasants did not have the resources to rent additional land. Hence, the prevalence of small owner-peasants in northern China was actually caused by the infertility of the land and the peasants' poverty. Therefore, the peasants in northern China were poor even though they owned land. Tawney predicted that as modern industry and finance expanded, what had happened in southern and eastern China would happen in northern China too and the number of owner-peasants would diminish.[105]

Tawney's theory was later confirmed by William Hinton, who found that the poor quality of the land was one of the reasons for the comparative dispersion of land ownership in the Long Bow Village of Lucheng County of Shanxi. "Whereas in many parts of China it took only half an acre or less to support one person," he noted, "in the southern districts of Lucheng County it took about one acre." He further concluded, "In general, in every country in the world the highest concentration of land holding is to be found in the richest, most fertile valleys, and the lowest concentration in the poorest mountain regions where the surplus possible from one man's labor is least, and hence the rate of exploitation is the lowest."[106] John Buck agreed that the agricultural productivity in northern China is much lower than that in southern China.[107] Elizabeth Perry's study of the Huai River region further confirms that low tenancy did not mean economic prosperity for the peasant.[108]

Despite the lack of marked land accumulation, Chinese intellectuals believed that the process of rural pauperization was also intensified in northern China after the turn of the twentieth century. The novelist Wang Tongzhao testified that in Shandong Province, where German and Japanese influence had been strong, the rural bankruptcy began at approximately the beginning of the twentieth century, as it did in Haifeng and other places in southern China. One character in Wang Tongzhao's story "The Sunken Boat" (1927) lamented that the lovely, interesting, and elegant old days were gone forever.[109] In his novel *The Mountain Rain* (1933), an old peasant remarked that things did not begin to turn unpleasant until thirty years before.[110] In the postscript to *Mountain Rain,* Wang admitted that one of his purposes of writing the story was to describe the causes and effects of the breakdown of the villages in northern China.[111] Li Dazhao suggested that the tide of rural bankruptcy reached the north a little later than the south because the civil war did not expand to the north after the 1910s. After an analysis of related statistics, Li argued that the years between 1917 and 1920 already showed a clear tendency toward bankruptcy of the middle and small peasants and the accumulation of land by the big landlords.[112]

Again, it was Lu Xun who gave vivid literary expression to the rapid bankruptcy of the villages. He wrote in "Hometown" in 1921:

> Through a crack in the canopy, I peered into the distance. Scattered across the distant horizon, towns and villages came into view under the vast and graying sky: they were drab, desolate, devoid of any semblance of life. I was assailed by a depression against which I was utterly powerless.
>
> No! This was not the countryside I had recalled time and again for more than twenty years. The area I remembered was far, far more lovely.

He then added that he was not sure whether his hometown had been truly as lovely as he thought: it was probably nothing more than what lay before him. But there were definitely no signs of progress either.[113] The fact that he had to sell his old house and move the whole family to the city is also indicative of the general situation of the countryside. It was believed at that time that one of the major signs and causes of the rural bankruptcy was the transfer of large numbers of the population, both rich and poor, from the villages to the cities. The writer Zhou Libo noticed the existence of two different images of village life and village people in Lu Xun's mind: one based on his early memory, the other on what he saw when he grew up. Zhou remarked that "in his other works, he (Lu Xun) also wrote about the peaceful and happy village that had not been flooded by the mighty current of commodity and the honest and kind old peasants, but when he wrote like that he was merely recalling the good dreams of his childhood years. When he was older he witnessed the 'bitter and numb' desolate villages and the shortcomings of the peasant life."[114]

For the pastoral novelist Shen Congwen, rural decadence was best indicated by the loss of innocence and purity of the villagers. In 1934, he visited western Hunan, his native land, after an absence of eighteen years, and found that "everything is different [from before]": "On the surface it appears that everything has progressed tremendously, but after a careful examination, you would find the tendency of decadence in the transition. The most obvious fact is that the uprightness, simplicity and the beauty of humanity has almost disappeared completely."[115] He decided to write a novel to depict how "twenty years of civil war have heavily pressed the character and soul of the peasants who were the first to be affected, and have deprived them of their previous simplicity, diligence, peace and uprightness" and how "excessive taxes and levies and opium have sunk the peasants into destitution and laziness."[116]

Authors of many other essays and novels of the 1920s and 1930s confirmed that the Golden Age described by Peng Pai, Wang Tongzhao, Lu Xun, and Shen Congwen did not begin to disappear until after the turn of the century. Liang Shuming wrote in 1936 that the process of rural destruction had started "several decades" earlier and had accelerated only "two or three decades" before.[117] Liang was particularly upset about spiritual bankruptcy, namely, the erosion of Confucian values. The leading Communist theoretician Zhang Wentian argued in 1933 that the process of rapid pauperization began after the Sino-Japanese War of 1894 and 1895.[118] In an article written in 1927, the writer Ye Shengtao observed that the peasants were in a more difficult position now than they were three or four decades earlier.[119] Lao Tongbao, the bankrupt peasant in Mao Dun's 1932 story "The Spring Silkworm," frequently recalled the prosperous years of the previous three decades.[120] In Wu Zuxiang's "The Great Peace Under the Heaven" (1934), the peace and prosperity of Fengtan Village did not begin to collapse until several decades before.[121]

The Portrayal of Rural Poverty

The living conditions of the poor peasants were widely depicted in stories and articles of the 1920s and the 1930s. Lao Tongbao in Mao Dun's "The Spring Silkworm" (1932), Huang Erguan in Hong Shen's "The Fragrant Rice" (1931), and Xi Dayou in Wang Tongzhao's *Mountain Rain* are good examples of small bankrupt landholding peasants, while Lu Xun's Ah Q might indicate how poor a landless peasant was. Lao Tongbao and Huang Erguan became bankrupt despite a good harvest. Both Mao Dun and Hong

Sheng's stories were set in southern China, while Wang Tongzhao was one of the few famous writers who wrote about northern China. Xi Dayou in *Mountain Rain* was originally an honest owner-peasant in Shandong who later became bankrupt mainly because of the extortion of the warlord troops. Wang Tongzhao's other stories, such as "The Sunken Boat," vividly described a major event taking place in Shandong at that time: the migration of large numbers of bankrupt peasants from Shandong to northeast China. He attributed this event to wars, banditry, heavy rent and taxes, and natural disasters.[122] Unlike these owner-peasants, Lu Xun's Ah Q experienced no bankruptcy. He was miserable from the very beginning. He had no land, no family, no house, and had to work as a farmhand and live in the Land and Grain Temple of the village. As early as 1927, a critic found that poverty was the central theme of Lu Xun's stories about rural China.[123]

The peasants' poverty not only became the central theme in stories written by left-wing writers such as Mao Dun, Lu Xun, and Hong Shen, but also attracted the attention of writers without clear political stands, such as Luo Shu and Shen Congwen. Both Luo Shu's "Twice-Married Woman" and Shen Congwen's "The Husband" tried to explore how poverty affected the dignity, mentality, and emotional life of the peasants.[124] In "Twice-Married Woman," a couple who had lost their land and house decided that the wife had to be sold to another man so that both of them could survive. In "The Husband," the peasants in the mountainous villages were so poor that they had to send their women, even newlywed wives, to serve the merchants and soldiers traveling along the river. A husband who went to visit his wife in the boat had to sleep alone in a separate corner while his wife slept with other men in the main section of the boat. For Shen Congwen, the most painful thing was not the mental and emotional injuries suffered by the husband, but the transformation experienced by the wives: The life of a prostitute quickly turned these previously innocent and simple village women into vulgar persons.

The left-wing artists also made their contribution to creating visual images of the poor peasant. Extremely active were a group of woodcarvers, who were patronized, guided, and encouraged by Lu Xun. Lu Xun endorsed woodcarving because he felt that both the Chinese traditional painting and the Western oil painting of the modernist school did not care much about social reality, while modern Western, especially Russian, woodcarving is close to life and hence easily accepted by the masses. Moreover, "woodcarving is easy to do."[125] Woodcarving became Chinese art's revolutionary genre, and the woodcarvers were all leftist revolutionaries. The movement traced its origin to an exhibition in Shanghai in 1931, which displayed some woodcarving works by the young left-wing artists for the first time.[126] Though it was not until after 1937 that the woodcarvers began to make the peasant one of their foci, some of them did try to depict the miserable conditions of the peasant before 1937, when most woodcarvers were still residing in the cities. This becomes obvious through a glance at the titles of their works created during the period of 1931–1937. Probably as a result of the disastrous flood in southern China in 1931, at least four works created by different artists before 1936 were entitled "Flood"; the titles of other works about rural China produced during that period included "Life After a Great Disaster" (Duan Ganqing, 1935); "Where Is Our Home," and "Famine" (Duan Ganqing, 1935); "We Are as Poor as before Even Though We Have just Had a Harvest" (Lu Zhou, 1936); "The Symphony of Hunger" (Zhang Ying); "Collapse on the Road because of Hunger" (Zhang Hui); and "The Hungry Throng" (Luo Qingzhen).[127]

The titles of academic works about the living conditions of the peasants were no less striking than those of the artistic works. The first volume of *Zhongguo nongcun* [Rural China] (1934–1935) contained articles such as "The Present Agricultural Crisis of China," "A Case of Rural Decline in Shangyu of Zhejiang," "The Villages of Longyan [Fujian] in Turmoil," "The Villages of Linwu of Hunan Under the Heavy Pressure of Taxation," "The Peasants of Fengyang [Anhui] Under All Kinds of Burden," and "A Case of Imperialists' Invasion of Rural China." In 1933, the left-wing economist Feng Hefa published his two-volume *Collected Materials on the Chinese Rural Economy*. Two years later, a two-volume continuation was added.[128] The four volumes represented the best collection of reports and investigations on rural conditions of various parts of China before the mid-1930s, and most of the articles included offered quite miserable portraits of rural China.

The Issue of Class Difference

It seems that all groups of intellectuals agreed that the peasants were poor, but they had different assessments about the extent of the gap between the rich and the poor in rural China. Some argued that there was no major difference. Sun Yat-sen at one time maintained that there were only the very poor and the slightly poor in China.[129] Sun's follower Liao Zhongkai agreed that there was no marked difference between the rich and the poor and argued that there were very few big landlords in rural China. He attributed this to the backward communication system of China.[130] Liang Shuming, who insisted that there was only professional difference but no class difference in Chinese society, suggested that the real difference was between the cities and the villages because the educated and the rich had all moved to the cities.[131] In the early 1920s, even some Communists supported this view. Qu Qiubai, for example, argued in mid-1923 that there was no marked class differentiation in

China.[132] The purpose of making such an argument was to support the United Front policy and show approval of the slogan of national revolution.

However, there were also many intellectuals who maintained that class exploitation did exist in China and that it was one of the most important sources of the sufferings of the peasantry. As early as the first decade in the 1900s, the anarchists led by Liu Shipei argued that the landlords were the "big robbers" and "a big calamity for the peasants."[133] In the foreword to *Hengbao*, Liu Shipei wrote that "our peasants are pitiful. They have no land. When they rent land from the tyrants, they have to pay fifty percent of their harvest as rent."[134] In the 1920s and 1930s, it became more and more popular among the left-wing intellectuals to emphasize class difference, to make comparisons between the poverty of the poor peasants and the wealth of the landlords, and to suggest that the poor were poor because they were exploited not only by outsiders such as the imperialists and warlords, but also by the landlord class, whom they believed formed the power base of the warlords and imperialists. Because of the dramatic regional differences existing in rural China at that time, supporters of the two contrasting views had no difficulty in finding living data to verify their respective positions.

Shen Dingyi argued in 1920 that high rent had made the lives of the peasants miserable. After paying the rent, the peasants had nothing left for themselves, and sometimes they were in debt to the landowner after paying everything they had.[135] Shen's report was confirmed several months later by the May Day special issue of the *Weekly Review* he and Dai Jitao edited. The issue contained articles about the living conditions of the peasants in Zhejiang, Hubei, and other places. Although the method of exploitation differed from place to place, peasants everywhere were extorted heavily by the landlords.[136] Both Li Dazhao and Peng Pai tried to show that just as the common people became poorer and poorer, the landlords became richer and richer.[137] Later left-wing commentators also found much evidence of class exploitation in Lu Xun's novels.

The theme of class difference and class exploitation was developed to a new degree in the 1930s by the young left-wing writers like Wu Zuxiang, Ye Zi, and Ai Qing, and the left-wing social scientists such as Chen Hansheng, Qian Junrui, Qian Jiaju, Feng Hefa, and Xue Muqiao. In Wu Zuxiang's 1932 story "Young Master Gets His Tonics," Chen the Baldheaded, a landless peasant who went to Shanghai for a living, had to sell his blood to Guanguan, a student in Shanghai who happened to be the son of a landlord from the same village, after the latter was injured in an accident. After Guanguan returned to the village, the wife of Chen the Baldheaded became Guanguan's wet-nurse, providing him with her milk every day as nutriment. Chen the Baldheaded later had to return to the village and became a bandit and was finally executed under the order of Guanguan's uncle.[138] Here milk and blood became powerful metaphors for the exploitation of the peasants by the landlords. Ye Zi published his first story "The Harvest" in 1933, in which he tried to answer a question that bothered a lot of intellectuals at that time: why were the peasants still poor and hungry even though they had a harvest? Landlords and officials were blamed for their excessive exploitation of the peasants.[139] Ai Qing, the leftist poet, in his famous poem "Dayanhe— My Wet-Nurse," written in 1933 while he was in prison, contrasted the life of his landlord family and that of Dayanhe, his wet-nurse, a poor peasant. The young poet, after taking all the milk Dayanhe had to offer, was taken back to his parents' home, where he found and enjoyed all kinds of strange things that he had never seen in Dayanhe's home. He saw "the red-lac-quered, floral-carved furniture," and "the ornate brocade on my parents' bed." His buttons were made of silk and mother-of pearl, he "sat on a lacquered stool with a small brazier set underneath," "ate white rice which had been milled three times," while Dayanhe, his wet-nurse, had to live a totally different life: "she washed our clothes... she carried the vegetables, and rinsed them in the icy pond by the village... she sliced the turnips frozen through and through...she stirred the swill in the pig's trough... she fanned the flames under the stove with the broiling meat...she carried the baling baskets of beans and grain to the open square where they baked in the sun."[140]

The left-wing social scientists led by Chen Hansheng and Qian Junrui tried to prove the existence of class difference and class exploitation with data collected from the villages. From the late 1920s to the early 1930s, they conducted investigations in various parts of China. In Chen Hansheng's native Wuxi County of Jiangsu, through a three-month investigation of seventy-seven villages and eight towns, they found that the landlords, who formed 5.7 percent of the total number of households, owned 40.5 percent of the land; the rich peasants, making up 5.8 percent of the total number of households, occupied 19.9 percent of the total land, while the poor peasants, who made up 68.1 percent of the total number of households, owned only 17.7 percent of the total land. In Guangdong, Chen Hansheng found that colonial and feudal exploitations were the main causes of the peasants' poverty and the major obstacle to the development of agriculture in China.[141]

Independent sociologists such as Li Jinghan and Fei Xiaotong, and some Nationalist scholars, although rejecting class struggle, supported the Communist view that there was class difference and class exploitation in rural China. Li Jinghan, basing his views on many years of rural investigation, realized that the "major aspect of the rural economic problem" was "the unfairness of rural social structures and institutions." The heart of the problem, according to Li, lay in the land system. He believed that this unfairness was the source of class conflict.[142] Fei Xiaotong, through his investigations in 1936, found that the land distribution of Kaixiangong was very unequal.[143]

Fei mentioned in 1981 that between 1936 and 1949, landlords occupied 56.5 percent of the total land of Kaixiangong. As a result, seventy-five percent of the families living in the village had to live on rented land and borrow money at usurious rates.[144] In his 1939 book, Fei emphasized that the land system was a serious problem and that it should be reformed. He repeatedly stated that taxes and rent were a heavy burden for the poor peasants, which was also the major cause of conflicts between the landlords and peasants. He further argued that these problems existed not only in the village he investigated, but also in every other part of China, and that they were especially serious in central China.[145]

The difference between the Chinese intellectuals who argued for the existence of class difference and those who argued against its existence is similar to the classic controversy between Robert Redfield and Oscar Lewis about life in rural Mexico, where Redfield found a folk society based on communitarian values and community solidarity, whereas Lewis saw a society torn by conflicts over access to land and a history of political struggle.[146] It also resembles the controversy between the Russian Communists and populists in the late nineteenth century concerning the social stratification of rural Russia. The populists emphasized solidarity and the precapitalist nature of the Russian commune and the possibility of using it as the base of a future Communist society, whereas Lenin and his followers contended that capitalism had already penetrated into rural Russia, and that the communes had already split into rich, middle, and poor strata, which would finally lead to a rural society based on class division.[147]

If the Mexican debate was basically academic, the Russian debate was very much political. The Chinese debate, like the Russian one, was deeply linked to political struggles between the various groups of intellectuals. Different groups of intellectuals often adopted different criteria about class differentiation, which led to different conclusions as to whether marked class difference existed in China. This is well indicated in the different assessments drawn from the same case study by a Communist scholar and a non-Communist scholar. The study was conducted by a non-Communist scholar in a village in Sanhe County of Hebei. According to the investigation, the village had 3,800 *mu* of land and about 170 families. The land distribution was as follows (p. 44):

The non-Communist investigator concluded that the land distribution was "quite equal" and that the living conditions of an ordinary family in the village were "not too bad" because each family averaged twenty-two *mu* of land. This assessment was strongly criticized by a left-wing scholar, whose calculations (based on the same statistics) showed that the ten richest families, which made up six percent of the total number of households, owned nearly fifty percent of the total amount of the land; while the poor families, meaning those who owned less than ten *mu* of land, owned less than ten percent of the total amount of the land, although they formed more than one-third of the total number of households. He then concluded that the land distribution was not equal. As for the living conditions of the peasants, the left-wing scholar argued that it was absurd to talk about the "ordinary family" with the average amount of land, because not every family owned the average amount of land.[148]

Number of Families	Amount of Land Owned by Each Family
5	200 *mu*
5	100 *mu*
3	80 *mu*
1	60 *mu*
11	40 *mu*
30	30–40 *mu*
30	20–30 *mu*
20	10–20 *mu*
45	less than 10 *mu*
20	0 *mu*

The assessment of the rural class stratification of Dingxian of Hebei and Zouping of Shandong indicates similar differences in the criteria held respectively by Communist and non-Communist scholars. Liang Shuming insisted that the land distribution in Zouping and Dingxian was equal because more than ninety percent of the households owned land.[149] The Communist scholar Chen Hansheng did not agree. Chen argued that although most families in Dingxian owned land, some of them owned much more land than others.[150] Surprisingly, some members of Liang's group tended to agree with the Communists rather than Liang Shuming. As mentioned earlier, Li Jinghan, the chief sociologist in Dingxian, agreed that class differences were one of the most serious problems of rural China. Wang Xiangchen, a writer affiliated with Yan Yangchu's Dingxian experiment, noted that there were marked class differences in the village he served.[151]

Current Research

Almost all Chinese intellectuals based their writings on the conditions of a specific area of China rather than the whole of China: Mao Zedong on Hunan and Jiangxi; Peng Pai on Guangdong; Fang Zhimin on Jiangxi; Lu Xun, Mao Dun, Ye Shengtao, and Wang Luyan on Zhejiang; Wu Zuxiang on Anhui; Fei Xiaotong on Jiangsu and Yunnan; Wang Tongzhao on Shandong; Liang Shuming on Henan and Shandong; and Yan Yangchu and Li Jinghan on Hebei. In their provinces, they usually covered only one or several counties rather than the whole province. Yet they all tended to take the small area they wrote about as the miniature of the nation, despite their awareness of the existence of marked regional differences in land distribution, land tenure, commercialization, and other aspects. Statistics were rare, and those available were often not very accurate.[152] Moreover, very few of those intellectuals were trained economists or sociologists. Therefore, one is justified to ask, were the images of the poor peasant created by the Chinese intellectuals reliable reflections of reality or merely the results of their imagination? Did the golden age described by the Chinese intellectuals really exist in rural China before the foreigners arrived or was it simply a myth created as a counterpoint to the prevailing disorder? And if rural bankruptcy did occur, were the reasons provided by the Chinese intellectuals accurate or off the mark?

Contemporary Chinese historians agree that rural bankruptcy did occur and that imperialism was its chief cause, or at least one of its most important causes. In fact, almost all the traditional peasant rebellions as well as modern peasant movements since 1840 have been interpreted wholly or partially as resulting from foreign invasion and the ensuing rural pauperization. For example, some scholars have tried to explain the Boxer Rebellions in terms of this process of rural bankruptcy.[153] In general, Chinese economic historians emphasize the detrimental effects of foreign trade and commercialization on the Chinese rural economy.[154] Since the 1980s, some Chinese scholars have begun to reexamine and reevaluate rural conditions during the first half of the twentieth century. They have not overturned the general conclusions, but they have challenged some specific viewpoints. For example, a few scholars have found that the differences in landholding between the rich and poor in pre-1949 China had been somewhat exaggerated by the Communist Party. The official Communist view, which was first stated in 1950 by Liu Shaoqi, holds that the landlords and rich peasants, who formed less than ten percent of the rural population, occupied seventy to eighty percent of the land, whereas the peasants, who made up more than ninety percent of the rural population, controlled only twenty to thirty percent of the land.[155] A recent study indicates that the landlords and rich peasants owned fifty to fifty-two percent of the land, while the peasants occupied forty-eight to fifty percent of the land, and that in the several decades before 1949, the general tendency was not land accumulation, but land dispersion.[156]

In the Soviet Union, studies concerning the social-economic history of rural China can be divided into two periods: the period before the breakup of Sino-Soviet relations and the period after. During the first period, theoreticians and scholars of the two Communist parties had so much influence on each other that it was impossible to draw a line between the two groups. Before 1949, the official Soviet view about rural China had tremendous influence on the Chinese Communist and leftist intellectuals. Besides the relevant works of political leaders such as Stalin, Trotsky, and Bukharin, and the documents of the Comintern, important works published during this period included Ludwig Madjar's work on rural economic relations, E. F. Kovalev's work on rent, and others.[157] From 1949 to the breakup of Sino-Soviet relations in the 1960s, Soviet studies on rural China basically followed the lines drawn before 1949.

The period after the breakup of Sino-Soviet relations saw a strong interest in reexamining the accepted views about rural China. A. C. Mugruzin, the chief Russian expert on modern Chinese rural economy, argued that in the first half of the twentieth century, landlords and rich peasants actually occupied about fifty percent of the arable land of China, not seventy to eighty percent, as estimated by Soviet and Chinese scholars in the previous period. Among them the landlord class owned thirty-five to forty percent of the land. His estimate is actually very close to that made by Joseph Esherick in the early 1980s, which held that in pre-1949 China, the landlords, who constituted four percent of the total rural households, owned thirty-nine percent of the land.[158] Mugruzin further argued that the penetration of capitalism in rural China was not evident at that time and that there were very few proletarians in rural China.[159] Although he agreed that rural pauperization did occur and listed semifeudal exploitation as the major factor,[160] his study implies that the Chinese peasants were not as poor as many Chinese intellectuals believed in the 1920s and 1930s, and that the exploitation by foreigners and landlords was not as severe as estimated before. As a result, he argued, the main difference in rural China was not between the landlords and the peasants, but between those who owned property and those who did not.[161]

In a recent work, Mugruzin argued that the Chinese rural economy in the first several decades of the twentieth century actually contained two contradictory tendencies: there were factors resulting in some growth in production, but there were also factors resulting in reduction in production and diminished productive forces. He argued that these two tendencies demonstrated different forces in different regions and among different social classes. He criticized previous Chinese and Russian studies for overemphasizing the tendency of pauperization, collapse, and stagnation while neglecting the tendency of growth. On the basis of his calculation and comparison of per capita grain production, money income, and land possession of the 1920s, 1930s and the 1950s, he concluded that the level of agricultural production of the 1920s to 1930s was actually higher than that of 1952 and only slightly lower than that of 1957. "Therefore, the 1920s and 1930s can hardly be simply described as 'stagnation,' not to mention 'decline'." He further concluded that there was growth in agricultural production during those years, and its growth rate was higher than that of the population growth.[162]

Among scholars in the West, views on this issue are much more diverse. There has been much controversy about two important issues relating to the images of the peasant created by the Chinese intellectuals. First, did the living conditions of the Chinese peasants improve or deteriorate during the first half of the twentieth century? Second, was Western presence, foreign trade, or imperialism beneficial or detrimental to the Chinese rural economy during that period?[163] Scholars in two influential schools—namely, the world system school and the moral economy school—have advanced arguments that are closest to those held by most Chinese intellectuals. The two theories share a negative evaluation of the role of imperialism in the "frontiers" or colonies. They agree that rural bankruptcy did occur in China, and that imperialism or foreign trade played the most important part in it. Frances Moulder, for example, finds that Western trade expansion and the ensuing incorporation of China into the world system was an important factor in causing rural problems in southern China, which led to the Taiping Rebellion in the mid-nineteenth-century.[164] This explanation of the cause of the Taiping Rebellion is very similar to that provided by Karl Marx, Li Dazhao, and most other Chinese Communist scholars.[165] Eric Wolf interpreted the twentieth-century peasant wars in six countries, including China, in terms of the expansion of the capitalist system and its devastating effects on the lives of the peasants in the frontier.[166] Robert Marks, Kamal Sheel, and Ralph Thaxton all found that the moral economy theory fit in well with the conditions of modern China. The theory explains the modern peasant movement in terms of the destruction of traditional moral economic institutions by Western expansion and the change of rural social structure and class relations. Robert Marks argues that the peasants in Haifeng, although benefiting from an expanding market brought about by imperialism in the beginning, suffered badly later from the breakdown of the sugar market and the ensuing changes in land tenure relations.[167] Kamal Sheel believes that the penetration of international capitalism caused the collapse of the trade and cultivation of tea, indigo, tobacco, and cotton of rural Jiangxi, which led to the change in land relations and the decline of the regional economy.[168] Thaxton argues that "the new pressure on peasant livelihood owed their origins mainly to the fiscal crisis induced by the world powers."[169] These scholars tend to agree with the Chinese intellectuals about the existence of a golden age, when the foreigners had not arrived and the old order still prevailed.

Next in line are a group of scholars who agree that Chinese rural economy did decline during that period, but they attribute this more to domestic factors than to foreign penetration. One of the earliest representatives of this group is R. H. Tawney. He remarked in 1932 that "it is difficult to resist the conclusion that a large proportion of Chinese peasants are constantly on the brink of actual destitution."[170] His statement that the position of the Chinese peasantry was "that of a man standing permanently up to the neck in the water, so that even a ripple is sufficiently to drown him"[171] has since been widely quoted. He tried to show that the situation was caused by heavy taxation, warlordism, bad credit relations, minute land holdings, poor soils, and population pressure. Tawney's views have been echoed by some later studies. James Thomson, for example, attributes China's rural crisis to population pressure and the failure to release the pressure through industrialization, and to natural and man-made disasters such as floods, famine, rebellion, economic dislocation, civil strife, and banditry. Although he mentions the destruction of the traditional handicraft economy by the flow of factory goods, he obviously agrees that it was mainly China's internal problems that caused the rural crisis.[172] Mark Selden notices the deterioration of living conditions in rural Shaanxi and argues that warlordism, famine, and class differences were the major factors responsible for rural poverty.[173] Victor Lippit emphasizes the exploitation of the peasants by the rural upper class who seized the major part of the peasant surplus through rent, taxation, and usurious interest rates.[174] Edward Friedman, Paul Pickowicz, and Mark Selden also agree that interior rural China experienced a long-term economic decline, but they do not believe foreign trade played any role in the decline; on the contrary, they argue that world market penetration was actually beneficial to the rural economy.[175] Besides the various internal factors frequently mentioned by the Chinese intellectuals, such as warlord wars, landlord exploitation, and natural disasters, some scholars, such as Joseph Esherick and Prasenjit Duara, find that the reform programs carried out by the government were a heavy burden for the peasants and formed one of the factors responsible for the increase in rural poverty.[176]

Then there are also some Western scholars who argue that the Chinese rural economy neither developed nor deteriorated in the first half of the twentieth century: it was in stagnation. Dwight Perkins and Albert Feuerwerker both argue that there was no growth in Chinese rural economy: although the output increased, it occurred at the same rate of population growth, which led to stagnation in per capita income. But these scholars also argue against the notion that the Chinese rural economy deteriorated during that period. They believe that tenancy rate and rent levels remained approximately the same during the period.[177] Douglas Paauw takes the same position, arguing that not only the agricultural sector, but the whole economy was in stagnation during the so-called Nanjing Decade (1927–1937).[178] Arthur Young, although claiming that the whole economy was in progress rather than stagnation, agrees with Paauw that most of agriculture "was relatively stagnant during the decade despite important trends that were beginning to bring about a forward movement."[179] Philip Huang also takes this position. He argues that mainly because of population pressure, the history of the rural economy of the Yangzi Delta was characterized by a pattern of "involutionary growth," "involutionary commercialization," "commercialization without development" or "growth without development."[180] Obviously, they all attribute the stagnation mainly to population pressure and/or the lack of technological breakthrough rather than external factors.

Finally, there is a group of scholars who claim that the Chinese rural economy was developing during the first half of the twentieth century and, as a result, the living conditions of the Chinese peasantry actually improved rather than deteriorated. One of the earliest proponents of this view is Ramon Myers. His study of the rural economy of northern China convinced him that the following popular propositions were all wrong: that during the first half of the twentieth century village land distribution became more unequal; that peasant living standards deteriorated steadily after China began to trade with the West; and that peasants were cruelly exploited by the wealthy classes of the cities. He found that the peasant economy of northern China "performed remarkably well" during that period and that the agricultural problems of China had nothing to do with rural socioeconomic relationships.[181] Two studies published in 1989 supported this view. Thomas Rawski maintains that Chinese rural economy developed in the prewar years. He estimates that agriculture developed at an average rate of 1.5 percent, which was 0.5 percent higher than population growth. This led to increase in output and income per capita and to rising living standards.[182] Loren Brandt estimates that rural labor productivity increased between forty and sixty percent during the period between 1870 and 1937, which indicates that the rural economy was improving rather than declining. He maintains that land concentration was not increasing during the period; that the terms of tenancy had improved for the tenant by the 1930s; and that more income went to the lower classes than to the landlords.[183] This group of scholars tends to believe that foreign trade actually exerted beneficial influences on Chinese rural economy. David Faure, for example, although avoiding a quantitative statement about whether the Chinese rural economy was developing or declining in pre-liberation Jiangnan and Guangdong, argues that foreign trade was a positive factor in the rural economy. He found that the tenants in a commercialized area could be much better off than the owner-peasants in a noncommercialized area, owing to the opportunities provided by the market.[184]

The debate is still going on and to date has neither proved nor disproved the image of the poor peasant portrayed by Chinese intellectuals in the 1920s and 1930s and after. Because of the lack of reliable data, the true nature of the development of rural economy and the peasant income change in the whole of China over the decades under discussion probably will never be indicated in solid statistics.[185] However, while it may be difficult to show statistically whether an average Chinese peasant became poorer or richer during the period, suffice it to say that the various disasters described by the Chinese intellectuals, including the decline of household industry, warlord wars, government and landlord exploitation, and flood and drought did happen in many parts of China during the period, and understandably these did result in terrible suffering on the part of the peasants. Moreover, for our purpose, it is much more important to trace what the Chinese intellectuals believed to be true than to prove whether what the Chinese intellectuals believed was actually true.

Poverty and Ignorance

It did not take much imagination for the Chinese intellectuals to relate the ignorance of the peasants to their poverty. The question was, does ignorance cause poverty or vice versa? As early as 1907, a revolutionary pointed out "the poor are ignorant because they are poor."[186] A writer suggested in the 1920s that it was intellectual famine that caused the peasants to suffer from poverty. Therefore, rural education would solve the problem.[187] Many others, however, believed the issue was not so simple. They viewed it more like a vicious circle. Hong Shen, the famous playwright, wrote a play in 1916 to call for contributions to a popular education program. He translated its title into English as *Poverty or Ignorance, Which Is It?* He believed education was the way to change the lives of the poor. But how could the poor afford education? One character in the play commented that the offspring of rickshaw drivers would always be rickshaw drivers because they had no money to send their children to school.[188] Liang Shuming also saw a vicious circle of poverty, ignorance, and the lack of political power. "The more ignorant, the weaker, the poorer; the poorer, the weaker, the more ignorant," he argued.[189] However, he seemed to believe that poverty was a greater concern. As to the matter of how to initiate rural work, he wrote that "the natural order is to start with economy; only after the development of economy can there be necessity and possibility for political and educational reform."[190]

Yan Yangchu found that the Chinese laborers in France were extremely eager to learn. They attended classes every evening after a whole day's hard work. Some even missed their supper to attend class, and they learned extremely quickly. Thus he realized that the people of the lower class were ignorant, not because they were not willing or not able to learn, but because they were denied the opportunity of learning.[191] Most left-wing intellectuals agreed with Yan that it was poverty that made the peasants ignorant. Mao Zedong is reported to have realized this even before the May Fourth Movement.[192] Peng Pai had come to this conclusion by 1921.[193] Li Dazhao had similar views: the peasants worked in the fields from dawn to dark, and when they happened to be free, there were no educational facilities in the village available for them.[194]

Understanding the complexities of the relationship between the ignorance and the poverty of the peasants convinced the intellectuals that education alone could not solve the problem of ignorance because education could not be separated from the social-economic system. As a result, Peng Pai later ridiculed himself for initially dreaming of instigating social revolution through education.[195] Other leading Communists such as Mao Zedong and Zhang Guotao were enchanted with mass education at first but ended up becoming revolutionaries instead. Yan Yangchu felt it necessary to make the transition from mass education to rural reconstruction. Fei Xiaotong found the literacy movement hardly helpful if rural society itself did not change.[196] The Communist intellectuals began to criticize the mass education movement in the 1920s for attaching too much importance to supra-class education.[197] Left-wing social scientists in the 1930s argued that poverty was the cause of all other problems in the village and criticized Yan Yangchu and his followers for attaching equal importance to the four biggest problems in the village they perceived: ignorance, poverty, illness, and selfishness.[198]

THE POWERFUL

Related to the poverty of the peasants, the theme of the peasants as a potentially powerful revolutionary force emerged during the 1920s and the 1930s, especially among left-wing intellectuals. In fact, as early as the period of the Boxer Rebellion, a few Chinese intellectuals had already realized that the peasants could become a powerful revolutionary force if proper leadership was provided. A few years later, the anarchists Liu Shipei, Zhang Ji, and others became true believers in the peasants' power. In their writings published in 1907 and after, they advocated "the laboring people's revolution" and "peasant revolution."[199] They suggested that the anarchist revolution in China should start with the peasant revolution because peasants not only formed the great majority of the Chinese population, but were also imbued with a sense of solidarity and a tradition of rebellion against oppressive authority. Their writings traced peasant rebellions in Chinese history to prove that "the revolutionaries came from the peasantry."[200] Many revolutionary intellectuals began to praise the peasant rebels in Chinese history.[201] Those revolutionaries led by Dr. Sun Yat-sen attached special importance to the secret societies, whose members were mostly peasants.

However, it was not until the 1920s and 1930s that it became a popular belief among the Chinese intellectuals that the peasants were truly powerful. If, previously, the large peasant population of China was considered a huge burden by many intellectuals, now that population became an immense resource for revolution and development. Many factors contributed to this transformation of perception. These included the support shown by the peasants to the Northern Expedition, the import of new revolutionary ideologies, especially the influence of the Russian Revolution, the demands for the further development of the national movement, and the manifestation of peasant power by traditional style peasant rebellions[202] and modern peasant movements led by pioneer intellectuals. The Communists and the left-wing Nationalists began to pay serious attention to the peasant during their cooperation between 1924 and 1927. After their split in 1927, the Communists began to exploit to the fullest extent the potential of the peasants' revolutionary spirit. At the same time, other groups of intellectuals began to explore the use of the peasants' power to further their own agenda.

The revolutionary intellectuals attributed the peasants' revolutionary spirit mainly to their miserable living conditions. As early as 1904, a revolutionary argued that the propertyless were prone to revolution because they had nothing to lose. Therefore, the poorer China became, the more revolutionaries there would be, and the earlier the revolution would succeed. He even announced that only the poor had the right to revolution.[203] Li Dazhao argued in 1920 that hunger is the driving force of social change. Since the peasants in northern China were suffering from natural disasters, and the warlords, tycoons, and politicians still refused to help them, it seemed to him that great social changes were imminent.[204] Chen Duxiu pointed out in 1923 that foreign goods, soldiers and bandits, natural disasters, and the officials and gentry "may well prompt the peasantry to join the revolution."[205] Peng Pai wrote in 1926 that the hardships and bitterness experienced by the peasants had equipped them with "self-awareness" and a willingness to join the peasant associations.[206] The Communist Manifesto to the Peasants written in 1920 stated that the life of the Chinese peasants was as miserable as that of the Russian peasants before the Russian Revolution and that the peasants were full of grievances. The Pingxiang Uprising of that year was cited as evidence of the peasants' resentment and the dawn of the revolutionary age.[207] The same argument was made in the January 1924 Manifesto of the Nationalist Party.[208]

This observation was probably partially based on the personal experiences of the revolutionary intellectuals themselves. For many of them, the poverty of their own families as well as the nation was one of the most important factors in convincing them that revolution was the only way out. According to Madame Sun Yat-sen, "Many times Dr. Sun has told me that it was in those early days, as a poor son of a poor peasant family that he became a revolutionary. He was determined that the lot of the Chinese peasant should not to be so wretched, that little boys in China should have shoes to wear and rice to eat."[209] Fang Zhimin also vividly described how the poverty of his own family and of other people influenced his thinking in his formative years. When he was still a student at the family school of the land-lord Zhang Niancheng, he was already constantly bothered by the question "Why are the rich always so rich and the poor always so poor!?"[210] One of his poems written in 1922 starts with the sentence "around me there seem to be innumerable people crying!" and ends with "Yes, I should come to your rescue, I will go with you."[211] In his autobiography, he wrote about how the debt his parents incurred to send him to school became a heavy burden for the whole family. He concluded, "because of my own economic status and my acceptance of the new trends of thought, I harbored deep resentment toward the bloodsuckers in the society....On the other hand, I had pro-found class sympathy toward the poor workers and peasants."[212] In order to change the miserable conditions of the poor peasants, he opted for revolu-tion. For the intellectuals from poor families, it was very easy to relate their personal or family misfortunes to the sufferings of other poor people and the terrible state of the nation. For those from well-to-do families, it took a little more political understanding for them to move along the same path as those from poor families.

Organization and Consciousness

Nonetheless, peasants were believed to be potential, not actual revolutionar-ies. They needed to be inspired, mobilized, and organized by the intellectu-als. If the revolutionary intellectuals or political activists were able to awake by themselves, then the peasants had to be awakened by others.[213] If not guided by intellectuals, the peasant rebellion would lead to no more than wild and rampant violence. Such discourse was widespread among the edu-cated Chinese as early as the time of the Boxer Rebellion,[214] and it became increasingly so in the late 1920s and after. In the Communist Manifesto to the Peasants written in 1920, the peasants were described as able to be awak-ened and willing to listen to propaganda. The document called on the revo-lutionaries to go to the countryside to enhance the peasants' political consciousness.[215] Peng Pai felt that poverty-striken peasants were waiting to be mobilized by revolutionaries like himself. He was very eager to get more comrades to help him with this, saying repeatedly that if the peasant move-ment in Haifeng failed, the reason would be that his fellow revolutionaries did not come to help him in his efforts.[216]

It was generally agreed that it took organization and political conscious-ness to make a powerful revolutionary force out of the amorphous peasant masses. The intellectuals believed that they were the ones who could bring these entities to the peasants. In the first decade of the twentieth century, the anarchists advocated the creation of "the association of the laboring people" and urged revolutionary intellectuals to go to the laboring people and merge with them.[217] In the 1920s, more and more intellectuals came to realize that whether the peasants were powerful or powerless depended to a large degree on the attitude of the intellectuals, who were believed to hold the key to changing the peasants through organization and education. Therefore, there was always a discourse about the powerlessness of the peasants that accompanied the discourse about their power. The peasants were powerless in the past because the intellectuals neglected them and they became powerful now only with the help of the intellectuals. Dr. Sun Yat-sen made this very clear in two of his speeches delivered in August 1924. In his first speech he argued that the first thing the peasants should do was to organize themselves. He described the peasants without organization as "a pan of sands," predicting that "if the peasants organize themselves with the help of the government, then they would reestablish their status and gain happiness."[218] In his second speech, which was made to the students of the Peasant Movement Institute, he told the students that because the peasants were lacking in education, they had been indifferent to national affairs, hence it was the responsibility of the graduates of the institute to educate the peasants about their duties and rights to the nation, to teach them the Three Principles of the People, so that the whole class of peasants would be awakened and join the revolution. He also reiterated the importance of organization in this speech.[219]

Sun Yat-sen's views were shared by his followers Liao Zhongkai, Tan Yankai, Chen Gongbo,[220] and Shen Dingyi. Shen decided in December 1927 that he would "dig deeply among the masses, to plant the ideas of the Three Principles of the People in so firm a foundation that they cannot be pulled up, and to instill among the masses a trust in party leadership." He argued that "the adult farmers in every village should be members of the farmer's association."[221]

Liang Shuming also argued that the two most important tasks of his rural reconstruction movement were the development of the peasants' self-consciousness and the creation of village organizations. He explained that self-consciousness meant that the peasants should be aware that they had to rescue themselves. After they achieved self-consciousness, they had to generate organization, which he defined as groups formed by many people with a common aim and armed with a sense of order and the spirit of moving forward. Organization was necessary, he argued, because all the rural programs required collective efforts. He expected that "the unorganized peasants, under the leadership of intellectuals, would unite to strive for economic self-defense and independence."[222] Yan Yangchu fully agreed with him. Yan attributed the lack of organization among the peasants to their selfishness, which he believed could be overcome through education in four fields: literature and art, means of livelihood, hygiene, and citizenship.[223] He attached particular importance to citizenship education in enhancing the peasants' political consciousness. "It is not enough to turn an illiterate peasant into 'someone who can read'; it is of first importance to make him a citizen with democratic ideas," he argued.[224]

The Communists were also concerned with the peasants' need for organization and their political consciousness. However, when the Communists talked about consciousness, they usually meant both national consciousness and class consciousness. In other words, the Communists wanted a different kind of peasant organization, one based on class difference and class consciousness, and they believed that it was the duty of the revolutionary intellectuals to help the peasants become organized and transform their consciousness. The peasants needed to be awakened to their class consciousness because they were not able to recognize their own class interest. As early as 1920, Cai Hesen argued that the problem of the Chinese revolution was not that China had no classes, but that the Chinese workers and peasants had no class consciousness—because they attributed their poverty and misery to "fate." "If their class consciousness is awakened," he predicted, "then the momentum would be as strong as that of [the working class] of western and eastern Europe."[225] Qu Qiubai believed that the peasant revolutions in the past failed because the peasants were not well organized and lacked democratic ideas; "There was no revolutionary class to lead them then, as there is today with the Chinese proletariat in the vanguard."[226] Fang Zhimin argued in early 1927 that the peasants were not strong in the past because they were not united, commenting "Now the peasants have understanding, but it will not do if they are not united."[227] Zhou Enlai, in an article written in 1928, emphasized that since seventy-five percent of the party members were peasants, the party was not built on a strong proletarian class base, and so needed to emphasize eliminating peasant consciousness as well as petty-bourgeois consciousness.[228] In a letter to the Red Army of Jinggangshan led by Mao Zedong and Zhu De written in September 1929, Zhou Enlai pointed out that since the Red Army was composed mainly of destitute peasants rather than workers, it was necessary to promote proletarian consciousness to overcome peasant consciousness.[229] Two decades later, in a speech to the writers, Zhou reiterated this point and argued that the peasants possessed some backward characteristics that could only be eliminated through patient reform with the help of "us"—the revolutionary intellectuals—although he also praised the peasants for their merits: courage, diligence, endurance, and simplicity.[230]

In stories from the 1930s and 1940s, left-wing writers began to devote themselves to depicting the process of the peasants' consciousness transformation. *The Mountain Rain* by Wang Tongzhao was one of those stories. Wang Tongzhao told his readers that besides describing the causes and facts of rural bankruptcy, he also wanted to trace the process of the peasants' awakening in this novel. The destitute peasant Xi Dayou, after abandoning his village and experiencing many new things and meeting many new people in the coastal city, began to understand "why the Japanese factory is willing to spend ten thousand silver dollars a day to hire laborers; why our own villages has become so desolate; why we are not able to keep out the foreign merchandise and why we are constantly bullied by foreigners." Mao Dun found in Xi Dayou a transformation from "peasant consciousness" to "proletarian consciousness" due to changes in his life.[231] In the 1940s, the famous peasant writer Zhao Shuli also paid much attention to the transformation of the peasant consciousness. Zhao's peasant characters usually had a dark side. In many cases, this dark side was reflected in their "feudal consciousness," which Zhao believed could only be overcome through constant education. In "The Story of Li Youcai," a peasant called Little Yuan was originally an activist in the struggle against the landlord, but after he was made the village official under the new regime, he began to act like a landlord. The peasant masses, except for a few "awakened" ones, were still subservient and not aware of their own rights, hence were powerless when confronting these "new landlords." In Zhao's opinion, the peasants had to undergo a process of consciousness transformation. Otherwise the revolution would simply end up with a new group of landlords replacing the old one.

The emphasis on organization is understandable since organization is important for any political movement. The obsession with the transformation of consciousness, however, is somewhat surprising. This is especially so for the Communists because the emphasis on consciousness is contradictory to the teachings of classic Marxism. In his classical study on Li Dazhao, Maurice Meisner pointed out that Li Dazhao's thought in its pre-Marxist stage was marked by a strong voluntaristic spirit, which "resulted in his explicit rejection of certain deterministic features of Marxism in his first encounter with the theory."[232] As previously indicated, in this aspect, Li Dazhao was not alone among the Chinese intellectuals, whether Communists, Nationalists, or members of other groups. This feature drew the Chinese intellectuals close to two leading international Communists. One is Lenin, who strongly emphasized the role of the consciousness of the revolutionaries in the revolution; the other is Antonio Gramsci, who also wrote about the importance of consciousness. Gramsci defined culture as "the attainment of a higher awareness, with the aid of which one succeeds in understanding one's own historical value, one's own function in life, one's own rights and obligations," which sounds very similar to the Chinese intellectuals' discourse on consciousness. Gramsci's strategy for achieving such a culture or consciousness is also very similar to that adopted by the Chinese intellectuals. According to Gramsci:

> The fact is that only by degrees, one stage at a time, has humanity acquired consciousness of its own value and won for itself the right to throw off patterns of organization imposed on it by minorities at a previous period in history. And this consciousness was formed not under the brutal goad of physiological necessity, but as a result of intelligent reflection, at first by just a few people and later by a whole class, on why certain conditions exist and how best to convert the facts of vassalage into the signals of rebellion and social reconstruction.[233]

Yet there is a crucial difference between Gramsci and the Chinese intellectuals in their concepts of consciousness. Gramsci was talking about replacing the capitalist consciousness of the masses with the proletarian consciousness or, in his own words, to replace the capitalist hegemony with an alternative hegemony, while the Chinese intellectuals all focused on getting rid of the so-called feudal consciousness of the peasantry and indoctrinating them with a new consciousness, be it the Three Principles of the People or socialism. For Gramsci, the transformation of consciousness is important because Western Europe is so developed that the capitalist class has established not only a political state, but also a civil society, which makes it very hard, if not impossible, to achieve a Communist victory through pure violent revolution. The reason why the Chinese intellectuals emphasized the transformation of consciousness was precisely the opposite: they wanted to use consciousness to make up for the underdevelopment of Chinese capitalism and the backwardness of Chinese society.

Various methods were adopted to awaken the peasants' consciousness.[234] For the Communists, the best way was by class struggle itself. Mass assemblies, parades, slogan shouting, trial and execution of the landlords, land confiscation and redistribution, and military struggle with the landlords and the Nationalists—all contributed to the increasing awareness of class consciousness among the peasants. Education, especially political indoctrination, was emphasized too. This could take many forms, including meetings, classes, and performances. In left-wing writer Yu Dafu's articulation, being involved in the peasant movement and taking part in actual struggle activities were active methods of arousing the peasants, whereas education was a passive method.[235]

For the non-Communist intellectuals, education, or the passive method, was taken as the major and even the sole way of arousing the peasants. The rural reconstructionists attached great importance to education. Citizenship education formed an important part of Yan Yangchu's mass education program in Dingxian. Besides formal teaching, Yan also promoted mass literature and peasant drama, supervised by Sun Fuyuan, a famous writer and editor, and Xiong Foxi, a Harvard-trained playwright, respectively. Sun edited 600 "mass reading books," while Xiong wrote and directed several plays to expose the evil behavior of the immoral gentry and the ignorance and superstition of the villagers, and to indoctrinate the peasants with Yan Yangchu's teachings.[236] They also made use of history. Scholars affiliated with the mass education association spent many years studying Chinese history from the Xia Dynasty to the Song Dynasty and chose forty national heroes from that period to use as role models for the masses.[237] The mass education association also published a magazine for the peasants, which appeared every ten days during the twelve years between 1925 and 1937. The articles were usually short and the language simple. Besides agricultural techniques, the magazine carried a column labeled "citizenship education," as well as stories and legends aimed at educating the peasants. It also reported to the peasants the current affairs of the nation and the world. For a long period, Dr. Sun Yat-sen's will was reprinted on the first page of each issue. There was also a short editorial in every issue; topics in 1926 included "It is not that the Republic is not Good"; "The Republic is still Good no Matter What"; "Why We Have to Have a Nation"; "Peasants Should Be Strongly Interested in National Affairs too"; "How Can Peasants Help Eliminate the Domestic Turmoil"; "The National Day and the Peasants"; "We Peasants should not Look Down Upon Ourselves"; "Despotism and Republicanism in the Villages." The topics of 1929 and 1930 included "How to Eliminate the Superstition of the Peasants"; "Who Dare to Say that the Common People are not Patriotic"; "The Country-bumpkins and Civilization"; "The Awakening of the Peasants"; and "The Country-bumpkins and Politics."

The Portrayal of the Powerful Peasant

The 1920s generation of Chinese intellectuals realized that ignorance, lack of organization, and many other weak points of the peasants could be overcome by better organizational and educational work offered by the intellectuals and that the peasants could be turned into a powerful revolutionary force. The events of 1926 and 1927 proved to many that this understanding was right. Madame Sun Yat-sen described vividly how the awakened and organized peasants moved Dr. Sun Yat-sen:

> I remember clearly the First All-Kwangtung Peasants' Conference in Canton in July 1924.[238] There for the first time we saw the people of

China...coming to participate in the revolution. From all the districts of Kwangtung, the peasants came, many of them walking miles and miles, barefooted, to Canton. They were ragged, tattered. Some carried baskets and poles. I remember I was deeply moved.

Dr. Sun was moved also. When we reached home, he said to me: "This is the beginning of the success of the revolution," and he told me again the part the oppressed people of China must play in their own salvation.[239]

Probably it was this new understanding of the revolutionary potential and spirit of the peasant that made Chen Duxiu feel it necessary to reassess the Boxer Rebellion in September 1924. He realized that his 1918 assessment of the Boxer Rebellion was not fair. He now felt that the xenophobia, superstition, and barbarism of the Boxer rebels were all forgivable, given the crime foreigners committed in China and the superstition and barbarism of the whole world at that time. "What really deserves our resentment is the civilization of the warlords, bureaucrats, unscrupulous merchants, university professors and journalists who are subservient to the foreigners, not the barbarism of the xenophobic Boxers!" he wrote. He said now he had to admit that the Boxer Rebellion was the solemn and stirring prelude to the Chinese national revolution.[240] He now listed the 1898 Reform, the Boxer Rebellion, the 1911 Revolution, and the May Fourth Movement as the four important national movements of the petty bourgeoisie.[241]

The left-wing Nationalist Liao Zhongkai had reached the same conclusion several months earlier than Chen Duxiu. Liao argued that China had had two revolutions; the first was the Boxer Rebellion and the second the 1911 Revolution. Unlike many other educated people of his generation, who attributed the failure of the Boxer Rebellion to the Boxers' stupidity, Liao put the blame on the Qing officials.[242] Li Dazhao also wrote about the Boxers in a sympathetic tone. To him it was understandable that the Boxers destroyed everything foreign, because the rebellion was actually not just a result of political, religious, racial, and cultural conflicts, but also "possesses economic meaning, and to some extent, it was a reaction to the oppression of industrial economy."[243] In another article, he called the Boxer Rebellion a "national revolutionary movement," although he also mentioned the peasants' weak points, notably, their ignorance and superstition.[244] In 1925, the Communist theoretician Qu Qiubai defined the Boxer Rebellion as "a primitive peasant rebellion," "a class struggle launched by the oppressed and exploited class of China against the foreign capitalist class," and "an anti-imperialist national liberation movement." In his opinion, the Boxers had many shortcomings, but were brave and patriotic and their actions wholly justified, considering the foreign aggression China had suffered.[245] In 1926, the left-wing Nationalist Gan Naiguang called the Boxer Rebellion "an ardent great peasant resistance."[246] After the Communists broke with the Nationalists in 1927 and retreated to the villages to lead peasant revolutions, the Communist Party began to fully rehabilitate the reputation of the Boxers and promote the Boxer Rebellion as "an anti-imperialist movement."[247]

If the "Boxer bandits" were revolutionaries, then what were the current bandits? Under the new circumstances, many revolutionary intellectuals began to write and talk favorably about the peasant rebels, or "bandits" and secret societies. Both Li Dazhao and Wang Ruofei paid special attention to the revolutionary potential of the Red Spear Society in northern China.[248] As early as 1925, the United Front dispatched peasant movement personnel to Henan to infiltrate and reorganize the Red Spears.[249] Chen Duxiu wrote in 1926 that the Red Spears rebellion was as significant as the Taiping and Boxer rebellions and referred to them as the latest in a long history of Chinese peasant rebellions.[250] Mao Zedong argued in 1926 that the rural vagrants of China who formed secret organizations were capable of fighting very bravely. "If a method can be found for leading them, they can become a revolutionary force," he predicted.[251] In 1926, one newspaper article argued that "those who look like bandits and robbers are actually a peasant revolutionary army." Lu Xun, although continuing to call the Boxers "bandits," agreed with this author.[252]

This new understanding of the revolutionary spirit of the peasantry even convinced the head of the Department of Peasant Affairs of the Nationalist Party, the left-wing Nationalist Gan Naiguang, in 1926 that the peasantry actually formed the class base of both the Nationalist Party and the national revolution, just as the workers formed the class base of the Communist Party. Unlike most other Nationalists, who supported a four-class alliance theory or a "revolution of all the people," Gan argued that the peasants were the main revolutionary force, while all other groups—workers, merchants, and so on—were their allies, although he insisted that whenever there were conflicts between the national interest and the class interest, the national interest should prevail.[253] He based his theory on the argument that imperialism, China's primary enemy, was supported by the warlords and bureaucrats, who were in turn buttressed by a class of local tyrants and evil gentry. Therefore, to overthrow imperialism, it was necessary to first overthrow the Chinese lackeys of the imperialists, and the class best suited to this task was the peasantry because they formed the great majority of China's population and their resistance would be the most powerful. He cited the Taiping Rebellion and the Boxer Rebellion to prove his point.[254]

It was probably also on the basis of this new understanding of the revolutionary spirit of the peasants that an argument was made as to whether Lu Xun's Ah Q was still a true image of the Chinese peasant. In 1928,

Qian Xingtun, a left-wing literary critic, argued that Ah Q represented the peasant of the past era—the era of the 1911 Revolution. It was not an accurate image of the peasant of the new era—the era of the May Fourth Movement, the May Thirtieth Movement, and the Northern Expedition—because in the previous decade Chinese peasants had demonstrated their revolutionary spirit.[255]

Mao Dun came to Lu Xun's defense by saying that the peasant movement had a history of only two to three years. Therefore, when Lu Xun wrote the stories in his *Cheering from the Sideline* before the Northern Expedition, the Chinese villages were exactly as Lu Xun described in his novels. Even after the Northern Expedition, there were still many peasants like those whom Lu Xun described.[256] Mao Dun still held this view five decades later. In his autobiography, he argues that the development of the peasant movement was not even among different regions of China. The revolutionary spirit of the peasants in the Lake Tai area, including Jiangsu and Zhejiang Provinces, was not as strong as that of the peasants of Hunan, Hubei, and Jiangxi. The peasants' awakening was also a slow process. In the Lake Tai area, according to Mao Dun, it took ten years.[257] Another reader agreed with Mao Dun that Qian's criticism was problematic. He argued that the revolutionary peasants depicted in Qian's article existed only in the South, or one-third of China's territory. The peasants in the North were still naive, unorganized, uneducated, and superstitious. They knew nothing about revolution, not to mention revolutionary spirit! Ah Q was still alive and he still represented the majority of the Chinese peasants. He predicted that it would take at least five more years for all the Ah Qs to disappear in China.[258]

Lu Xun himself was even more pessimistic about the peasants' revolutionary spirit than that reader. He wrote in 1926, "I wish people are right to say that what I wrote about was a past era, but I am afraid that what I saw was not the past, but the future, or even two or three decades from now."[259] Lu Xun was too critical to see the revolutionary spirit of the peasants: his feelings toward them as reflected in the novels never went beyond sympathy and well-meaning criticism. A contemporary critic commented that "he does not ask the peasants to fight against their fate, neither does he ask the youth to return to the villages to reform the countryside."[260] In 1928, Feng Xuefeng, a leading Communist literary critic, divided the progressive intellectuals into two groups: one formed by those who turned against the old culture and society and their previous status by joining the socialist movement, the other composed of those who sympathized with the revolution, but still could not totally break with the past and were not sure about their own belief in revolution. Feng placed Lu Xun into the second group.[261] After a thorough study of the peasant characters created by Lu Xun in his various stories, Mao Dun concluded that they all belong to "the children of traditional China."[262]

All these evaluations of Lu Xun are quite different from the eulogistic one made by Mao Zedong in 1937. The truth is that Lu Xun was a representative of the writers of the early 1920s. Besides Lu Xun, writers emerging during that decade who wrote about the peasant included Ye Shengtao (Zhejiang), Xu Yunuo (Henan), Pan Xun (Zhejiang), Peng Jiahuang, Xu Jie (Zhejiang), Wang Renshu (Ba Ren, Zhejiang), Wang Tongzhao (Shandong), Xu Qinwen (Zhejiang), Jian Xian'ai (Guizhou), Feng Wenbing (Feiming, Hubei), Wang Luyan (Zhejiang), Sheng Congwen (Hunan), Tai Jingnong, and others. Some of these writers, including Xu Yunuo, Pan Xun, Peng Jiahuang, and Xu Jie, stopped writing around 1926, which means their literary career ended before the emergence of the radical peasant movement in 1927. Accordingly, like Lu Xun's novels, most of their stories focused on the ignorance, superstition, and subservience of the peasants. Their characters demonstrated little revolutionary spirit. Although some of their characters were not content with their lives and tried to escape the bleak world of their villages, their adventures always ended up with failure. Both critics and the writers themselves believed that what they wrote was exactly what was happening in the villages at that time. For example, Mao Dun praised Xu Jie and Peng Jiahuang for their "pure objective attitude."[263]

Lu Xun and some of his fellow writers of the early 1920s seem to have never experienced the transformation of thought as Mao Dun did, who belonged to the 1920s generation in the beginning, but then caught up with the radical writers of the 1930s. Mao Dun initially was very pessimistic about the peasants' revolutionary spirit and the future of the land revolution. According to Zheng Chaolin, during one of his visits to Mao Dun immediately after the collapse of the First United Front in 1927, Mao Dun "complained about the positions the Party had adopted after the August 7 Conference [1927] and opposed the policy of organizing peasant insurrections everywhere. He said that if one insurrection failed, the peasants would no longer be prepared to participate in insurrections, even if the situation became revolutionary. That was the first time I had heard a comrade come out clearly against the new policies of the Central Committee," Zheng comments.[264] Mao Dun's pessimism about the Chinese revolution in general was reflected in his first trilogy, composed of three novels—*Shattered Illusion, Vacillation,* and *Pursuit*—and his famous and controversial essay "From Guling to Tokyo." His pessimism about the peasant revolution in particular is expressed in the story "Mud," which is his first centered on the peasant. The story begins with the arrival of a small Communist guerrilla force at a village to mobilize the peasants. The villagers, however, are very scared, believing the Communists will force them to practice "sharing wives." Then Chiang Kai-shek's army arrives and the guerrillas retreat. Chiang's army loots the village and executes Uncle Huang, the only literate person in the

village, for having helped the Communists. Instead of being aroused, the villagers are relieved because everything becomes normal again and "there were
to be no more new and incomprehensible terrors in store."[265] Fifty years
later, Mao Dun criticizes himself for making the peasants look too backward
in this story. Because of his "obsolete thinking," Mao Dun was ostracized by
the party after the Northern Expedition.[266]

But Mao Dun was not going to remain an enemy of the party for long.
In 1932 and 1933, he completed his village trilogy of "The Spring
Silkworm," "The Autumn Harvest," and "The Last Days of Winter." In
these stories he created some young, politically conscious, and rebellious
peasant characters, whose images were totally different from the ones he portrayed in "Mud." The author frequently likened these people to the Taiping
Rebels.[267] The Chinese peasant rebellions in history also drew Mao Dun's
attention. In 1930, he wrote a story about the rebellion led by Chen Sheng
and Wu Guang at the end of the Qin Dynasty. The rebellious peasants,
especially their leaders, were highly praised. He also applied modern revolutionary concepts to this ancient event. For example, he adopted the concept
of class to describe the peasants involved in the rebellion.[268]

Mao Dun's transition was probably as much an outcome of his own
awakening as of pressure from his fellow left-wing writers and the
Communist Party. There was a strong tendency among left-wing writers in
the early 1930s to shift attention from urban intellectuals to the revolutionary
peasants. Along with the march of the Communist revolutionaries into the
villages, peasants and their revolution became the focus of the left-wing writers who stayed in urban centers. These left-wing writers, including Jiang
Guangci, Hong Shen, Ding Ling, Wu Zuxiang, Ye Zi, Sha Ting, Qiu
Dongping, and others, had all experienced the peasant movement of the late
1920s and were now armed with a revolutionary ideology. They played a very
important role in turning the party propaganda about the revolutionary spirit
of the peasants into vivid literary images. Peasants in their works were no
longer as naive and weak-minded as Ah Q and others in the stories created by
the writers of the 1920s. This new trend began in the years between 1928 and
1930, with the rise of the so-called revolutionary literature or propaganda literature, led by Jiang Guangci. Jiang Guangci's novel *The Roaring Land*, published in 1930, was considered the first literary work depicting the awakening
of the peasants and their revolution. The story, like many others by Jiang, followed a formula: a revolutionary intellectual, who is the son of the local landlord, returns to his village to lead the peasant revolution. He is assisted by a
young villager who has worked as a miner and a female student who is the
niece of another local landlord. Together they manage to mobilize the peasants and organize them into peasant associations. The young peasants are all
awakened and militant, while the old ones are subservient, superstitious, and

backward at the beginning, but in the end, realize that the young peasants are right and they too join the revolution.[269] In the same year, Yang Hansheng published his *The Underground Spring*, which was also about the peasant movement during the Northern Expedition. Mao Dun remarked that the story was very much like Jiang Guangci's works, implying that it is full of political propaganda but mediocre in artistic quality.[270]

In fact, even before the publication of *The Roaring Land*, some stories about the peasant movement during the Northern Expedition had already been published, including *The Dusty Shadow* by Li Jingming, published in Shanghai in 1927, based on the true story of the revolutionary intellectual Zhou Shuiping, who led the unsuccessful peasant movement of Jiangyin County of Jiangsu during the Northern Expedition and was executed by the warlord Sun Chuanfang.[271] The tragic result of the movement and the story put "heavy pressure" on Lu Xun and made him "very uncomfortable."[272]

After 1930, the revolutionary peasant became a fashionable subject in left-wing literary writings. In Hong Shen's "The Bridge of Five Degree Holders" (1930), the peasants of a village in Southern China who were suffering from a severe drought won their struggle against the powerful Zhou family by destroying the Zhou family's bridge, which was believed to be related to the fortune of the Zhou family, but blocked the passing of the boat with a water pump used for irrigation. Li Quansheng, the small landholding peasant who led the struggle, was very brave and determined.[273] Ding Ling, like Mao Dun, had been famous for her stories about young intellectuals, but now she also shifted her attention to the peasants. In "The Tianjiachong Village," written in 1931, she described how a revolutionary intellectual, who was a daughter of a landlord, awakened the consciousness of Zhao Desheng, a landless peasant, and other villagers. The young female revolutionary in the story advised the peasants, "How could you fail the battle [against the landlords]? You have so many people! Look ahead from here, then go ahead, then look ahead again, from here to the place far, far away—in all those places with chimney smoke, those who live in hut and pit, those who stand by the cattle pen—all those powerful and strong men are your comrades!" The young revolutionary was later arrested, but the now aroused villagers began to fight. According to Ding Ling, the novel was based on a true story.[274] "The Flood," another work by Ding Ling, written in the same year and also based on real events, concerned the same theme. The peasants' fight against the flood finally led them to confront the corrupt and inept government.[275] One contemporary critic commented that the most valuable contribution of "The Flood" was the belief in the power of the masses.[276] Wu Zuxiang's "One Thousand and Eight Hundred Piculs" (1933) described how the organized poor peasants looted the 1800 piculs of grain stored in the temple of a landlord clan.[277] The peasant Xi Dayou in Wang Tongzhao's *The*

Mountain Rain decided to join the revolutionaries after his ideological transformation.[278] Xi Dayou represented a break from the peasant images created
by Wang Tongzhao a few years earlier.[279] Ai Qing, while in prison, wrote a
beautiful long poem to praise the peasant rebels led by Chen Sheng and Wu
Guang at the end of the Qin Dynasty.[280] This radical trend in the revolutionary literature even influenced writers who were not directly involved with the
League of Left-wing Writers. Wang Luyan, for example, published two
novels, *The Village* and *The Wild Fire (The Angry Village)*, both in 1936, in
which he depicted the peasant rebellions and created the characters of many
revolutionary peasants who were totally different from the helpless and subservient peasant characters he had created previously.

Ye Zi might be the best representative of those left-wing writers who
dealt with the revolutionary peasants in the 1930s. He devoted most of his
short literary life to writing about the peasant revolution of the late 1920s
and early 1930s. All heroes and heroines in his stories have strong revolutionary spirit. The young generation seems immediately receptive to revolution. The old peasants are more like Lu Xun's characters in the beginning;
they are hardworking, enduring, and subservient, but in the end they are all
taught by experience that revolution is the only way out. In fact, it was the
norm to write about the generational or age differences and conflicts among
the peasants. The older people, whether a father, a mother, or an older
brother, are usually still not politically conscious and are not ready to fight,
but the son and the younger sibling are often of a totally different type. They
are politically aroused, brave, and resolute. To some extent, the differences
between the old and the young peasants in the stories of the 1930s mirror the
differences between the writers of the 1920s and the radical writers of the
1930s. Mao Dun depicted the differences and conflict between a father and a
son in "The Autumn Harvest," and Wang Luyan described the differences
and conflict between an elder brother and a younger brother in *The Wild
Fire*. However, it was Ye Zi who made the most extensive use of this formula. In "The Harvest" (1933) and "The Fire" (1933), the hardworking and
docile old peasant Uncle Yun Pu has illusory hopes about the landlords and
the officials and is against the revolutionary activities of his son Liqiu in the
beginning, hoping the landlord and official will leave some grain for his
family after being served a good meal. However, after all his grain is taken
away and his son arrested and executed, he joins the revolt without hesitation. In "Outside the Wire Entanglement" (1933), Uncle Wang initially
curses his two sons for their rebellious activities. After the Nationalist Army
takes his property, burns his house, and kills his daughter-in-law and two
grandchildren, he is in such despair that he wants to hang himself, but
changes his mind at the last second and decides to join his two revolutionary
sons. The next morning, the author wrote, Uncle Wang is "on the way to the

direction where the sun rises." In "The Guide" (1933), Aunt Liu, an old peasant who has worshipped Guanyin for over forty years, finds it hard to hold on to her belief after the Nationalists kill her three sons. She ends up disguising herself and leading a brigade of the Nationalist Army to a trap set by the Red Army, before the Nationalist Army executes her in the end.[281]

Despite the bloody and tragic scenes in his stories, Ye Zi, compared to Lu Xun, was much more optimistic about the peasants' consciousness and much more confident about what path the peasants should take. On Ye Zi's novels Lu Xun offered these comments: "The writer has fulfilled the current task, he has responded to the oppressor: Literature is militant!"[282] In fact, it was the peasants, rather than literature, that were really militant. Most of Ye Zi's novels were based on true stories. For example, Uncle Yun Pu and his son Li Qiu in "The Harvest" and "The Fire" were Ye Zi's uncle and cousin, respectively. The latter was executed in 1931 for joining the local peasant movement.[283] Led by his youngest uncle, a Communist student returned from the provincial capital Changsha, Ye Zi's whole family participated in the peasant movement in Hunan from 1925 to 1927, and underwent the blood and fire of the fierce class struggle. Thirteen members of his family died for the movement after its failure, and his mother became mentally deranged after being forced to witness the execution of his father and sister.[284] Ye Zi admitted that his novels were short of artistic flavor, but were full of flaming enthusiasm and bloody and tearful facts. "Sometimes I wanted to jump into my stories to fight the enemy," he declared.[285]

The strong interest of the left-wing writers in the peasants' revolutionary spirit continued in the 1940s. Important revolutionary literary works on peasants during that decade included *The Heroes of Mountain Luliang* (1945) by Ma Feng and Xi Rong, and a series of stories written by the peasant writer Zhao Shuli, among which the most successful were "The Marriage of Little Erhei," "The Story of Li Youcai," and "The Transformation of the Lijiazhuang Village." *The Heroes of Mountain Luliang* was about how the peasants of northern China joined the resistance against the Japanese invaders, and Zhao Shuli's novels described the peasant life in the Communist base area in Shaanxi. Mao Dun commented that the characters in *The Heroes of Mountain Luliang* represented "the peasants who had stood up and who could never be enslaved again," while the peasants in "The Story of Li Youcai" were those who had destroyed the feudal remains and were marching toward their total freedom; the peasants in "The Transformation of the Lijiazhuang Village" already possessed "a strong national consciousness," "a clear awareness about who to love and who to hate and a will to fight," and "the creative power."[286] Two important novels appeared in 1948 to depict the land reform being carried out in north China: *The Sun Shines over the Sangkan River* by Ding Ling, and *The Hurricane* by Zhou Libo. Both depicted the birth of a group of peasant heroes. In addition to novelists, playwrights and poets also devoted themselves to portraying the new image of the peasant. The most famous play about the new peasant during the period was *The White-Haired Girl*, written by He Jingzhi and Ding Yi, based on a real story, and one of the best poems about the new peasant was "Wang Gui and Li Xiangxiang," written in 1945 by the peasant poet Li Ji. The *Yangge* (Rice Song) plays were also used to demonstrate and extol the power of the peasants.[287]

The woodcarvers joined the left-wing writers in creating the image of revolutionary peasants. After 1937, some woodcarvers went to Yanan, while others stayed in the area controlled by the Nationalist government. In the years that followed, they created two contrasting images of the peasant: one was the image of the peasants in the non-Communist areas, who were not very different from the prerevolutionary peasant—poor, oppressed, and exploited; the other was the image of the peasants in the Communist-controlled area, representing the new type of peasants—strong, happy, and awakened.[288]

Different Understandings of the Peasant Power

Although the great majority of Chinese intellectuals had come to the conclusion that the peasants were a powerful force, they had different views about how to utilize that force. Liang Shuming, for example, at first did not believe the peasants could be turned into revolutionaries. After the Communist peasant movement began, he saw the revolutionary peasants mainly as a negative and destructive force. He proposed rural reconstruction, with the purpose of counterbalancing the Communist peasant movement and turning the peasants into a peaceful constructive force. Liang criticized those Chinese revolutionaries who strove to find the "driving force" of revolution among the "peasants, workers, proletariat and the oppressed." "In their imagination, these people are the most deprived both politically and economically, therefore, they must want to change the current state of affairs so that they can get equal political and economic opportunities," he argued. Liang believed that this was erroneous because these people could not become true revolutionaries for two fundamental reasons. First, their problems were caused by personal misfortune rather than class difference. Therefore, they would be fighting for personal gain rather than class interest. As a result, as soon as they achieved some status, they would turn into nonrevolutionaries or counterrevolutionaries. Second, these people were mostly ignorant peasants from poor and remote villages. They possessed no new knowledge. Instead, their life was permeated with old habits. Therefore, if they rose to solve their own problems, they would move backward rather than forward. However, Liang did not deny that the peasants formed "a potential powerful force in the society," which could be tapped for the benefit of the nation under two conditions: first, if it was guided by the intellectuals; second, if it was used to build a new social order rather than destroying old forces.[289]

The warlords Chen Jiongming and Yan Xishan shared Liang Shuming's perception of the peasants. According to Peng Pai, Chen Jiongming once told him that "I am scared of the masses, especially the peasants." "He turned pale at the mere mention of the peasants," Peng commented. Chen believed that the peasants should always be pacified and never aroused or mobilized. Thus Peng Pai's work among the peasants terrified him.[290] During the Anti-Japanese War, Yan Xishan's followers suggested that the peasants of Shanxi be mobilized to join the fight against the Japanese, but Yan was reluctant because, he contended, "it is not a simple matter to organize the peasants. We lose a big opportunity if we don't organize the peasants, but if we do, we'll create for ourselves a lot of trouble." He added, "The peasants are like a fierce tiger, we have to have an electric whip that can bring the tiger under control [before we start mobilizing it]."[291] Like the Communists, Liang Shuming, Chen Jiongming, and Yan Xishan all believed that the peasants possessed violent revolutionary power, but instead of tapping this power, as the Communists tried to do, they preferred keeping that power in check.

The non-Communist intellectuals tended to focus more on the peasants' potential intellectual and productive power rather than their revolutionary power. Yan Yangchu was a good example. He mentioned that his experience with the Chinese laborers in France helped him realize both the "bitterness" and the "strength" of the "bitter strength,"[292] and that "their physical strength is above us (the intellectuals), while their intellectual strength is not below us. The only difference is the opportunity of education."[293] He realized that China's richest resource was neither coal nor iron, but the 300 million politically uneducated peasants and he advocated exploiting this "intellectual mine." He firmly believed that a proper education program would release the potential intellectual power of the Chinese peasants. "As soon as the 'intellectual mine' is exploited, the intelligence of the people would be promoted, and [China] would hold sway over the world."[294] He believed that the fate of a nation is totally determined by the intellectual level of its people.[295] Besides intellectual power, he also emphasized productive power, physical power, and the power of unity of the peasants. He argued that these four types of power could be exploited by education in the four fields of literature and arts, economics, public health, and citizenship.[296]

There were also a few intellectuals who were never fully aware of the peasants' power. Fei Xiaotong, for example, admitted in 1950 that he was not convinced that the peasants were truly powerful until early 1949, when he saw a long line of peasant carters sending food to feed the Communist soldiers at the front during a dark night. He was on his way from Beijing to Shijiazhuang to meet with Mao. "Marching toward the opposite direction were the peasants and their grain carts. There was a flag on each cart, but there were no escorting soldiers. They continued their march with the light of lanterns during the late night. Looking from afar they were like a line of red stars. This image moved me... it was an iron current, it was unparalleled power," he wrote. He then blamed himself for being unfamiliar with this power, for not understanding this power earlier, and for lacking confidence in the liberation of the people. After he returned to Qinghua University from this trip, he made two speeches about the "power of the people."[297]

The image of a potentially powerful peasantry, together with the discourse on the innocence and sacredness of the peasantry, the emphasis on consciousness, a common aversion toward capitalism and belief in socialism, has led many to view many of the peasant sympathizers, including Dr. Sun Yat-sen, Li Dazhao, Peng Pai, Mao Zedong, Yan Yangchu, Fang Zhimin, Tao Xingzhi, Liang Shuming, and many others, as having been strongly influenced by populism—for among the elements of populism are the beliefs that the people are pristine and powerful, that a modest educational stimulus would release the creative forces of the people, and that it is possible to avoid capitalism.[298] Although there was never an independent populist movement in China, as there was in Russia, populism did add much flavor to the ideological basis of the various peasant movements of China, whether Communist, liberal, functionalist, or Confucianist. However, these Chinese intellectuals could hardly be described as pure populists because few of them really believed that the people, or the peasants, could carry out the revolution without the leadership of the intellectuals. Maurice Meisner found in Li Dazhao's views a contradiction between a populist faith in the revolutionary spontaneity and energies of the masses and a voluntaristic belief in the decisive revolutionary role of the consciousness of the intelligentsia.[299] Kamal Sheel found the same contradiction in the mind of Fang Zhimin.[300] The same can be said about Mao Zedong, Peng Pai, and many other Communist intellectuals. Benjamin Schwartz reached the following conclusion nearly four decades ago: "That anarchistic variety of populism which insists on the spontaneous initiative of the people itself does not become deeply entrenched in China.... In general, it is the elitist rather than the anarchist brand of populism which wins in China. The notion that popular energies are to be tapped is certainly present, but it is linked to the conviction that their energies must be guided by those who know."[301]

The peasants were ignorant, innocent, poor, and powerful. These were the major aspects of the image of the peasant in the minds of the Chinese intellectuals during the first half of the twentieth century. But these were not all the elements in the image of the peasant. The ideas that the peasants were superstitious, physically weak, selfish, and so on, also formed part of the intellectuals' discourses about the peasants. However, most of these other elements in the image of the peasant can be related to the four dominant aspects in one way or another. The four aspects of the image of the peasant did not evolve equally at the same time. At the beginning of the century, most intellectuals were mainly concerned about the ignorance of the peasants, and only a few of them realized that the peasants were actually powerful when and if proper leadership and education were provided. By the 1920s and the 1930s, however, most intellectuals had come to agree that the peasants were truly powerful. While the peasants were still believed to be ignorant, most intellectuals now felt that such ignorance could be forgiven, since it was not their own fault. Moreover, they believed that such ignorance could be overcome with their help. At the same time, the view that the peasants were innocent and poor became widely accepted, as a result of the influence of new trends of thought and new events. On the whole, in the first two or three decades of the twentieth century, Chinese intellectuals managed to turn the image of the peasants from a basically negative one to an essentially positive one. The major features that formed the multifaceted peasant image created by the Chinese intellectuals in the 1920s and 1930s were passionately and concisely summarized by the legendary American journalist Edgar Snow in 1936, who described the Chinese peasantry as the "impoverished, underfed, exploited, illiterate, but kind, generous, courageous and just now rather rebellious human beings who are the vast majority of the Chinese people." [302]

This transformation of the peasants' image was accompanied by a transformation of the intellectuals' perception of their own roles and their relations with the peasants. At the turn of the century, most intellectuals acted as bystanding critics of the peasants. Starting from the 1920s and 1930s, however, many of them began to consider themselves representatives of the peasants, and the various groups of intellectuals even fought against one another for the right to represent the peasants. This transformation becomes obvious through a quick comparison between the writings about the rebellious peasants during the Boxer Rebellion and those about Boxers and the newly emerged revolutionary peasants during the 1920s and 1930s. The tone had changed. Instead of blaming and criticizing the peasants, the intellectuals now praised and extolled them. Moreover, the intellectuals now tended to blame themselves for whatever weaknesses the peasants possessed. The way of addressing the peasant was changed too. At the time of the Boxer Rebellion, the peasants were usually addressed as "they" and "them." However, by the 1920s and 1930s, many intellectuals began to address the peasants as "we" and "us." There was much discussion about the merging of the peasants and intellectuals, and some intellectuals believed they had actually successfully transformed themselves and had adopted the identity of the working class. If, at the beginning of the century, the peasants were mainly viewed as a source of the national crisis, by the 1920s and 1930s, many intellectuals had come to realize that the peasants could become a powerful positive force, or at least a potential positive force in the national movement. In the ignorance and poverty of the peasantry, the intellectuals found the guilt of the "old" society, which they intended to overthrow or reform. In the innocence, poverty, and powerfulness of the peasantry, the intellectuals found the force needed for overthrowing or reforming the "old" society.

The peasants' ignorance, innocence, poverty, and powerfulness were recurrent and universal features present as they were in the writings of intellectuals with different theoretical and political persuasions. As a result, all the images of the peasantry created during that period were multisided. However, that does not mean there were no crucial differences among the images created by different groups of intellectuals. Two major differences can be discerned among the images created by the various schools. The first difference was in the relative importance each group attached to each feature. For some pastoral writers, innocence or purity was the most important aspect of the peasants' image of their creation. The other features possessed only secondary importance. Yan Yangchu and his followers in the rural reconstruction movement argued that the four most striking traits of the peasant were ignorance, poverty, weakness, and selfishness. Although they also discussed the peasants' innocence and power, they believed that these were less important than the four features they listed. The left-wing intellectuals, however, believed that the most important features of the peasants' image were poverty and powerfulness. Because of the varying importance they attached to the various features, the portraits of the peasant produced by the various intellectual groups were quite different from one another.

The second major difference among the various groups of intellectuals was in the interpretations they offered. For example, while all agreed that the Chinese peasants were truly poor, they attributed this to different causes: some viewed imperialism, the external factor, as the chief or sole culprit; some argued that external and internal factors played equal roles; still others held that poverty was entirely an internal problem to China. As to the internal factor of rural poverty, Communist and left-wing intellectuals argued that it was composed of the warlords, including the new warlords led by Chiang Kai-shek, the compradors in the cities, and the landlords and gentry in the villages. The Nationalists would list only the old warlords and bandits. They would call the Communists red bandits, who they believed had prevented the Nationalist government from reunifying and reconstructing the nation. As discussed before, the relations between ignorance and poverty caused much controversy. The left-wing intellectuals attributed the peasants' ignorance to their poverty, which was in turn related to social injustice; but others held that it was ignorance that caused poverty. Regarding the peasants' power, the left-wing intellectuals emphasized the peasants' revolutionary spirit, but others, including Yan Yangchu, Liang Shuming, and the right-wing Nationalists, did not regard this as significant. While the latter also talked about the power of the peasants, they preferred to interpret it as something very different. As for that power demonstrated in the violent peasant movement, the left-wing intellectuals saw it as positive and revolutionary, while the right-wing Nationalists and many others considered it negative and destructive. Therefore, even if the various groups of intellectuals shared a same or a similar portrait of the peasant, they might still endow it with different meanings.

These two major differences indicate that some room did exist for the intellectuals to manipulate the image of the peasant to fit their own programs. The links between the images created by the various groups of intellectuals and their respective economic-political programs were quite obvious. Although those who argued for the existence of class difference in rural China did not necessarily support class struggle, those who argued against the existence of class difference were all against class struggle. Those who advocated agrarian revolution emphasized the revolutionary spirit of the peasants, while those who championed education and reform stressed the intellectual power of the peasants. The images of the peasant thus created were the outcome of the interaction between the perceived social reality on the one hand and a preexisting national program in the minds of the intellectuals on the other. This, in turn, would be used to justify each group's program for changing the fate of the nation.

4

The Nature of Rural Society

With Chiang Kai-shek's coup against the Communists in April 1927 and Wang Jingwei's purge of the Communists in July 1927, the First United Front between the Nationalists and Communists came to a bloody end. By the same token, the so-called Great Revolution of China that started on May 30, 1925, was regarded as having failed. Why did the revolution fail? Where was the way out, if there was any? Revolutionaries of all kinds, especially the revolutionary intellectuals who were compelled to retreat to their research rooms in the urban centers, were forced to ponder these questions. It did not take long for the various groups of revolutionaries to find that they were involved in a theoretical battle that was no less fierce than the military and political battles they had just fought and were still fighting. One of the most important topics they debated during that period was the issue of the nature of Chinese society—that is, whether modern China had become a capitalist society, a feudal society, a semifeudal and semicolonial society, or none of these.

Organizers, participants, and critics alike emphasized the importance of this debate to past and future revolutions. According to He Ganzhi, a Communist theoretician, the debate mattered because, on the one hand, it helped examine the reasons why the Great Revolution had failed and hence would help mold future policies, and, on the other hand, it provided opportunities for the various political parties to propagandize their own views and criticize those of others.[1] Wang Lixi, editor of *Dushu zazhi*, one of the most influential journals at the time, emphasized the importance of the debate to the search for revolutionary strategies. In 1931, he announced "in order to inquire into the right future of the revolution, we first need to answer: at

73

what social stage is China in at present?"[2] Qian Junrui, an active Communist participant in the latter phase of the debate, declared that "the purpose of our debate about the nature of Chinese rural society is not to conduct academic argument, but to determine the tasks and nature of the agricultural reform movement or peasant movement of contemporary China."[3] Mao Zedong also realized the importance of the issue. In 1939, he summarized the points put forth by Communist Party theoreticians and made a formal statement about the nature of Chinese society. According to Mao, "only when we grasp the nature of Chinese society will we be able to understand clearly the targets, tasks, motive forces and characters of the Chinese revolution and its prospective and future transition. A clear understanding of the nature of Chinese society, that is, of the conditions of China, is therefore the key to a clear understanding of all the problems of the revolution."[4]

The debate was carried out among the various factions of the Nationalist Party and Communist Party rather than between the two parties, because one of the most striking political features of the post-Northern Expedition era was the rise and fall of factions within the two parties. During the three years between 1927 and 1930, Chen Duxiu, Qu Qiubai, and Li Lisan were deposed as leaders one after another by the Chinese Communist Party. Factions within the party struggled not only for power, but also for the legitimacy of their theories and strategies. The three deposed leaders, for example, were believed to represent three different revolutionary strategies respectively: right opportunism, "left" putschism, and "left" adventurism—to follow the later official definitions of the Communist Party. The struggle finally led to the formation of the Chinese Trotskyite organization led by Chen Duxiu, as opposed to the Chinese Communist Party, from which Chen was expelled in 1929. The same factional struggles occurred within the Chinese Nationalist Party. One year after the collapse of the First United Front, two powerful factions, the Reorganization Group and the Third Party, were formed in Shanghai. All these factions, both Nationalist and Communist, were more or less involved in the debate about the nature of Chinese society.

Of crucial importance to understanding the nature of Chinese society was understanding the nature of rural Chinese society, because the rise of peasant power in South China, especially the peasants' demand for solution of the land problem, was one of the most important contributions to the breakdown of the First United Front.[5] After the collapse of the First United Front, the peasant problem—and especially the land problem—became the thorniest issue to demand the attention of all parties and factions and caused endless problems in their relations. Moreover, the nature of urban China was already quite clear because the Chinese cities had obviously become an integral part of the capitalist world by that time. What remained uncertain was the nature of rural Chinese society. During the first phase of the debate, which lasted roughly from 1928 to 1933, the major issues debated were the nature of Chinese society as a whole and the general social history of China, in which special attention was paid to rural Chinese society. During the second phase, lasting from 1934 to 1935 but continuing sporadically into 1937 and beyond, the nature of rural Chinese society became the focal point of the debate.

Although the Communists and leftists formed the majority of the participants, some scholars with other political affiliations also joined in. Nor was the debate confined to Chinese revolutionaries and scholars: Soviet and Japanese leftist theoreticians also contributed. Marxism provided the theoretical weapon for the great majority of the participants, and even many of the non-Communist scholars adopted Marxist theories and terms.[6] But there were also scholars who refused to accept Marxian views. Finally, the debate mainly took place during the period between the split of the First United Front in 1927 and the Japanese invasion of China in 1937. Its roots, however, can be traced to as early as 1920; and it lingered on for quite a while after 1937. Fei Xiaotong, for example, in his works written during and after the Second World War, still tried to define the nature of rural China. Wang Yanan, a contributor to *Dushu zazhi* and a supporter of the theory of a capitalist China in the early 1930s, changed his position in the 1950s and wrote a book to prove the theory of a semifeudal and semicolonial China, which by then had become the indisputable official theory of Communist China.[7] In the 1980s, historians in Mainland China started another debate on the issue.[8]

THE INDIGENOUS PIONEERS: 1920–1922

In November 1920, after escorting the British philosopher Bertrand Russell on a trip to Hunan Province, the Chinese philosopher Zhang Dongsun became Russell's loyal disciple and fully accepted Russell's idea that what China really needed at that moment was not socialism, but education and industry, because China's two biggest problems were believed to be ignorance and poverty. Zhang published several short articles and letters during and after that month, to propagate Russell's ideas, among which the most well known was a 500-character article entitled "One More Lesson Learned from My Trip to the Interior."[9] In these articles and letters Zhang Dongsun criticized the Chinese socialists for blindly accepting socialist ideas created for Western society by Westerners, without paying due attention to the differences between China and the West and the applicability of socialist theories to Chinese society. The reason for this, according to Zhang, was because those intellectuals were living in coastal seaports, therefore, what they saw was the industrial materialist civilization of the West that had been transplanted to China, which was totally different from the traditional agrarian culture that existed in the vast interior areas of China. In short, Zhang believed that the Chinese socialists were misled by the few tiny parts of China that had been urbanized, modernized, and Westernized.

Zhang Dongsun's writings greatly shocked the early Communists of China, because Zhang had been considered one of them. In the earlier months of that year, he was still a follower of socialism and in one of his articles he declared that "socialism is a philosophy of life and a worldview— it is also the most recent and most advanced philosophy of life and worldview."[10] He was among those who organized the first Marxist group in Shanghai[11] and he once even called for a Sino-Russian socialist alliance to overthrow the international capitalist system and establish a socialist world order.[12] After his change of position in November 1921, he indicated in his writings that he still hated capitalism, but only the foreign one. Since capitalism was believed to be the best way to develop industry, he proposed to establish Chinese national capitalism to compete with and gradually eliminate foreign capitalism, which was considered by him to be the cause of China's poverty. He still loved socialism as well, but no longer the Russian-style revolutionary socialism. He now turned to guild socialism, which proposed peaceful cooperation rather than violent class struggle between the capitalist class and the proletarian class. But even guild socialism could not appear in China in any time soon, because it could only be realized after the capitalist system was fully established and developed. He wrote, "Even the advanced nations have not realized this new system, not to mention China. It is still in doubt whether or not our sons and grandsons can see this system established in China."[13]

Zhang Dongsun's abrupt change of mind led to a debate about whether socialist revolution was applicable to China. Zhang Dongsun's view was supported by some of his comrades in the Research Clique, Beiping New Learning Association, and the Association for Spreading Learning,[14] including Liang Qichao, Shu Xincheng, and some others. Their critics were China's earliest Communists, including Chen Duxiu, Li Dazhao, Cai Hesen, Li Da, Shao Lizi, Chen Wangdao, Li Hanjun, Li Ji, Zhou Fohai, and others.

Although the focus of the debate was the applicability of socialism, it inevitably touched on the issue of the nature of Chinese society because Zhang Dongsun, Liang Qichao, and others argued that socialist revolution was not applicable to China precisely because China was not a capitalist society. According to Zhang Dongsun, China was still in the stage of universal poverty, and there was neither a capitalist class nor a working class in China, and, therefore, no social basis for socialist revolution. He argued further that

China had neither bourgeois politics nor capitalist economy. He asked: how could we establish the working-class dictatorship without a working class?[15] For the same reason, he was against the organization of the Chinese Communist Party. "What class will the party represent? If there is no class to back it, the party can never be organized," he wrote.[16] He agreed with Shu Xincheng that China had no qualifications for any -ism. Liang Qichao was the strongest supporter of Zhang Dongsun. He shared Zhang Dongsun's idea that China had neither a capitalist nor a working class.[17] He preferred calling the poor Chinese "vagrants" rather than "workers." In his opinion, China lacked the material preconditions for socialism, and China's problem was in production rather than in distribution. Should China develop socialism at all, it had to wait until after the full blossom of Chinese national capitalism, and there was no shortcut to socialism. He also emphasized the difference between Chinese society and Western society to support his point that class struggle was not applicable to China. In 1921 and 1922 and after, Liang Qichao developed the theory that Chinese society was characterized not by conflicts between capitalists and proletarians, but by conflicts between the class with guns and that without guns, and between the class with jobs and that without jobs. He vaguely admitted that China was a class society, but his definition of class was quite different from that of the Marxists.[18]

Almost all Marxist theoreticians China had at that time rushed to the defense of revolutionary socialism. Their articles appeared in a number of leftist journals published in Shanghai, and some other journals published in Beijing and elsewhere. They argued that although China was not a developed capitalist country, it had already become an integral part of the capitalist world and had established an elementary capitalist system. Therefore, a proletarian revolution was not only possible, but also necessary. Chen Duxiu, for example, attributed China's poverty to the development rather than underdevelopment of capitalism because it is the nature of capitalism to increase the wealth of one class while at the same time accelerate the pauperization of another. He found Zhang Dongsun's argument that China had no working class absurd. He angrily questioned, "If China has no workers, who plants the rice you eat? Who weaves the cloth you wear? Who builds the house you live in? Who makes the trains and ships you take? Who prints the newspaper you edit?"[19]

Li Ji tried to prove that China did have a few large capitalist enterprises, which he believed included the mines and banks owned by foreigners or jointly owned by Chinese and foreigners. As for landlords and rich peasants in rural areas, they were all small capitalists. Therefore, China was a country with deep-rooted small capitalists and burgeoning big capitalists, and the Chinese working class was suffering from the capitalist method of exploitation under the capitalist system.[20]

Li Da argued that China had already entered the age of industrial revolution and that the difference between Chinese society and Western society was in quantity rather than in quality. The so-called vagrants, who were very much despised by Liang Qichao, were actually unemployed workers and potential revolutionaries. According to him, the capitalist class in China was international, and almost all Chinese people belonged to the working class. Therefore, Chinese society was characterized by conflicts between the international capitalist class and the Chinese working class.[21] Cai Hesen agreed with Li Da that China had become a proletarian nation oppressed by an international capitalist class.[22] His slogan was that the class war in China was part of the class war of the world. Capitalists of the foreign powers and a few Chinese warlords, tycoons, and capitalists formed the capitalist class in China, while the great majority of China's population belonged to the proletarian class.[23] Like Li Da and Cai Hesen, Li Dazhao also viewed the class formation of China from a global perspective.[24]

Li Hanjun's argument was exceptional in that he held that economically China had already entered the age of capitalism, but politically it was still in the age of feudalism.[25] He was one of the very few who argued that there were feudal survivals in Chinese society before Stalin's theory about a semifeudal and semicolonial China reached China during the First United Front. Li's view would be further elaborated by the leftist Sun Zhuozhang in the early 1930s.

Mao Zedong, although not directly participating in the debate, expressed his ideas about the issue in a letter to his friends in France. Mao was a special correspondent for the *Changsha Dagongbao* while Bertrand Russell and Zhang Dongsun visited Changsha in November 1920. He had Russell's lectures reported in the newspaper.[26] He told his friends "Russell, speaking in Changsha...took a position in favor of Communism, but against the dictatorship of the workers and peasants. He said that one should employ the method of education to make the propertied classes conscious [of their failings]." Mao then said that he and his friends in Changsha found Russell's view "all right in theory," but "in reality it can't be done."[27] Mao viewed China as a capitalist society or, more accurately, he regarded China as part of the international capitalist system, which was composed of two international classes: the capitalists and the proletariat. Peng Pai also talked about the evil and wickedness of the capitalist system in 1921.[28] One comrade of Peng Pai remarked that Peng Pai's aim of launching the struggle against the landlords was "to overthrow the present capitalist system."[29]

All these arguments made by the early Communists were in accordance with the official guidelines of the newly established Chinese Communist Party. The program passed by the First Congress of the CCP in 1921 asserted that the aim of the party was to overthrow the bourgeois government with the revolutionary army and the proletariat and to eliminate capitalistic private ownership.[30] The party did not have any doubt at the time of its birth about the capitalist nature of the Chinese state and society. Otherwise its very existence would have become problematic. The Second National Congress of the CCP, held in 1922, recognized the existence of feudal warlords, but at the same time maintained that "Chinese capitalism has developed to such a degree that the Chinese bourgeoisie has been able to fight against the feudal warlords for their own class interest." It also emphasized that the imperialists were behind the Chinese feudal warlords and together they were blocking the development of Chinese national capitalism.[31] To a large extent the resolution of the Second National Congress of the CCP signaled the transition from the theory of a capitalist China to the theory of a semifeudal and semicolonial China.

The socialists all believed that China did not have to wait till the full development of capitalism to launch the socialist revolution. In fact, many of them doubted the possibility of further developing capitalism in China because of the encroachment of foreign powers. They suggested that through a socialist revolution China skip the developed capitalist phase and jump directly from an elementary or colonial capitalist society to a socialist society. It was not necessary to develop Chinese national capitalism, the socialists argued, because on the one hand, Chinese national capitalism and foreign capitalism were equally evil and, on the other hand, socialism could help build a modern industry as fast as capitalism, while at the same time avoiding the evils of capitalism and creating a rational and equal society. Li Dazhao, for example, argued that the experience of the Soviet Union had proved that the socialist system could do better than the capitalist system in developing industry and agriculture.[32] If Zhang Dongsun, Liang Qichao, and their supporters really wanted to develop industry, the socialists asked, why didn't they choose socialism instead of capitalism?

No sophisticated theories were provided by either side in the debate. The Chinese Marxists did not know very much about Marxism at the time, and this was evident in their arguments. For example, almost all Marxists classified the peasants, especially the poor peasants, as proletarians. This point was to cause much controversy among the Marxists themselves later. No serious efforts were made to analyze the nature of traditional China. Li Hanjun brought up the issue of a feudalism–capitalism dichotomy, but he did not amplify his theory. Contemporary historians in mainland China, while praising the Marxists for their brave defense of revolutionary socialism, admitted that their knowledge of Marxism was insufficient and many of their arguments were naive and inaccurate.[33]

No matter how naive the debate might have been, it did bring up some important issues that would continue to be debated in later times. As far as the nature of Chinese society is concerned, the debate touched on three major points. First, was China a capitalist society? Were there both a capitalist class and a working class in China? Second, was there a fundamental difference between rural China and urban China and between *neidi* (interior) and *kouan* (coastal ports)? Zhang Dongsun and many others noticed that the urban–rural difference was so dramatic that it actually made the Chinese cities and villages different kinds of society; they argued that it was important not to neglect the rural and interior areas in discussions about the nature of Chinese society. The Marxists, however, insisted that no fundamental difference existed between coastal urban centers and interior rural areas and that China as a whole had become an integral part of the capitalist world. The Communists would discard these positions in later debates. The third issue concerned whether imperialism and national capitalism were friends or enemies. Zhang Dongsun and Liang Qichao attributed China's problems to imperialism and proposed to develop national capitalism in order to eliminate foreign capitalism. The socialists, however, paid more attention to class division than national difference. In Li Da's words, capitalists, whether native or foreign, were all voracious tigers, and national capitalism was a plague as dangerous as foreign capitalism.[34] This position would also be discarded by the Communists in later debates.

The debate about socialism ended in 1922, but the interest in the nature of Chinese society continued. For example, after 1922, *Xinqingnian*, now an organ of the Chinese Communist Party, continued to publish articles discussing socialism and the nature of Chinese society. Some participants of the debate, such as Chen Duxiu, Li Da, Cai Hesen, and Li Ji, became leading figures in the later debate about the nature of Chinese society, with their views more or less modified. As far as their views about the nature of current Chinese society and the Chinese revolution are concerned, Chen Duxiu and the other early communists can be viewed as Trotskyites before Trotskyism reached China. Or, in Benjamin Schwartz's word, they were "Proto-Trotskyists."[35] It was probably not a coincidence that after the collapse of the First United Front, some of these Communists, including Chen Dixiu and Li Ji, accepted the Trotskyite view that China had already become a capitalist society. For many of them, the Trotskyite interpretation of the nature of Chinese society was not new or foreign at all, but their own view that had been suppressed during the First United Front. Zhang Dongsun and Liang Qichao never actively joined the debate again, but their views had great influence on the non-Marxist scholars who wrote about the nature of Chinese society from the late 1920s to the 1940s.

THE SOVIET PREDECESSORS: 1924–1928

During the First United Front, the nature of Chinese society became an important issue to the leaders of the Soviet Union and the Comintern because it directly determined what kind of revolution China should and would have: a feudal China would require a bourgeois revolution; a semifeudal and semicolonial China needed a bourgeois democratic revolution; and a China with an Asiatic mode of production or a capitalist system would necessitate a proletarian revolution. This issue caused a heated debate in the Soviet Union during the First United Front, and the debate escalated after the collapse of the First United Front, when the Chinese revolution became one of the three major issues that caused the final split between the Stalinists and the Trotskyites.[36] The debate about the nature of Chinese society produced three contrasting views in the Soviet Union: one arguing for a China with an Asiatic mode of production, another for a capitalist China, and still another for a semifeudal and semicolonial China.

Two Hungarian Communists who lived in the Soviet Union, Evgenii Varga and Ludwig Madjar, represented the theory of a China with an Asiatic mode of production. In 1925, Evgenii Varga began the debate about the Asiatic mode of production in China with an essay denying that China was feudal. He claimed that China was ruled by a class of scholar-elite, that China could not develop capitalism because of the existence of the "tyranny of the clan" in villages, and that political power in China came from the control over massive public works. This view was later embraced by Karl Wittfogel and elaborated by Madjar.[37] Madjar was sent to work in the Soviet consulate general in Shanghai in 1926. After he returned to Moscow, he was made the deputy to the head of the Comintern's Far Eastern section. From this position he wrote *A Study of Chinese Rural Economy*, a book first published in 1928 and reprinted in 1931 and praised at that time as the first powerful attempt at subjecting the contemporary Chinese land system to Marxist analysis. He argued that China at the time of the arrival of the Westerners was still a society with the Asiatic mode of production, whose chief features were the absence of private land ownership and the presence of a special form of taxation (a mixture of rent and tax). However, due to the influence of commercial capitalism, the Asiatic mode of production had long been in erosion. The arrival of Western imperialism brought about more fundamental changes, and current China was in transition from the Asiatic mode of production to capitalism. Although remnants of the Asiatic mode of production still widely existed and were still important in determining the strategy of the Chinese revolution, capitalism was growing rapidly and had made China a capitalist country by destroying the economic basis of the Asiatic mode of production.[38]

Karl Radek and Leon Trotsky and their followers in the opposition group embraced the theory of a capitalist China. They shared Varga and Madjar's view that there was no feudalism in China. However, they did not accept the theory of the Asiatic mode of production. Instead, they argued that China had long been a capitalist society. Radek had been a member of the opposition group since 1923 and 1924, and he served as president of the Sun Yat-sen University in Moscow from 1925 to 1927. In his lectures given at the university, he argued that because of the erosive influence of commercial capitalism, whose chief features were free transaction of land and money rent, feudalism had disappeared in China since the Qin and Han dynasties.[39] After the Opium War, commercial capitalism developed to a new stage, and industrial capitalism also emerged. Therefore, capitalism had dominated in both urban and rural areas of China. To him, the peasant struggles in rural China were against the bourgeoisie rather than the feudal elements.

Trotsky began to write about China during the First United Front, but his most important writings about China were all produced after the collapse of the First United Front in 1927. Trotsky's views on the nature of Chinese society differed fundamentally from those held by Stalin and Bukharin in several aspects, especially in his definition of the capitalist class of China and his denial of the existence of feudalism in China. According to Trotsky, contrary to Stalin and Bukharin's theory, there were no contradictions between imperialism and the Chinese national bourgeoisie because the latter were simply agents and representatives of the former; neither were there any contradictions between the Chinese urban national bourgeoisie and the rural landlord class because the two classes were closely linked. The landlords were capitalists rather than feudal forces, rural China was dominated by urban China, and there was actually no feudalism in China. Together the imperialists, the national bourgeoisie, and the rural landlords formed the capitalist class of China, which was the target of the revolution.[40]

Stalin and his supporters severely criticized the views of a China with an Asiatic mode of production and a capitalist China, and instead insisted that China was a semifeudal and semicolonial society. Madjar's book carried a long official editor's introduction written by its publisher in which Madjar's major views were roundly attacked, although there was praise for the book's abundance of materials. The introduction, based mainly on materials provided by Madjar himself, argued that private land ownership had existed in China for a long time and that the peasants had long been bonded to the land by the landlords and exploited by them. Permanent tenancy, which Madjar considered a remnant of the common land ownership of the premodern rural community and a unique Chinese phenomenon, did not exist widely in China and was not unique. Because of this, Madjar's conclusion that China was in transition from the Asiatic mode of production to capitalism was incompatible with China's social realities: the chief features of the Asiatic mode of production—the absence of private land ownership, the rule of rural communities, and the combination of agriculture and handicrafts in the households—were either totally absent or present but not of much significance in China. The introduction's inference was that China at that moment was a semifeudal society. Warlords and the incessant wars between the warlords were cited as examples of the vestiges of feudal institutions. The official introduction admitted that after the Qin unification, China was more centralized and despotic than other feudal societies, but argued that this did not contradict the concept of feudalism at all: it was feudalism with special Chinese features. It was further suggested that the most important basis of the centralization of China was not the irrigation system, as the proponents of the Asiatic mode of production argued, but the struggles with other ethnic groups.[41]

The debate on the Asiatic mode of production was suppressed in the late 1920s in the Soviet Union and in 1931 it was officially declared that the Asiatic mode of production as described by Madjar and others did not exist in China. Those who insisted on its existence were classified and persecuted as Trotskyites. It was treated not as an academic issue, but a political one, because the theory of the Asiatic mode of production was believed to be detrimental to the Comintern's efforts at spreading revolution to the colonies and semicolonies since "a geographically distinct mode of production arguably could render Comintern leadership unnecessary."[42] Because of severe political pressure, Madjar declared in 1930 that while he would no longer insist that China at the time of the arrival of the Westerners was a society with the Asiatic mode of production, he still believed that the Asiatic mode of production represented a special stage in the development of human society.[43]

The official introduction to Madjar's book pointed out the same contradiction in Radek's writings: on the one hand, Radek described many feudal features of China. On the other hand, he refused to call China a feudal society.[44] More severe attack on Radek came directly from Stalin, who argued that Radek was wrong in overemphasizing the role of commercial capitalism in Chinese history and in defining current China as a capitalist society. According to Stalin, commercial capitalism had existed in rural China for a long time, but had never played a dominant role in the economy; instead, it was characterized by primitive accumulation and was closely linked with the rule of landlords; it also inherited from the landlords the medieval method of exploiting and oppressing the peasantry. What dominated the current rural economy of China were the survivals of feudalism, which were protected by the imperialists and represented by the warlords, governors, and military and nonmilitary bureaucrats.[45]

The debate about the nature of Chinese society was closely intertwined with the differences in revolutionary strategies of the three sides, especially between the Stalinists and the Trotskyites. Based on their respective analyses of the nature of Chinese society, the Stalinists insisted that the Chinese revolution was a national-democratic revolution aimed at overthrowing imperialism and feudalism, but Trotskyites argued that it should be a proletarian revolution against the capitalists, both foreign and Chinese. The Stalinists believed that the Nationalist Party was a bloc of four classes (workers, peasants, petty bourgeois, and national bourgeois), but Trotsky maintained that it was a bourgeois party. Trotsky's theory about a capitalist China led him to a entirely different analysis about China's class relations, which in turn led him to the conclusion that it was impossible to unite all of China's classes to fight imperialism and warlordism because of the close links between the national capitalists, the imperialists, and the rural landlord class. By the same token, the land revolution in China was considered a revolution against the capitalist class rather than feudal forces, and the Chinese capitalists would therefore surely stand against the land revolution.[46] The proponents of the theory of the Asiatic mode of production supported the Trotskyite strategy because they believed that the "Asiatic" China had a weak and underdeveloped bourgeoisie, unable to assume the leadership of the revolution, and, therefore, the peasants and the proletariat had to lead the revolution, which could be socialists in its aims. Because of this, many supporters of the theory of the Asiatic mode of production were persecuted as Trotskyites.[47] Before 1927, based on their theory about national revolution and class alliance, Stalinists ordered an alliance between the Chinese Communists and Nationalists. This policy was probably also linked to the abandonment of internationalism and world revolution and in their stead the search for allies against the Western powers and the pursuit of Russian national interest by the Stalinists.[48] The Trotskyites, who still upheld internationalism and world revolution, strongly argued against such an alliance and proposed an "independent class policy" based on an "independent class organization."[49] After 1927, the Stalinists continued to champion a democratic-bourgeois revolution in China, while the Trotskyites argued for a proletarian revolution and proposed national assembly as a temporary strategy.

THE DEBATE AMONG THE CHINESE MARXISTS

During the First United Front of 1924–1927, through the Comintern, the Stalinist theory of national revolution, which emphasized that China should first complete a bourgeois-democratic revolution before entering the stage of proletarian-socialist revolution and implied that the present China was a semifeudal and semicolonial society, was widely accepted by both the Nationalists and Communists in China. This theory provided justifications for the United Front Policy and conformed well with the slogans of the First United Front: "Down with the Imperialists" and "Down with the Warlords," with imperialists representing the colonial forces and warlords the feudal forces. Both Chen Duxiu and Li Da changed their position about the nature of Chinese society. They abandoned their previous views of the capitalist nature of Chinese society and argued instead for a semicolonial and semifeudal China. Chen Duxiu wrote in 1926 that "the National Revolution has two meanings: national revolution and democratic revolution, namely, the overthrow of foreign imperialism and the native semi-feudal forces." He divided all Chinese people into two factions. One was the democratic faction, or the red faction. The other was the semifeudal faction, or the anti-red faction.[50] Li Da, in his *Contemporary Sociology*, published in 1926, pointed out that China was a semifeudal and semicolonial country; therefore, "although the target of the Chinese democratic revolution is imperialism, the feudal class that serves imperialism or the representatives of the imperialists within our weak nation should also be overthrown."[51]

Mao Zedong had also abandoned his belief in a capitalist China and accepted the new theory by early 1926. In an essay written in December 1925, he divided the Chinese population into five classes: the big bourgeoisie, the middle bourgeoisie, the petty bourgeoisie, the semiproletariat, and the proletariat. He made specific assessments about the rural population on the basis of this five-class theory, which he believed could be applied to any country. "As regards the countryside," he wrote, "the big landlords are the big bourgeoisie, the small landlords are the middle bourgeoisie, the owner-peasants are the petty bourgeoisie, the semiowner tenant peasants are the semiproletariat, and the farm laborers are the proletariat."[52] Such a classification indicates clearly that at that time he still believed that both Chinese society in general and rural China in particular were capitalist in nature. He mentioned nothing about feudal or semifeudal forces. However, only one month later, he wrote another article in which he described the big landlords as "the only secure bulwark of feudal and patriarchal society," but he continued to classify the other classes of rural China as either bourgeoisie or proletariat.[53] In another important essay written in September 1926, Mao argued that China was "an economically backward semicolony" where "the feudal-patriarchal class (the landlord class) in the villages" formed "the greatest adversary of revolution" because it constituted "the only solid basis for the ruling class at home and for imperialism abroad." He now included more people into the feudal category than he had several months earlier. The warlords, the local bullies, bad gentry, greedy bureaucrats, and corrupt officials were all viewed as components of feudal forces.[54]

The semicolonial and semifeudal theory was accepted not only by the Communists, but also by many Nationalists, especially the left-wing Nationalists. Gan Naiguang, for example, argued that China was a semicolony with strong feudal survivals, reflected in warlord politics, the power of the evil gentry, local tyrants and corrupt officials, the backward agricultural and industrial level, and localism and patriarchy.[55]

These typical Stalinist arguments would be followed by the theoreticians of the Chinese Communist Party in their debate with the Nationalists and the Trotskyites after 1927. During the First United Front, although not everyone liked Chen Duxiu and Mao Zedong's interpretation of feudal forces, it was generally agreed that both colonialism and feudalism did exist in China. The revolutionary theoreticians, Nationalist and Communist alike, all tried to prove that China was a weak nation with strongly entrenched feudal characteristics threatened by foreign powers. The theory of a capitalist China proposed by Communist scholars in the pre-United Front years was temporarily forgotten.

The debate about the nature of Chinese society among the various groups after 1927 was an extension and development of both the debate among Chinese intellectuals and the debate in the Soviet Union before, during, and immediately after the First United Front. The collapse of the First United Front, on the other hand, provided both occasion and purpose for the participants of the debate.

The First Phase: 1928–1933

There were three major groups in the first phase of the debate, lasting from 1928 to about 1933. Each group was named after its journal and was affiliated with a political party or faction: The *Xinshengming* (New Life) and *Qianjin* (Forward) group with the Nationalist Party; the *Xinsichao* (The New Thought) group with the Communist Party Central Committee; and the *Dongli* (the Driving Force) group with the Chinese Trotskyites. Besides these three groups, leaders of the Third Party, although not directly participating in the debate, also expressed their views about the nature of Chinese society.

The Xinshengming Group. Within the Nationalist Party, the issue of the nature of Chinese society was first raised by three short-lived journals that appeared in 1928 and 1929: *Shuangshi* (Double Ten), *Geming pinglun* (Revolutionary Review), and *Qianjin*. After the three stopped publishing in 1929, their message was carried on by another journal, *Xinshengming*, which existed from November 1928 to December 1930. The contributors to these journals were mostly left-wing Nationalists.

Shuangshi was one of the first journals to raise the issue of the nature of Chinese society. *Qianjin* was directly affiliated with the Nationalist Party's Department of Propaganda, headed by Gu Mengyu, a prominent economist and left-wing Nationalist. Using the pseudonym Gongsun Yuzhi, Gu was both the editor of and chief contributor to the journal. As a learned man

fluent in German, English, and French, and with a Ph.D. in economics from
the University of Berlin, Gu was said to be very familiar with Marxism,[56]
although he never became one of its proponents.[57] Gu argued that the
Chinese revolution should not adopt the method of class struggle and land
revolution because China was not a class society. He probably predated
Liang Shuming in suggesting that Chinese society had only professional differences, but not clearly defined class differences—hence the Communist
theory about a semifeudal and semicapitalist China was baseless. He argued
that the structure of Chinese society had undergone little change since the
collapse of feudalism in pre-Qing times. This structure had three major features: (1) an underdeveloped monetary system; (2) commercial capital and
usury that formed the major forms of capital (industrial capital was insignificant); and (3) free land transactions. These features had remained unchanged
since the Opium War, despite the political and economic influence of foreign invasion. Gu maintained that the economy and society of China
belonged to the stage of incipient capitalism, but that feudal ideas still had
tremendous influence; hence he defined China as "an incipient capitalist
society dominated by feudal ideas."[58] Although politically Gu was hostile to
Marxism, academically he was strongly influenced by it, and his views about
the nature of Chinese society were often expressed in Marxian concepts. One
might consider his theories somewhat contradictory, since an incipient capitalist society cannot be compatible with a classless society. It should be mentioned that the contributors to the journal did not agree with one another
about the nature of Chinese society. While Gu Mengyu basically denied that
China was a feudal society, other contributors believed that China was still a
society dominated by feudal forces.[59]

   Geming pinglun was created by Chen Gongbo, another left-wing
Nationalist. Both Chen and Gu belonged to the Wang Jingwei clique of the
Nationalist Party and both later became important leaders of the anti-
Chiang Kai-shek Reorganization Group. Chen and Gu founded two different journals instead of one because they could not agree with each other
whether the authors should use their real names or not.[60] However, that was
not their only difference. *Geming pinglun* was more radical than *Qianjin*.
While Gu Mengyu and *Qianjin* denied the existence of classes and the
applicability of class struggle in China, Chen Gongbo and *Geming pinglun*
argued that the national revolution of China should adopt the methods of
mass movement, democratic collectivism, and class alliance. The two journals represented two different groups within the Wang Jingwei clique. The
Geming pinglun group wanted to overthrow the military dictatorship of
Chiang Kai-shek through revolutionary organization and activities, while
the *Qianjin* group put more faith in public opinion than in political organization. The supporters of *Geming pinglun* were mainly students and young

intellectuals, whereas *Qianjin* was more welcomed by high-ranking politicians and intellectuals.[61]

Ironically, although Chen Gongbo was a fierce enemy of the Communists at that time, to a large extent he agreed with the Communists in their analysis of the nature of Chinese society. He defined China as a semicolonial society with strong feudal structures.[62] He argued that the feudal forces included the landlords, the bureaucrats, and the warlords, all of whom oppressed the general populace, including the newly born bourgeoisie.[63] The only major difference between him and the Communists was that he considered the Comintern to be the third reactionary force in China, in addition to imperialism and feudalism, because it was committed to strengthening the Communist Party and destroying the Nationalist Party and therefore hindered the national revolution, just as imperialism did.[64]

While *Shuangshi, Qianjin,* and *Geming pinglun* were all controlled by the left-wing Nationalists led by Wang Jingwei, *Xinshengming* was created by Chiang Kai-shek's theoreticians, including Dai Jitao, Shao Lizi, Chen Guofu, Chen Bulei, and Zhou Fohai, with the purpose of "interpreting the Three Principles of the People and enhancing the spirit of the Three Principles of the People."[65] All the books published by the Xinshengming Press had light blue covers, because blue is the symbol of the Nationalist Party.[66] Although at that time power struggles and personal animosities were rampant between Wang's group and Chiang's group, there seemed to be no fundamental difference between them in their understanding of the nature of Chinese society because many left-wing Nationalists, including Gu Mengyu, Chen Gongbo, and Tao Xisheng, were soon to become the most important contributors to *Xinshengming.* In fact, the right-wing Nationalists did not really participate in the debate. In Chen Gongbo's words, this was because the rightists had no knowledge of the theories. He also took that as the reason why the Communist theoreticians took the wayward left-wing Nationalists rather than the Nanjing government as their primary target in the debate.[67]

Among the contributors to *Xinshengming,* Tao Xisheng showed the greatest interest in the debate about the nature of Chinese society. He was undoubtedly also the most productive writer of this group. Born in 1899 in a gentry family in Hubei Province, he attended Beijing University, became involved in the May Thirtieth Movement in 1925, and, in 1927, was invited to Wuhan to work in a military school run by the United Front, where he stayed for about a year. According to his own accounts, it was during this period that he realized how destructive the Communist peasant movement was. He was very sympathetic with the victims of class struggle in the rural areas. Once he risked his own life to rescue five peasants who were about to be executed for being enemies of the peasant association.[68] Fifty years later, he commented that his one-year experience in Hubei during the First United

Front made him realize that "the Communist theory about a semi-feudal and semi-capitalist China was far-fetched and was made to fit their policy and strategy of 'peasant movement and land revolution.' It was not based on objective analysis of and scientific research on the structures and problems of Chinese society."[69]

As early as 1925, he published an article about the social structure of China, in which he analyzed the origin, development, and decline of the literati to demonstrate that the literati and the peasantry formed the two main classes of Chinese society. In 1928, he began to write more on this topic and in the following year collected his articles in a book, *A Historical Analysis of Chinese Society*, which was widely read and reprinted eight times between January 1929 and March 1933.[70] His important works also included *Essays on Chinese Social Phenomena* (1931), *Chinese Society and Chinese Revolution* (1932), and *Retrospect and Prospects of China's Problems* (1932). His basic argument was that it is difficult to find a pure capitalist society or a pure feudal society because every society is a mixture of elements of different social formations. To him, China had developed commercial capitalism since ancient times, and China after the Opium War was no longer a feudal society. However, feudal forces were still very powerful in Chinese society. What were these feudal forces? They were the institutions and ideas affiliated with the literati class, which, according to him, was similar to the feudal aristocracy and included two groups: the landlords and bureaucrats.[71]

Tao's biggest problem was that he was inconsistent and often contradictory. One commentator from the Trotskyite group attributed this to his blind plagiarism of the ideas of others.[72] A left-wing historian argued that it was because he frequently adapted his theories to changes in the prevailing political scene.[73] In his first book, *A Historical Analysis of Chinese Society*, Tao argued first that China had never had a feudal period in the strict meaning of the term "feudalism," then in the latter part of the book he stated that to the end of the Qing Dynasty China had been a feudal society, and the feudalism of China was not very different from the feudalism of medieval Europe.[74] Later he developed the so-called five-stage theory about Chinese history. According to this theory, after middle Qing, China became a commercial capitalist society or a semifeudal society oppressed by the imperialists.[75]

Tao believed that his theory was totally different from either the theory of the Stalinists or that of the Trotskyites.[76] However, his understanding of the nature of Chinese society was actually a mixture of the ideas of the Stalinists and the Trotskyites. His theory about commercial capitalism was not different from that of the Trotskyites, and his theory about a commercial capitalist society where the development of capitalism was hindered by both the feudal forces and imperialism was very similar to that of the Stalinists. Therefore, he was severely criticized by both sides. The Trotskyites criticized him for emphasizing the feudal forces in modern China, and the Stalinists criticized him for exaggerating the role of so-called commercial capitalism in premodern China.[77]

The Dongli Group. Some Chinese students in Moscow accepted Trotsky's theory about the Chinese revolution and became Trotskyites immediately after Chiang Kai-shek's coup of April 1927, which indicated to them the inaccuracy of Stalin's theory of a semifeudal and semicolonial China as well as the fallacy of the United Front policy stemming from this theory. By the winter of 1928, Trotskyites were said to be everywhere among Moscow's Chinese students. It was reported that at one point nearly half of the Chinese students in Moscow were Trotskyites.[78] The Chinese Trotskyite Wang Fanxi estimated that at one time nine-tenths of the former students at the Communist University for Toilers of the East in Moscow were Trotskyites.[79] But Trotskyite organizations did not appear in China until 1928, formed mainly by veteran Communists who had been purged by the Chinese Communist Party and by students returned from Moscow. From 1928 to 1930, four Trotskyite groups were formed in China. The first one was formed in 1928 by some returned students from the Sun Yat-sen University. They published a journal named *Our Views* [Women de hua], therefore they were called the "Our Views group."[80] The second group was led by Chen Duxiu and was formed in October 1929. Chen had become very resentful of Stalin and the new leaders of the Chinese Communist Party, who blamed him for all the failures the party experienced in 1927 and deposed him in August of the same year. Chen liked Trotsky's writings[81] and decided to cooperate with Trotsky and form a new organization. His group was the largest among the four Chinese Trotskyite organizations. Their "Our Political Manifesto" declaring the birth of their organization was signed by eighty-one persons.[82] Their organ was entitled *The Proletariat* [Wuchanzhe], and they were therefore called "The Proletariat group." As many of its members were veteran Communists, the group was also referred to as "The Seniors Group." Two other groups were formed around the end of 1929 or spring 1930. One was called "The October group," the other "The Combat group," both named after their respective journals, and both were created by students who had returned from Moscow.[83]

Although the Trotskyites had four different organizations with fierce power struggles among them, their political principles and theories, including their understanding of the nature of Chinese society in general and rural Chinese society in particular, were not very different from one another. They were all loyal followers of Trotsky, devoting most of the pages of their journals to his writings. Wang Fanxi, leader of one of the four groups, admits that "it seems to me in retrospect that the 'struggle' between these four groups was waged over trivial and petty issues with exaggerated intensity...we deliberately exaggerated our differences in order to justify the existence of our various factions."[84] After reading the political principles of all four groups, Trotsky found that there were no fundamental differences among them and suggested that they create a unified organization.

According to Zheng Chaolin, among all the elements in Trotsky's theory, his thesis—"that not feudal remnants but capitalist relations were predominant in China, that China had long been capitalistic, that China's backward rural economy was dominated by urban capitalism, and that Chinese society was already bourgeois; so...China's revolution...would be proletarian-socialist"—was one of those more difficult for the Chinese Trotskyites to accept. Chen Duxiu was among those skeptics,[85] which indicates that Chen, although very much influenced by foreign theories, was not a blind follower of Stalin or Trotsky. His abandonment of the theory of a capitalist China and acceptance of the theory of a semifeudal and semicolonial China during the First United Front, and his subsequent abandonment of the latter and reacceptance of the former after the collapse of the United Front, were evidently sincere and painful.

Chen's conversion to Trotskyism, or rather his return to his former position, was well reflected in his views of the nature of Chinese society expressed in a letter in 1929 to the Central Committee of the Chinese Communist Party, in which he argued that because of the long-lasting erosion of commercial capitalism and the penetration of international capitalism into the villages, the whole economic structure of rural China was dominated by commodity economy. The cities dominated the villages rather than vice versa. As a result, capitalist economic relations prevailed in rural China. The Northern Expedition further destroyed the political power of the feudal elements; the capitalist class had managed to establish their political rule over other classes, and had even forced the imperialists to make some concessions. Therefore, China had become a capitalist society both economically and politically; feudalism had become "the survivals of the survivals."[86] A few months later, in "Our Political Manifesto" of "the Proletariat Group," written by Liu Renjing and Chen Duxiu, the Chinese Trotskyites elaborated on their views about the nature of Chinese society.[87]

The reorganized Trotskites published a journal entitled *Dongli*. The first issue of the journal appeared in July 1930, its second issue in September, and then the Nationalist government closed the journal down. Although short-lived, the journal was very influential at that time, with its clear-cut Trotskyite stand. It was edited by Wu Jiyan, Chen Duxiu's nephew; the chief theoretician of the journal was Yan Lingfeng, a returned student from the Sun Yat-sen University of Moscow. In the first issue, Yan published an article entitled "Chinese Economy: Capitalist or Feudal"; in the second issue, he contributed another article. These two articles, together with his responses to his critics, were collected in a book entitled *Studies on the Economy of China*, published in Shanghai in June 1931. He published another book in the next year.[88]

In his various works, Yan Lingfeng did not deny there were still feudal survivals in China, but he argued that what dominated Chinese society was petty bourgeoisie rather than feudal survivals. According to him, the great majority of Chinese peasants were small-scale commodity producers and belonged to the petty bourgeois class. They were no longer feudal peasants. He criticized the Stalinist argument that imperialism played a double role in China: on the one hand, it destroyed the traditional subsistence economy and spread commodity economy; on the other hand, it blocked the development of national capitalism, and for its selfish purpose it even allied with feudalism and acted as the protector of the feudal survivals. Yan believed that imperialism had to develop capitalism in the colonies because at the stage of imperialism, colonial countries exported not only commodities, but also capital. He maintained that there were no contradictions between imperialism and Chinese national capitalism, as assumed by the Stalinists. He also pointed out that rural China had become an integral part of the capitalist world: the subsistence economy had been totally destroyed; the small peasants were now closely connected with the outside world by the market system; commercial capital and usury in rural China did not belong to feudalism, but were part of the capitalist system because they were related to urban capital and their function was to destroy feudalism in rural areas; rent in kind was not a feudal survival, but a stimulant to the development of capitalism.

Another influential Trotskyite theoretician was Ren Shu, who published *Introduction to Chinese Economy* in Shanghai in January 1931.[89] Although Ren Shu and Yan Lingfeng often attacked each other,[90] their views on the nature of Chinese society were basically the same. One of Ren Shu's major innovations was to analyze the development of capitalism in China by tracing the decline of traditional technologies and institutions and the rise of modern technologies and institutions. For example, he argued that the Chinese sailing ship (junks) represented feudal economy and steamships represented capitalist economy; when he found that in 1926, ninety-eight percent of the commodities in China were carried by steamships, and only two percent by junks, he concluded that capitalism made up ninety-eight percent of the Chinese economy, and feudalism only two percent. He made the same comparison between the old-style Chinese private banks (*qian zhuang*) and modern banks, and found that modern banks had rapidly replaced the traditional banks as the most important financial institutions. He also studied the development of the silk industry and found that, in 1928, silk produced by traditional methods, which to him represented feudalism, made up only ten percent of the total output, whereas silk produced in modern factories, which he believed represented capitalism, made up ninety percent of the total output.

Yan Lingfeng and Ren Shu raised several issues that were to become the focal points of the second phase of the debate, including the validity of using technological change to determine the change of the nature of a society; the role of imperialism in the development of capitalism in China, especially rural China; the relationship between commodity economy and capitalism; and the status of rural classes.

The Xinsichao Group. Both the Xinshengming group and the Dongli group challenged the Stalinists' theory about Chinese society that emphasized both colonial and feudal characteristics. However, the attacks of the Xinshengming group were not very efficient because they did not go beyond the Stalinist views. Their views about the nature of Chinese society turned out to be not as different from those of the Stalinists as they believed them to be. The real challenge to the Stalinist theory came from the Trotskyites, as many of them were among the best-trained Marxist theoreticians China had at that time, well versed in both classic Marxist works and foreign languages, especially Russian. Most Trotskyites lived on theory-making rather than on practical revolutionary activities. The Nationalist scholars liked to comment, not without bias, that the real authorities on Marxism were all Trotskyites. The Trotskyites themselves were also very proud of their knowledge of Marxism. Although the Chinese Trotskyites did little more than repeat what Trotsky and Radek said about Chinese society and the Chinese revolution, supporting their views with more data, they necessitated serious response from the Stalinists, since the Trotskyites offered entirely different views on the nature of Chinese society, on the reasons for the failure of the First United Front, and on future revolutionary strategies. A CCP ideologue made it very clear that the participation of the CCP in the debate about the nature of Chinese society was mainly a response to the Trotskyite challenge.[91]

Before the emergence of Trotskyite organizations in China in 1928, the Chinese Communist Party, following Stalin, had already begun to attack the Trotskyites in the Soviet Union on their views about the nature of Chinese society and the strategy of the Chinese revolution. For example, the Resolution of the Sixth National Congress of the Chinese Communist Party passed on July 9, 1928, reiterated that the current Chinese revolution could only be a bourgeois-democratic revolution rather than a socialist revolution or continuous revolution, as proposed by the Trotskyites, because the unification and independence of the nation had not been achieved, the private land ownership of the landlords had not been destroyed, and the semifeudal remnants had not been eliminated.[92] Before the Sixth Party Congress, Stalin's theory about Chinese society had not been accepted by everyone, although it had been widely propagated in China. Some believed that China was still a feudal society, and some argued that China was a society with strong vestiges of the Asiatic mode of production.[93] The Sixth Party Congress made Stalin's views about the nature of Chinese society the official theory of the Chinese Communist Party. In 1928, the Communist leader Cai Hesen declared his acceptance of Stalin's theory.[94] Obviously, Stalin's theory was quite different from Cai's 1921 argument of a "proletarian Chinese nation" oppressed by "an international capitalist class." A resolution passed by the Central Committee of the Chinese Communist Party in September 1929 defined the "semifeudal" character of Chinese society as follows: "Capitalism has played a dominant role in the Chinese land system (free transaction of land), but feudal exploitation still dominates the relations between landlords and peasants (examples include rent in kind and labor rent), therefore, the economic relations of rural China are semi-feudal."[95]

After the rise of the Chinese Trotskyite organizations, Li Lisan, who replaced Qu Qiubai as the de facto leader of the Chinese Communist Party after the Sixth Party Congress, and the new central committee of the party, responded to the Trotskyite challenge. In an article written in December 1929 and published in the journal *Bolshevik*,[96] Li attacked the views of Chen Duxiu and his followers. He started with the role of imperialism in the development of capitalism in China. He argued that the Trotskyites were wrong in believing that imperialism might make concessions to China and help China develop capitalism because it was in the interests of the imperialists to ally themselves with the reactionary feudal forces, from warlords to local landlords, to divide China and prevent China from developing a national market and industrial capitalism. According to Li, the ultimate purpose of imperialism was not to help China develop capitalism, but to turn China into a market and raw material base of the powers. As a result, on the one hand, imperialism had helped destroy the subsistence economy and develop commodity economy in China, which were beneficial to the development of capitalism; on the other hand, it protected the feudal mode of production and prevented China from developing the capitalist mode of production.

Li Lisan argued that the Trotskyite view about commercial economy was also wrong. According to the Trotskyites, the development of commercial capitalism would destroy feudal relations, and commercial capitalism could even become an independent social form to replace feudalism. Li agreed that commercial capitalism could help destroy the feudal system, but he did not believe that commercial capitalism could become an independent mode of production, because the only effect of the development of commercial capital would not be to change the old mode of production, but would lead to landlords exploiting the peasants even more with the old methods and cause rural society to become stratified. Only the development of industrial capitalism could finally overthrow the feudal system and replace it with capitalism.

Li's conclusion was that the current Chinese economic structure still conformed to the Marxist definition of feudalism, with the peasants as the owners of the tools and methods of production, and the landlords as the owners of the land. The relations between the landlords and the peasants were relations between lords and subjects, based on the land ownership system and extraeconomic exploitation. Li mentioned some special features of Chinese feudalism, such as the free transaction of land and the control of political power by literati bureaucrats rather than by the landlords themselves. He maintained that although these features made Chinese feudalism somewhat different from the feudalism of medieval Europe, they did not affect the basic feudal nature of Chinese society.

The journal *Xinsichao,* which represented the official views of the Chinese Communist Party, was first published in November 1929 in Shanghai and continued to exist until July 1930. Its authors mainly elaborated on the views of Li Lisan and the Comintern, and strove to prove and propagate the theory of a semifeudal and semicolonial China. Like Li Lisan, their primary targets of criticism were the Trotskyites. The chief contributors to *Xinsichao* included Pan Dongzhou, Wang Xuewen, Wu Liping, Xiang Shengwu, and Li Yimang.[97] According to He Ganzhi, it was Pan Dongzhou and Wang Xuewen who first created the Chinese phrase "ban fengjian ban zhimindi," meaning semifeudal and semicolonial.[98] They defined Chinese rural economy as a semifeudal economy, because rural China had already been dominated by commodity economy, which was neither pure feudal nor pure capitalist, but a mixture of and a transitional form between the two. They defined the rural economy as a semicolonial economy because foreign interests now dominated the Chinese economy. Pan Dongzhou attributed the bankruptcy of national industry and the crisis of rural economy to foreign financial capital, which he believed had helped destroy China's national economy, and had acted as the protector of landlords, gentry, warlords, and bureaucrats.[99]

Two famous former Communists lent their support to the Chinese Communist Party. One was Li Da, the famous Marxist theoretician. Although no longer a party member by that time, he continued to hold the official Communist view about the nature of Chinese society. He published a book in 1929 in which he continued to advocate the theory of a semifeudal and semicolonial China and the national democratic revolution.[100]

The well-known novelist Mao Dun also joined the debate and supported the official Communist line. Like Li Da, he had also left the party. The debate that took place in 1930 greatly interested him, and he decided to write a novel to express his views. The novel he wrote was *Twilight,* published in

1933. Its hero, Wu Sunpu, was the owner of a silk factory, an ambitious national industrialist, with dreams of developing China's national industry. However, the economic inroads made by foreigners, which became ever more severe with the Great Depression, coupled with the monopoly of the national economy by the bureaucratic bourgeoisie and the incessant fighting among the warlords, made the development of native Chinese industry very difficult. As a result, his dreams were shattered; he was reduced to frantic efforts to protect his own individual interests. He faced pressure from two sides: the compradors, who represented the interests of the foreign business-men, and his workers, who were struggling for their own livelihood and rights. In the end he was forced to his knees by a powerful comprador—one of his own countrymen in the pay of foreign businessmen.

Mao Dun later said he wrote the novel to expose the misleading theories of the Trotskyites and the bourgeois scholars about the nature of Chinese society.[101] On another occasion he wrote:

> I wrote the novel in order to make the following responses to the Trotskyite and bourgeois scholars through the use of vivid descrip-tion: There is no way that China can develop its own capitalism. Because of the oppression of imperialism, feudal forces and the bureaucratic and comprador classes, China had become increas-ingly semi-colonial and semi-feudal...the future of the Chinese national bourgeoisie was very gloomy. They were weak and waver-ing. At that time they had only two options: to surrender to the imperialists and became compradors, or to compromise with the feudal forces.[102]

Though the novel was set in the city, Mao Dun's original plan was to include the village in the plot. One of the reasons why he chose to write about a silk factory was that such a factory connects the city with the village.[103] In his own words, his intention was to compose an "urban–rural symphony" or an "urban–rural trilogy." For the rural part, he planned to write about the peas-ant revolt, the Red Army, and the bankruptcy of the rural economy. In the afterword of *Twilight*, he explained that he had to cut the rural component because of his own health failing.[104] But in an interview conducted forty years later, he said that he had to do so because he was not familiar enough with the village conditions at that time. Because of the absence of rural life in *Twilight*, he called it a novel with hemiplegia.[105] *Twilight* enjoyed great influ-ence at the time, and the Communists actually used the novel as a textbook to teach revolutionary theories to its junior members.[106]

The Third Party. The Third Party, or the Chinese Revolutionary Party [*Zhonghua geming dang*], was created immediately after the 1927 defeat by a group of former Nationalists and Communists. Its leaders were the former Nationalist Deng Yanda and the former Communist Tan Pingshan. Both Deng and Tan held important positions in the short-lived Wuhan government. Ironically, while Communist comrades both at home and abroad criticized Tan Pingshan for neglecting the land problem in 1927, Deng Yanda's Communist friends highly praised him for being a strong supporter of the land revolution.[107] Among the leaders of the Nationalist Party, Deng was one of the very few who really appreciated the power of the peasantry. He even followed Gan Naiguang in arguing that the Communist Party was a proletarian party and represented the interests of the workers, while the Nationalist Party represented the interests of the peasants, and, as a result, the Nationalist–Communist United Front would naturally lead to an alliance between workers and peasants.[108]

According to their political declaration, the Third Party's understanding of the nature of Chinese society was very similar to that of the Chinese Communist Party. The declaration argued that both feudalism and capitalism had distinct economic, political, and social features. Feudalism was defined as a system in which the subsistence economy played the dominant role and the landlords used political force to occupy the land and exploit the peasants by plundering their products and forcing them to do free labor; in which the occupation of the land by the landlords led to their monopoly of political, military, and economic power; and in which there were marked social stratification and class differences. Capitalism was believed to have a set of different features.

Based on their definitions, it was argued that the backward northwestern and southwestern areas and the vast rural areas of China still belonged to the feudal stage, but the coastal cities had already entered the capitalist stage. However, since more than seventy percent of China's population lived in rural areas, feudalism was still the dominant force in China. At the same time, the party also recognized that China had become a semicolonial country because the national economy was controlled by foreign powers, which inhibited the development of national capitalism in China.[109] Such an understanding of the nature of Chinese society may have influenced the short-lived anti-Chiang Kai-shek Fujian government of the early 1930s, in which the Third Party members played an important role. The minimum political program released by the Fujian government defined China as a "semi-feudal society under the rule of the imperialists."[110]

Dushu zazhi: All Groups Coming Together. By the end of 1930, the major journals of the various groups, including *Qianjin, Geming pinglun, Xinshengmin, Dongli,* and *Xinsichao,* had all stopped publication. Most were banned by the Nanjing government. In April 1931, a new journal entitled *Dushu zazhi* [Study Magazine] appeared, and it carried on the debate for another two years. *Dushu zazhi* was published by the Shenzhou Guoguang Press, which was affiliated with Chen Mingshu, a former general of the Nationalist army, but at that time a dissident of the Nationalist Party who was actively engaged in propagating socialism and creating the Social-Democratic Party of China. The editors of *Dushu zazhi* were a couple named Wang Lixi and Lu Jingqing, both were poets. Wang was a member of the Nationalist Party and a former member of the anti-Bolshevik Group in Jiangxi,[111] but at the time of debate he was a follower of Chen Mingshu. Although the previous journals were all controlled by particular political groups and were not open to contributors with different political orientations, *Dushu zazhi* was much more receptive to people with different views.[112] The editors declared that their intention was to break up the monopoly that certain factions had over the debate.[113] Wang Lixi, the editor, "liked to think of himself as a second Tsai Yuan-pei [Cai Yuanpei], and employed writers from right across the political spectrum, including the pro-Kuomintang rightist Tao Hsi-sheng, members of the Stalinist faction, and even Trotskyists."[114]

Probably because of its inclusiveness, among all the journals involved in the debate during that period, *Dushu zazhi* was undoubtedly the most influential.[115] From 1931 to 1933, *Dushu zazhi* published four special issues on the social history of China. Much criticism and personal attack were exchanged, not only between people with different political affiliations, but also between people within the same political groups. Many contributors declared that they did not belong to any political party, but almost all of them had to choose the views of one of the political groups since virtually no new views about the nature of Chinese society emerged. Some Trotskyite participants later recalled that most of the articles were critical of Stalinist views and that the Trotskyites defeated the Stalinists in the debate,[116] which implied that the representation of the views of the various groups in the journal was not balanced. A simple survey of the background of the authors of the four special issues of *Dushu zazhi* indicates that at the time of the debate, among the total of twenty-nine authors, six were Trotskyites, three were Trotskyite sympathizers, one was possibly Trotskyite, three were CCP members, two were possibly CCP members or supporters, five belonged to Tao Xisheng's Xinshengming group, one was a foreigner, four were independents (one Trotskyite supporter, one CCP supporter, two social-democrats), and four unidentified (see Table 1). The table tends to support the claim by some Trotskyites that they contributed more to the journal than the other groups. However, Wang Xuewen, an active Communist participant in the debate, recalled that after the CCP leaders found out the connections between Shenzhou Guoguang Press and the "anti-Bolshevik group," presumably meaning the anti-Communist background of its editor Wang Lixi, they prohibited the party and Youth League members from contributing articles to

Dushu zazhi.[117] Therefore, the unbalanced representation may have been caused by the CCP rather than the editor of *Dushu zazhi*. The second half of the Trotskyite claim, that the Trotskyites defeated the CCP in the debate, is even more difficult to prove.

Table 1
General Information about the *Dushu zazhi* Special Issues

Name of Author	Number of Articles	Views about the Nature of Current Chinese Society	Political Affiliation at the time of debate	Political Affiliation after 1949
Bai Ying	1	semifeudal, semicapitalist		
Chen Bangguo	3	capitalist		
Dai Xingyao	1	capitalism with feudal survials (bureaucrats)	Xinshengming	
Du Weizhi	1	capitalist	Trotskyite	mainland, jailed died in 1992
Hu Qiuyuan[1]	2	colonial pre-capitalist or semi-colonial feudalism	Japan Group[2]	Taiwan
Ji Lei	1	irrelevant (general theory)		
Jing Yuan[3]	2	backward capitalist	Trotskyite	mainland, recanted
Li Ji	3	capitalist	Trotskyite	mainland, recanted
Liang Yuandong[4]	1	irrelevant (ancient China)	Xinshengming CCP	mainland
Liu Mengyun[5]	1	semifeudal, semicolonial	CCP	mainland
Liu Suhua[6]	1	semifeudal, semicolonial	CCP	Died in the Civil War (1946–1949)
Ren Shu	2	capitalist	Trotskyite	
Sun Zhuozhang	2	capitalist economic base and feudal superstructure	Independent[7]	drowned in 1932 in Putuo, Zhejiang
Tao Xisheng	2	semicolony with strong feudal forces	Xinshengming	Taiwan
Tanaka Tadao	1	irrelevant (critical review)	Japanese	
Wang Boping	2	capitalist	Trotskyite[8]	Taiwan
Wang Lixi	3	irrelevant (ancient China general review)	Independent	died in Henan in 1939
Wang Yanan	1	capitalist	Japan group	mainland, changed his views

Table 1 (Cont'd.)
General Information about the *Dushu zazhi* Special Issues

Wang Yichang	4	capitalist	Independent (Trotskyite)	
Xiong Deshan	3	irrelevant (ancient China)	CCP	died in Guilan during the Anti-Japanese War
Yan Lingfeng	2	capitalist	Trotskyite	Taiwan
Yu Shen	1	backward capitalist	possibly Trotskyite	
Zhang Hong	1	semifeudal	possibly CCP	
Zheng Xuejia[9]	1	capitalist	Japan Group	Taiwan
Zhong Gong	1	semicolonial, semifeudal[10]	possibly CCP	
Zhou Gucheng	1	transitional: traditional-modern: national-international	Xinshengming	mainland
Zhou Shaocou	1	irrelevant (ancient) China)		
Zhu Bokang[11]	1	semi-colonial, semifeudal	Xinshengming	mainland
Zhu Xinfan	2	semifeudal, semicolonial	independent (CCP)	died in 1946
Total: 29	48			

1. He was basically a Trotskyite sympathizer at that time, but later became associated with the Nationalist Party. For more information, see Benton, *China's Urban Revolutionaries,* 96.

2. This group included some Chinese students in Japan who had a very close relationship with Wang Lixi. It was not a strictly political group and the members did not necessarily share the same views about the nature of Chinese society.

3. Jing Yuan was Liu Renjing.

4. For Liang's life story, see Yao Dianzhong, "Liang Yuandong jiaoshou zhuan," 208–219.

5. According to Chen Hansheng, Xue Muqiao, and Feng Hefa (*Jiefangqian de Zhongguo nongcun,* 267), Liu Mengyun was Zhang Wentian.

6. For Liu's life, see Wang Xuewen, "Sanshi niandai Shanghai wenhua zhanxian de yixie douzheng qingkuang," 46–47; *Zhongguo shehui xingzhi wenti lunzhan ziliao xuanbian,* Vol.1, 10.

7. For more information about Sun, see Gao Jun, "Zhongguo shehui xingzhi wenti de lunzhan," 9.

8. For Wang's life story, see Zheng Chaolin, "Chen Duxiu and the Trotskyists," 175; Yueh Sheng, *Sun Yat-sen University in Moscow and the Chinese Revolution,* 171–172.

9. Zheng Xuejia was a Trotskyite at that time, but later became associated with the Nationalist Party.

10. Indirect evidence for his CCP identity is provided by Yu Shen, another participant, who called Zhong Gong "Stalinist" and classified Zhong and Liu Mengyun (Zhang Wentian) into the same group.

11. For more information about Zhu, see the book advertisement in *Zhongguo shehui shi de lunzhan,* Vol. 3; Wang Shunsheng and Yang Dawei, *Fujian shibian,* 166.

The table indicates that, contrary to the claim of the editors, very few authors were truly nonpolitical academicians. Those who did not hold any political stand before the debate became involved in politics immediately after they joined the debate. Usually they identified with or were identified by others with one or two of the political groups based on their views. A good example was Wang Yichang. He was a virtual nobody before the debate. Even the editors did not know who he was.[118] His articles in *Dushu zazhi* brought him considerable fame, and led to his close affiliation with Wang Lixi and Tao Xisheng,[119] but his views about the nature of Chinese society had always been very close to those of the Trotskyites. In fact, in his first article published in *Dushu zazhi,* he openly attacked both the Xinshengming and Xinsichao groups for failing to notice the rise of capitalism and the fall of feudalism in China.[120] In the second phase of the debate, he was more clearly identified with the Trotskyites because of his views, although there is no evidence that he had ever joined any Trotskyite groups.

Another contributor, Zhu Xinfan (also called Zhu Qihua, Zhu Peiwo and Li Ang), called himself a "nonpartisan international revolutionary," but since he was a strong supporter of the Stalinist theory about the nature of Chinese society and a fierce critic of the *Xinshengmin* scholars and the Trotskyites, he was regarded as a blind follower of the Stalinists. However, the Communists never considered him their comrade. In a book published in 1940, he claimed that he was one of the delegates to the first national congress of the Chinese Communist Party in 1921 and that he was the chief interpreter for the Soviet advisor Mikhail Borodin during the First United Front. In this book he also strongly attacked the Stalinists.[121] According to his own account, at the time of the debate, he held an official position in the Nanjing Nationalist government. Some said that he had been Zhou Fohai's secretary and the editor of a Nationalist journal. Many of his books were not his own products, but compilations of Stalinist works.[122] He was probably just a player, making use of popular interest in the debates as an easy source of income and fame, but as long as he played with Stalinist views, he was perceived as a serious Stalinist.

The young Sichuanese Sun Zhuozhang also called himself a "nonpartisan revolutionary." He had studied in France and had been involved in the formation of the Social-Democratic Party of China there.[123] He argued that China had already become a capitalist country economically, but was still feudal politically because the capitalist production forces had not been able to dismantle the backward feudal political system. In his opinion, this was perfectly compatible with the Marxist theory about the contradiction between superstructure and economic base. He and a few others believed that his theory was original and unique. However, Li Hanjun had developed such a theory ten years earlier, during the debate on socialism. Sun was probably not aware of Li's theory at that time since Li's views were only made public in a very short article published in *Xinqingnian*. Some participants called Sun an eclecticist who tried to combine both the CCP and Trotskyite theories. It would be difficult to classify him as belonging to any of the political groups at that time, although it is probably safe to call him a "leftist."

Compellingly, during the first five years of the debate, as far as the nature of the current Chinese society was concerned, the debate produced only two contrasting views: one held that China was already a capitalist society, and the other was that China was a semifeudal, semicolonial society. In other words, the Chinese participants of the debate were followers of either Stalin or Trotsky. The Communist Party, the various factions of the Nationalist Party, and the Third Party basically shared an understanding of the nature of Chinese society, though they all strove to demonstrate that they had totally different views from one another. In fact, they were not as different as they wanted the public to believe. This can probably be attributed to two important factors. First, most of the participants from the Nationalist Party, including Gu Mengyu, Chen Gongbo, and Tao Xisheng, belonged to the left wing of the party. Both Chen and Tao were former Communists.[124] The founders of the Third Party, Deng Yanda and Tan Pingshan, were former left-wing Nationalist and Communist, respectively. They all seemed to have differentiated the Chinese Communist Party from Marxist theory. They did not like the CCP, but they still talked in Marxian terms: Marxism was the only grand revolutionary theory they were familiar with at that time. Second, the main slogan of the First United Front was "Down with the Imperialists and the Warlords," which was created according to the theory of a semifeudal and semicolonial China. All three groups agreed that there was nothing wrong with the slogan or the theory. The United Front failed, not because the slogan and the theory were wrong, but because that slogan and theory were betrayed by their former revolutionary allies. Now that they all wanted to portray themselves as the true successors of the National Revolution, they had to continue to adhere to that slogan along with the theory on which it was based.[125]

The real difference among the Communist Party, the left-wing Nationalists, and the Third Party was reflected in their understanding about which elements represented the semifeudal or feudal forces in China. For example, both Mao Zedong and the left-wing Nationalist Tan Yankai believed that there were "local bullies and evil gentry" in China, but they could not agree about just who "the local bullies and evil gentry" were. Tan argued that they were the people who overtly allied with the opposing warlords, but for Mao they were members of the rural ruling class.[126] The three groups differed in their revolutionary strategies, especially their attitudes toward the peasants. The left-wing Nationalists and the Third Party were very suspicious of the revolutionary strategies, especially the land revolution suggested by the Comintern, but they did not have much doubt about the Comintern's theory on the nature of Chinese society and Chinese revolution.

Contemporary mainland Chinese historians still emphasize the similarities between the theories of the Nationalist theoreticians and the Trotskyites in order to classify them into what they consider a single "reactionary" group.[127] Leaving aside the judgmental term "reactionary," analysis of their writings at the time reveals that, generally speaking, the Nationalists were close to the Trotskyites in their view of the nature of ancient China because they were not against the theory of "commercial capitalism." However, their view of the nature of current Chinese society was quite different from that of the Trotskyites and more similar to that of the Chinese Communist Party because they did not deny the existence of feudal forces or feudal influence. The Nationalists could not accept the Trotskyite theory about the capitalist nature of current Chinese society mainly because behind it stood the ghost of proletarian revolution.

The similarities between the three groups' theories of the nature of current Chinese society, especially between the views of the Nationalists and the Chinese Communist Party, were first pointed out by the Trotskyites, who had decided to discard not only the strategies proposed by the Comintern, but also its theory of the nature of Chinese society. The Trotskyites attributed the Third International's failed strategies to its faulty evaluation of the nature of Chinese society. The Chinese Trotskyites declared that Stalin's views of Chinese society and Chinese revolution "have no difference at all from the views of the Third Party, the Reorganization Faction, and even Chiang Kai-shek, because all these people are making a great fanfare about anti-feudal forces."[128] The Trotskyite Li Ji found the debate between the Nationalist Tao Xisheng and the Stalinist Zhu Xinfan ridiculous because their views were actually the same.[129] The Trotskyite sympathizer Wang Yichang, in reviewing the debate, classified Chen Gongbo, the leader of the Reorganization Group, and Deng Yanda, the leader of the Third Party, with the Communist Xinsichao group and found the views of the Xinsichao group and the Xinshengming group very much the same.[130]

The similarities between the views of the Stalinists, the left-wing Nationalists, and the Third Party were also manifested in the fact that throughout the debate, the Stalinists made the Trotskyites, rather than the other two groups, their major target of attack. Li Lisan's important article and the articles published in *Xinsichao* were all responses to the open letter by Chen Duxiu and Liu Renjing, while the majority of the articles by the Stalinists published in *Dushu zazhi* were responses to the works of the Trotskyites Yan Lingfeng and Ren Shu. When the Communist theoretician He Ganzhi attempted a thorough study of the whole debate in 1937, he included only the Xinsichao and the Dongli groups and wholly neglected the other groups.

While differences existed not only between groups, but also within groups, those latter differences tended to focus on less fundamental issues. Moreover, mainly depending on the unity and discipline to each group, some had more internal differences than others. A contributor to *Qianjin* who belonged to the Nationalist group later recalled that Gu Mengyu was lenient and liberal enough to publish an article criticizing Gu's own views.[131] The three leading theoreticians of the Nationalist group—Gu Mengyu, Chen Gongbo, and Tao Xisheng—although in general agreement about the nature of Chinese society, had very different views about class and class struggle in China. Gu Mengyu denied the existence of classes and the applicability of class struggle in China; Tao Xisheng and Chen Gongbo recognized the existence of classes in China, but doubted the applicability of class struggle. The Trotskyites also quarreled constantly among themselves, though as far as the nature of Chinese society was concerned, their views were quite similar. The most serious difference within the Trotskyite group seems to have been between Yan Lingfeng and Ren Shu on one side and Liu Renjing on the other. In 1931, Liu Renjing published a short review of Ren Shu's *Introduction to Chinese Economy* and Yan Lingfeng's *Studies on Chinese Economy,* in which he accused the two authors of neglecting two important factors that blocked the development of capitalism in China—one was imperialism, the other was feudal remnants. He argued that they were wrong in suggesting that capitalism had developed to the same level in China as that in other capitalist countries. He agreed with them that China had already become a capitalist country, but he preferred to define China as "a backward capitalist country."[132]

The confusion of concepts added to the intensity of the debate. The central issue in the debate was whether or not feudalism still existed in China. But what is feudalism? It seems that everyone had his or her own definition, and the same person might have different definitions at different times.[133]

Geographically, this phase of the debate was mainly conducted in Shanghai. Most of the leading participants resided in Shanghai, to enjoy the relative safety provided by the international concessions, and almost all of the influential books and journals were published in Shanghai, which was China's center of publication at that time. Beijing and Tianjin also figured prominently in the debate because of the various publications based there. Heated debates were frequent among university students and professors .[134]

Rural China was the core of the debate. All groups agreed that capitalism had already dominated the urban economy of China. If there were any feudal vestiges in the cities, they were quite insignificant. The real battle between the groups was fought in the countryside. He Ganzhi and Sun Zhuozhang rightly remarked that the issue of the nature of rural society was the focus of all debates.[135] All groups devoted much attention to the villages, and some studies even ignored the cities completely. Those who argued for a capitalist China had to prove that urban or foreign capitalism had already penetrated into the villages and had fundamentally changed rural life. Those who argued for a semifeudal and semicolonial China had to prove that despite the penetration of urban capitalism, rural life had not been fundamentally changed and there were still strong feudal elements.

The Second Phase: 1934–1937

Largely because of the importance of the nature of rural Chinese society to the whole debate and the fact that there were actually only two contrasting views in the debate, the second phase of the debate was centered on only one issue: the nature of rural Chinese society. The social history of China and the nature of Chinese society as a whole attracted much less attention during the second phase than during the first phase. Moreover, the second phase of the debate involved only two groups: the CCP group and the group that supported Trotskyite views. Besides the theoretical and political importance of the nature of rural society, two other factors also contributed to the rise of the debate. One was the introduction of the writings on Chinese rural society and economy by foreign scholars; particularly important were the works by the Russian scholar L. Madjar, the American scholar John Lossing Buck, and the Japanese scholar Tanaka Tadao. The other was the transfer of financial capital from the cities to the villages following the bankruptcy of urban industries caused by the Great Depression.

Ironically, since it was impossible for both the Chinese Communist Party and the Trotskyists to have their own research institutions and their own journals openly in the areas controlled by the Nationalists, the CCP group disguised themselves as non-Communists, while the Trotskyite group was composed of real non-Communists. The CCP scholars were able to carry on their activities under the guise of researchers of the Academia Sinica headed by Cai Yuanpei, an academic leader known for his tolerance of diversity. Chen Hansheng, an underground Communist who had earned a Ph.D. in history in 1924 from the University of Berlin, was the leader and guiding spirit of this group. Chen worked with Li Dazhao at Beijing University from 1924 to 1927 and later went to Moscow to work as a research fellow in the Institute of Peasant Movement Studies of the Comintern, where he became involved in a debate with Madjar.[136] He believed Madjar's argument about rural China was wrong, but lacked solid evidence to prove that rural China was still dominated by feudalism rather than capitalism.[137] He returned to

China in 1928 and a year later was invited by Cai Yuanpei to head the Institute of Social Sciences of Academia Sinica based in Shanghai, a position he maintained till 1934. During this period he recruited some young leftist scholars to conduct investigations in the villages of twenty-four counties, with the purpose of proving the semifeudal and semicolonial nature of China's rural society.[138] Their direct protector in Academia Sinica was Yang Xingfo, then general secretary of Academia Sinica and a former follower of Deng Yanda. It was due to Yang's support that the investigative reports of Chen Hansheng's group were published, and it was because of Yang's assassination by Chiang Kai-shek in June 1933, as well as the suspicion and persecution of the Nationalist scholar Fu Sinian, that Chen Hansheng had to resign his position in Academia Sinica in 1934.[139]

Before he left China in late 1934 for Tokyo to work for the Comintern as a secret agent under the legendary red spy Richard Sorge, Chen organized his followers into the Chinese Association of Rural Economy Studies and became its chairman. The association published a journal entitled *Zhongguo nongcun* [Rural China] from October 1934 to December 1936; its chief contributors included young scholars such as Qian Junrui (Tao Zhifu), Sun Yefang, Xue Muqiao, and Feng Hefa. These scholars were so active that Chen's absence seems to have affected very little the work of the association.

The other side of the debate was represented by the journal *Zhongguo jingji* [Chinese Economy], which was affiliated with the Chinese Association of Economic Studies and edited by Deng Feihuang, a former member of the Reorganization Group. The chief contributors to the journal included Wang Yichang, Zhang Zhicheng, Wang Yuquan, Zhang Zhiming, and Wang Jingbo. They supported the Trotskyite views on the nature of rural Chinese society, although there is no evidence that any of them were affiliated with Trotskyite organizations.

The general argument between the two sides about whether rural China was semifeudal and semicolonial or capitalist was based on their differences on many specific issues. The first issue was what determined the nature of rural China: production forces or production relations? The *Chinese Economy* scholars argued that Marxism held that production forces form the base of a society and hence determine the nature of the production relations and the nature of the society. Since many new agricultural methods, equipment, and technology had been imported into China, and more and more poor peasants had become wage laborers employed on farms using these new importations, capitalist rural production forces had been created in China; therefore, rural China had become a capitalist society. The *Rural China* scholars, however, insisted that although production forces should be taken into account, it is production relations—namely, the method of property ownership, the status of each class in the production, and the method of distribution—that determine the nature of a society. This was because "the nature of a social-economic structure (which means the sum total of production relations) can only be determined by its own features," not by the features of its material base. According to Marxism, production forces are not always compatible with production relations and hence it would be misleading to determine the nature of production relations on the basis of production forces. They argued that the Soviet Union was a socialist country not because it had more advanced production forces than capitalist countries, but because it had more advanced production relations. Therefore,

> when we analyze a feudal society, our main concern is to observe whether in the dominant economic system of that society, the exploitation of surplus products is based on land ownership, whether the direct producer is independent, and whether the relations between the owners of the means of production and the direct producer are based on extra-economic power, etc. We do not take into consideration whether the society uses 'manual pestle' or 'junks'.[140]

Fruitful conclusions in the debate about the relative importance of production forces and production relations in determining the nature of rural China were virtually impossible. Even if both sides agreed on this issue, the nature of Chinese rural society would remain obscure because it was even more difficult for them to agree on exactly what kind of production forces or production relations China had at that time. There was not even agreement on the definition of production forces. Wang Yichang, the leader of the *Chinese Economy* group, argued that production forces were the human-invented technologies used in the exploitation of nature and natural resources. His follower Zhang Zhicheng elaborated on his point and proposed that production forces were composed of three elements: means of production, or tools; labor; and technology. However, Xue Muqiao of the *Rural China* group believed that production forces had both technological and social aspects, with social relations also forming an important component.[141] Furthermore, the two sides had different assessments about the importance of modern technology and organization in rural China. The *Rural China* group argued that capitalist production forces, including machines and other modern agricultural technologies, existed in limited areas only, and most rural areas were still at the pre-capitalist stage. The *Chinese Economy* group, however, emphasized the importance of imported modern farming methods and equipment to the rural economy.

As for rural production relations, the two groups could not agree on the roles of the various rural classes and the relations between them. The *Rural*

China group classified the landlords and rich peasants, especially those considered "local tyrants and evil gentry," as semifeudal elements. The small landholding peasants and landless peasants were regarded as semifeudal producers. The *Chinese Economy* scholars viewed the landlords as feudal remnants but rich peasants as rural capitalists, the small landholding peasants as independent capitalist producers, and the poor peasants and landless peasants as members of the rural proletariat.[142] As a result of their different perceptions of the roles and nature of each class, the general schemes for classification of the rural population were also different. Wang Yichang of the *Chinese Economy* group proposed a two-step classification. The first step was to divide the whole rural population into the landlord class and the peasant class; the second step was to further divide the peasant class into the capitalist class and the labor class. According to Wang, the relations between the landlords and peasants were feudal in nature, but the relations between the rural capitalists and the rural labor class were of a capitalist nature.[143] The *Rural China* scholars argued that rural classification was not so simple because there were many other classes between the rural capitalists (rich peasants) and the rural proletariat, including the middle peasants and poor peasants. They insisted on dividing the rural population into five classes: landlord, rich peasant, middle peasant, poor peasant, and farm labor.[144] Wang Yichang called this classification "a complete mess" because it confused feudal relations with capitalist relations and unnecessarily differentiated the poor peasants from farm laborers, both of whom, according to Wang, formed the rural proletarian class.[145]

Rural usury also caused some controversy between the two groups. The *Rural China* group argued that usurers were affiliated with both the capitalist forces and the landlord class, and that they were not always incompatible with the feudal elements. The *Chinese Economy* group saw usurers as representatives or agents of urban capitalists and imperialists, and therefore they were capitalist elements. Related to the role of usurers and merchants was the issue of commodity economy, which had been a hot topic since the beginning of the debate. The *Rural China* group maintained that commodity economy alone could not determine the nature of a society because it could only change the exchange system of a society, but not its production system. Commodity economy or commercial capital could exist in any form of society. In China, commercial capitalists and feudal elements had joined forces to establish a political and economic united front; therefore, the development of commercial capitalism sometimes strengthened rather than weakened the position of feudal elements. This was well reflected in the fact that many Chinese landlords were at the same time businessmen and usurers. The *Chinese Economy* scholars, however, reiterated the significance of the development of commodity economy in rural areas. According to them, if the landlords and peasants had to rely on external markets, then rural China was a part of the capitalist world.

This in turn led to another round of debate on the relative importance of cities and villages in China's economy. Did the cities dominate the villages, or vice versa? The *Chinese Economy* group firmly believed that the urban centers had established their dominant roles over the rural areas; therefore, if the cities were capitalist, so were the villages. The *Rural China* group did not deny that the cities had dominated the villages economically, but they argued that urban capitalists, although dominating the villages, had failed to fundamentally change the production relations of the rural areas. Cities and villages remained different. To them, the fact that the rural economy was controlled and dominated by urban capitalists did not necessarily mean that the rural economy itself was capitalist in nature.

The different perceptions of the two schools about the role of the rich peasants and the small landholding and landless peasants were closely related to their different views about land rent. According to Marxist theory, feudal rent is quite different from capitalist rent. The former is based on feudal land ownership, which involves landlords who own the land and peasants who do not own land but have to rent land from the landlords. The latter is based on capitalist land ownership, which involves landlords who own the land, rural capitalists who rent the land for capitalist production, and rural workers who provide their labor for rural capitalists in exchange for wages. As a result, feudal rent is paid to landlords by tenants; such rent includes the total surplus value created by the tenants and often even includes part of the products needed by the tenants and their families for survival. Capitalist rent is paid to landlords by rural capitalists, and it includes only part of the surplus value created by rural workers; the other part of the surplus value is kept by rural capitalists as the average profit. The debate about land rent started in the previous period. The Trotskyites argued that the rent paid by the Chinese peasants was capitalist in nature because it was paid in cash rather than in produce, and that it was the surplus value extracted from the rural proletariat by the rural capitalists. The Communist Party theoreticians held that rent in cash was not incompatible with feudalism because it was merely a simple modified form of rent in produce. Moreover, in China, rent in cash had just emerged and rent in produce was still the dominant mode. Furthermore, the CCP theoreticians argued, the rent paid by the Chinese peasants included all the surplus value they created and usually such rent also included part of the products needed for the peasants' survival. The peasants were not entitled to keep any part of the surplus value as their average profits. Such exploitation was semifeudal in nature rather than capitalist, and the Chinese peasants were feudal tenants rather than rural capitalists.[146]

The role of imperialism in China's rural economy, especially the relations between imperialism and national capitalism in rural China, and the relations between imperialism and rural feudal forces, remained a heated topic in the debate. The two sides were adamant about their previous positions, with those on the *Chinese Economy* side arguing that imperialism would cause the inevitable disappearance of feudalism and the rise of capitalism in China. On the one hand, they reasoned, imperialism and feudalism were totally incompatible with each other; on the other hand, there was no difference or contradiction between imperialism and Chinese national capitalism. A slightly different view was voiced by Wang Jingbo, a member of the *Chinese Economy* group, who argued that even if rural China did not have a capitalist mode of production, it was still a capitalist society because it was controlled and dominated by imperialism or international capitalism. In his words, "China is a colony; and a colony is the countryside of international capitalism."[147] The *Rural China* group maintained that imperialism actually played a double role in the transition from feudalism to capitalism in rural China. As for Wang Jingbo's view, Qian Junrui and Zhou Bin of the *Rural China* group pointed out that even though rural China was dominated by international capitalism that did not necessarily mean that rural Chinese society itself was capitalist.[148] They cited India and other colonies as examples to show that a dominant foreign capitalist system could work well in a pre-capitalist context.

The differences in the general understanding of the nature of rural society led the two groups to different interpretations of the current rural pauperization and bankruptcy of China. The *Chinese Economy* group viewed that bankruptcy as both proof and a natural result of the development of capitalism in rural China. The *Rural China* group, on the one hand, opposed attributing the rural bankruptcy to feudal exploitation alone, and on the other hand, rejected the idea of interpreting it entirely in terms of capitalist development. They stressed the combined effects of external factors such as the invasion of foreign capital and the shift of world agricultural depression, and internal factors such as the commercialization of agricultural production, the domination of China's national economy by the imperialists, and the semifeudal exploitation.[149]

Finally, the two groups could not agree on matters relating to the study of rural economics. Should rural economists focus on the land problem or capital problem, production relations or production forces? The differences between the two groups were largely caused by their different understandings of the nature of China's rural crisis. Wang Yichang of the *Chinese Economy* groups proposed that rural economists should shift their attention from social relations (production relations) to relations between humans and nature (production forces, especially technology). The *Rural China* scholars argued that the most urgent problem in rural China was still the land problem, which the First United Front failed to solve; therefore, they contended, rural economists should study production relations, especially the issue of land redistribution.[150]

The *Chinese Economy* group proposed that since rural China had already become part of the capitalist world, the most urgent issue was capital distribution rather than land distribution. They either declared that "the issue of land redistribution had become history since the end of the Great Revolution in 1927,"[151] or argued that although the land problem was still an urgent issue, as a colonial capitalist society the true enemy of China was foreign capitalism rather than native feudalism, and the land problem could only be solved after, rather than before or simultaneously with the overthrow of foreign capitalism.[152] Accordingly, they believed that the subject of rural economics was capital rather than land, production forces rather than production relations.[153] They proposed greater focus on the technological aspects of production, such as agricultural techniques and the revenue and expenditure of agricultural management.

These two approaches were believed to be represented respectively by John Lossing Buck's *Chinese Farm Economy*, published in 1930, and Chen Hansheng's *The Production Relations and Production Forces of Rural Guangdong*, published in 1935. Buck's book focuses on the management of individual farms or rural households, especially on the technical issues of the farms, such as the utilization of land, the size of the farms, and its effects on efficiency, tenancy, fertilizer and livestock, revenue, and expenditure. Chen's book concentrates more on social relations in the countryside and emphasizes the landlords' exploitation of the peasant. Wang Yichang and Han Dezhang of the *Chinese Economy* group proposed a shift from the Chen approach to the Buck approach, which meant a shift from topics such as rural classes, usury, and rent to topics like soil, crops, livestock, tools, fertilizer, and measures. Qian Junrui of the *Rural China* group, however, called for a movement from the Buck approach to the Chen approach, arguing that rural economics should be an integral part of theoretical economics rather than an extension of agricultural science.[154] In other words, the *Rural China* group wanted to concentrate on agrarian issues, while the *Chinese Economy* group preferred to focus on agricultural issues.

Except for Wang Yichang, a veteran of the debate, all the other participants during this phase were new faces. However, the issues were basically the same as in the first phase. The two groups were loyal successors of the Xinsichao group and the Dongli group, respectively. The main difference was that they narrowed their scope from China as a whole to rural China alone. The biggest change on the CCP side was that they now paid much more attention to field investigation and relied more on materials collected directly from the villages to prove their arguments. The major change on the Trotskyite side was that they were now more scholars than revolutionaries. After the two large-scale arrests by the Nanjing government in 1931 and 1932, the Trotskyite organizations were heavily decimated and most of their leaders had been put into prison. That group of scholars who continued to argue along the Trotskyite line during the second phase of the debate seems to have banished politics, especially the idea of revolution, from their minds. There is no evidence that any of them had ever been revolutionaries before. They preferred to call themselves economists, whose duty it was to find ways of increasing productivity within the capitalist system. Therefore, their opponents in the debate charged they had abandoned the revolutionary message of the Trotskyite participants of the first phase of the debate and had fallen into reformism.

Although this new phase of debate may have taken on a more academic appearance than the first phase, in essence it was still a political debate waged between the revolutionaries and reformers. Generally speaking, if the CCP scholars during this phase were better armed with solid data than the Trotskyites, the Trotskyites once again proved themselves to be better students of Marxist theories, with bountiful quotations from Marxist classics to buttress their arguments.

THE NON-MARXIST AND ANTI-MARXIST VIEWS

Many non-Marxist scholars felt that the whole debate among the Marxists was baseless and absurd. They tended to stress the uniqueness of Chinese society and refused to apply Marxist or other foreign concepts, such as feudalism, class, or the Asiatic mode of production, or foreign grand theories such as Marxist unilinear evolutionism, to the study of Chinese society. In this they were true successors of Zhang Dongsun and Liang Qichao. However, unlike Zhang and Liang, they were more like external critics than direct participants in the debate. In the process of their criticism they tried to form their own theories about the nature of Chinese society in order to replace the foreign theories. Unlike the Marxist participants, this group of scholars did not act collectively, nor did they seem to share common political views. Some were considered conservatives, while others were regarded as liberals. Some of them were traditional Chinese scholars, and others were academically trained social scientists. The representatives of this group included Qian Mu, Hu Shi, Liang Shuming, and Fei Xiaotong. What they had in common was a shared aversion to the revolutionary ideologies.

Qian Mu, in his *Guoshi dagang* [An Outline History of China], written in 1929, argued that since the Qin Dynasty China had been neither a feudal nor a capitalist society, because while there were no hereditary feudal lords or major differences between the rich and the poor in China, and the relationship between the landlords and the tenants was regulated by state law rather than feudal bonds, it was also the case that traditional Chinese political ideology did not allow for the development of capitalism. He criticized those who debated whether China was a feudal or capitalist society for blindly following the pattern of European history without paying enough attention to the uniqueness of Chinese history.[155] He brought up the issue of feudalism again in his *Guoshi xinlun* [A New History of China], in which he stressed the positive effects of Confucianism on China's social justice. He maintained that there had been no strictly stratified class system in China since the Qin and Han Dynasties. In Chinese society there had been neither a hereditary aristocracy nor a class of serfs such as those in eighteenth- and nineteenth-century Europe. Theoretically, there was mobility among the four main social groups of China: the literati, the peasantry, the craftsmen, and the merchants. Therefore, he rejected the use of the term "feudalism" to define Chinese society. He did not like the term "despotism" either, because he believed that Confucianism proposed to limit rather than strengthen the power of the emperor.[156]

Hu Shi made his first serious response to the Marxist debate in an article written in 1930. Based on his well-known argument about issues and isms, he proposed piecemeal reform to eliminate China's five national enemies: poverty, disease, ignorance, corruption, and disorder. According to Hu, Chinese society was neither capitalistic nor feudal, but a society enfeebled by those five "enemies":

> This enumeration of our five enemies does not include capitalism, because we cannot yet talk about capitalism in China. Nor the capitalist class, because we have only a few fairly well-to-do people, but certainly no capitalist class. Nor feudalism, because feudalism in China ended 2,000 years ago with the formation of the First Empire. Nor imperialism, because imperialism cannot injure a country that is not first devastated by those five devils.[157]

To support his conclusions, Hu cited Li Jinghan's investigation of Beijing village families and information about villages in Sichuan and Anhui. In a speech delivered in America in 1941, Hu Shi further argued that Chinese feudalism was successfully abolished during the Han Dynasty rather than during the Qin, as he had claimed in his 1930 article. Chinese society after Han had seen no real class divisions, and not even any enduring differences between the rich and the poor.[158]

Liang Shuming also emphasized the uniqueness of Chinese culture and society, summarizing his theory about the nature of Chinese society in a book published in 1937. He defined China as a society based on Confucian ethics, in which there were only professional differences, but no class differences. The aristocracy and serfs of medieval Europe and the capitalists and workers of modern Europe had no parallels in China. In China there was no monopoly of property and therefore no exploitation of one class by another. He attributed this to three factors: one was the free transaction of land, which made monopoly of the land very difficult; another was the rule of inheritance, which was not based on primogeniture but required the property to be equally divided among all children—a factor that also helped to avoid the monopoly of property; the last was the lack of machines, which made it unnecessary to accumulate large amounts of wealth to build large-scale factories.

Obviously, the concepts of feudalism and class adopted by Qian Mu, Liang Shuming, and Hu Shi were quite different from those used by the Marxist scholars. To the former, feudalism meant the contracted political structure of medieval Europe, and class meant the unbridgeable gap between the aristocracy and the commoners of medieval Europe. They did not consider the relations between landlords and peasants feudal and did not regard warlords and landlords as feudal forces, as many revolutionary intellectuals did. On the issue of feudalism, the Marxists and non-Marxists actually adopted two different sets of definitions and created two unrelated discourses using the same terminology. The non-Marxist scholars had much less internal controversy concerning the concept of feudalism and its existence in China; they all based their concept of feudalism on the social features of medieval European society and Western Zhou China. Marxists of all kinds agreed that China had gone through a period of feudalism, but they could not agree about whether current China still possessed feudal traits. In order to support their argument that feudalism did exist or had existed in China, Chinese Marxists had to base their concept of feudalism more on the social features of China rather than those of medieval Europe. In short, the non-Marxist scholars adopted a universal concept of feudalism in order to argue against the universality of both feudalism and the Marxist scheme of social evolution, whereas Marxist scholars had to localize and nationalize the concept of feudalism in order to prove the universality of both feudalism and the Marxist scheme of social evolution.

The young sociologist Fei Xiaotong also agreed to some extent with Liang Shuming. In fact he was accused by some people of plagiarizing Liang Shuming's theory about the nature of Chinese society.[159] In a book written in the 1940s, he made his first effort at generalizing about Chinese society by discussing its nature. Following Qian Mu and Liang Shuming, he emphasized the uniqueness of Chinese society. As a functionalist, his theoretical weapon was anti-evolutionism. To him, the debate about the transition from feudalism to capitalism was meaningless.[160]

In summary, there were two major approaches to the issue of the nature of Chinese rural society: Marxist and non-Marxist. Although the first round of the debate, which took place in the early 1920s, was carried out between Marxists and non-Marxists, the most important part of the debate, which occurred between 1927 and 1937, was conducted among various groups of Marxists. The non-Marxists became onlookers or, at most, external critics. This was so because the debate between 1927 and 1937 was closely tied to the theory and strategy of past and future revolutions: it was mainly an argument among revolutionaries. The great majority of the non-Marxists were nonrevolutionaries. Therefore, it was difficult for them to find common ground with the doctrinally oriented revolutionary theoreticians.

There were clearly three levels of differences among the intellectuals who addressed the issue of the nature of Chinese society. At the first level were the differences between the Marxist and non-Marxist intellectuals. They did not even share a common system of definitions and concepts that provided the theoretical bases of the debate. At the second level were the differences between the Trotskyites and the other three groups of revolutionary intellectuals, namely, the Chinese Communist Party, the Reorganization group, and the Third Party. They all accepted Marxist theory and its system of definitions and concepts, but had different understandings of the definitions of feudalism and capitalism and of their manifestations in China. At the third level were the differences among the Chinese Communist Party, the Third Party, and the Reorganization group. They agreed with each other about the existence of feudal elements in China, but used different terms to define such elements; and disagreed with each other as to what exactly composed those feudal elements.

Whether Marxist or non-Marxist, all those who wrote about the nature of Chinese society and Chinese rural society took the debate as a political matter rather than a purely academic endeavor. Everyone tried to establish logical relations in one way or another between their views of the nature of Chinese society and their political strategies. Their starting points were their strategies and programs for rebuilding the nation rather than China's social realities. No one conducted any serious investigations during the first phase of the debate. During the second phase, some of them, especially the CCP scholars, began to conduct investigations in the villages. However, their conclusions had already been reached before they went to the villages. They were determined to find data to support, rather than challenge, those conclusions.

The various views that emerged during the debate about the nature of Chinese rural society formed an important part of the Chinese intellectuals' efforts to grasp something that could justify their grand programs for China in general and rural China in particular. Each group of intellectuals strove to define Chinese rural society in such a way as to provide the basis for its transformation to a new society as envisioned by that group, and transformed in a manner of their prescription or preference. That they spent so much time and energy in debate on the issue of the nature of Chinese society reflected well the influence of the May Fourth Movement and the New Culture Movement.[161] The debate was the combined result of several factors: the rise of the modern Chinese intelligentsia, the spread of Marxism, and the increasing acceptance of the social sciences in China. During the New Culture Movement and May Fourth Movement, Chinese intellectuals were mainly concerned about the importation of foreign ideas; now they endeavored to link those imported ideas with the realities of China. Many Chinese intellectuals now firmly believed that the development of human society is determined by a set of social laws, and therefore it is possible to find the best program for China's future through the study of China's present. As a result, instead of looking to heaven for mandate, as the traditional Chinese peasant rebels did, modern Chinese revolutionaries turned to society itself for legitimacy and guidance. In other words, to the modern Chinese intelligentsia, the laws of society are the modern mandate of heaven. The debate indicates how modern Chinese revolutionaries have differed from both the traditional literati and the traditional peasant leaders, and how twentieth-century Chinese revolutions and reforms have differed from traditional Chinese peasant rebellions and dynastic changes.

5

Patterns of Intellectual–Peasant Relations

The Chinese intellectuals created various images of the peasant and offered various theories about the nature of Chinese rural society as part of their effort to justify their respective programs for the peasantry and rural China. However, in order to put their programs into practice and utilize and transform the peasants, the intellectuals could not simply stay in their study rooms and indulge in mental exercises. To test their theories about peasant and rural China and activate their revolution or reform plans, they had to go to the countryside to meet the peasants in person. This gave rise to the question: what kind of relationship should the intellectuals have with the peasants? This topic figured prominently in the intellectuals' writings of that period. Different groups had different ideas about this, with most using either imported theories or traditional practices to justify their respective patterns.

FROM ALIENATION TO REUNION

The Transformation of Identity

In his 1936 interview with Edgar Snow, Mao Zedong recalled that shortly after the 1911 Revolution, he joined the revolutionary army in Changsha for a short time, hoping to help complete the revolution. He had the following to say about his life in the army: "My salary was seven yuan a month—which is more than I get in the Red Army now, however—and of this I spent two yuan a month on food. I also had to buy water. The soldiers had to carry water in from outside the city, but I, being a student, could not condescend to carrying, and bought it from the water peddlers."[1] This statement reveals that, on the one hand, the new generation of students like Mao was quite different from the old literati, which regarded soldiering as one of the lowliest occupations. On the other hand, these new students still maintained some of the features of the traditional literati, such as their contempt for manual labor. However, for our purpose, the importance of this statement lies in Mao's identifying himself as a student, rather than a farmhand, his previous status. Five years earlier, when he was thirteen years old, Mao was forced to quit school to work in the field all year long. One of his early friends recalled that some days his father ordered him to carry farmyard manure from his village to the faraway field fifteen times a day.[2] His life as a laborer lasted for about two years, during which he is said to have proved himself to be as capable and hardworking as an adult peasant in all kinds of farm work.[3]

If Mao's talk with Edgar Snow in 1936 indicates how he changed from a farmhand or a semifarmhand to a student, then his "Talks at the Yenan Forum on Literature and Art" made six years later convey how he overcame his identity as an intellectual and reemerged as a member of the working class:

> If you want the masses to understand you, if you want to be one with the masses, you must make up your mind to undergo a long and even painful process of tempering. Here I might mention the experience of how my own feelings changed. I began life as a student and at school acquired the ways of a student; I then used to feel it undignified to do even a little manual labor, such as carrying my own luggage in the presence of my fellow students, who were incapable of carrying anything, either on their shoulders or in their hands. At that time I felt that intellectuals were the only clean people in the world, while in comparison workers and peasants were dirty. I did not mind wearing the clothes of other intellectuals, believing them clean, but I would not put on clothes belonging to a worker or peasant, believing them dirty. But after I became a revolutionary and lived with workers and peasants and with soldiers of the revolutionary army, I gradually came to know them well, and they gradually came to know me well too. It was then, and only then, that I fundamentally changed the bourgeois and petty-bourgeois feelings implanted in me in the bourgeois schools. I came to feel that compared with the workers and peasants the unremoulded intellectuals were not clean and that, in the last analysis, the workers and peasants were the cleanest people, and even though their hands were soiled and their feet smeared with cow-dung, they were really cleaner than the bourgeois and petty-

bourgeois intellectuals. That is what is meant by a change in feelings, a change from one class to another.[4]

Those who believed that Mao was an innate peasant leader, who always had feelings for the working people and placed his hopes on the peasantry from his earliest years, would find this statement hard to accept. The fact is that after Mao left his village and became a student of what was considered a "modern" school at the age of sixteen, especially after he entered the First Provincial Normal School in Changsha in 1913, he seemed to gradually forget his status as a peasant youngster and strove to find a place among the urban intelligentsia. In a letter written in 1917, Mao followed the traditional Chinese literati and classified all human beings into two types: gentlemen and "small persons." He considered intellectuals like himself to be gentlemen and the peasants "small persons." Although he argued then that gentlemen should have mercy for small people and treat them as fellow countrymen,[5] it was not until after he became a revolutionary and had some experience in urban revolution that he fully understood the necessity of returning to the peasants. In his own words, he did not "fully realize the degree of class struggle among the peasantry" (meaning the value of the peasants as a component force of class struggle) until 1925, which happened after he observed the militant peasant movement following the May Thirtieth Movement during a sick leave in his native village in Hunan.[6] This was confirmed by Zhou Enlai, who recalled that sometime before 1925, when informed of the rural work done by Tao Xingzhi, Mao replied that the party was too busy with work in the cities and could not send people to the villages.[7] To be sure, Mao did not totally ignore the peasants before 1925, but neither did he make them the focus of his attention, as he did after 1925.[8] Stuart Schram found it curious that "although of peasant origin, he had been so long in rediscovering the peasantry."[9] Within the Communist Party, there were quite a few who returned to the countryside or redirected their attention to the peasants earlier than or contemporaneously with Mao. These included Li Dazhao, Shen Dingyi, Wei Baqun, Peng Pai, Liu Zhidan, Deng Zhongxia, Yun Daiying, and others.[10]

The path Mao took from a village boy to an urban intellectual and his subsequent return to the village and the peasants was shared by many Chinese intellectuals of his generation. His change of sentiment and identity was also a common experience among the intelligentsia, especially the revolutionaries. If Mao's statement was more concerned with the change of "subjective identity," or how the intellectuals felt about their alienation from and reunion with the working class, Lu Xun's relationship with his peasant friend Run Tu, described in his famous story "Hometown," was indicative of the change of "objective identity," namely, how the peasants

sensed the change of their relationship with the intellectuals. Lu Xun, heir
to a bureaucratic family,[11] and Run Tu, the son of a peasant who worked in
Lu Xun's house, were close friends when they were young and used to call
each other "brother," but when Lu Xun returned to his hometown as an
established intellectual and government official after an absence of twenty
years and met Run Tu again, Lu Xun could not detect any trace of their
old friendship and Run Tu, now a poor peasant, began to call Lu Xun
"Master" and asked his son to kowtow to Lu Xun. "I shuddered [upon
hearing that] as I realized what a wretched, thick wall now stood between
us," Lu Xun wrote.[12]

The change of subjective and objective identities of the intellectuals
described by Mao Zedong and Lu Xun were well analyzed by Fei Xiaotong
in 1947:

> at college, even if they [the students from villages] fail to learn any
> new knowledge or technology, their life style and value system
> must undergo dramatic changes, hence they feel that they have
> become different from the villagers, that they are no longer able to
> associate with the rustic villagers, whose language is crude and dull
> and whose appearance is repulsive. Even though the students are
> willing to condescend to living with the villagers, others would see
> them as different persons from whom they used to be and would
> treat them with increased respect. As a result, the students would
> be treated like guests in their own homes, making it impossible for
> them to continue to live at home.[13]

Returned Students

The great majority of modern Chinese intelligentsia of Lu Xun's and Mao
Zedong's generations, especially the Communist revolutionaries and the
early champions of the peasants among them, were either directly from the
village, like Mao, or from families or areas close to the peasants, like Lu Xun.
For example, according to a recent collection of official biographies, among
the thirteen delegates attending the first congress of the Chinese Communist
Party, seven were from ordinary peasant families; two were from landlord
families; three were from county seats of the interior and rural Hubei
Province; only one, Chen Gongbo, born in Guangxi and raised in
Guangzhou, was of truly urban origin.[14] According to Li Rui, those of Mao's
close friends during his student years in Changsha who later became
Communists and died for the revolutionary cause were mostly from rural
areas. Li believed that their rural background made Marxism-Leninism more

acceptable to them and played a role in the formation of their revolutionary spirit and character.[15]

A quick survey of the background of other prominent Communist and non-Communist intellectuals who were involved in the early peasant movement indicates a similar pattern. Dr. Sun Yat-sen was born in a village in Guangdong and considered himself the son of a poor peasant;[16] Li Dazhao was born and raised in a rich peasant family in Hebei; Peng Pai was from a landlord family in Guangdong; Shen Dingyi was from a landlord family in Zhejiang; Deng Yanda was born and raised in a village in Guangdong;[17] Yan Yangchu was from the interior and rural Bazhong County of Sichuan; and Tao Xingzhi was born into a poor peasant family in Anhui.[18] It was these intellectuals with rural roots who first proposed to go or return to the village.

The general tendency was not only for intellectuals with rural origins to return to the village, but also for them to return to their own villages. Early examples included Shen Dingyi and Peng Pai, who began to organize the peasants in their native communities in the early 1920s. Other early examples included Wei Baqun of Guangxi;[19] Mao Zedong and Liu Dongxuan of Hunan;[20] Ruan Xiaoxian, Huang Xuezeng, and Zhou Qijian of Guangdong;[21] Fang Zhimin of Jiangxi;[22] and Zhou Shuiping of Jiangsu.[23] Some anarchists also went to Xiangshan County of Guangdong, the erstwhile home of their late leader Liu Shifu, to organize peasant associations and establish peasant schools.[24]

Yun Daiying, the general editor of *Zhongguo qingnian* [Chinese Youth], argued in 1924 that both the students who returned to their native villages for summer vacation as well as the primary school teachers in the villages could most easily be drawn into the peasant movement. He called on the local intellectuals to help with the work of their own villages.[25] In the same year, Ruan Xiaoxian made seven suggestions about the peasant movement to the Communist Youth League, including that "the leaders of the movements should be natives. If they are not natives, they should have native guides."[26] Seven years before, Li Dazhao had made the call for all urban students to go to the village. Yun Daiying's and Ruan Xiaoxian's call was different from that of Li Dazhao in that Yun and Ruan targeted a special group of urban students, namely, those who had their roots in the villages, and urged them to return to their own villages. Yun and Ruan saw the trend more clearly than Li Dazhao, probably because they had the advantage of observing the rural work of intellectuals like Shen Dingyi and Peng Pai. Actually, most of the intellectuals who went to the villages to carry out reform or revolution before the Northern Expedition were the so-called returned students.

During the Northern Expedition, peasant movements in various parts of China continued to be led by "returned students." At the provincial level, the peasant movement in the southern provinces was tightly controlled by native

Communist intellectuals—Peng Pai in Guangdong, Mao Zedong in Hunan, and Fang Zhimin in Jiangxi. The peasant movement at the county and village levels was also mainly led by local intellectuals. For example, in Guangdong, the peasant movement at the district level was headed by the so-called "big four of the peasant movement" —Peng Pai, Zhou Qijian, Huang Xuezeng, and Ruan Xiaoxian. Except for Ruan, all the others were sent back to the district whence they came.[27] Returned students also led the peasant movement of Guangning,[28] Lechang,[29] and Hainan of Guangdong;[30] Pingle of Guangxi;[31] Xingguo,[32] Donggu,[33] and Xunwu of Jiangxi;[34] and Rucheng,[35] Yueyang,[36] and Sangzhi of Hunan.[37]

The Peasant Movement Institute in Guangzhou and Wuhan played a special role in training peasant leaders. Those provinces with more graduates of the institute were usually also the provinces where the peasant movement developed more quickly than others.[38] Initially, the special status of the returned students was a great asset to the peasant movement. As H. Chapman observed, these students helped protect the peasant movement because these intellectuals "were protected by a false analogy, which ranked them with the old-time Chinese scholars—their persons being regarded by all classes as almost sacred and their opinions as entitled to peculiar respect—so that they were able to engage in seditious propaganda, even mild rioting, for which others would be imprisoned and shot."[39]

A general survey (Table 2) of the Communists who led the peasant uprisings after the breakdown of the First United Front in 1927 indicates that most of them were also returned students.[40]

TABLE 2
A Survey of the Communist Leaders of Major Peasant Uprisings from 1927 to 1929.

Name	Native Place	Education	Urban Experience	Place of Uprising	Time of Uprising
Peng Pai+	Haifeng (Guangdong)	College (Waseda Univ.)	Tokyo	Haifeng (Guangdong)	Late 1927
Zhang Shanming*	Dapu (Guangdong)	Technical school; Univ. of the Toilers of East	Guangzhou; Moscow	Hai-lu-feng (Guangdong)	April,Sept., Oct. 1927
Gu Dacun*	Wuhua (Guangdong)	Professional School	Guangzhou	Wuhua and adjacent areas	August, 1928
Yang Shanji*	Hainan (Guangdong)	college(Univ. of the Toilers of East)	Guangzhou; Moscow	Hainan (Guangdong)	Sept. 1927
Feng Ping*	Hainan (Guangdong)	Shanghai Culture Univ.; Univ. of the Toilers of the East	Shanghai; Guangzhou; Moscow	Hainan (Guangdong)	Sept. 1927
Wang Wenming*	Hainan (Guangdong)	college (Shanghai Univ.)	Shanghai	Hainan (Guangdong)	Sept. 1927

TABLE 2 (Con't)
A Survey of the Communist Leaders of Major Peasant Uprisings from 1927 to 1929.

Name	Native Place	Education	Urban Experience	Place of Uprising	Time of Uprising
Feng Baiju*	Hainan (Guangdong)	middle school	Nanjing; Shanghai	Hainan (Guangdong)	Sept. 1927
Lei Jingtian*	Nanning (Guangxi)	Xiamen Univ.; Daxia Univ.	Naning; Xiamen; Shanghai	Youjiang (Guangxi)	Dec. 1929
Wei Baqun*	Donglan (Guangxi)	military school; Peasant Movement Institute	Guilin; Guiyang; Guangzhou	Donglan (Guangxi)	Dec. 1929
Zhu Jilei*	Pinghe (Fujian)	middle school; Peasant Movement Institute	Xiamen; Guangzhou	Pinghe (Fujian)	March 1928
Guo Diren*	Longyan (Fujian)	middle school Peasant Movement Institute	Xiamen; Guangzhou	Longyan (Fujian)	April 1928
Deng Zihui*	Longyan (Fujian)	middle school	Japan	Longyan (Fujian)	April 1928
Zhang Dingcheng*	Yongding (Fujian)	higher primary school	county seats of Yongding & Dapu	Yongding (Fujian)	June 1928
Fu Bocui*	Shanghang (Fujian)	Tokyo School of Law and Politics	Japan	Shanghang (Fujian)	June 1928
Guo Muliang	Shanghang (Fujian)			Shanghang (Fujian)	June 1928
Chen Geng+	Chong'an (Fujian)	middle school	Fuzhou	Chong'an (Fujian)	1928
Fang Zhimin*	Yiyang (Jiangxi)	technical school	Nanchang; Jiujiang; Shanghai	Yiyang and Hengfeng (Jiangxi)	Jan. 1928
Shao Shiping*	Yiyang (Jiangxi)	college (Beiping Normal Univ.)	Nanchang; Beijing	Yiyang and Hengfeng (Jiangxi)	Jan. 1928
Huang Dao*	Hengfeng (Jiangxi)	college (Beiping Normal Univ.)	Nanchang; Beijing	Yiyang and Hengfeng (Jiangxi)	Jan. 1928
Zeng Tianyu*	Wan'an (Jiangxi)	college (China Univ.)	Nanchang; Tokyo; Beijing	Wan'an (Jiangxi)	Dec. 1927

TABLE 2 (Con't)

A Survey of the Communist Leaders of Major Peasant Uprisings from 1927 to 1929.

Name	Native Place	Education	Urban Experience	Place of Uprising	Time of Uprising
Zeng Yansheng*	Ji'an (Jiangxi)	college (Shanghai Univ.)	Nanchang; Shanghai; Nanjing	Wan'an (Jiangxi)	Dec. 1927
Gu Bai	Xunwu (Jiangxi)	middle school	Meixian; Guangzhou	Xunwu (Jiangxi)	March 1928
Mao Zedong*	Xiangtan (Hunan)	normal school	Changsha	(Hunan) and (Jiangxi)	Sept. 1927
Yu Bimin+	Pingjiang (Hunan)	military school Peasant Movement Institute	Guangzhou	Piangjiang (Hunan)	Sept. 1927
He Long*	Sangzhi (Hunan)	no formal education	Changsha and other places	Sangzhi (Hunan)	March 1928
Zhou Yiqun+	Tongren (Guizhou)	college; military academy	Guiyang; Shanghai Tokyo; Guangzhou	Sangzhi (Hunan)	March 1928
Luo Nachuan*	Pingjiang (Hunan)	middle school	county seat of Pingjiang	Pingjiang (Hunan)	March 1928
Hu Zi*	Huangmei (Hubei)	college (Dongnan Univ.)	Wuhan; Nanjing	Huangmei (Hubei)	Sept. 1927
Xiao Renhu	Huanggang (Hubei)	Zhonghua Univ.; Whompoa military academy Peasant Movement Institute	Wuhan; Guangzhou	Mianyang (Hubei)	Sept. 1927
Deng Chizhong*	Mianyang (Hubei)	middle school Peasant Movement Institute	Wuhan	Mianyang (Hubei)	Sept. 1927
Zou Zisheng	Lixian (Hunan)			Gong'an[1] (Hubei)	Sept. 1927
Fan Xueci	Gong'an (Hubei)			Gong'an (Hubei)	Sept. 1927
Yang Yunxiang	Gong'an (Hubei)			Gong'an (Hubei)	Sept. 1927
Pan Zhongru*	Huangpi (Hubei)	Whompoa military academy	Wuhan; Guangzhou	Huang'an-Macheng (Hubei)	Nov. 1927

TABLE 2 (Con't)

A Survey of the Communist Leaders of Major Peasant Uprisings from 1927 to 1929.

Name	Native Place	Education	Urban Experience	Place of Uprising	Time of Uprising
Wu Guanghao*	Huangpi (Hubei)	Whompoa military academy	Guangzhou	Huang'an-Macheng (Hubei)	Nov. 1927
Dai Kemin*	Huang'an (Hubei)	normal school; Peasant Movement Institute	Wuhan	Huang'an-Macheng (Hubei)	Nov. 1927
Cao Xuekai*	Huang'an (Hubei)	college (Zhonghua Univ.)	Wuhan	Huang'an-Macheng (Hubei)	Nov. 1927
Cheng Kesheng*	Zaoyang (Hubei)	middle school	Wuhan; France	Zaoyang (Hubei)	Nov. 1927
Wang Weizhou*	Xuanhan (Sichuan)	technical school; military school	Chengdu; Russia; Shanghai	Xuanhan-Wanyuan (Sichuan)	April 1929
Li Jiajun*	Wanyuan (Sichuan)	college (Tongji Medical College)	Shanghai	Xuanhan-Wanyuan (Sichuan)	April 1929
Wang Bolu*	Xinyang (Henan)	Peasant Movement Institute	Wuhan	Xinyang (Henan)	Nov. 1927
Zhang Yanwu*	Huangchuan (Henan)	Peasant Movement Institute	Wuhan	Huangchuan, etc. (Henan)	Feb. 1928
Ma Shangde* (Yang Jinyu)	Queshan (Henan)	Technical school	Kaifeng	Queshan (Henan)	Oct. 1927
Zhou Weijiong	Shangcheng (Henan)	Central military-political school	Wuhan	Shangcheng (Henan)	May 1929
Xu Qixu	Macheng (Hubei)			Shangcheng[2] (Henan)	May 1929
Shu Chuanxian*	Huoshan (Anhui)	Tokyo Advanced Industrial school	Anqing; Japan; Guangzhou	Lu'an-Huoshan (Anhui)	Nov. 1929
Zhou Juanzhi*	Lu'an (Anhui)	middle school	Anqing	Lu'an Huoshan (Anhui)	Nov. 1929
Wang Ruofei+	Anshun (Guizhou)	college	Guiyang; Japan; France; Moscow	Central Jiangsu (Jiangsu)	May 1928

TABLE 2 (Con't)

A Survey of the Communist Leaders of Major Peasant Uprisings from 1927 to 1929.

Name	Native Place	Education	Urban Experience	Place of Uprising	Time of Uprising
Yan Pu*	Wuxi (Jiangsu)	college (Nanfang Univ.)	Wuxi; Shanghai	Wuxi (Jiangsu)	Nov. 1927
Hang Gaoren	Wuxi (Jiangsu)	Peasant Movement Institute	Guangzhou	Wuxi (Jiangsu)	Nov. 1927
Hu Gongmian*	Yongjia (Zhejiang)		Shanghai and other Places	Yongjia (Zhejiang)	late 1929
Yu Fangzhou*	Ninghe (Tianjin)	college (Nankai Univ.)	Tianjin	Eastern Hebei	Oct. 1927
Liu Zhidan*	Bao'an (Shaanxi)	middle school; military academy	Guangzhou	Weihua (Shaanxi)	May 1928

* born in a village

+ born in a county seat

‡ born in a city

1. Lixian of Hunan is adjacent to Gong'an of Hubei.

2. Macheng of Hubei is adjacent to Shangcheng of Henan.

This survey, although covering only the major ones of the several hundred Communist peasant insurrections following the Chinese Communist Party Central Committee's directive issued on August 7, 1927, suffices as a foundation for several general conclusions to be drawn. First, most of the insurrections were led by intellectuals with at least a middle-school education. Among the individuals surveyed, He Long was the only one who did not have any formal education. Second, most of the intellectuals were originally from rural areas. Some were from villages, others from county seats. Not a single one was born and raised in a big city. Those from county seats were often related to the surrounding villages in one way or another. Zhou Yiqun, Wang Ruofei, and Peng Pai, for example, were from landlord families who had houses in county seats but left their fields in the villages to be cultivated by their tenants. Third, most of the intellectuals chose to return to their native areas to launch uprisings. For most insurrections, at least one of the key leaders was local born.

This survey covers only the peasant uprisings. The Communists also launched many soldier uprisings during that period. The leaders of the soldier uprisings were not necessarily native sons because the army units were frequently transferred from one area to another. However, most of those uprisings were supported by local party leaders and the peasant forces they controlled. The Communist leaders later argued that the Nanchang Uprising and the Guangzhou Uprising failed mainly because the military leaders failed to get the support of the local peasants,[41] while the Autumn Harvest Uprising led by Mao Zedong was considered a model for soldier–worker–peasant alliance. The Pingjiang Uprising of 1928 led by Peng Dehuai was greatly assisted by the peasants of Pingjiang, organized by local intellectuals such as Luo Nachuan and Hu Yun. In Guangxi, the soldier uprising led by Yu Zuoyu, Li Mingrui, Deng Xiaoping, and Zhang Yunyi gained strong support from the Youjiang peasant movement led by Wei Baqun. Zhang Yunyi later remarked that "if we [the rebel soldiers] had not gone to Youjiang to join the revolutionary masses, it would have been very difficult for us to create the Seventh Red Army and to strengthen and develop our forces within a short time." [42] In Shaanxi, the soldiers and local peasants led by natives and nonnatives joined in launching the Weihua uprising. The support of local peasants was widely believed to be essential for the success of the soldier uprisings.

Those non-Communist intellectuals interested in the peasantry and who went to the countryside after 1927 showed the same inclination for their native villages. Shen Dingyi was still very active in his home village in Xiaoshan County of Zhejiang. His bid for national power ended in failure, and he then lost his provincial position, but he would never lose his village, to which he could always return.[43] Fu Bocui was another peasant leader whose experiences were very similar to those of Shen Dingyi. Like Shen, Fu was also from a landlord family. He had studied in Japan in the mid-1910s. In 1918, Fu became a lawyer and returned to his native county—Shanghang of Fujian— to practice law. He became famous among the students and local people for his courageous and successful struggles against corrupt officials. He joined the Communist Party right after Chiang Kai-shek's coup in April 1927 and became a prominent Communist leader in western Fujian. He then voluntarily reduced his tenants' rent and ordered other landlords to do the same. However, when the party asked him to distribute his land among the tenants, he refused on the grounds that such radical measures would cause attack from the Nationalist government, and that the partition of land ownership would block technological improvement. At a local party conference presided over by Mao Zedong in 1929, Zhang Dingcheng and others criticized his stand. In 1930, he was expelled from the party for disapproving the official policies about land distribution and other matters. After that, he returned to his home village, Jiaoyang of Shanghang, located on the boundary of three counties and surrounded by high mountains. During the next two decades, with a population of about 5,000 and an army of about 700 soldiers, he mediated between the Nationalists and the Communists and managed to keep his small domain an independent kingdom.[44] Like Shen, although lacking support from either the Nationalist Party or the

Communist Party, Fu remained a powerful local figure simply because of his local connections and influence.[45]

In southwestern Henan Province, the rural reconstruction movement in the four counties of Zhenping, Neixiang, Xichuan and Dengxian was led by four natives—Peng Yuting, Bie Tingfang, Chen Zhonghua, and Ning Xigu, respectively. Although Bie Tingfang, the least educated among the four, had the strongest military force and it was mainly his power that enabled the implementation of many of the rural reconstruction projects, it was the intellectual Peng Yuting who masterminded the local autonomy and rural reconstruction programs carried out in the region. Peng, a native of Zhenping, was well educated and well traveled, and was a high-ranking official before returning home in 1926. After both Peng and Bie died, Chen Zhonghua took over. Chen was a native of Xichuan who had attended schools in Shanghai and Kaifeng.[46] Ning Xigu, the leader of the Dengxian County, was a native of Dengxian and a graduate of the Huangpu Military Academy in Guangzhou.[47]

Two other rural reconstructionists, Wu Chaoshu and Feng Rui (Feng Tixia), also chose to return to their rural birthplaces. Wu, from Hainan, was a former consul-general in Washington D.C. In the early 1930s, he resigned from his position as the head of the Legislative Yuan and returned to Hainan to help with the rural development project. Feng Rui was an agronomist from Guangdong who worked in Dingxian for some years. In the early 1930s, he returned to Guangdong to oversee a rural reconstruction project.[48]

The rural reconstructionists Liang Shuming and Yan Yangchu did not return to their own villages. Liang, born and raised in Beijing, did not have a village to which he could return; Yan, a native of Sichuan, chose to go to Dingxian of Hebei.[49] However, the rural reconstruction project in Henan, where Liang later worked, was started by three natives: Wang Bingcheng, Peng Yuting, and Liang Zhonghua. Liang Shuming was their employee. Likewise, the project in Dingxian was also initiated by the native Mi family.[50] Yan Yangchu himself admitted that the particular reason for his choosing Dingxian as the base of his experimental program was because the mass education movement had already spread to fifteen counties of the Baoding district before he arrived there. In addition, the peasants of Baoding, especially Mi Digang, invited him to go there and assured Yan that they would give him full support.[51] In these two cases, because the locals who initiated the projects were relatively insignificant persons, they were later overshadowed by outsiders who possessed more resources and greater fame. It was often the case that if those who went to the countryside were nonnative intellectuals, they had to communicate with the local people through native intellectuals in the initial phase. For example, when the sociologist Li Jinghan started his investigation project in Dingxian, he was far from successful with the peasants because his investigators were all nonnative college graduates. Later he decided to use the graduates of local schools. These native intellectuals were far more successful in collecting data because they enjoyed the trust of the peasants.[52]

Researchers interested in rural society also tended to return to their native locales to conduct investigations. The sociologist Fei Xiaotong made field trips to many areas of China, including Guangxi and Yunnan, but his most famous fieldwork was conducted in the Kaixiangong village in his home county, Wujiang of Jiangsu. In the preface to Fei's *Peasant Life in China,* his mentor Bronislaw Malinowski remarked that one of the unique features of Fei's book was that "it is the result of work done by a native among natives."[53] Malinowski explained that here the word "native" simply meant that Fei was born and raised in the area he studied.[54] Truly there is hardly a better word than "native" to describe the relations between Fei and the people of Kaixiangong. Other Chinese sociologists and anthropologists followed the same pattern. Martin Yang's *A Chinese Village* is about the life of his own village, Taitou of Qingdao, Shandong.[55] Lin Yaohua [Lin Yueh-hwa]'s *The Golden Wing* depicts his own family and his home village in Gutian of Fujian.[56]

Even foreign scholars who studied Chinese villages had to follow this pattern. The American sociologist Daniel Harrison Kulp II was the author of *Country Life in South China,* a book about the social life of the Fenghuang [Pheonix] village of Chao'an County, Guangdong. Investigation and data collection were mainly conducted during the summers of 1918 and 1919 by his students who came from the Chaozhou area. Kulp himself paid a visit to the village in 1923, accompanied and assisted by a college student from that village. It has even been rumored that Kulp never actually visited the village and that all the investigation was done by his students from that area.[57]

John Lossing Buck's studies on Chinese farm economy and land utilization have been very influential. However, little of the data contained in the books were collected by Buck himself; instead, they were provided for him by the Chinese native intellectuals—Buck was the guide, compiler, analyzer, and synthesizer. His *Chinese Farm Economy* was based on seventeen surveys, containing data about 2,866 farms (households) in seventeen localities. All surveys were conducted by his students in their native communities. His project on Chinese land utilization, which started in the early 1930s, was also completed with the help of native intellectuals. Buck realized from the very beginning that "the selection of capable Regional Investigators was the foundation of the study." Most of his investigators were "graduates of middle schools and could speak the same dialect as that of the farmers to be interviewed."[58] Buck's preference for native investigators was preceded by that of the Chinese anarchist Liu Shipei. Liu emphasized about a decade earlier that "the sufferings of the peasants differ from place to place.... Therefore, a native's description about the conditions of the people of his place would be different from hearsay."[59]

It is interesting to note that the Communist Yun Daiying and many other revolutionary and reform leaders attached special importance to the role of village school teachers in carrying out rural programs. A 1928 CCP document stipulated that rural teachers in particular should be encouraged to join the peasant movement.[60] Another CCP document, published in September 1926, called the village primary school teachers "the natural guides of the peasants," and urged the party to win them over.[61] The Communist peasant leader Ruan Xiaoxian expressed the same views in an important article written in the same year.[62] There were not many professions suitable for a returned intellectual in the village other than that of village school teacher. Therefore, most returned students became village school teachers. As teachers they enjoyed the villagers' respect, trust, and support. Some of the rural teachers returned first to teach in the village and were only later drawn into the revolutionary or reform programs. Others became revolutionaries or reformers first, then returned to the villages and became teachers as a convenient guise.

Examples of the important role of village teachers in the rural revolution were plentiful. Ruan Xiaoxian reported in 1926 that in Hunan there were more than 100 primary school teachers who were helping with the local peasant movement. Because of this, Ruan foresaw a bright future for the peasant movement of Hunan.[63] Deng Zihui and Zhang Dingcheng recalled that right after the collapse of the First United Front in 1927, in Longyan and other counties of western Fujian, the Communist Party did not have many peasant members. However, at the same time, the primary school teachers of all the villages were mostly Communist party members or leftists. As a result, the work of the party was all based in the primary schools.[64] Deng Zihui, the leader of the peasant uprising in Longyan County, and Zhang Dingcheng, who led the uprising in Yongding County, were themselves primary school teachers prior to the uprisings. In Huang'an County of Hubei, almost all rural school teachers were Communists during the period of the First United Front. This was one of the most important reasons why Huang'an became a Communist stronghold after 1927.[65] In Shimen County of Hunan, after the breakup of the United Front in 1927, the local Communists— who were mostly intellectuals—went to the middle schools and primary schools to take positions as teachers and used the schools as their bases to prepare for peasant uprisings.[66] In Weinan County of Shaanxi, the Communists gathered in three local schools and made Xuanhua Higher Primary School the base of the local party branch.[67] When the Weihua Uprising was defeated, the local party branch transferred the intellectual party members from the city to the villages to work among the peasants. As a result, the primary school teachers and principals in northern Shaanxi were mostly Communists or members of the Communist Youth League.[68] In his "Xunwu Investigation," written in May 1930, Mao Zedong explained why middle school and primary school students and primary school teachers were so active in the local Communist movement. Mao found that most of these people belonged to the class of small landlords who, "in years with declining standard of living, must incessantly sell land in order to survive. This group has a very miserable future ahead.... They are enthusiastic for revolution."[69] However, revolution was not the only choice for rural school teachers. As will be indicated, the intellectuals involved in the rural reconstruction and mass education movements, such as Liang Shuming, Yan Yangchu, and Tao Xingzhi, attached even greater importance to village school teachers in transforming rural China. Village school teachers played a very important role in their reform programs.

The intellectuals who returned to their areas of birth enjoyed many advantages: they had a keen understanding of local conditions; they were familiar with local culture and spoke the dialects; and, finally, they had an array of connections. Family or lineage support was particularly important in the development of many peasant movements. Peng Pai and Fang Zhimin, for example, received much support from their family members, relatives, and friends in their native communities.[70] Living and working among their own people gave the revolutionaries special strength and a sense of security. After Fang Zhimin launched a peasant uprising in his native area in late 1927, the Nationalist government sent a regiment of soldiers to the area to deal with him. He and his followers had only two and a half guns, and were in no position to resist the strong enemy. Finally they were surrounded in a small mountainous area. Yet Fang flatly rejected the idea that the guerrillas should move to another area to avoid being eliminated, reasoning that by staying they could always rely on the local people, whereas in a new area, they would be total strangers to both the place and the people and hence it would be much easier for the enemy to eliminate them.[71] It turned out that Fang made the right decision. The enemy regiment failed to eliminate his small forces. Local and familial support also played an important role in many non-Communist projects. The reform project of the Zhaicheng village of Dingxian, Hebei started out as a business of the Mi family.[72] Fei Xiaotong's fieldwork in Kaixiangong was assisted by his sister, who was working with the peasants as an expert on silk-making.

The Communist leaders attached so much importance to native cadres that when the Red Army moved to a new area, one of the first things it would do was to look for local party branches or party members, and whenever the main forces of the Red Army had to retreat from an area, the party would leave some party leaders with good local connections in the area to "continue the struggle." For example, when the Red Army of Youjiang area in Guangxi had to leave for the central base area in Jiangxi, the party decided that natives Wei Baqun and Chen Hongtao would stay in Youjiang. When the Red Army decided to leave Jiangxi, Mao Zedong instructed Zhang Dingchen, a native of western Fujian, to return to his birthplace. To remain in an area where fierce class struggle had just been carried out without a powerful military force of one's own was an extremely dangerous undertaking. Natives had advantages, but they had disadvantages too. Usually they had many local enemies, who, after the retreat of the Communist forces, would return to seek revenge. Even if the revolutionaries themselves could escape, their families would often become easy targets. These disadvantages were noticed by the Communist leaders as early as the initial phase of the land revolution. In northeastern Jiangxi, for example, the three Communist leaders, Fang Zhimin, Shao Shiping, and Huang Dao, once decided to switch their bases. Huang Dao, a native of Hengfeng County, would work in Yiyang County. Fang Zhimin, a native of Yiyang County, would work in Hengfeng County. The local party committee ordered that switch because Fang Zhimin was "too big a target in Yiyang and would attract the attention of the enemy."[73] Shao Shiping, a native of the seventh district of Yiyang, was transferred to its ninth district, after a dangerous confrontation with his enemies in his native village. Later he was transferred to Hengfeng to replace Fang Zhimin. They still worked in their home areas, but not their native villages. It was hoped that this arrangement would ward off the disadvantages of working in one's native place while still enjoying some of its advantages. On many occasions, the revolutionaries left behind in their native communities after the retreat of the main forces of the Red Army did not survive. In Guangxi, both Wei Baqun and Chen Hongtao were killed not long after the retreat of the Red Army. But there were successful cases of such arrangements as well. One was the triumph of the Communist guerrilla forces on Hainan Island, where "the red flag was never toppled" between 1927 and 1950. Another example was the success of the Communist forces in western Fujian led by Zhang Dingcheng and Deng Zihui. When the Communist forces in southern China had to make another march to the north in 1937, the Communist Party again left some prominent leaders in their homelands to "continue the struggle." Huang Dao stayed in Jiangxi to lead the Communist forces in northern Fujian and northeastern Jiangxi. Tu Zhengkun was left in Pingjiang of Hunan to manage the local office of the New Fourth Army and the local party work.

During the Anti-Japanese War, besides leaving behind a small number of local-born party members to continue the struggle in the south, the Communists also emphasized the importance of local knowledge and local cadres in their new base areas in northern China. In the southern Hebei base area created by the Eighth Route Army forces led by Xu Xiangqian, Li Qingyu, a local veteran Communist, was chosen to head the government because he "was familiar with local conditions and enjoyed the respect of the local people."[74] He Long, head of the central Hebei base area, realized that his most urgent task was to train local cadres, "because they have a better knowledge of local conditions and customs than those from other provinces."[75] In the Shanxi–Chahar–Hebei base area, two natives were selected to head the Border Region Administrative Committee. In the northern Jiangsu base area, three local Communists were chosen to lead the administrative and military organs. A survey of 210 New Fourth Army cadres stationed in northern Jiangsu indicated that 140, or two-thirds, of them were natives of Jiangsu. Chalmers Johnson called the use of natives "standard Communist practice," which formed "one of the methods by which the Communists advanced local civil-military cooperation."[76] In contrast, the lack of reliable local cadres hindered the Communist mobilization efforts in the Huaibei area.[77]

In many areas, local-born intellectuals played as important a role in establishing revolutionary base areas in northern China as their southern comrades did. The northern Shaanxi base area was originally created by intellectuals such as Liu Zhidan, Xie Zichang, Gao Gang, and Xi Zhongxun, who were all natives of Shaanxi and educated in urban schools. In Shanxi, native-born Bo Yibo was a key figure in building Communist power. During the Anti-Japanese War, the warlord Yan Xishan, famous for his "sense of locality," was so impressed by the two leading Communists from Shanxi that he declared, "The resistance war of Shanxi should rely on Bo Yibo in political aspect and on Xu Xiangqian in military aspect."[78] In Shandong, before the Eighth Route Army arrived, the local Communists had already created the powerful Shandong Column.[79]

Though largely confined to northern China during the Anti-Japanese War, the party did not forget southern China and was always ready to send those cadres of southern China origins back to their birth places to reestablish Communist power. In 1940, Zhuang Tian, a military leader who had taken part in the Long March and who was then stationed in Yanan, was sent to Hainan Island to help Feng Baiju with military affairs: he was chosen because he was a native of Hainan.[80] In 1945, when the Anti-Japanese War was approaching its end, the Central Committee of the party decided to send Zhang Dingcheng, the former leader of the western Fujian base area, together with more than 300 cadres from western Fujian and eastern Guangdong, back to southern China to reestablish the Communist base area in western Fujian, eastern Guangdong, and southern Jiangxi.[81] Six months earlier, Shao Shiping, the former leader of the northeastern Jiangxi base area, had already been sent back to Jiangxi to reestablish a Communist government there. Li Xiannian, a veteran Communist from Hubei, was sent back to the Hubei–Henan border area in 1939 to reestablish a base area in the region formerly controlled by the Hubei–Henan–Anhui Soviet.

To some degree, the experiences of the returned students are very similar to the rites of transition analyzed by Van Gennep and Victor Turner. According to them, the transition of individual status in small-scale societies follows three stages: separation, margin (liminal), and aggregation. The first stage, separation, represents the detachment of the individual or group either from an earlier fixed point in the social structure or from a set of cultural conditions. During the intermediate phase, the liminal period, the status of the individuals and groups concerned is ambiguous, and they traverse a realm that has few or none of the attributes of the past or coming state. In the third stage the passage is consummated. The individuals or groups are in a stable state once more and, by virtue of this, have rights and obligations of a clearly defined and structural type and are expected to behave in accordance with certain customary norms and ethical standards.[82] If the path of the returned students is taken as a rite of passage, then, clearly, the beginning of a higher level education, which usually accompanied the beginning of urban experience, represents separation from their previous status and conditions. After a short liminal period for the students, which involved mainly psychological and intellectual changes, they acquired the status of intellectuals, and, according to tradition, began to assume responsibility for the national fate as well as the people's livelihood, while at the same time enjoying respect from the people. In this case the students' journey or pilgrimage to the schools in the cities served two functions: one was to differentiate the students from the other villagers, and the other was to unite and homogenize the students from various parts of China so that they would return to their villages with similar ideas and a sense of comradeship.

The Awakening and Reunion

Not all intellectuals with rural origins voluntarily returned to the countryside. It took the kind of transformation of sentiment and identity described by Mao Zedong to bring some intellectuals back to their villages. From an individualistic point of view, the intellectuals had nothing to gain but everything—including even their lives—to lose by returning to the village. In fact, few of those Communists who returned to organize peasant uprisings following the breakdown of the First United Front survived. Hence it was believed by the revolutionary intellectuals that only those who put the fate of the nation and class above their own happiness and lives had the courage to return. Identity transformation was important not only for the Communists, but also for the non-Communist peasant sympathizers. The non-Communist Tao Xingzhi went through a similar identity change as the one described by Mao Zedong:

> I was born a Chinese commoner. However, more than a decade of school life gradually drew me toward the direction of a foreign aristocrat.... Fortunately, my roots as a Chinese and commoner are deep, hence, after a period of awakening, I now rush back to the Chinese masses like the Yellow River runs wild.[83]

The non-Communist writer Lao Xiang's experiences are similar to those of Tao Xingzhi. One of his books was entitled *The Yellow Soil* because he believed that yellow soil symbolized country life. Urban dwellers, he suggested, despised the peasants because of their closeness to the yellow soil; the peasant who wanted to have a better life had to first divorce himself from that. As a village boy, he had begun to despise the yellow soil after he started attending an urban school. After living in the city for more than a decade, he felt that he had gradually turned into a city dweller and did not want to visit his native village. However, he soon found that it was not so easy to rid himself of the yellow soil. He could avoid thinking of it during daytime, but at night it was often in his dreams. After a period of time, his feelings about urban life began to change and he felt a longing for the yellow soil. Finally, in 1933, he decided to join Yan Yangchu and went to a village in Dingxian to help with the rural reconstruction.[84]

Both Tao Xingzhi and Lao Xiang attributed their "awakenings"—their change of feelings—to their deep rural roots. For others, the awakening was the combined effect of rural roots and urban experiences. Fang Zhimin, for example, recalled that when he was a little boy in the village school, he did not know either what imperialism was or what patriotism meant. After entering the higher primary school, he gradually came to understand patriotism; however, it was not until he had actually witnessed the behavior of foreigners in the big cities that he finally became a steadfast patriot and Communist. In Nanchang, he saw how Westerners controlled China's postal service. In Jiujiang, he saw how the foreigners had obtained concessions on Chinese territory, how foreign warships navigated freely in China's inland waters, and how foreign teachers in the missionary school earned much higher salaries than the Chinese teachers. In Shanghai, he saw the French Park with signs prohibiting Chinese and dogs from entering. "I've come across many offensive instances like these and some even more so than these," he wrote. "Each time I was incensed and became more determined to strive for the liberation of the Chinese nation." The way to liberate

China, according to Fang, was to awaken all the masses to fight against the hated imperialists.[85]

Urban experiences had contradictory effects on rural intellectuals: it drew them away from the villages, but at the same time pressed them back to the peasants. The students from the villages were supposed to find in the cities a life different from and better than the ones they had left behind; they were also to transform themselves from peasants to persons of higher status. However, many discarded such notions once they became aware of the nation's plight and decided to devote themselves to the urgent cause of national salvation. To do so, they had to return to the countryside, to their places of birth.

Revolutionary intellectuals considered one's attitude toward the working class, including workers and peasants, an important criterion differentiating progressive from backward intellectuals. For an intellectual to become a qualified Communist, the transformation of sentiment described by Mao Zedong was requisite. Mao told his young followers in 1939, "In the final analysis, the dividing line between revolutionary intellectuals and non-revolutionary or counter-revolutionary intellectuals is whether or not they are willing to integrate themselves with the workers and peasants and actually do so....If he is willing to do so and actually does so, he is a revolutionary; otherwise he is a non-revolutionary or a counter-revolutionary."[86] Mao was quite confident that he himself had completed this transformation of identity.

The close connection between the early Chinese intelligentsia and the countryside is not surprising in a country with a large peasant population and undeveloped urban centers, where it had been possible throughout history for peasants to enter the upper class through education, and where the educated class had never been confined to the cities, as was the case in many other cultures. Among the leading Chinese intellectuals who devoted themselves to the peasant movement in the early twentieth century, Liang Shuming stood out as one of the very few born and raised in an urban environment, and because of that he later considered his engagement in the peasant movement one of the four major surprises in his life.[87] Although the intellectuals no longer considered themselves peasants after they left their home villages, their blood relationship with the peasants gave them considerable advantage in communicating with the peasants. This common blood origin, together with the merging of the intellectuals' interest in building a strong and independent nation and the peasants' interest in finding better lives, formed the dual bond that made the relationship between the intelligentsia and the peasantry in China somewhat different from that which existed in some other peasant societies. For example, in early modern Europe, most of the intellectuals who "went to the people" came from the upper class who viewed the people as "a mysterious Them."[88] In Russia, the earliest populists in the nineteenth century were mostly of urban and aristocratic origins because of an impassable gulf between the aristocracy and the serfdom that had existed before. After the emancipation of the serfs, however, the new generation of populists began to appear more similar to the Chinese intellectuals: those who launched the "To the people" movement were believed to be mainly of non-aristocratic origins, and hence better understood the sufferings and the power of the peasantry. In India, due to the traditional caste system and the new colonial education system, the intelligentsia and the peasantry were separated by marked social and cultural barriers. Many Indian nationalist intellectuals in the early twentieth century found themselves in embarrassing positions because they could no longer speak the language of their own people.

Urban Origins of the Peasant Movements

Although the majority of Chinese intellectuals interested in the peasantry were rooted in the villages, the various peasant movements they led all originated in urban centers. This is compatible with the fact that almost all the leading intellectuals of the various movements went through a period of urban living. It is also compatible with the argument that the peasant movement represents the last stage of the Chinese national movement. The ideologies that provided the theoretical basis for the peasant movements, such as Communism, liberalism, functionalism, and neo-Confucianism, were all first developed in the cities. In fact, most of them had their roots in foreign soil. In addition, the first phase of almost all the peasant movements took place in the cities. Sporadic Communist or socialist peasant movements began quite early, but for quite a while did not get official recognition within the party, which initially paid much more attention to the labor movement.[89] Even the early sporadic peasant movements were influenced by events that occurred in urban locales. In May 1923, when Peng Pai had successfully organized 200,000 peasants into peasant associations in Guangdong, he declared, "the class struggle of the urban working class had now spread to the villages."[90] In fact, Peng Pai's interest in the peasantry may be traced back to his student years at Waseda University in Japan.[91] During the First United Front, the Communist Party started to pay serious attention to the peasants; after the collapse of the First United Front in 1927, rural China became increasingly important to the party as land revolution was made an official policy.

The mass education movement began in cities such as Changsha of Hunan, Hangzhou and Jiaxing of Zhejiang, Yantai and Qufu of Shandong, and Wuhan of Hubei, and did not begin to spread to rural areas until 1926, when Yan Yangchu decided to move his base to Dingxian of Hebei.[92] Yan Yangchu believed that there were two good reasons for starting the mass education movement in towns and cities. First, it would help urban people become aware of how difficult and monotonous rural life was. Second, it could help gain support from society and educational institutions. He argued that in order to be successful in the countryside, they first had to be successful in the cities, because without the leadership of the cities, nothing could be accomplished in the countryside.[93] In Liang Shuming's case, Liang's Confucian philosophy developed while he taught in Peking University in the late 1910s and early 1920s. After resigning from the university in 1924, he ran schools in Caozhou and Qufu of Shandong and Guangzhou of Guangdong. He did not start his rural project until the late 1920s.

Sociological research on the peasantry was also preceded by research on urban society. Li Jinghan, the sociologist who investigated the peasants of Dingxian in the late 1920s and 1930s, recalled that immediately after he came back to China upon his graduation from an American university, he began investigating the lower classes and other groups in Beijing, which he carried on for four years. Then he realized that the great majority of the Chinese population was living in the villages, and the real "people" were in the countryside rather than in cities; consequently he shifted his attention from the city to the village.[94] Likewise, the community studies carried out by the functionalist school originated in urban Chicago; when such ideas came to China, they were first taught in urban universities, with the earliest case studies carried out in the noisy streets of Beijing. Probably because of the influence of Professor Robert Ezra Park of the University of Chicago, Fei Xiaotong argued in 1933 that to understand social change, one should study the cities and not the countryside, for rural change would come from the natural and inevitable pattern of villagers temporarily going to the city and then returning home with new ideas and attitudes.[95]

All these intellectual movements were nationalistic; they originated in the cities because the intellectuals in the cities were the first subjected to new ideas. Focus began to shift from the cities to the villages because in China a national movement could not be truly national without the participation of the peasants. The urban theories, once brought to rural China, were often made rural as a result. Hence Marxism or Leninism became Maoism; urban mass education became rural mass education; urban community studies became rural community studies. The process of importation also led to a process of creation.

AREAS OF DIFFERENCE

The strong connections between the Chinese intellectuals who returned to the village and the peasantry did not guarantee an easy integration of the two groups, considering their fundamental differences. The intellectuals who returned to the village straddled the rural and urban worlds. To some extent, they were also intermediaries between the foreign and Chinese worlds. No matter how strongly the intellectuals sympathized with the peasants, in the eyes of the peasants they were often strangers with strange ideas as well as members of the ruling class. Intellectuals often felt wronged because peasants did not respond to their actions and ideas with the enthusiasm they expected. They felt a strong bond with and affection for the peasants, but such feelings were generally not reciprocated, at least not at the beginning.

Affecting the intellectual–peasant relations were several areas of difference that kept them apart. One of the most important was language. For a nonnative intellectual, the linguistic difference between him or her and the peasants was that of different dialects or between Mandarin and the dialect. The Communist leader Qu Qiubai, a native of Jiangsu, lamented that he could not communicate with the Jiangxi peasants because they did not share a "common language."[96] The famous woman writer Xie Bingying described a similar experience. Xie, together with five other female students, were among the student army of the Central Political-Military School at Wuhan sent to rural Hubei to fight the rightist rebellion. At the village, the six of them wanted to talk to the local women. But only two could communicate with the peasants. The other four were from northern China and hence could not understand the Hunan–Hubei dialect.[97] In July 1927, a Communist cadre working among the Red Spears reported from northern Henan that since most cadres were from southern Henan, they could not work effectively because of language difficulties.[98] It was also reported in June 1926 that, for similar reasons, when the peasant movement activists of Haifeng County of Guangdong moved to neighboring Puning County, they found it very hard to carry on their work.[99]

Such problems also plagued the foreign and Chinese intellectuals involved in the rural reconstruction projects, as in Lichuan County of Jiangxi. The people of Lichuan speak a dialect that is different from both Mandarin and that of neighboring Fujian. This linguistic barrier is believed to have been one of the factors that caused the failure of the project.[100] Yan Yangchu, who started his mass education work among the Chinese laborers in France during World War I, later realized that it was fortunate for him that the Chinese laborers there were all from northern China because otherwise it would have been impossible for him to communicate with them.[101] His Dingxian base was also in northern China, yet when Yan Yangchu made his first speech to the villagers of Dingxian, this famous speaker found that it was still difficult to get his idea across because he was not familiar with the local jargon.[102] Liang Shuming made a wise decision to go to the villages in Henan and Shandong in northern China. Had he gone to the villages in

Guangdong, as he had originally expected, he would have had to bring an interpreter with him.

For a local-born intellectual, the linguistic difference between him or her and the peasants was that between the more formal speech and the vernacular. Peng Pai lamented in 1921 that education had become a privilege of the upper class and, as a result, even in the same district with all inhabitants speaking the same language (or dialect), the poor people, because of their lack of education, could not understand what the educated people were saying.[103] Peng Pai's first encounter with the villagers of Haifeng was just such an experience. He went to a village near the county seat of Haifeng in 1922 to mobilize the peasants. He met several peasants during the first two days, but no one wanted to talk to him. He realized that one of the reasons why the peasants avoided him was because his speech was too cultured and hence much of what he said was unintelligible to them.[104] Mao Zedong also noticed such linguistic difference between local intellectuals and the masses. However, writing almost two decades later than Peng Pai, he attributed the difference to a deficiency in learning of the intellectuals rather than the peasants. He said in a speech, "If someone enters primary school at seven, goes to middle school in his teens, graduates from college in his twenties and never has contact with the masses of the people, he is not to blame if his language is poor and monotonous." If the intellectuals refused to learn from the masses after graduating from school, Mao claimed, they would never be able to improve their language.[105] In another speech, Mao said: "Since many writers and artists stand aloof from the masses and lead empty lives, naturally they are unfamiliar with the language of the people. Accordingly, their works are not only insipid in language but often contain nondescript expressions of their own coining which run counter to popular usage."[106] Obviously, for Mao, the linguistic difference was not just an issue of language skills, but rather one of attitude on the part of the intellectuals.

In a recent article, the sociologist Fei Xiaotong also discussed the linguistic problems he encountered as both a local and a nonlocal intellectual when he was with the peasants. He made three important field trips in his lifetime. The first was to the mountainous area inhabited by the Yao minority people in Guangxi in 1935; the second was to his native county Wujiang of Jiangsu in 1936; and the last was to the Lu village in Yunnan during the Anti-Japanese War. He felt that because of linguistic differences, the knowledge he gained from the three trips was different in each case. "In the Jiangcun village [in his native county], on the whole, I could communicate with my subjects without the help of a third party; in the Lu village, I could not have my own way as I did in the Jiangcun village; in the mountainous area inhabited by the Yao people, I could not do without the help of those who could speak Mandarin."[107] He was arguing against the idea that one should not conduct anthropological work among one's own people. Obviously he believed that linguistically it is much more convenient for an anthropologist to work in his native land than in other places. However, even there, he was not free of linguistic problems. "Although we all speak the Wu dialect, much of what they said was not very intelligible to me, and it was more difficult for them to understand what I was saying,"[108] Fei wrote.

Clothing was another area of difference between intellectuals and peasants. The intellectuals liked to wear long gowns, or Western suits, or the so-called Sun Yat-sen suit (Chinese tunic suit, later known as Lenin garb and then as the Mao suit). These were either impractical or too formal and expensive for the peasants. The peasants' clothing, which Mao refused to wear while a student, usually consisted of loose-fitting trousers and a tunic-like garment made of handwoven cloth. The differences were obvious. In many regions, peasants were often barefooted or had only straw sandals to wear, whereas intellectuals would always wear shoes. When Peng Pai first went to a village in Haifeng in May 1922, he wore a white hat and a white Western-style student uniform. On the first day, he met two peasants. The first mistook him for a tax collector, and the second thought he was an army officer or a soldier. The next day, another peasant guessed that he had come to the village to collect debts. None of them would grant him conversation. After two days, Peng Pai realized that besides his formal speech, his clothing also played a role in betraying his status and scaring the peasants away.[109] When Luo Nachuan, the peasant leader of Pingjiang County of Hunan, first went to visit the paper makers in a mountainous area in the 1920s, he was mistaken for a geomancer because he wore a long gown and a pair of glasses. Fortunately, he found it useful to pretend to be one and told the workers that a great change was coming.[110] On this matter of clothing, Mao Zedong found that there was a time lag between the students and other sections of the population in adopting the new style. The students were the first, the young peasants and young workers were next, and the rest lagged behind. Adoption of the new style was also linked to economic status. The poor could not afford such changes.[111]

The intellectuals and peasants also had different attitudes toward physical labor. The peasants did not necessarily enjoy such work, but they had to do it for survival. The intellectuals, however, disclaimed any work involving physical labor. Yan Yangchu was very upset to notice that the "village youth, before they started their school education, were able to help their parents with collecting firewood and night soil, watching the buffaloes and plowing the field, and were true laborers, but as soon as they entered school, became educated and were exposed to urban culture, they turned into vagrants who were not content with rural life but could not survive in the cities; they could work with neither their minds nor their hands."[112] When Qu Qiubai and his family refused to wash their own clothes and cook their own food despite their not being able to afford a servant,[113] and when the student-soldier Mao Zedong had to spend some portion of his meager income to buy water, they were merely following the social norms. After the October Revolution in Russia, the idea of "the sanctity of labor" took hold in China and some intellectuals began to attribute social injustice to the division between mental work and manual work. Out of a sense of guilt about their own lifestyle and a sense of sympathy toward the laborers, many students embraced the "New Village" ideal of half-study/half-work and began to adopt a different attitude toward physical labor. However, this failed to eliminate a basic difference: intellectuals still basically labored with their minds, while peasants and workers did so with their hands.

Finally, the intellectuals and peasants also had different beliefs. The May Fourth generation of Chinese intellectuals, especially the revolutionaries among them, was mostly iconoclastic, believing that religion, superstition, and even traditional thought should be wiped out before China could modernize, whereas the peasants still upheld their traditional belief systems and continued to worship their various gods and deities, deceased ancestors, and the Son of Heaven. While the intellectuals had already become obsessed with social Darwinism, Socialism, Anarchism, Marxism, liberalism, and all imported -isms, the peasants were still using geomancy and fate to explain the world and their lives within it. Many Communist intellectuals were disappointed that the peasants had a hard time accepting the idea that class exploitation was the main cause of their poverty. Instead, the peasants believed that fate determined their poverty.[114] The sociologist Li Jinghan found in the 1930s that superstition had managed to maintain its indisputable authority among the peasants:

> If there is no rain, they would pray to the Dragon King; if the locusts come to destroy their crops, they would pray to the Bala; if the river runs wild, they would pray to the God of the River; if they are poor and in dire need of money, they would pray to the God of Wealth; if their women are infertile, they would pray to the Goddess; if they are seriously ill, they would pray to the God of Medicine. They are indifferent to the public welfare of the village....However, when it comes to renovating temples, remolding golden statues, and arranging ceremonies for the gods and fairies, they would vie with each other to donate and often times their donations would be well beyond what they can afford. Their life is dominated by the belief in fate and heaven, which is far different from the belief in the omnipotence of science and man's power in conquering nature.[115]

In his study of the Chinese Revolutionary Party, Edward Friedman pointed out the essential difference between the belief systems of the intellectuals and the peasants. The peasants might join the revolution led by the intellectuals, but they tended to experience the revolution differently. The peasants continued to act on millennial, religious, and mystical notions after the 1911 Revolution.[116] Mugruzin found that Chinese peasants possessed a strong belief in absolute power. During the warlord period, peasants longed for the return of the emperor. They believed that the only reason there were so many corrupt officials and evil gentry was because of the emperor's absence.[117] This was confirmed by Li Dazhao, who recorded in 1917 that after the 1911 Revolution, the intellectuals all believed that the old imperial system would vanish and never be resurrected; the peasants in the countryside, however, were not so sure. They predicted that a new emperor would soon appear.[118] As late as 1926, a peasant magazine published by Yan Yangchu's mass education association still had to persuade the peasants that current problems were not caused by an emperor's absence, but by the lack of a true republican system.[119]

The differences in belief systems were linked to the issue of the relations between the great tradition and the small tradition, as first defined by Robert Redfield in his *Peasant Society and Culture*. Although most scholars agree that the two traditions did exist in China, they hold different opinions of the relations between them. Arthur Wolf argues that there has always been a vast gulf between the religions of the elite and those of the peasantry; Maurice Friedman believes that the elite and the peasantry in traditional China formed a "community of ideas."[120] Chinese intellectuals tend to agree more with Friedman than with Wolf. Even the Communist intellectuals held that there had been much consensus between the great tradition and the small tradition, although that is not very compatible with their class analysis perspective. They argued that the consensus was the outcome of deliberate indoctrination of the peasantry by the elite.[121] One recent study by a Chinese scholar confirms that in China the two traditions were based on the same principles, albeit expressed in different ways.[122] However, when the modern intelligentsia broke with the traditional elite and the great tradition, they also severed the consensus between the great tradition and the small tradition. They wanted to destroy the old consensus based on old principles and establish a new consensus based on new principles. Before the new consensus could be reached, there would have to be the bridging of the virtually impassable gap between the modern intelligentsia's beliefs and the peasantry's.

Since it was impossible for the peasants to learn the intellectuals' ways immediately, the intellectuals had to adopt the peasants' ways in many circumstances, in order to minimize their differences and in turn gain the peasants' trust. Hence, when Shen Dingyi returned to his village to launch the rent resistance movement in 1921, he decided to adopt the peasants' clothes and speak the local dialect. In 1928, when he again returned to his village, he worked with the villagers day after day. Keith Schoppa commented that Shen's strategy of working with the peasants "went to the heart of local values."[123] Peng Pai realized after his first two days of encounter with the peasants that he had better translate the formal terms he used into terms more easily understood and he had better wear simpler clothes.[124] Peng Pai's personal experiences plainly indicate how an intellectual striving to educate the peasants would first have to adopt the peasant way of life. In July 1921, when he began organizing the Association of Laborers' Sympathizers, he was still talking about educating the peasants in order to eliminate the differences between the educated and the uneducated, but in June 1923, one year after he went to the countryside, he told his friend that "I have been assimilated by the uneducated class."[125] He believed that he had eliminated the differences between himself and the peasants, though he had achieved it the other way round. During the First United Front, Peng taught his students in the Peasant Movement Institute to use colloquial rather than formal language when talking to the peasants, to be patient with them, and not to act differently from the peasants.[126] In early 1928, he surprised the survivors of the Guangzhou Uprising by wearing "the clothes of an ordinary peasant and straw sandals" while giving a speech at a mass meeting.[127] In 1924, Yun Daiying urged the students who intended to do rural work to learn the language of the peasants so that they could better spread their ideas.[128] In the Honghu area of western Hubei, the Communist intellectuals who returned to their home villages after the collapse of the First United Front chose to wear ragged short gowns and torn straw hats; they also genuinely helped the peasants with their harvesting, plowing, and fishing.[129]

Like Shen Dingyi, Peng Pai, Yun Daiying, and others, Mao Zedong also stressed the importance of eliminating the various areas of difference. In 1921, he wore a grass hat, lumber jacket, and grass shoes while working among the Anyuan miners. The next year he again put on rough clothes to pretend to be a construction worker.[130] He wore "peasant clothes made of blue hand-woven cloth" or "a ragged cotton-padded jacket of the common people" and "straw sandals" while marching toward the Jinggang mountains after the Autumn Harvest Uprising in 1927.[131] His appearance was so close to that of a peasant that some of his soldiers took him for a hired laborer and asked him to carry their loads.[132] In speeches made during the Rectification Campaign, he urged intellectuals to learn the language of the masses.[133] He also called on them to do farm work with the peasants.

During the Anti-Japanese War, the Communist political workers in the villages were ordered to equip themselves with knowledge of local politics, economic conditions, and any specific grievances within the villages. They were asked to dress and talk like peasants, and to pay attention to the problem of local superstitions.[134] Intellectuals were encouraged to go to the villages to learn from as well as teach the peasants.[135] Before Zhuang Tian and some other southerners left for Hainan in 1940, Zhou Enlai urged those who could not speak the Hainan dialect to learn it because "no one can work well without mastering the dialect."[136]

The rural reconstructionists Liang Shuming and Yan Yangchu also called for the elimination of the differences between the intellectuals and the peasants. Liang argued that the purpose of his movement was to "let the villagers transform the revolutionary intellectuals, and let the revolutionary intellectuals transform the villagers." He predicted that "when the differences between them are finally eliminated, China's problem will be solved."[137] Yan Yangchu argued that those who wrote for the masses should first study their language.[138] When Yan himself worked with the Chinese laborers in France during World War I, he decided to use colloquial rather than classical Chinese.[139] Yan also asked the intellectuals to do physical labor. He pointed out that since the educated people do not labor and the laborers do not read, every Chinese is "half a man." An ideal "new man" would be one who is both educated and skillful at labor.[140] In this he was quite close to the anarchist Liu Shipei, who envisioned in a 1907 article a society in which "everybody is worker, peasant and literatus at one and the same time, and everybody has equal rights and responsibilities."[141] Yan argued that the purpose of his mass education movement was to help the peasants rid themselves of ignorance and eliminate the differences between the educated and the uneducated. However, in order to civilize the peasants, the intellectuals had to learn to live the life of the peasants first.[142]

Many intellectuals were sincere in changing their language, clothing, and attitude toward labor, but they were not sincere about changing their beliefs. On the contrary, they wanted desperately to indoctrinate the peasants in their own faith. To do this, however, they had to first hide their differences to gain the peasants' trust. Both Peng Pai and Yun Daiying warned students who planned to go to the villages not to show any disrespect toward the gods and ancestor spirits worshipped by the peasants. Peng Pai said in 1926, "When we work in the villages, the first step is to gain the confidence of the peasants... And you can't gain their trust if you attack their belief in gods. There are times when we not only do not insult their gods, but even worship along with them. This doesn't mean that we capitulate to religious superstition, but only that some concessions are necessary to even begin to do our work."[143] Ironically, his warning against attacking religion and superstition may have contributed to the rise of the cult of Peng Pai, which was indicated by the peasants addressing him as the "Buddha" or the "Eternal One."[144] Yun Daiying in a 1924 article listed six inappropriate methods in dealing with the peasants, including the inclination "to ignore the mentality of the peasants and indulge in speeches about eliminating superstition and reforming rites."[145] These were wise warnings because attacking the beliefs of the peasants could ruin the intellectuals' program. The Mi brothers of Zhaicheng Village of Dingxian once botched their reform program because they offended the villagers by destroying the village temple.[146]

On the whole, none of the intellectual groups was able to attain a complete fusion with the peasantry. The sociologist Fei Xiaotong recalled that he failed to do so with the villagers of Kaixiangong, and he attributed that failure to the class difference between him and the villagers.[147] Similarly, Yan Yangchu also failed in his Dingxian base area. The sociologist Li Jinghan left vivid descriptions about the intellectuals' experiences in Dingxian:

> "To integrate with the peasants" is easy to say and to accept as a slogan. When you try to put it into practice, however, there will be problems.... The peasants dare not integrate with you in the beginning.... When they finally feel that you really like to be with them, they would approach you earnestly and sincerely. Then they would allow you to enter their homes and sit on their *kang* [stove-cum-bed], prepare tea for you, invite you to eat together with their families, and even ask you to stay overnight. At this point, it can be said that you have achieved the goal. However, you now feel uneasy and distressed about the outcome because his smell makes you uncomfortable; you find it hard to sit on the brick bed because it is dirty; the simple food is hard to swallow; other unhygienic conditions and their habit of wasting too much time on social intercourse all make it unbearable for you. Granted you can continue as you have to, it is inevitable that you would be reluctant and find it painful.[148]

More than any other group, the Communists attached importance to winning the hearts of the peasants, but even they were not able to achieve genuine integration. The hardest task of the Communists was to conceal their differences in belief from the peasants. Evidence shows their followers did not pay due attention to Peng Pai's and Yun Daiying's warning against disrespecting the religious beliefs of the peasants, and on many occasions, this was detrimental to the relations between the Communists and the peasants. Zhang Dingcheng and Deng Zihui admitted that in western Fujian, during the Northern Expedition, the peasant associations destroyed quite a few statues of the Buddha, which caused deep resentment among the peasants. This policy continued in the period after 1927 and further alienated the party from the masses.[149] The peasants of Hunan complained to Mao Zedong in 1927 that everything the peasant association had done was good, except destroying the temples and the figures of the gods. Mao replied that he was against such antireligious policies.[150] In the Sichuan–Shaanxi base area created by Zhang Guotao, Communists alienated the local peasants by excessive iconoclastic actions such as smashing the statues of Buddha and destroying the temples.[151]

The Communists believed that both intellectuals and peasants have their strong as well as weak points, and a complete person is one with the strong points of both groups but free of the weak points of either. According to Zhou Enlai, Mao Zedong was just such a complete person. In a speech delivered in 1943, Zhou held that "Comrade Mao Zedong's style of work incorporates the modesty and pragmatism of the Chinese people; the simplicity and diligence of the Chinese peasants; the love of study and profound thinking of an intellectual; the efficiency and steadiness of a revolutionary soldier; and the persistence and indomitability of a Bolshevik."[152] The Communist Party and the Red Army were believed to be institutions that could help both the intellectuals and peasants eradicate their weak points and transform into more well-rounded persons. Upon entering the party, intellectuals and peasants all became proletariat, hence theoretically there would no longer be differences between intellectuals and peasants within the party.[153] However, in reality, such differences were never completely eliminated.

On the one hand, the intellectuals' love of the peasants would not automatically eliminate their differences from the peasants. On the other hand, it was equally impossible to promote the peasants to the psychological and intellectual levels of the intellectuals as quickly as many intellectuals wished. A total elimination of the main differences between the intellectuals and the peasants, either through one assimilating the other, as anticipated by Yan Yangchu and the early Peng Pai, or by combining the strong traits of both groups to attain a new common identity, as Liang Shuming and the Communists wished, remained an ideal. Before the differences could be eliminated and the ideal achieved, there would still be a gap, which meant that the intellectuals still had to pay attention to managing their relationship with the peasants. Therefore, several interrelated issues had to be solved upon the intellectuals' arrival at the village. How would they place themselves within the village social structure? With whom would they identify— the villagers as a whole, or some special groups within the village? What kind of relationship should they have with those they wanted to identify with?

CLASS ALLIANCE

Communist intellectuals tackled these issues from the point of view of class analysis, class alliance, and class struggle. When Li Dazhao wrote in 1919 that the intelligentsia should integrate with the working class, and in 1920 that the intelligentsia should be the vanguards of the masses and the masses should be backup forces of the intelligentsia, he still followed the traditional educated and uneducated classification and made no effort to define and classify who constituted the intelligentsia and the masses.[154] Later, Communist intellectuals developed more precise classifications. The masses would not be viewed as a monolithic bloc; instead, they were to be divided into different classes. So would the intelligentsia. The integration of revolutionary intellectuals and the peasants would theoretically be achieved through a reclassification of both the intelligentsia and the masses. The Communist slogan called for a worker–peasant alliance rather than an intellectual–peasant alliance, with workers as the leaders, and peasants the allies of the revolution. However, in reality, there were not many workers in the party and even fewer in the party leadership. Actually, intellectuals had always controlled the Communist Party. The worker–peasant alliance had in reality always been an intellectual–peasant alliance.

Chen Duxiu, Peng Pai, and Mao Zedong were among the pioneers in analyzing the different classes of Chinese rural society and the intellectuals. Chen Duxiu wrote two articles to discuss the issue in 1923. In the first article, he divided the Chinese rural population into four classes and ten groups; he claimed that the great majority of the Chinese peasantry could be drawn into the national revolution. In the second article, he defined the intelligentsia as petty bourgeoisie but emphasized that it could not be an independent class because it had no economic base, and furthermore that intellectuals could be revolutionary, nonrevolutionary, or counterrevolutionary. He suggested that the revolutionary intellectuals could play a special role in the national revolution by uniting all the other classes, including the merchants, workers, and peasants. Chen envisioned a national rather than social revolution. He believed in the theory of two-stage revolution, which viewed the Chinese workers and peasants as too weak at that moment to lead the revolution and China as still at the stage of national revolution, not class revolution. Only after the development of capitalism reached certain levels should the Communists begin to talk about a proletarian revolution. He concluded that intellectuals and peasants could cooperate in the national revolution.[155]

Peng Pai made his classification in 1925. He did not try to classify all the rural population, but only the peasants. He divided the peasants into four classes: landowning peasant, semilandowning peasant, tenant-peasant, and rural laborer. Unlike Chen Duxiu, who believed that social revolution could not start until after the completion of the national revolution, Peng Pai maintained that social revolution and national revolution were not incompatible. Class struggle could actually help the national revolution. Based on his experiences with the Haifeng peasant movement, he believed that the peasants had played and would continue to play a crucial role in the national revolution.[156] It was incumbent on the intellectuals to draw the peasants into the revolution by performing the role of instigator, organizer, and leader.[157]

Mao Zedong's several articles about class analysis and the role of the peasantry in the revolution appeared in 1926, in which he proposed a classification of rural population similar to that made by Chen Duxiu. He preferred dividing the rural population into eight groups instead of ten, but, more to the point, his rationale for class analysis was totally different from Chen Duxiu's. Mao's chief concern was to differentiate enemies from friends. He proposed class revolution under the guise of national revolution. According to him, for the national revolution to be victorious, class revolution was necessary, which in turn required the revolutionary party to make class alliances and engage in class struggle. In this he was a supporter of Peng Pai and was opposed to Chen Duxiu's two-stage revolution theory. He concluded that the enemies of the national revolution were the warlords, bureaucrats, compradors, big landlords, and reactionary intellectuals who cooperated with the imperialists. The friends of the revolution included the petty bourgeoisie, the semiproletariat, and the proletariat—peasants were included in this group of friends. The intelligentsia could be broken down into several classes: the reactionary intellectuals, who were among those targeted by the revolution; the petty bourgeoisie, who were possible allies of the revolution; and the revolutionary intellectuals, who were slated to be the leaders of the revolution. The roles of intellectuals and peasants in the revolution were thus clearly defined. Putting it differently, a section of the intelligentsia would lead a section of the rural population to fight another section of the intelligentsia and another section of the rural population. By defining the revolutionary intellectuals as the leading group within the working class, Mao blurred the division between the traditional educated and uneducated.[158] From Li Dazhao to Chen Duxiu, Peng Pai and Mao Zedong, the Chinese Communists' perceptions of the roles of the intellectuals and peasants in revolution were strongly influenced by Lenin's theory about the intellectuals as revolutionary vanguards and peasants as potential revolutionary allies. Rural class analysis, with the aim of forming an intellectual–peasant alliance, became an obsession of the revolutionary intellectuals after the breakdown of the First United Front and the start of the land revolution. Even the writer Yu Dafu wrote an article about the rural classes in September 1927.[159]

Between 1927 and 1937, the Communist Party adopted a five-class theory that divided the rural population into landlords, rich peasants, middle peasants, poor peasants, along with rural workers. The official line was to rely on the poor peasants, along with rural workers, to try to win over the middle peasants, neutralize the rich peasants, and fight against the landlords. The party emphasized the alliance of workers and peasants. Since the Communist Party was actually controlled by revolutionary intellectuals rather than workers, this worker–peasant alliance policy was tantamount to a reaffirmation of the intellectual–peasant alliance.

Benjamin Schwartz provides an excellent analysis of how the Communists tried to prove that the intellectual–peasant alliance was actually a worker–peasant alliance. According to Schwartz, the party theoreticians developed several concealment devices to elide the contradictions between the Marxist theory of worker–peasant alliance and the Chinese reality of intellectual–peasant alliance. The first was to equate the Communist Party with the working class and the Communist leadership of the peasant movement with proletarian hegemony. The second was to equate the rural proletariat with the proletariat proper. As an example of this, in the period of the Jiangxi Soviet, the party attached great importance to creating a rural proletarian class mainly composed of agricultural laborers and promoting that class to the leading position.[160] The third device was to emphasize the "soviet" as a genuine proletarian political institution and to use it as another proof of "proletarian hegemony" within the Soviet areas.[161]

In practice, this class-alliance theory and method led to widespread family conflicts. Many revolutionary intellectuals were from landlord or rich peasant families,[162] but now they had to return to the villages to unite with the poor peasants to fight against their own families. This was a great advantage for the peasant movement, because, as Lucien Bianco pointed out, the family status and educational background of these intellectuals greatly facilitated their penetration of the local political game.[163] But to the families of these intellectuals, this usually meant misfortune and tragedy. For the intellectuals from upper-class families, to join the Communist revolution meant to turn against the family. To turn one's back on one's own family became fashionable for revolutionary intellectuals. Such acts ranged from disavowing marriages arranged by one's parents, redistributing one's family property to the poor, to killing one's own relatives. When Peng Pai began his peasant work in Haifeng in 1922, his mother cried upon hearing what he intended to do and scolded him for trying to destroy his own family. His eldest brother hated him deeply. So did all other members of the family and the clan, except two of his brothers.[164] Later Peng Pai gave his share of the family land to the tenants for free. Shen Dingyi and Fu Bocui also turned against their families and classes by reducing the rent of their tenants. Wei Baqun in Guangxi sold some of his family's belongings to buy guns and ammunitions for the peasant armed forces.[165] In 1925, Huang Dao led the peasants of his village to attack the powerful local leader Huang Wenzhong, a landlord of Huang Dao's own lineage. Huang Wenzhong's house was pulled down and his rice looted.[166] Yan Pu, known as the "the good-hearted third young master" and "the immortal one" to the local peasants, and "the Peng Pai of Jiangsu" to his Communist comrades, was born to a big landlord family in Wuxi of Jiangsu. He was called a "prodigal" by his relatives because he always encouraged and helped tenants seek rent reduction and other concessions from his own family.[167] Zeng Tianyu, a Communist from Jiangxi, asked his landlord father to give his land to their tenants. When his father refused, he got his father to give him his share of the property so that he could at least give that away.[168] Usually, the revolutionaries who worked in their home villages were more likely to have family conflicts than those working in other areas. However, if the revolutionary happened to be the patriarch of the family or clan, like Shen Dingyi and Fu Bocui, it was easier for him to take steps against his own economic interest without causing major family problems.[169]

On many occasions, turning against the family led to consequences involving more than property. Fang Zhimin rebelled against his adoptive father, the landlord Zhang Niancheng, and forced him to flee to Shanghai, where he later died a miserable death. He also had to execute his own fifth paternal uncle, Fang Gaoyu, a landlord and moneylender who opposed the rent reduction policy during the First United Front, and later, during the agrarian revolution, refused to donate money and food to poor peasants.[170] Zhou Weijiong, an important leader of the Hubei-Henan-Anhui base area, likewise executed his ninth maternal uncle, Qi Zizhou, who was a landlord and regarded as an enemy of the revolution. Zhou's action was wholeheartedly supported by his cousin and comrade Qi Dewei, Qi Zizhou's nephew.[171] Such actions were perfectly consistent with the traditional belief in placing righteousness above family loyalty and with the modern theory of class struggle. They indicated to the peasants that their leaders had truly subordinated personal interests and lineage ties to class interests and were wholly devoted to the revolution. Execution of reactionary blood relatives thus became a brutal, painful yet very efficient means of establishing the authority of the revolutionaries.

To turn against one's own family and class provided a serious challenge to many Communist intellectuals throughout the revolution. Those intellectuals who led and participated in land reform after the Anti-Japanese War still found themselves torn between the party and the people on the one side and their family on the other. According to William Hinton, the students and young teachers who joined the land reform in Lucheng County of Shanxi were either directly or indirectly connected to the landlord class "whose overthrow was the object of all their work."[172] The party took many measures, such as criticism and self-criticism, to make sure that the intellectuals with upper-class backgrounds severed all attachments to their pasts and took a firm stand with the workers and peasants. However, as Hinton observed:

> For many intellectuals, taking a new stand was no abstract question to be decided by cool reasoning simply on its economic or political

merit. Their own families had been or soon would be under attack. Some of their parents had already been beaten to death by angry peasants. Some of them were apt to end up in charge of land division in areas where their own property lay. They had to face the possibility of accusations and actions leading to the destruction of their homes and families.... Many participants found that they could not sleep at night. They lost their appetites and burst into tears when they faced their choice, or confronted past mistakes.[173]

Having the courage to turn against one's own family and class was taken as a touchstone for distinguishing a real revolutionary intellectual from a fake. He Long recalled that during the Northern Expedition of 1926, Zhou Yiqun, an intellectual from a landlord family in Tongren County of Guizhou, brought a propaganda team to He's army, then stationed in Hunan. Upon their meeting He apologized to Zhou for confiscating the rice Zhou's family had stored while He's army was stationed in Tongren. Zhou replied, "It doesn't matter. I hope your revolutionary soldiers got enough to eat. The more you confiscated, the better." He Long, who was looking for Communists at that moment, knew immediately that Zhou was a Communist and it turned out that he was right.[174] It was Zhou who later introduced He into the Communist Party in 1927. The two of them remained intimate comrades until Zhou was killed in 1932. Peng Pai mentioned that when the peasant association of Haifeng decided to launch a rent-reducing movement in 1923 after a big flood, the students and intellectuals in the county seat, most of whom were from landlord families, withdrew their support of the peasant association under pressure from their families.[175] Fang Zhimin had a similar experience. While in higher primary school, he organized a youth association composed of students from both poor and rich families. After several rounds of struggle with local tyrants and corrupt officials, the members from rich families all turned against the association and became supporters of their families.[176] If Zhou Yiqun's reply to He Long convinced He that Zhou was a true revolutionary, then the change of attitude of the Haifeng students and intellectuals and those of Fang Zhimin's association indicated to Peng and Fang that these people were only pseudorevolutionaries. According to Zheng Weisan, a leader of the peasant uprising in eastern Hubei, the revolutionary intellectuals from landlord families in Huanggang County of Hubei had to stand the test of the bloody campaign against the local upper class people during the land revolution of 1927–1937: "Some of them resolutely turned against their former class and stood with the peasants; but a few of them... openly refused to work for the committee to try the local tyrants and evil gentry."[177] In Xingguo County of Jiangxi, Li Ting, a revolutionary and a returned student, found the peasants suspicious of his intentions and indifferent to his exhortations because his grandfather was a landlord. Finally, an old peasant confronted him at a meeting: "You asked us to organize peasant associations and overthrow the local tyrants and evil gentry. Then what kind of person is your grandfather?" Li replied without hesitation: "He is one of the evil gentry." "Then how should we deal with him?," the old peasant asked. "No difference. We should overthrow him." The peasants gave him a big round of applause. From that point, the peasants knew that Li was a real revolutionary and began to consider him one of their own and to give him their whole-hearted trust and support.[178] In early 1928, Hu Yun, a guerrilla leader of Pingjiang County in Hunan, took her followers to her own village, where her husband's wealthy family and relatives lived, to distribute stored rice and land to the poor peasants. Furthermore, "in order to reveal her determination to support the revolution forever," she set fire to her grandiose house with more than one hundred rooms. As a result, "her revolutionary resolve was praised by the poor peasants."[179] In spring 1927, the peasant movement of southern China became increasingly radical and violent and many family members of the leading Nationalists and Communists were attacked. In Hunan, Tan Yan-kai's son-in-law, a member of a wealthy family in Changsha, was arrested and fined; Tang Shengzhi's father was harassed by labor union pickets; He Jian's father-in-law was punished;[180] Xia Xi's father was arrested and his family's belongings confiscated. Tan, Tang, and He, all Nationalists, chose to become renegades of the revolution. But Xia Xi, a leading Communist in Hunan, remained a leader of the revolution. Ironically, many of these real revolutionaries, including the woman revolutionary Hu Yun, were later executed by their own comrades, though their only crime was that they came from landlord families.

Perceiving themselves as the vanguard of the proletariat, the Chinese Communist intellectuals found it convenient and satisfying to justify their relations with the peasants by invoking the theory of class alliance. According to that theory, the positions of the two revolutionary allies— the intellectuals and the peasants— were not equal. The proletariat, or the intellectuals, was the leader, while the peasants were the followers. The class alliance theory was actually not very different from the traditional theory about those who ruled and those who were ruled. The peasants, although larger in number and greater in power, did not know what direction to follow. The intellectuals, in the guise of the proletariat, would perform the function of guide for the peasants. The revolutionary intellectuals were aware that both the intellectuals and peasants were important in the revolution, but they were important in different ways.

Much scholarly attention has been paid to the respective roles played by the intellectuals and peasants in the Chinese revolution. The moral economy school tends to view the Chinese peasant revolution as a result of the Chinese social crisis and the peasants' response to it. The peasants joined the revolution not because they were persuaded and mobilized by the intellectuals, but because the traditional institutions that guarantee their subsistence were destroyed. James Scott remarks that while external forces may be essential for revolution in the countryside, those forces require conditioning to the rural environment in order to play any significant role in its precipitation.[181] Kamal Sheel does not deny the leading role played by the Marxist intellectuals in the peasant revolution in northeastern Jiangxi. However, he emphasizes, first, that these intellectuals were not outsiders but mostly natives with a strong rural background; and, second, they managed to put the peasant movement on the right course only by facilitating the fusion of local issues and problems with their revolutionary concerns.[182] Some moral economists argue that the peasants were capable of making their own revolution without the intellectuals. Robert Marks, for example, maintains that the reason why the modern peasant movement was different from the traditional peasant rebellions was because the rural social structure had changed due to the penetration of imperialism. It did not have much to do with the organizational and educational work of the revolutionary intellectuals. In his words, "their [the peasants'] history did not begin when Peng Pai walked into the countryside." Peng Pai was simply a spokesman for the peasants. He was the medium for the transmission and articulation of the peasants' demands, but not the source of those demands.[183] Ralph Thaxton finds that the peasants in north China "turned toward anarchism and revolution on their own, without outside Communist party instigation, mainly because revolution was becoming the only act that held out hope for survival."[184] Though the peasant culture had revolutionary potential, peasant revolution was impossible in traditional China because "Only in the twentieth century, and mainly after the fall of the Qing order, would there emerge the unique set of political circumstances making folk revolution possible through a powerful mass movement."[185] James Polachek argues that intellectuals such as Mao Zedong did not add anything new to the traditional forms of peasant resistance, but instead simply tried to help one section of the peasantry to fight against another section in order to appeal to the former and draw them into the revolution. In his words, Mao Zedong "simply enlarged on an old millenarian dream that bore the stamp of Hakka society."[186] These scholars, instead of stressing Communist mobilization and indoctrination of the peasants, choose to emphasize the influence of the peasant culture on the Communist movement, and they explain the success of the Communist peasant movement in terms of the Communist promotion of the peasant demands.

Opposing the moral economists are scholars such as Roy Hofheinz and Chen Yungfa, who attribute a much more important role to the intellectuals in making the revolution than the moral economists claim. They maintain that the intellectuals did not just lead, but actually initiated or made the revolution. Hofheinz's study of the Haifeng peasant movements brought him to a conclusion opposite of that reached by Marks. Hofheinz claims that the movement actually did not have much to do with either the rural social structure or the peasants. Instead, it was conceived and imposed on the peasants by revolutionary intellectuals such as Peng Pai.[187] This view has been supported by some Chinese revolutionary intellectuals. In answering the question about why the Red Army and Soviets were created in about ten counties in Hubei but not in the other thirty-odd counties of the same province after 1927, Zheng Weisan, a leader of the Hubei–Henan–Anhui base area, commented that the key factor in creating the Red Army and Soviets was the existence of a fair number of revolutionary intellectuals in these ten counties.[188] The leaders of the southern Jiangxi base area also emphasized the role of native revolutionary intellectuals in the local revolution.[189] The former Communist Gong Chu believed that it was the local Communist intellectuals rather than the peasants who created the peasant movement in northern Guangdong.[190]

The perception of the majority of Communist intellectuals of their own role in the revolution was somewhere between those two extreme views. Their assessment was quite similar to the moral economy theory in that the Communist intellectuals did not believe that they created the conditions for revolution. Nor did they believe they created the revolution and class struggle. Peng Pai claimed in 1923 that "the animosity between the rural classes has existed for a long time, the only reason why the revolution has not broken out is because no one has come to mobilize the peasants."[191] Fang Zhimin, in his autobiography written while awaiting execution, remarked that "Hengfeng was like a revolutionary powder keg. I make no attempt to conceal the truth that I was the ignitor. I walked into Hengfeng and ignited the fuse of the powder keg; the keg exploded—the revolutionary insurrection broke out immediately."[192] Mao Zedong, in his famous Report on the Peasant Movement in Hunan, declared the following:

> In a very short time, several hundred millions peasants in China's central, southern, and northern provinces will rise like a fierce wind or tempest.... They will, in the end, send all the imperialists, warlords, corrupt officials, local bullies, and bad gentry to their graves. All revolutionary parties and all revolutionary comrades will stand before them to be tested, to be accepted or rejected as they decide. To march at their head and lead them? To stand behind them or to stand opposite them and oppose them? Every Chinese is free to choose among the three, but by the force of circumstances you are fated to make the choice quickly.[193]

They all perceived that peasant violence was imminent and that it would occur whether other people wanted it or not. However, that did not mean that the revolutionary intellectuals could do nothing for the peasants. Their perception of their own roles in the peasant movement closely paralleled the roles assigned to the intellectuals by Lenin. Peng Pai called himself an "instigator" and repeatedly asked his comrades to come to help him with the instigation, which he considered conducive to the success of the revolution. He later created the famous Peasant Movement Institute in Guangzhou and many other training programs in other places, whose function it was to train "instigators." Fang Zhimin likened himself to an ignitor. Likewise, Mao Zedong held that a revolutionary could choose to lead the peasants.

Although these Chinese revolutionaries emphasized the material basis of the social structure and social change, they did not believe that the deterioration of the material conditions of the peasants or the change of social structure would automatically lead to a modern socialist revolution. To them, the peasants would not become revolutionaries just because of the crisis of social structure; they had to be awakened, taught, and led into the revolution. If the revolutionary intellectuals did not provide proper leadership, then the peasants could do no better than the traditional peasant rebels such as the Taiping rebels and the Boxers. The peasantry had revolutionary potential, but it was up to the intellectuals to exploit that potential.[194]

This assessment of the role of the revolutionary intellectuals in the peasant movement is largely compatible with the facts. At the same time the Communist peasant movement was taking place, there were many other non-Communist peasant riots and uprisings in China, which had entirely different goals from those of the Communist peasant movement.[195] It is in that sense that Barrington Moore remarked that "the conservative half-truth that 'outside agitators' make riots and revolutions—a half-truth that becomes a lie because it ignores the conditions that make agitators effective—finds strong support from Chinese data."[196] Scholars like Benjamin Schwartz, Kung-chuan Hsiao, William Hinton, Lucien Bianco, Eric Wolf, and Elizabeth Perry also agree that the intelligentsia were not simply articulators of the masses, that the intellectuals were not always committed to promoting the peasants' interests, and that, without outside influence, the peasant rebels would have remained rebels and could never become revolutionaries by themselves.[197] Interestingly, Fernando Galbiati, another expert on Peng Pai, holds a view different from both Hofheinz and Marks but similar to the Chinese Communists regarding the intellectuals' role in the Communist peasant movement. He agrees with Marks about the deterioration of the living conditions of the peasants,[198] but does not believe that this would automatically have led to a successful peasant revolution. Intellectuals like Peng Pai made the peasant movement viable by contributing to it modern organization, social power, and political structure. Though the party was close to the peasants, and sometimes the party's policies reflected a strong rural bias, it was also always cautious about the negative aspects of peasant mentality.[199]

TEACHER–STUDENT RELATIONSHIP

The intellectuals engaged in the rural reconstruction movement adopted a different pattern of intellectual-peasant relationships from the Communists. This movement was led by a loose organization made up of individuals who acted independently in different areas. As far as their relationship with the peasants was concerned, they were all against the Communist class alliance pattern because they did not believe in class struggle, many of them did not even admit that there were class differences in China. Instead, most of them adopted the traditional teacher–student dichotomy and expanded it to include the whole rural society. The majority of the leaders in the rural reconstruction movement gave their primary attention to building schools. These were not schools in the usual sense since they were not just a part of the society, but the centers of society, and they incorporated the whole society. As Liang Shuming expressed it; "a village or township school is not just a school.... The best way to say it is that it is a school, but at the same time it is also a rural organization. Take the township school for example ... this school is extremely large ... it includes all the villages and people of the township." [200]

Liang Shuming contended that the two most serious problems of rural China were the lack of political consciousness and the lack of organization. The best way to deal with these two problems was to build village and township schools. These schools would instill in the peasants a sense of political consciousness and bring the isolated households and villages into an organization. Liang suggested building different kinds of schools to incorporate everyone in the villages: schools for adults, women, children, old men, and old women, respectively, as well as kindergarten.[201] In Zouping County of Shandong, where Liang Shuming was based, various levels of schools actually replaced the various levels of government. There were village schools, township schools, and county schools; the principals of the schools were concurrently the government leaders; the intellectuals were the teachers of the schools, and the peasants were supposed to be the students. According to Liang, the teachers' duties at these schools needed to be different from those of ordinary schools: "The village and township schools should provide education in its broad, general sense.... The duties of the instructors are not limited to teaching textbooks and teaching only the students within the schools." [202]

In 1933, Liang Shuming submitted his Draft about the Society-Centered Education System to the Ministry of Education of the Nationalist government, in which he maintained that education rather than political power should be the center of society because political power is based on military force and in a society dominated by political power, social change can only be brought about through violence, whereas education is based on rationality and can therefore lead to peaceful social change. He advocated "making the school the center of the local society and the teachers instructors of the society." Based on his experiences in Zouping County, he suggested entirely eliminating the barriers between the schools and society by incorporating school education and social education into a single education system of five levels: township school, district school, county school, provincial school, and national school.[203] The Nationalist government rejected his draft, with the Nationalist scholar Fu Sinian charging that the plan was wholly irrelevant to the question of dealing with the Japanese.[204] Liang's setback did not deter him. Years later, after the PRC was established, at a meeting of the Political Consultative Conference in September 1953, he suggested the Communists adopt his education plan to mobilize the peasants for the purpose of socialist reconstruction. The next day he was roundly scolded by Mao Zedong, and his education plan became one of the three issues that caused his separation from Mao and his complete oblivion in the next three decades.

Similar policies were adopted in Yan Yangchu's Dingxian Experiment. One of Yan Yangchu's followers summarized ten principles of the new education they were trying to promote. Among them:

1. Change the role of the school—"school is not the warehouse or store of knowledge, but the center of society and the service station of reconstruction."
2. Expand the range of education—"rural schools should open their doors to provide appropriate education for all the villagers."
3. Extend the time limit of education—"education should cover the whole life of a person."
5. Increase the number of locations for education—"the whole countryside should be taken as the location of education."
10. Amplify the social responsibility of the teacher—"the teachers of the rural schools are not only transmitters of knowledge...they are also leaders of reconstruction and organizers of the society."[205]

In Yan Yangchu's program, three types of education were proposed: the school type, the family type, and the social type. His aim was to incorporate everyone in the village into his educational institutions. The scope of their learning, which included cultural education, economic education, health education, and political education, also went far beyond the standard curriculum.[206] What was taught was different from both traditional Chinese education and the newly imported Western education; it was also different from the Communist concept of education that emphasized class consciousness and the rural education proposed by some agricultural experts that stressed the spread of farming techniques. Like Liang Shuming, Yan Yangchu was also the chief administrator of the county.

The rural reconstruction school ignored class analysis and class alliance. They considered the peasants an inseparable whole, and wanted to identify with all the villagers. As Liang Shuming repeatedly stated, the aim of rural reconstruction was to include everyone in the village and to strengthen solidarity among the villagers, not divide them. Yan Yangchu insisted that the popular education movement should be impartial and have no relationship with religions,[207] parties, or -isms, otherwise its scope would be narrowed.[208] He rejected the idea that mass education meant the education of the poor and hence was the equivalent of class education.[209]

Yan did admit that an upper class and a lower class existed in China. However, his "class" was not defined in economic, but in educational terms. The upper class comprised a small group of educated people who disdained the lower class formed by the great mass of uneducated people. The division between the two classes was believed to be the cause of China's problems. To solve these problems, the educated upper class had to go to the masses to study them and teach them and try to incorporate them into the upper class.[210] In short, to Yan, the only class difference in China was that between the class of teachers and the class of students.

Yan's and Liang's views were shared by Tao Xingzhi, who also adopted a broad definition of education in his training of village school teachers. He wanted the village school to be the center for reforming rural life, and the village school teachers to be the leaders of that reformation. He had very high expectations of the village teachers: "A good village teacher should possess: first, the skills of the peasant; second, a scientific brain; third, the spirit of social reform.... Such teachers are the moving spirits of reforming rural life."[211] Tao actually believed that China's future lay on the shoulders of village school teachers. He wished he could train one million village teachers and establish one million village schools in order to transform one million villages. If that could be achieved, he predicted rural China would be transformed.[212]

Rural education and the teacher–student pattern were also among the major topics discussed at the three national conferences on rural reconstruction. At the Third National Conference on Rural Reconstruction held in

1935, one of the topics was how to make the village school teachers the key force of rural reconstruction. The participants suggested making the village school the keystone for rural reform. According to this idea, the village school teachers would not only teach the schoolchildren, but also their parents. As one of their documents announced, "The primary school teachers engaged in rural reform should pay attention to all kinds of issues, make themselves the absolute leaders and organize the masses into a closely-knit unity."[213]

To eliminate the barriers between school and society through mass education was widely viewed by the intellectuals as a necessary means for improving the social-cultural conditions of the masses as well as strengthening national solidarity. The young Mao Zedong was a strong supporter of mass education before he became a Marxist. As early as 1917, when he was still a student at the First Normal School of Hunan, he was actively engaged in creating a night school for the workers. According to Mao, one of the reasons for creating a night school was to eliminate the barrier between school and society. He also shared the vision of school as society or society as school proposed by Yan Yangchu and Liang Shuming.[214] After he joined the Communist Party, Mao continued to support the local mass education movement led by Li Liuru and Fang Weixia.[215] In 1922, when Yan Yangchu went to Changsha to launch a mass education campaign, Mao was one of the volunteer teachers who helped him.[216] Many other Communists were also strong supporters of the mass education movement. In Beijing, around the days of the May Fourth Movement, a group of students led by Zhang Guotao and others established an association of mass education, speech groups of mass education, and night schools.[217] Many Communists might never divest themselves of their enthusiasm for mass education, but in later years they no longer considered it the most effective means of changing China.

OTHER PATTERNS

Some researchers tended to consider themselves objective observers and the peasants their research objects. Although their sympathy for the peasants was as strong as anyone's, they did not intend to stay in the village and become directly involved in practical work. For instance, Fei Xiaotong twice refused to give up his research to do practical work in the village.[218] Their bases were the universities and research institutes in the urban centers, from which they made frequent and temporary trips to the village to conduct fieldwork. In Fei Xiaotong's words, what they were interested in was "reliable information" and "a common-sense judgment" based on the information,[219] which they believed they could achieve through community studies. He also believed that there was no contradiction between their objective research and their desire to give voice to the grievances of the peasants. Finally, Fei firmly believed that social science could help direct social change so that its results would be beneficial to the people.[220]

The Communist Chen Hansheng was another researcher who tried to act as an impartial social scientist and give the appearance of being interested in nothing else except information about local conditions. He made this point very clear to the American leftist journalist Agnes Smedley while they were on a trip to the villages of Wuxi County of Jiangsu in 1929. On the boat to their destination, they met landlord Zhu, the most powerful local tyrant. Zhu invited them to his house and Chen accepted, explaining to Smedley that if they rejected the invitation they would never be able to conduct their investigation. The day they arrived at Zhu's home, they found that a wedding ceremony was going on at the same time that the Zhus had arrested some poor peasants and detained them in their house. Smedley was surprised to find that Chen Hansheng remained quite calm and indifferent about what had happened and urged Chen to help free the peasants. Chen replied that it would be dangerous for an outsider to interfere and that they had better pretend not to see anything if they did not want their investigation interrupted. Smedley saw many more disconcerting scenes, which were "common sights" to Chen Hansheng.[221] Chen and his followers tried to remain impartial researchers while in the field, although their ultimate goal was to help one class overthrow the other.

The primary purpose of a researcher was to collect factual information from the peasants—no easy task. Researchers of all groups agreed that it was very difficult to obtain reliable information from the peasants, who were often suspicious of the researchers' intentions, believing that they were working for the government and their research was for the purpose of tax collection. As a result, the peasants often refused to provide any information or gave false statements. Therefore, the researchers, just like the practitioners, had to make it their priority to gain the peasants' trust and cooperation. Li Jinghan, the sociologist who spent seven years in Dingxian investigating rural life, wrote that "they (the peasants) feared an imminent disaster when asked about the number of people in their families, land and properties, etc., all linked to money-collecting and forced labor."[222] Mao Zedong, who was also concerned with this issue, considered it a prerequisite for an investigator to gain the trust of the masses. In a 1941 speech to a group of Communists sent to investigate women's lives, he taught them how to get the masses to tell the truth: "the key is to make friends with the masses; do not act like a detective.... If the masses do not tell you the truth, the blame is on you, not on the masses."[223]

The foreign and Chinese missionaries involved in the rural reconstruction movement, although basically following the teacher–student pattern, attached more weight to the peasantry's religious education. Missionary organizations in China began to pay attention to secular matters such as poverty and illiteracy in the early 1920s. In fact, Yan Yangchu, a Christian himself, started his mass education program while he was affiliated with the YMCA, though he later severed his relations with the church. Although there was much discussion among the missionaries about a rural program, and a few even started to experiment with a mass education program during the 1920s, it was not until the 1930s that the church began to be directly involved in the rural reconstruction movement. The most famous base of the church was a district in Lichuan County in southern Jiangxi, an area recovered from the Red Army in the mid-1930s. Financially the project was supported by the Nationalist government; theoretically and methodologically it was strongly influenced by Yan Yangchu and his Dingxian model. Yan actually sent a group of experts to Lichuan to help with the church program.

The main difference between the church program and Yan Yangchu's experiment was that Yan Yangchu gave no attention to religion, whereas the church strove to imbue its program with a religious spirit whenever possible. Yan Yangchu preferred a school-centered society, while the missionaries wanted to build a church-centered society. In late 1930 and early 1931, the National Christian Council of China [NCCC] invited Kenyon Butterfield, an agricultural specialist and the proponent of "rural community parish" to China for a visit. Butterfield suggested that the church in China focus on building "community-parish, with a self-supporting rural church, indigenous in its methods, led by a specially trained pastor" who was to be both "a preacher and a community leader and builder." This suggestion was fully accepted and endorsed by the church. In a meeting held in early 1933, the National Christian Council of China urged that each member church experiment in at least one rural community parish and train rural workers. It is reported that after the meeting "all over China men were eager to work out a synthesis that partook of both the rural community parish of Kenyon Butterfield and the model *hsien* of James Yen."[224] The more well-known cases included George Shepherd's experiment in Fujian and Hugh Hubberd's experiment in Hebei. In 1935, the NCCC reiterated that the primary purpose of the Lichuan project was "the establishment of a Christian rural Community by uniting kindred minds in a common effort and life, on the basis of a Christian self-sacrifice, love and service, combined with scientific methods."[225] As one missionary put it, the responsibility of the rural missionary was to "make real Christians, but intelligent, healthy, public spirited, patriotic, economically independent, cooperating Christians." Clearly, they wanted to be the peasants' teachers, but not ordinary secular teachers because, in addition to secular subjects, they also wanted to teach the peasants religion.[226]

If this missionary–native pattern reflected strong foreign and modern influence, other patterns indicated continuity of native traditions. In southwestern Henan, local leaders Peng Yuting, Bie Tingfang, Chen Zhonghua, and Ning Xigu were more like traditional rulers of the peasants, although they preferred to call themselves rural reconstructionists.[227] This was especially true for Bie Tingfang, who was called a local despot by many local peasants, probably because there were too many bandits in that area when the local rural reconstruction started. In 1929, 6,000 bandits from the neighboring Deng County attacked the county seat of Zhenping. They burned 9,000 houses and kidnapped 12,000 people.[228] Peng Yutin returned to his native Zhenping that year to deal with the problem of banditry. Bie Tingfang's career started as a local militia leader whose chief duty it was to fight the bandits. Likewise, Chen Zhonghua was invited back to his village from the county seat by his fellow villagers to help quell the bandits.

In such an environment, there was no clear division between the impoverished peasants and bandits and, as a result, the peasants were often considered potential bandits by the local gentry, who naturally wanted strengthened military power to keep the peasants under control. Peng Yuting created a normal school to train village schoolteachers and village leaders. However, unlike their counterparts in Zouping and Dingxian, the schoolteachers in southwestern Henan had little power, which was confined to the village leaders and military officers. These local leaders relied heavily on coercion, persecution, and exploitation of the peasants. Like Liang Shuming and Yan Yangchu, these leaders also actually took over the local government. However, while Liang and Yan were experimenting with rule by teaching, Bie Tingfang opted for rule by killing and oppressing. In the early 1930s, Bie commanded about 60,000 militia men. His profile was very much like the local strongman model of elite behavior in peripheral regions proposed by some scholars: in such regions, the elites were more likely to command militia units, and their coercive resources were generally greater than those of the elites in the core areas.[229] Yan Yangchu remarked that the greatest achievement of the rural reconstructionists in southwestern Henan was the militia organization, and that, ironically, they failed to achieve results in social-economic improvement.[230] Bie Tingfang actually committed many brutalities and accumulated much wealth and was a wholly different kind of rural reconstructionist from Liang and Yan.[231] Because of their heavy hand in suppressing the local bandits as well as opponent power holders, two of the four leaders, Peng Yuting and Ning Xigu, were assassinated.

The leaders of the Chinese peasant movements in the first half of the twentieth century had similar backgrounds and experiences. The patterns of intellectual–peasant relations formed an integral part of the rural programs of the various intellectual groups. These patterns were created on the basis of the intellectuals' understanding of the rural society and the peasantry and the intellectuals' perception of their own roles in changing rural society.

The similarities among the various patterns of intellectual–peasant relationship are evident. On the one hand, they were all based on the intellectuals' deep sympathy for the peasants; on the other hand, they all strove to justify their control over the peasants. They shared a fundamental assumption: the peasants were too ignorant and weak to control their own fate, and it was the intellectuals' responsibility to save them by leading them, or through teaching or research.

The major difference among them was in their views about with whom they should identify and how. The Communist intellectuals made it very clear that they intended to identify with the poor people of the village. On many occasions, this led to an unusual alliance between the youths of rich families and the poor peasants. If they had to make concessions to the landlords, as happened during the Anti-Japanese War, the Communists made it very clear that it was a temporary tactic, not a matter of principle. The non-Communist intellectuals, on the other hand, tended to claim that they identified with all the villagers.

The difference between the Communists and non-Communists was very similar to that between the populists and the Communists in prerevolutionary Russia, with the populists arguing for the people as a unified whole, and the Marxists standing with the lower classes. However, since the 1930s, many non-Communist intellectuals have been repeatedly accused by the Communists of siding with the ruling class instead of the people as a whole, which was believed to be the reason for their lack of mass support. For example, Communist intellectuals attacked Liang Shuming for relying on warlords and local gentry and for acting in their interest. The same accusation was directed toward Yan Yangchu in the 1930s. Fei Xiaotong was also criticized for neglecting class differences in the villages and emphasizing the gentry's role in his rural development program. These accusations can be attributed to differences between the Communists and the non-Communists in their attitude toward the local gentry. The Communists perceived the peasants and the traditional rural upper class as deadly enemies; hence, to ally with the peasants meant to help the peasants fight against the landlords and gentry. Any attempt at mediating between the classes and maintaining the status quo was thus deemed as serving the interests of the upper class. Many non-Communists, however, viewed the relations between the peasants and the gentry as a symbiotic one and believed that the gentry actually played a positive role in rural society. The rural reconstruction movement relied heavily on the gentry. Likewise, Fei Xiaotong contended that local leaders were the bridge between the local peasants and nonnative intellectuals; hence they were indispensable to local reform.[232] Fei also claimed that the gentry class could be reformed and could perform a leading role in the industrialization of China if they chose to relinquish their land, change their old lifestyle, and invest their money in industry.[233]

6

Conclusion

On their bloody road to rescue the Chinese nation, a generation of frustrated but awakened Chinese intellectuals came across the Chinese peasantry, among whom they found both the causes of and remedies for China's national crisis. The Chinese nation, rather than the Chinese peasantry, was both the starting point and the end of all the intellectuals' peasant movements in China during the first half of the twentieth century. Despite all the differences among the various intellectual groups in their perceptions of the peasantry, Chinese rural society, as well as their relations with the peasantry, they shared two basic goals: first, to promote the peasants' cultural and economic conditions; second, to draw the peasants into their political and national movements. In other words, they all wanted to transform as well as to utilize the peasants. These two goals were the foundation of the various peasant movements the intellectuals tried to promote, and the fulfillment of these two goals was crucial to the success of their respective national movements. If the peasants' conditions remained unchanged, the intellectuals believed, the Chinese nation would fail to develop as well, and if the Chinese peasants, who formed the great majority of the population, remained outside of the national movement, there would be no national movement. Although many intellectuals were physically confined to small villages in remote areas during this period, they were emotionally and intellectually focused on the greater Chinese nation: both the actual tattered nation of the present and the ideal nation they imagined for the future.

The Chinese intellectuals themselves never denied the close connections between their peasant movements and their grand purpose of rescuing the nation. On the contrary, all groups of intellectuals strove to portray

167

themselves as true nationalists or patriots and their opponents as mere pre-
tenders, and to prove that their peasant movement was the best method to
save and rebuild the nation, while their opponents' was doomed to failure.
Liang Shuming, for example, called his rural reconstruction theory the last
resort for reviving the Chinese nation and believed that both the Communist
and capitalist methods were dead ends for China. Yan Yangchu argued that
his mass education movement was the best way to rescue the nation. In his
words, to help the peasants to a fuller development of their powers "was pro-
foundly worthwhile, for their own sake, but especially for the sake of building up the nation from its foundations"; he added, "rural reconstruction is
national reconstruction, and national reconstruction, rural reconstruction."[1]
Fei Xiaotong repeatedly emphasized the impact of China's national crisis on
his personal academic career. He stated that the sole purpose of his research
was to help rescue the nation, his specific concern was to improve the living
conditions of the peasants, and that his research subject was determined by
the needs of the nation.[2] He believed that his rural industrialization program,
by shortening and eliminating the gap between China and more developed
countries, was the most effective way to modernize the nation. The
Nationalists depicted themselves as orthodox nationalists because they were
the champions of the national revolution, which theoretically incorporated all
Chinese except a handful of evil warlords. All intellectuals considered their
peasant movements as part of their national movements. For many of them,
the peasant movement *was* the national movement.

The Communists, because of their obsession with class struggle, were
viewed by others, especially the Nationalists, as being unfaithful to the
nation, since the latter held that a class revolution would lead to internecine
wars within the nation and hence was incompatible with the national revolution. There had also been the charge that the Chinese Communists were
wavering internationalists vacillating between Stalin and Trotsky. The
Communists themselves, however, argued that class struggle was the most
effective way to achieve national revolution, and that there was no contradiction at all between their class revolution and national revolution. The
Communists reconciled these two revolutions by first proposing a "nation-
class" theory, which argued that China was a proletarian nation oppressed
and exploited by foreign capitalist nations, and that, therefore, in China,
class revolution and national revolution were one and the same. Later, the
"nation-class" theory was replaced with a "class-nation" theory, according to
which the Chinese upper classes, by their treacherous actions of cooperating
with the foreigners to oppress and exploit their compatriots, ceased to be
Chinese nationals and became lackeys of the foreigners—only the lower
classes of China, they argued, were true members of the Chinese nation.
Thus, their class revolution and national revolution were still believed to be

one and the same. The only difference was that, by defining class enemies as the traitors of the nation and hence lumping more Chinese into the imperialists' camp, their nation had become smaller than that of the Nationalists. The difference between the groups that opposed class struggle and those promoting it was that they defined the Chinese nation differently: the former chose a cultural and racial definition of the nation, while the latter preferred to define it along class lines.

The Communists' claims have been supported by many scholars who have studied Communism and nationalism in China and the world. Eric Hobsbawm's contention that "Marxist movements and states have tended to become national not only in form but in substance, i.e., nationalist" is perfectly applicable to the Chinese Communist peasant movement.[3] Anthony Smith defined the Communism of Yugoslavia, Vietnam, and China as "national communism" that "seeks the support of a peasantry threatened by alien rule."[4] Eric Wolf remarked that the Chinese Communists were able to harness peasant energies for "ends never dreamed of by the peasantry,"[5] and that the Chinese Communist revolution, although carried on with the aid of the peasants, was not made "for the sake of peasantry."[6] Chalmers Johnson, based on his study of the Communist-peasant relations during the Anti-Japanese War, suggested that the Chinese Communist Party should be viewed as the leader of a war-energized, radical nationalist movement and the Chinese Communist version of Marxist-Leninist ideology as an adjunct to Chinese nationalism. He concluded that "the Communist rise to power in China should be understood as a species of nationalist movement."[7] Lucien Bianco observed that there was "a serious ambiguity" in the Chinese Communist–peasant movement: "though sincere in its concern for the plight of the peasantry and in its will to better it, the Communist elite used the mobilization of the peasants and the promise of liberation as a means to serve an end which held much less interest for those peasants: the independence, power and might of the nation."[8]

The fact that the chief concern of the intellectuals involved in the peasant movements was the nation rather than the peasants does not necessarily mean that the intellectuals were merely making use of the peasants. It only means that when the intellectuals perceived a clash between the interests of the nation and those of the peasants, they would usually put the former above the latter. In his analysis of the relations between the Chinese Communists and the peasants, Benjamin Schwartz pointed out that on the one hand there was little doubt that Communist leaders had risen to power by addressing themselves to the immediate needs of the Chinese peasants; on the other hand, he noted, it would be wrong to assume that the Communist leaders embodied the aspirations of the Chinese people and that they would automatically continue to express the needs and aspirations of the masses. In his words, "the needs of the masses have a time dimension."[9] Schwartz's conclusion applies to non-Communist intellectuals as well. The Nationalists chose to neglect the interests of the poor peasants after 1927 because they perceived that their interests clashed with the interests of the whole nation. In order to maintain a multiclass alliance against the imperialists, which they believed was crucial in winning the national revolution, the peasants' interests had to be sacrificed. The Communists, however, saw no such clash of interest. They decided to buttress the poor peasants' demands because they perceived that by doing so they would be able to draw the powerful peasants into the national movement. However, during the Anti-Japanese War, when the Communists perceived that the United Front of various classes was absolutely essential to the existence of the nation, they decided immediately to abandon their previous radical policies and adopted a milder policy toward the rural rich. The nation's interests were always supreme; in the name of the nation, the peasants' interests could be either promoted or sacrificed. In that sense, it would not be too much of an exaggeration to say that the intellectual-led peasant movements during the first half of the twentieth century were not genuine peasant movements since peasants themselves never became the center of such movements. To borrow Hugh Seton-Watson's words, such movements can only be called movements of peasants, but not peasant movements.[10]

Nor does the premise that the intellectuals utilized and transformed the peasants necessarily mean that the peasants were always passive subjects waiting to be acted on by the intellectuals. The peasants themselves often showed their approval of a certain policy by giving their full support to it or their disapproval by being indifferent or offering resistance. As Fernando Galbiati puts it, "Once the decision to make revolution with, if not for, the peasants was taken, the peasants were put squarely amid the KMT–CCP conflict and eventually tipped the scales in favor of the party that took up their cause and seemed able to give them their dream."[11] The intellectuals, in order to garner the support they desperately needed, had to make concessions to the peasants. The peasants, in turn, would give their support to those intellectuals they believed had real concern for the peasants' welfare.

Leften Stavrianos observes that in the national liberation movement of the third world, three ideologies were vying for the support of the peasantry: religious revivalism, reform, and socialist revolution. He related these three different approaches to class differences. Religious revivalism represented the interests of the archaic dynastic and landed class. This was a conservative reaction, though it could also be progressive and even revolutionary. Reform was the approach taken by the Westernized merchants, teachers, clerks, officials, and military officers. Their rhetoric was often revolutionary, but their objectives were reformist. The poor peasants and radical intellectuals chose the path of socialist revolution.[12] Stavrianos thus affirmed that all three groups were nationalists, though of different stripes. This classification fits well with China's situation during the first half of the twentieth century, when conservative reformers such as Liang Shuming wanted to reestablish the lost Confucian tradition; liberal reformers such as Yan Yangchu and Fei Xiaotong intended to create socialism and democracy in China through non-violent means; and Communist revolutionaries firmly believed in class struggle. If the conservative and liberal reformers are grouped together, then there were only two groups of intellectuals in China: reformers and revolutionaries. To adopt Gramsci's concepts, the reformers preferred the war of position—a movement of gradualism, moderation, and molecular changes controlled from the top, while the revolutionaries championed the war of movement, which emphasized popular initiative and radical challenge. These were two different roads for building the nation-state.[13] The history of the Chinese peasant movement during the first half of the twentieth century was in a sense the history of the struggle among the various groups. The long struggle ended in 1949, with the Communists claiming a total victory and the reformers suffering a total defeat.

The intellectuals' primary concern with the Chinese nation as a whole along with their ideologies for liberating and building the nation strongly influenced their understanding of the Chinese peasantry. Despite the rural origins of most of the intellectuals who wrote about the peasantry, their writings about the Chinese peasantry and rural China indicated a strong urban bias. The intellectuals' views and perceptions of the Chinese peasantry were determined more by what kind of "ism" they embraced than by what facts they found in the countryside. Those intellectuals who went or returned to the villages were not intellectuals as such, but intellectuals with specific persuasions, be it Communism, socialism, or Nationalism, and they acquired all these "isms," or "national myths"—to adopt Chalmers Johnsons's phrase—through their education and urban experiences.[14] Their debate about rural China really was an application of their urban theories to the rural world, and their struggles in the countryside were a continuation of their struggles in the cities. The different beliefs held by the various groups of intellectuals not only gave birth to different policies and strategies, but also led to different perceptions and views of the characteristics of the Chinese peasantry, the nature of Chinese rural society, and of the ideal intellectual–peasant relations. In other words, the differences among the Chinese intellectuals in their perceptions of the peasantry and rural society were to a large degree determined by the differences in their policies toward the peasantry, which were in turn determined by the differences in their visions and views about what kind of nation they wanted to have and how they planned to achieve this ideal nation.

The links between the intellectuals' perceptions of the peasantry, their policies toward the peasantry, and their perceptions of the Chinese nation as a whole are first indicated in the images of the peasant they created. Although the great majority of the intellectuals agreed that ignorance, innocence, poverty, powerfulness, and other features combined to form the image of the Chinese peasant, they attached different importance to and provided different explanations for the various features. The Communists emphasized the poverty and latent power of the peasantry and attributed the poverty of the peasantry mainly to class exploitation because they championed a class-based nation and wanted to use the peasants to achieve their goal. Most non-Communist intellectuals, however, tended to attach different importance to each of the features, deemphasized class exploitation, and interpreted poverty in terms of other factors.

The protracted debate among the Chinese intellectuals about the nature of Chinese rural society represented another attempt at applying the grand theories to rural China. The participants were all aware that what they were debating was not an academic issue, but a political one, because their views of the nature of Chinese rural society were directly linked to their policies toward the peasantry. Those who adopted Marxist theory in interpreting rural Chinese society were mostly self-proclaimed revolutionaries, yet they were proponents of different revolutions and, accordingly, they held different views of the nature of Chinese rural society. Intellectuals affiliated with the Chinese Communist Party, which called for an antifeudal and anti-imperialist national democratic revolution, believed that rural China was a semifeudal and semicolonial society, while the Trotskyites, who anticipated a proletarian revolution in rural China, argued that rural China was already a capitalist society. Those who opposed the adoption of Marxist theory and believed in the uniqueness of rural Chinese society were all reformers. By denying the applicability of revolutionary Marxist theory to rural China, they denied the feasibility of an agrarian revolution in China.

The intellectuals' theories of ideal relations with the peasants were also closely related to their policies toward the peasantry as well as their grand theories about and plans for the Chinese nation. The Communist revolutionaries wanted to form a militant intellectual–peasant alliance, with the intellectuals as leaders and the peasants as loyal followers who would provide the physical power needed to complete the revolution. The reformers, however, felt no need for a militant alliance with the peasants. They tended to perceive themselves as teachers, patrons, rulers, and researchers while the peasants were their students, protégés, subjects, and objects of research. Intellectuals of all groups shared the view that the peasants themselves were not able to act independently and rationally. Whether as a force for revolution or for reconstruction, the peasants needed to be guided, taught, ruled, and/or protected by the intellectuals.

The images of the peasant, the theories about the nature of rural society, and the ideal patterns of intellectual–peasant relations created by the intellectuals were all used to support and justify their policies toward the peasants. These policies, in turn, were linked to what the intellectuals planned for the Chinese nation. The various groups of intellectuals chose to ally themselves with different strata of the rural population and used different methods to achieve their ideal society and nation. There were clear differences between the proponents of violent social revolution and the supporters of peaceful reform, and between those who were determined to identify with the lower strata of the peasantry and those who claimed to identify with all strata of the rural population. The connections between the intellectuals' perceptions of the peasantry and their rural programs were not always obvious and an outsider might find them hard to understand. Hence, after the collapse of the First United Front, the leader of the Third Party, Deng Yanda, found it difficult to understand why the CCP, which believed that China was still a semi-feudal and semicolonial society, insisted that the proletariat rather than the bourgeoisie be the leader of a national democratic revolution, and why the Trotskyites maintained that rural China was a capitalist society yet argued that the right strategy at that time was to form a national assembly rather than launch a proletarian revolution. Although some non-Communists also accepted the idea of the existence of classes and class exploitation in rural China, they proposed to solve the problem in a peaceful way. In other words, the links between the intellectuals' perceptions of the peasantry and their policies toward the peasantry were mainly based on the beliefs and theories each intellectual group embraced; hence, it was often true that only those who held the same beliefs could see the coherence of their respective theories.

The competition and conflict among different perceptions of the peasantry and different rural programs did not stop completely with the Communist victory in 1949. Shortly after the founding of the PRC, the Communists, who had been perceived as the champions of the peasants' concerns, decided to ruthlessly squeeze the peasants to build the cities because the Communist leaders now believed that industry, especially heavy industry, was the key to the continued existence and further development of the Chinese nation. This policy, at the time of its birth, was criticized by former reformers like Liang Shuming and Fei Xiaotong, who felt that the Communist policy of exploiting the peasants was detrimental not only to the interests of the peasants, but also to those of the nation. Therefore, at any one given moment, there were always different perceptions of the relations between the interests of the peasants and the interests of the nation. To a large degree, these different perceptions led to the differences in the agrarian and agricultural policies adopted by the various groups of intellectuals.

The Communist victory in the pre-1949 period does not necessarily mean that their radical methods would be successful in the future; neither does the reformers' failure in the pre-1949 period imply that reform methods would always result in failure in rural China. Unfortunately for Chinese peasants, however, the Communist victory led to a misperception among the Communist leaders, especially Mao Zedong, that their revolutionary methods would work well under any and all circumstances and that reforms would inevitably be ineffective and therefore should be discarded. Mao's contempt for the reformers was well demonstrated in his dispute with the reformer Liang Shuming in 1953, during which Mao openly ridiculed Liang for "showing off his proficiency with the ax in front of the master carpenter." The competition and hostility between the revolutionaries and reformers before 1949 carried over into the post-1949 period. Thus the Communists continued their violent revolutionary methods when the revolution was already over and initiated a number of major programs that ended in disaster. Tumultuous policy changes during the first decade of the PRC offer a series of examples. Although land reform had constructive results in the early 1950s, the Communist leaders were not content. Whatever their reasons—whether impatient, heady with success, or foolish—they launched the Great Leap Forward, which failed miserably and led to widespread suffering and hardship. It is both tragic and ironic that it was the Communists who caused the greatest famine in rural China in Chinese history. The Communists continued to carry out class struggle in rural China even though the rural ruling class had been wholly eliminated immediately after the establishment of the People's Republic. If the reformers' mistake before 1949 was to insist on reform when the circumstances required revolution, then the Communists' mistake from the mid-1950s to the late 1970s was to adhere to their revolution when conditions no longer warranted such methods.

It took roughly twenty years for the Communist leaders to realize that their revolutionary methods were no longer compatible with the changed circumstances. Those twenty years formed one of the most painful periods for the Chinese peasants in Chinese history. The fact that the Chinese peasants meekly endured the cumulative bitterness without rebellion can be attributed to their traditional passivity, the prestige and authority of the Communist Party among the peasants established in the pre-1949 period, and the tight and extremely effective social-political control exerted over the villages by the party. The highly acclaimed rural reforms initiated in the late 1970s after Mao's death were mainly based on two new policies: decollectivization of the land and development of rural industry. In part, the peasants initiated the policy of decollectivization and the party and government later approved and promoted it. The policy reflects and satisfies a centuries-long desire of every Chinese peasant: a piece of land that they can call their own. The policy of rural industry, on the other hand, was first proposed by intellectual reformers in the revolutionary era. It had been strongly advocated by the sociologist Fei Xiaotong and others since the 1930s.

The spirit of reform since the late 1970s in China is the same as that of the reform and revolution in pre-1949 China: on the one hand, the government satisfies the demands of the peasants; on the other hand, it tries to transform them. Although the official media has given equal praise to the policy of decollectivization and that of developing rural industry, their effects and significance are actually quite different. Decollectivization of land is essentially a retrogressive policy. It resulted in an increase of agricultural production in the first few years of the reform only because of the traditional enthusiasm of the Chinese peasants in tilling land of their own. However, such enthusiasm alone can only create limited growth during a limited time period. To bring about sustained agricultural growth requires the application of advanced technologies, but decollectivization made technological improvement impossible because agricultural tracts are too fragmented. If no progress is made in rural industry, in many areas where decollectivization has been carried out and where the peasants have been bound to their small pieces of land, agricultural production entered a new round of stagnation after a few years of limited growth. Progress in rural industry, on the other hand, has brought about unlimited growth in some areas, including considerable changes even in areas where decollectivization has not been carried out. Decollectivization seemingly provides a temporary solution to the peasants' subsistence problem, while rural industrialization apparently has the possibility of utterly changing the face of rural China and the Chinese peasantry. At last, reformers have been granted a chance to demonstrate the value of their programs in a society created by revolutionaries.

Notes

Notes to Chapter One

1. John Fitzgerald, *Awakening China*, viii.

2. Li, Oufan, *Zhong xi wenxue de huixiang*, 12, 15–16.

3 Helen Siu, Furrows, 23–24.

4. Kathleen Hartford, "Will the Real Chinese Peasant Please Stand Up?," 99.

5. Ibid., 98–99; Myron Cohen, "Cultural and Political Inventions in Modern China: The Case of the Chinese 'Peasant'," 151–170; Charles Hayford, *To the People: James Yen and Village China*, 62, 113; Charles Hayford, "The Storm over the Peasant: Orientalism and Rhetoric in Construing China;" Charles Hayford, "What's so Bad about The Good Earth?," 4–7.

6. Eric Wolf, *Peasants*, vii.

7. Karl Polanyi, *Primitive, Archaic and Modern Economies: Essays of Karl Polanyi*; A.V. Chayanov, *The Theory of Peasant Economy*.

Notes to Chapter Two

1. *Zhu Ziqing xuanji*, 192–193. Quoted in Vera Schwarcz, *Chinese Enlightenment*, 21–22.

2. Chang Kuo-tao [Zhang Guotao], *The Rise of the Chinese Communist Party*, Vol. 1, 39–41.

3. Li Dazhao, "Wan'e zhiyuan." In *Li Dazhao quanji*, Vol. 3, 298.

4. However, many have pointed out that the Chinese traditional literati were actually less alienated from the peasantry than their counterparts in other parts of the world. See V. G. Kiernan, *Imperialism and Its Contradictions*, 158–159; Angus McDonald, *The Urban Origins of Rural Revolution*, 63.

5. For discussions of the similarities and differences between the Russian and Chinese intelligentsia, see Benjamin Schwartz, "The Intelligentsia in Communist China: A Tentative Comparison," 164–181.

6. Xiang Peiliang. "Lun guduzhe." In *Liushinianlai Lu Xun yanjiu lunwenxuan*, Vol.1, 50.

7. For Lu Xun's denial of the existence of a true Chinese intelligentsia, see "Lu Xun zhi Xu Xusheng"; for his criticism of educated Chinese, see "Zhi Xiao Jun di wu xin," "Zhi Xiao Jun di jiu xin"; Feng Xuefeng, "Guanyu zhishifenzi de tanhua—pianduan huiyi," 149–159.

8. Feng Xuefeng, "Lu Xun xiansheng jihua er wei wancheng de zhuzuo," 164.

9. Zhou Enlai, "Wo yao shuo de hua." In *Liushinianlai Lu Xun yanjiu lunwen xuan*, Vol. 1, 496–497.

10. Benjamin Schwartz, "The Intelligentsia in Communist China: A Tentative Comparison," 172. See also his Introduction to *Reflections on the May Fourth Movement: A Symposium*, 4–5, for more discussion.

11. Benjamin Schwartz, "The Intelligentsia in Communist China: A Tentative Comparison," 172–173.

12. Yip Ka-che, "Nationalism and Revolution: The Nature and Causes of Student Activism in the 1920s."

13. Li Zehou, "Lue lun Lu Xun sixiang de fazhan," 543–544.

14. Vera Schwarcz, *The Chinese Enlightenment*, 24.

15. For a recent discussion about Gramsci's concepts, see Paul Ransome, *Antonio Gramsci*, chap. 7.

16. Aleksander Gella, "An Introduction to the Sociology of the Intelligentsia," 25.

17. Chalmers Johnson, however, believed that the Chinese peasantry did not enter the nationalist movement until the outbreak of the Sino-Japanese War in 1937. Chalmers Johnson, *Peasant Nationalism and Communist Power*.

18. Eric Wolf, *Peasant Wars of the Twentieth Century*, 289.

19. Hans Kohn, *The Idea of Nationalism*, 4.

20. Tom Nairn, *The Break-up of Britain*, 41.

21. Peter Burke, *Popular Culture in Early Modern Europe*, 9–15.

22. For the Chinese intellectual movement of studying the culture of the people, see Hung Chang-tai, *Going to the People*. According to Peter Burke (*Popular Culture in Early Modern Europe*, 21–22), in early modern Europe, "people" were defined as everyone in a particular country, or the uneducated, or the peasants. When Chinese intellectuals of the early twentieth century called for going to the people, usually it meant going to the peasants.

23. Joseph Stalin, *Marxism and the National and Colonial Question*, 15.

24. Peter Alter, *Nationalism*, 49–50.

25. Karl Marx, "Revolution in China and in Europe." *Karl Marx on Colonialism and Modernization*, 63–70.

26. Li, Dazhao, "Daying diguozhuyi qinlue zhongguo shi," 593.

27. Qiao Xuwu, "Ji Bai Lang Shi," 417; Edward Friedman, *Backward Toward Revolution*, 151–156.

28. Robert Marks, *Rural Revolution in South China*, chapter 6.

29. William Hinton, *Fanshen*, 54.

30. Barrington Moore, *Social Origins of Dictatorship and Democracy*, 188.

31. One proponent of this argument is Jin Yaoji, *Zhongguo xiandaihua yu zhishifenzi*, 77.

32. Aleksander Gella, "An Introduction to the Sociology of the Intelligentsia," 15.

33. V. F. Li., ed., *Intelligentsiia i sotsial'nyi progress v razvivaiushchikhsia stranakh Azii i Afriki*, 18–21.

34. Within the Communist Party, there was much controversy about how to distinguish a leftist from a rightist during the First United Front. Some argued that a leftist was someone who sympathized with the Communist Party; others said a leftist was someone who served the interests of the masses; a third group held that a leftist was someone who was against imperialism. In Borodin's view, a leftist was someone who supported solving the land problem. *Xiandai shiliao*, Vol. 1, 86–87. A similar view had been advocated by the Guangdong District Committee of the CCP even before the Northern Expedition. Chang Kuo-tao, *The Rise of the Chinese Communist Party, 1921–1927*. Vol. 1, 600. Fang Zhimin shared this view in 1927. Fang Zhimin, "Fanyou yundong yu wuren."

NOTES TO CHAPTER THREE

1. Chen Duxiu, "Anhui aiguohui yanshuo," 15–16.

2. Sun Zhongshan, "Minsheng zhuyi sidagang," 318–319.

3. "The British Rule in India" (1853, 6, 25). *Karl Marx on Colonialism and Modernization*, 88–89.

4. Chen Duxiu, "Kelinde Bei," 415–420. See D.W.Y. Kwok, *Scientism in Chinese Thought, 1900–1950*, 70–71; James P. Harrison, *The Communists and Chinese Peasant Rebellions*, 46; and Paul Cohen, *History in Three Keys*, 227–230, for further discussions.

5. Sun Zhongshan, "Zai Riben Rihua xueshengtuan huanyinghui de yanshuo"; "Zhi Beijing canyiyuan zhongyiyuan dian.".

6. Sun Zhongshan, "Zhina baoquan fenge helun," 61.

7. Chen Chunsheng, "Chen Shaobai xiansheng yu Xianggang Zhongguo ribao."

8. Guominbao, "Da Xijiangsanshi wen," 208-209.

9. *Zhongguo xunbao,* "Zhongguo qingzhong lun."

10. "Yihetuan yougong yu zhongguo shuo," 59, 62.

11. For more discussions, see *zhongguo jindaishi zhengminglu,* 449–452.

12. Zhang Guotao [Chang Kuo-tao], *The Rise of the Chinese Communist Party,* Vol. 1, 309–310.

13. Sun Zhongshan, "Genzhe yao you qi tian," 719.

14. Li Dazhao, "Qingnian yu nongcun," 180.

15. Li Dazhao, "Dongxi cunluo shenghuo de yidian," 352. Li called the old-style private school Ziyuepu.

16. Zhang Guotao, "Zhishi jieji zai zhengzhi shang de diwei ji zeren," 98.

17. Peng Pai, "Haifeng nongmin yundong," 111.

18. Peng Pai, "Haifeng zongnonghui dui shiju xuanyan," 27.

19. Peng Pai, "Peng Pai gei Li Chuntao" (1923, 6, 5), 32.

20. Eighty to ninety percent of the Chinese Laborers in France came from Shandong; the rest were from Zhili (Hebei), Henan, Jiangsu, Anhui, and other provinces. See Chen Sanjing, *Huagong yu Ouzhan,* 7, 35.

21. Yan Yangchu, "Pingmin jiaoyu," 47.

22. Yan Yangchu, "Zai zhouhui shang de jianghua," 182.

23. Yu Bida, "Nongren de changchu he duanchu."

24. Liang Shuming, "Xiangcun jianshe dayi," 683-684.

25. Lu Xun, "Po 'esheng lun," 28.

26. Lu Xun, "Nala zouhou zenyang," 162-163.

27. Lu Xun, "Lun zhaoxiang zhilei," 183.

28. Lu Xun, "Suiganlu sanshiqi," 309-310.

29. Lu Xun, "Zailun Leifengta de daodiao," 194.

30. See the next section for more discussions on their views of the relations between poverty and ignorance.

31. Quoted in Keith Schoppa, *Blood Road: The Mystery of Shen Dingyi in Revolutionary China,* 121.

32. Keith Schoppa, *Blood Road,* 97.

33. For discussions, see Ouyang Fanhai, "Lun Ah Q zhengzhuan," 514–544; Ai Wu, "Lun Ah Q," 435–441; Li Bo [Zhou Libo], "Tan Ah Q," 347; Yuan Liangjun, *Lu Xun yanjiushi,* Vol. 1, 97–98.

34. Lu Xun, "Jiwaiji shiyi—Yingyiben duanpianxiaoshuo zixu," 389.

35. Wang Yao, *Lu Xun zuopin lunji,* 285, 299.

36. Li Dazhao, "Qingnian yu nongcun," 182-183.

37. Yan Yangchu, "Nongcun yundong de shiming," 293.

38. Zheng Tianting, "Zhuiji 1928 nian Liang xiansheng zuo xiangzhi shijiang," 24–26.

39. Peng Pai, "Peng Pai gei Li Chuntao" (1922, 11, 18), 11.

40. Deng Zhongxia, "Lun nongmin yundong."

41. Bi Da, "Nongren tong shangren de bijiao."

42. Hung Chang-tai, *Going to the People: Chinese Intellectuals and Folk Literature 1918–1937*, 6, 14, 167.

43. John Fitzgerald, *Awakening China*, 135–137.

44. Ba Ren, "Lu Xun de chuangzuo fangfa," 295.

45. Quoted from Su Xuelin, *Ersanshi niandai zuojia zuopin*, 316–317.

46. Ling Yu, *Cong biancheng zouxiang shijie*, 200.

47. Jeffrey Kinkley, *The Odyssey of Shen Congwen*, 103.

48. Ye Shengtao, "Bei'ai de zhongzai," 130.

49. See Hung Chang-tai, *Going to the People*, 14, for discussion.

50. Lin Yutang, *My Country and My People*, x–xi.

51. Ibid.

52. Lu Mingzhuo, *Li Dazhao sixiang yanjiu*, 256.

53. Peng Pai was an example. See Robert Marks, *Rural Revolution in South China*, 167; Li Chuntao, "Haifeng nongmin yundong jiqi zhidaozhe Peng Pai," 312.

54. Li Dazhao, "Qingnian yu nongcun," 183.

55. Li Dazhao, "'Shaonian Zhongguo' de 'shaonian xingdong'," 320.

56. Li Dazhao, "Diji laodongzhe," 451.

57. Li Dazhao, "Guangming yu hei'an," 186.

58. *Tianyi*, Nos. 8–10.

59. Wang Chengren and Bai Shengxiang, "Shilun xinhai geming shiqi zichan-jieji gemingpai dui nongmin de fadong he lingdao," 35.

60. Zou Rong, *Gemingjun*, 658; Liu Shipei, "Beidianpian," 752; Huang Kan, "Ai pinmin," 786–790.

61. Chang Yu, "Lun Laiyang minbian shi," 652–658.

62. Chen Duxiu, "Zhongguo nongmin wenti," 512–514.

63. Deng Zhongxia, "Zhongguo nongmin zhuangkuang ji women yundong de fangzhen."

64. "On the People's Democratic Dictatorship," 415.

65. *Guangdong nongmin yundong ziliao xuanbian*, 145.

66. "Gao nongmin shu" (1924, 8). The Peasant Department of the KMT CEC.

67. Liao Zhongkai, "Zai Guangzhou Zhongguo guomindang zhuidao Liening dahui de yanshuo," 609; "Zai shijing binggongchang qingnian gongren xuexiao de yanshuo," 628; "Nongmin yundong suodang zhuyi zhi yaodian," 698–703; "Gemingpai yu fangemingpai," 757.

68. *Guangdong nongmin yundong ziliao xuanbian*, 228–229.

69. Chen Duxiu, "Geming yu wuli," 1143.

70. Peng Pai, "Haifeng nongmin yundong," 105–106.

71. Fang Zhimin, "Wo congshi geming douzheng de lueshu," 9; "Gandongbei Suwei'ai chuangli de lishi," 198.

72. Zhang Wentian, "Zhongguo geming jiben wenti," 391–401.

73. Deng Yanda, "Zenyang qu fuxing Zhongguo geming—pingmin geming?," 172–173; "Shiliunian shiyiyue dui Zhongguo ji shijie geming minzhong xuanyan," 198–200; "Shijiunian jiuyue shiwuri dui shiju xuanyan," 204.

74. *Fujian shibian dang'an ziliao*, 17–18; 26.

75. Wang Ching-wei (Wang Jingwei), "The Difference Between Communism and Sun Yat-senism," 68.

76. Qi Shufen, *Jingji qinglue xia de Zhongguo*, Preface.

77. Qi Shufen, *Jingji qinglue xia de Zhongguo*, Preface to the 3rd edition.

78. Li Zixiang, "Laximan baogaoshu zhi nongcun bufen de yantao," 2–3.

79. Li Jinghan, *Zhongguo nongcun wenti*, 29.

80. Ibid., 28–29.

81. Hong Shen, "Xiangdaomi," 177–179.

82. Qian Moxiang and Shen Jichang, "Hong Shen de nongcun sanbuqu," 343, 345.

83. Mao Dun, "Chuncan," 282–283.

84. Luo Fu, "Ping 'chuncan',"1209–1210.

85. In *Modern Chinese Stories and Novellas 1919–1949*, 379, translated by Cyril Birch.

86. Ye Shengtao, "Duoshoule sanwudou."

87. Wang Tongzhao, *Shanyu*, 8–10.

88. Qi Shufen, *Jingji qinglue xia zhi Zhongguo*, 1.

89. Zheng Chaolin, *An Oppositionist for Life: Memoirs of the Chinese Revolutionary Zheng Chaolin*, 182.

90. Fei Hsiao-tung, *Peasant Life in China: A Field Study of Country Life in the Yangtze Valley*, 282.

91. Ibid., 1–2.

92. Fei Xiaotong, *Xiangtu chongjian yu xiangzheng fazhan*, 56–63.

93. James P. McGough, *Fei Hsiao-tung: The Dilemma of a Chinese Intellectual*, 7.

94. Hu Shih, "Which Road Are We Going?," 12.

95. Gu Mei, *Zhongguo nongcun jingji wenti*, 186–220.

96. Liang Shuming, "Jingyi qingjiao Hu Shizhi xiansheng," 38.

97. Hu Songping, ed., *Hu Shizhi xiansheng nianpu changbian chugao*, Vol. 3, 870.

98. Liang Shuming, "Xiangcun jianshe dayi," 606.

99. Peng Pai, "Haifeng nongmin yundong," 105–106; "Zai diliujie nong-minyundong jiangxisuo de jiangyan," 194; In "Haifeng nongmin qigao tongbao shu," 43, Peng declared that less than one percent of the peasants in Haifeng had their own land.

100. *Guangdong nongmin yundong baogao. In Guangdong nongmin yundong ziliao xuanbian*, 41–42.

101. For a glimpse at the regional differences in land accumulation, land tenure, rural finance, and many other aspects of rural China before the mid-1930s, see *Zhongguo nongcun jingji ziliao*, 2 vols, and *Zhongguo nongcun jingji ziliao xubian*, 2 vols.

102. For more information, see Li Dazhao, "Tudi yu nongmin," 621; Peng Pai, "Zai shenggang bagong gongren daibiao di sanshiliu ci dahui shang de baogao," 94–95; Frederic Wakeman, *The Fall of Imperial China*, 14–15.

103. For details, see Donald Gillin, *Warlord Yen Hsi-shan in Shanhsi Province, 1911–1949*, 57, 209.

104. Chen Hansheng, "The Good Earth of China's Model Province."

105. R. H. Tawney, *Land and Labor in China*, 37–38.

106. William Hinton, *Fanshen: A Documentary of Revolution in a Chinese Village*, 29.

107. John Buck, *Land Utilization in China*, 37.

108. Elizabeth Perry, *Rebels and Revolutionaries in North China*, 28, 30.

109. Wang Tongzhao, "Chenchuan," 99.

110. Wang Tongzhao, *Shanyu*, 8.

111. Ibid., 306-307.

112. Li Dazhao, "Tudi yu nongmin," 620.

113. Lu Xun, *Diary of a Madman and Other Stories*, 89.

114. Li Bo [Zhou Libo], "Tan Ah Q," 347.

115. Shen Congwen, "Changhe tiji."

116. Shen Congwen, "Biancheng tiji."

117. Liang Shuming, "Xiangcun jianshe dayi," 604.

118. Zhang Wentian, "Zhongguo geming jiben wenti," 367–369.

119. Ye Shengtao, "Chizhe de jiao," 206.

120. Mao Dun, "Chuncan"; "Qiushou," 280–281, 321.

121. Wu Zuxiang, "Tianxia taiping," 117–142.

122. Wang Tongzhao, "Chenchuan," 96.

123. Yi Sheng, "Disanyang shijie de chuangzao—women suo yingdang huan-ying de Lu Xun," 56–57.

124. Luo Shu, "Shengrenqi"; Shen Congwen, "Zhangfu," 313–333.

125. Lu Xun, "*Xin E hua xuan xiaoying*," 345.

126. For early history of the Chinese woodcarving movement and its political affiliation, see Tang Yingwei, *Zhongguo xiandai muke shi*; Ye Fu, *Muke shouce*, 102–142; Chen Yanqiao, *Lu Xun yu muke*; Li Yunjing, *Zhongguo xiandai banhua shi; Zhongguo xinxing banhua wushinian xuanji*, Vol. 1: 1931–1949, 3–23.

127. All these works are collected in *Banhua jicheng: Lu Xun cang Zhongguo xiandai muke quanji*, 5 vols.

128. *Zhongguo nongcun jingji ziliao*, 2 vols. and *Zhongguo nongcun jingji ziliao xubian*, 2 vols.

129. See Zhang Guotao, *The Rise of the Chinese Communist Party*, 331.

130. Liao Zhongkai, "Geming jixu de gongfu," 328.

131. Liang Shuming, "Zhongguo wenti zhi jiejue," 216–217.

132. See Zhang Guotao, *The Rise of the Chinese Communist Party*, 313.

133. Liu Shipei, "Beidianpian"; "Lun Zhongguo tianzhu zhi zui'e."

134. Liu Shipei, "*Hengbao* fakanci."

135. Xuan Lu [Shen Dingyi], "Nongjia"; "Duanping."

136. *Xingqi pinglun*, no. 48, 1920, 5, 1.

137. Peng Pai, "Haifeng nongmin yundong,"102–105; Li Dazhao, "Tudi yu nongmin."

138. Wu Zuxiang, "Young Master Gets His Tonic," 379.

139. Ye Zi, "Fengshou."

140. Ai Qing, *Selected Poems of Ai Qing*, 27–29.

141. For a recent treatment of the investigation, see Du Song, "Tudi geming zhanzheng shiqi Zhongguo nongcun jingji diaochatuan huodong shimo."

142. Li Jinghan, *Zhongguo nongcun wenti*, 22–23.

143. Fei Hsiao-tung, *Peasant Life in China*, 192.

144. Fei Xiaotong, *Jiangcun jingji*, 296.

145. Fei Hsiao-tung, *Peasant Life in China*, 189–191, 265, 283–284.

146. Robert Redfield, *Tepoztlan, A Mexican Village*; Oscar Lewis, *Life in a Mexican Village*.

147. V. I. Lenin, *The Development of Capitalism in Russia*.

148. Zhang Tiezheng, "Hebei Sanhexian nongcun shehui gaikuang," 475–487.

149. Liang Shuming, "Zhongguo wenhua yaoyi," 147–148.

150. For details, see Chen Hansheng, "Xiandai Zhongguo de tudi wenti," 47–48.

151. Lao Xiang [Wang Xiangchen], *Huangtuni*, 42.

152. For discussions of the regional differences in landholding and various rural surveys conducted in the revolutionary period, see Joseph Esherick, "Number Games."

153. Jian Bozan, "Yihetuan yundong," 1–6; Jin Chongji and Hu Shengwu, "Yihetuan shiqi de gejieji dongxiang," 449–450; *Zhongguo jindaishi zhengminglu*, 404–406.

154. Albert Feuerwerker, "China's Modern Economic History in Communist Chinese Historiography," 221–222.

155. Liu Shaoqi, "Guanyu tudi gaige wenti de baogao," 32–33.

156. Guo Dehong, "Jiuzhongguo tudi zhanyou zhuangkuang ji fazhan qushi"; Guo Dehong, *Zhongguo jinxiandai nongmin tudi wenti yanjiu*.

157. Kovalev argued that the Chinese rural economy was already in decline before the Anti-Japanese War. The Japanese occupation made the situation even worse. E. F. Kovalev. Arenda i Arendnye Otnosheniia v Kitae.

158. Joseph Esherick, "Number Games," 405.

159. A. S. Mugruzin. *Agrarnya otnosheniia v Kitae v 20–40-kh godakh xx v.*, 4; 21–22.

160. Mugruzin, Ibid., 185-186.

161. Mugruzin, Ibid., 188.

162. A. S. Mugruzin. *Agrarno-krestianskaia problema v Kitae v pervoi polovine XX veka*, 60–61, 66–71.

163. For recent reviews of the various debates on Chinese rural economy during the first half of the twentieth century, see "New Perspectives on the Chinese Rural Economy, 1885–1935: A Symposium," edited by Daniel Little and contributed to by Daniel Little, Thomas Gottschang, Thomas Wiens, Bin Wong, Kathleen Hartford, Scott Rozelle, Thomas Rawski, and Philip Huang, *Republican China*, 18(1), 1992, 23–177; Ramon Myers, "How Did the Modern Chinese Economy Develop?—A Review Article"; Philip Huang, "A Reply to Ramon Myers"; R. Bin Wong, "Chinese Economic History and Development: A Note on the Myers-Huang Exchange."

164. Frances Moulder, *Japan, China and the Modern World Economy*, 70, 152–157.

165. For Marx's view, see "Revolution in China and Europe" (1853,6,14). In *Karl Marx on Colonialism and Modernization*, 62–70; for Li Dazhao's view, see "Daying diguozhuyi qinlue Zhongguo shi," 801; "Sun Zhongshan xiansheng zai Zhongguo minzu gemingshi shang zhi weizhi," and "Makesi de Zhongguo minzu geming guan."

166. Eric Wolf, *Peasant Wars of the Twentieth Century*, chapter 3 and conclusion.

167. Hofheinz Roy, *The Broken Wave*, 139; Robert Marks, *Rural Revolution in South China*, chap. 5; 283–284.

168. Kamal Sheel, *Peasant Society and Marxist Intellectuals in China*, 43–65.

169. Ralph Thaxton, *China Turned Rightside Up*, 59.

170. R. H. Tawney, *Land and Labor in China*, 72.

171. Ibid., 77.

172. James Thomson, *While China Faced West*, 43.

173. Mark Selden, *The Yenan Way in Revolutionary China*, 7–8.

174. Victor D. Lippit, *Land Reform and Economic Development in China*.

175. Edward Friedman, Paul Pickowicz, and Mark Selden, *Chinese Village, Socialist State*, 277–280.

176. Joseph Esherick, "Number Games"; Prasenjit Duara, *Culture, Power and the State*, chap. 8.

177. Dwight Perkins, *Agricultural Development in China*; "Growth and Changing Structure of China's Twentieth Century Economy"; Albert Feuerwerker, *The Chinese Economy, ca. 1870–1911*.

178. Douglas Paauw, "The Kuomintang and Economic Stagnation, 1928–1937."

179. Arthur Young, *China's Nation-building Effort, 1927–1937*, 400.

180. Philip Huang, *The Peasant Family and Rural Development in the Yangzi Delta, 1350–1988*, 11.

181. Ramon Myers, *The Chinese Peasant Economy*, 15–17, 292–293.

182. Thomas Rawski, *Economic Growth in Prewar China*, 268, 320.

183. Loren Brandt, *Commercialization and Agricultural Development*, 132, 169–167, 171.

184. David Faure, *The Rural Economy of Pre-Liberation China*.

185. See Thomas Wiens, "Trends in the Late Qing and Republican Rural Economy: Reality or Illusion?," 63; and Philip Huang, "The Study of Rural China's Economic History" for discussion.

186. Huang Kan, "Ai pinmin," 786.

187. Wen Shan, *Xiangcun de huoyan*, 10, 21–22.

188. Hong Shen, "Pinmin canju," 2, 53–54.

189. Liang Shuming, "Shandong xiangcun jianshe yanjiuyuan sheli zhiqu ji banfa gaiyao," 226.

190. Ibid., 227–228.

191. Yan Yangchu, "Pingmin jiaoyu xin yundong," 32.

192. Zhou Shizhao, "Xiangjiang de nuhou," 100.

193. Peng Pai, "Laodongzhe tongqinghui de yuanqi," 1.

194. Li Dazhao, "Qingnian yu nongcun," 180.

195. Peng Pai, "Haifeng nongmin yundong," 110–111.

196. Fei Xiaotong, *Xiangtu Zhongguo*, 14.

197. For discussions see Huadong shifan daxue, *Zhongguo xiandai jiaoyu shi*, 34–36.

198. Wu Bannong, "Lun 'Dingxian zhuyi'"; Qian Jiaju, "Dingxian de shiyan yundong neng jiejue Zhongguo nongcun wenti ma?"

199. It should be mentioned that the anarchist peasant revolution is different from the later Communist peasant revolution. The anarchists wanted to eliminate private landownership and build a Communist system, but they planned to achieve this through peaceful means and were against peasant armed forces and a peasant regime. As a result, they tended to emphasize the power of resistance rather than the power of violence of the peasantry.

200. Liu Shipei, "Wuzhengfu geming yu nongmin geming." For further discussions, see Peter Zarrow, *Anarchism and Chinese Political Culture*, 106–108; Arif Dirlik, *Anarchism in the Chinese Revolution*, 103–104.

201. Wang Chengren and Bai Shengxiang, "Shilun xinhaigeming shiqi zichanjieji gemingpai dui nongmin de fadong he lingdao," 36, 38.

202. Many Communist leaders were influenced by the peasant rebellions taking place in their native communities. See Peng Pai, "Haifeng nongmin yundong," 102; Edgar Snow, *Red Star Over China*, 135–136; Zhang Guotao, *The Rise of the Chinese Communist Party*, 1–15; Agnes Smedley, *The Great Road: The Life and Times of Chu Teh*, 22–29.

203. Baihuadaoren [Linxie], "Guomin yijian shu," 921.

204. Li Dazhao, "Biange de yuandongli," 534.

205. Chen Duxiu, "Zhongguo guomin geming yu shehui ge jieji," 563.

206. Robert Marks, *Rural Revolution in South China*, 217.

207. *Jiefang qian de Zhongguo nongcun*, 108.

208. Leonard Hsu, *Sun Yat-sen: His Political and Social Ideals*, 131–132.

209. "Madame Sun Withdraws from Politics." *The China Weekly Review* (July 30, 1927), 22. In Song Qingling, *The Struggle for New China*.

210. *Fang Zhimin wenji*, 390.

211. Fang Zhimin, "Kusheng," 362–363.

212. Fang Zhimin, "Wo Congshi geming douzheng de lueshu," 15.

213. The differences and connections between the active, spontaneous, and popular awakening of the nationalist intellectuals and the passive, Machiavellian, and systematic awakening of the masses in the nation-building movements in colonial states were first explored by Benedict Anderson in his *Imagined Communities* (113–114, 163). John Fitzgerald, in *Awakening China,* analyzes how these two processes worked in China during the Nationalist Revolution. In *What Is to be Done*, Lenin expressed similar views about the awakening of class consciousness: workers and peasants, if left to their own, could only develop trade-union consciousness and petty-bourgeois demands for land respectively; therefore, the intellectuals would have to lead the revolution on behalf of the workers and the peasants.

214. See Luo Baoshan and Sang Bing, "Minzu zichanjieji yu Yihetuan yundong," 475–476.

215. *Jiefangqian de Zhongguo nongcun*, 108.

216. "Peng Pai gei Li Chuntao" (1922,11,18; 1923,7,19; 1923,7,30); "Peng Pai gei Liu Renjing" (1924,1,20).

217. "Lun Zhongguo yi zuzhi laomin xiehui"; "Zhang Ji jun you Lundun laihan."

218. Sun Zhongshan, "Nongmin dalianhe," 716.

219. Sun Zhongshan, "Genzhe yao you qi tian," 719–723.

220. See Liao Zhongkai "Nongmin yundong suodang zhuyi zhi yaodian," 698; "Nongmin jiefang de fangfa," 706; Angus W. McDonald, Jr., *The Urban Origins of Rural Revolution,* 260; Chen Gongbo, "Nongmin yundong zai Zhongguo guomin geming de diwei," 701.

221. Keith Schoppa, *Blood Road,* 213, 215.

222. Liang Shuming, "Xiangcun jianshe dayi," 616–162; *Xiangcun jianshe lilun,* 495.

223. Yan Yangchu, "Zhonghua pingmin jiaoyu cujinhui Dingxian gongzuo dagai," 247.

224. Yan Yangchu, "Zhi Cai Tinggan," 44.

225. Cai Hesen, "Cai Linbin Gei Mao Zedong," 53.

226. Qu Qiubai, "Guomin geming zhong zhi nongmin wenti," 390–391.

227. Fang Zhimin, "Zai Jiangxi diyici quansheng nongmin daibiao dahui shang de kaimuci," 219.

228. Zhou Enlai, "Jianjue suqing dangnei yiqie fei wuchanjieji de yishi," 8–9.

229. Zhou Enlai, "Zhonggong zhongyang gei Hongsijun qianwei de zhishi," 37.

230. Zhou Enlai, "Zai Zhonghua quanguo wenyi gongzuozhe daibiao dahui shang de zhengzhi baogao," 348-349.

231. Mao Dun, "Wang Tongzhao de Shanyu," 557–569.

232. Maurice Meisner, *Li Ta-chao and the Origins of Chinese Marxism*, 149.

233. Quoted in Paul Ransome, *Antonio Gramsci: A New Introduction*, 72. See page 129 for more discussion.

234. John Fitzgerald provides an excellent treatment of the intellectuals' awakening of the general masses of China during the National Revolution in his *Awakening China*.

235. Yu Dafu, "Nongmin wenyi de shizhi," 283.

236. For Sun and Xiong's achievements, see Lao Xiang, *Huangtuni*, 83–99; Yan Yangchu, "Zhongguo pingmin jiaoyu yundong de zongjie," 212–213; "Pingmin jiaoyu yundong de huigu yu qianzhan," 285–287.

237. Yan Yangchu, "Zhongguo pingmin jiaoyu yundong de zongjie," 213–214.

238. This conference was actually held in May 1925, two months after Dr. Sun's death. What Madame Sun referred to in this article must be another conference.

239. "Madame Sun Withdraws from Politics" (July 1927), 220. In Song Chingling, *The Struggle for New China*.

240. Chen Duxiu, "Women duiyu Yihetuan liangge cuowu de guannian," 769–771.

241. Chen Duxiu, "Ershiqi nian yilai guomin yundong zhong suode jiaoxun," 812.

242. Liao Zhongkai, "Gemingdang yingyou de jingshen," 652–653.

243. Li Dazhao, "You jingjishang jieshi Zhongguo jindai sixiang biandong de yuanyin," 436–437.

244. Li Dazhao, "Daying diguozhuyi qinlue Zhongguo shi," 592.

245. Qu Qiubai, "Yihetuan yundong zhi yiyi yu wusa yundong zhi qiantu," 340–353.

246. "Chuangkan de hua" (1926,8,1), *Nongmin yundong*, no. 1.

247. Rong Mengyuan, "Yihetuan fandi yundong."

248. For history of the Red Spear Society, see Elizabeth Perry, *Rebels and Revolutionaries in North China*, chap. 5; and Tai Hsuan-chih, *The Red Spears, 1916–1949*.

249. Elizabeth Perry, *Rebels and Revolutionaries in North China*, 213.

250. Du Xiu [Chen Duxiu], "Hongqianghui yu Zhongguo de nongmin baodong," 1073.

251. Mao Zedong, "An Analysis of the Various Classes among the Chinese Peasantry...," 308.

252. Gu Yuanzeng, "*Diguozhuyi yu diguozhuyi guojia de gongrenjieji yihouji*"; Lu Xun, "Xuejie de sanhun," 207, 211.

253. Gan Naiguang, *Zhongguo Guomindang de jige genben wenti*, 3, 37.

254. Gan Naiguang, "Shui shi guomingeming de zhulijun"; *Zhongguo guomindang de jige genben wenti*, 44–45, 51.

255. Qian Xingtun, "Siqule de Ah Q shidai," 69.

256. Mao Dun, "Du Ni Huanzhi," 197–217.

257. Mao Dun, *Wo zouguo de daolu*, Vol. 2, 738.

258. Qing Jian, "Ah Q shidai meiyou si," 92–93.

259. Lu Xun, "Ah Q zhengzhuan de chengyin," 379.

260. Yi Sheng, "Disanyang shijie de chuangzao—women suo yingdang huanying de Lu Xun," 56–57.

261. Feng Xuefeng, "Geming yu zhishijieji," 86–87, 90.

262. Mao Dun, "Lun Lu Xun de xiaoshuo," 430–438.

263. Mao Dun, "Zhongguo xinwenxue daxi—xiaoshuo yiji daoyan," 485–492.

264. Zheng Chaolin, *An Oppositionist for Life*, 190.

265. The story was published in 1929. For English translation, see Mao Dun, "Mud."

266. Zheng Chaolin, *An Oppositionist for Life*, 190.

267. Mao Dun, "Chuncan"; "Qiushou"; "Candong."

268. Mao Dun, "Dazexiang."

269. Jiang Guangci, *Paoxiao de tudi*.

270. Mao Dun, "Diquan duhougan," 331.

271. Su Xuelin, *Ersanshiniandai zuojia zuopin*, 328.

272. Lu Xun, "Chenying tici," 547.

273. Hong Shen, "Wukuiqiao."

274. Ding Ling, "Gei Daluxinwen bianzhe de xin," 104.

275. Ding Ling, "Tianjiachong"; "Shui."

276. He Danren, "Guanyu xin de xiaoshuo de dansheng—ping Ding Ling de 'shui'," 247.

277. Wu Zuxiang, "Yiqianbabai dan."

278. Wang Tongzhao "Shanyu," 293, 306.

279. Mao Dun, "Du Ni Huanzhi," 199.

280. Ai Qing, "Jiubaige."

281. Ye Zi, "Xiangdao."

282. Ye Zi, "*Fengshou* Xu," 358.

283. *Ye Zi yanjiu ziliao*, 14.

284. *Ye Zi yanjiu ziliao*, 1–2.

285. Ye Zi, "*Fengshou* zixu," 51.

286. Quoted in Tang Jinhai, "Lun Mao Dun wenxue piping de meixue jiazhi," 405–406.

287. William Hinton, *Fanshen*, 11.

288. For portraits of the "old" and "new" peasant created by the woodcarvers, see *Zhongguo xinxing banhua wushinian xuanji*, Vol.1. Representative works include "The Peasant" (Wang Liangjian, 1938); "He (She) Ate the Wrong Tree Leaves" (Wang Li , 1945); "After the Departure of the Rice-tax Collectors" (Li Hua, 1946); "The Commissioner for Relief Coming to the Village" (Lu Tian, 1946); "He Who Can Should Contribute His Labor" (Wo Zha, 1939); "Arise" (Li Hua, 1947); "Voting with Beans" (Yan Han, 1948); "Discussing the Household Plan" (Jiao Xinhe, 1938); "Drink" (Li Qun, 1940); and "Militia" (Wu Lao, 1942).

289. Liang Shuming, "Zhongguo wenti zhi jiejue," 206–220.

290. Peng Pai, "Guanyu Haifeng nongmin yundong de yifengxin," 60.

291. Li Guanyang, "Dui Yan Xishan de pouxi," 78–79.

292. The Chinese word for laborer, kuli, literally means bitter strength.

293. Yan Yangchu, "Guanyu pingmin jiaoyu jingshen de jianghua," 83.

294. Yan Yangchu, "Guanyu pingmin jiaoyu jingshen de jianghua," 89; "Zhonghua pingmin jiaoyu cujinhui Dingxian shiyan gongzuo baogao," 308.

295. Yan Yangchu, "Pingmin jiaoyu gailun," 89.

296. Yan Yangchu, "Zhi Cao Yanshen," 215–216; "Nongcun jianshe yaoyi," 38–47.

297. Fei Xiaotong, *Wo zhi yinian*, 6–8.

298. For discussions on populism or populist element in the thought of Chinese intellectuals, see V. I. Lenin, "Democracy and Narodism in China"; Benjamin Schwartz, "The Intelligentsia in Communist China"; Stuart Schram, *The Political Thought of Mao Tse-tung*, 79–80; Maurice Meisner, *Li Ta-chao and the Origins of Chinese Marxism*, 197–210; Daniel Kwok, "Mao Tse-tung and Populism"; Charles Hayford, *To the People*, xiv–xv; Kamal Sheel, *Peasant Society and Marxist Intellectuals in China*, 165; Hu Qiaomu, "Jinian Zhongguo gongchanzhuyi yundong de weida xianqu Li Dazhao."

299. Maurice Meisner, *Li ta-chao and the Origins of Chinese Marxism*, 197–210.

300. Kamal Sheel, *Peasant Society and Marxist Intellectuals in China*, 165.

301. Benjamin Schwartz, "The Intelligentsia in Communist China: A Tentative Comparison," 175.

302. Edgar Snow, *Red Star over China*, 71.

NOTES TO CHAPTER FOUR

1. He Ganzhi, *Zhongguo shehui xingzhi wenti lunzhan*, 57–59.

2. Preface to the Third Edition, *Zhongguo shehuishi de lunzhan*, Vol. 1.

3. Tao Zhifu [Qian Junrui], "Zhongguo nongcun shehui xingzhi yu nongye gaizao wenti," 3.

4. *Selected Works of Mao Tse-tung*, Vol. 2, 315.

5. For eyewitness accounts about how the Nationalist politicians and army officers changed their views of the Communists, the United Front, and the revolution, because of the rise of peasant power, see Gong Chu, *Wo yu Hongjun*, 47; Zheng Chaolin, *An Oppositionist for Life*, 130–131, 185; Aleksei Vasilevich Blagodatov, *Zhongguo geming zhaji: 1925–1927*, 177; Zhou Enlai, "Guanyu yijiuersi zhi yijiuerliu nian dang dui Guomindang de guanxi," 117; Hua Gang, *Zhongguo dageming shi*, 276; Chen Gongbo, *Kuxiaolu*, Vol. 1, 122–123; Wei Zhen, "'Marishibian' qinliji." For academic discussions of the issue, see Jiang Yongjing, *Baoluoting yu Wu Han zhengquan*, 311; Lei Xiaocen, *Sanshinian dongluan Zhongguo*, 76; Wu Tien-wei, "A Review of the Wuhan Debacle," 132; Harold Issacs, *The Tragedy of the Chinese Revolution*, 214; Robert North and Xenia Eudin, *M. N. Roy's Mission to China*, 97–98, 118.

6. For more information, see Wang Lixi, "Zhongguo shehuishi lunzhan xumu," and Zheng Xuejia, *Shehuishi lunzhan de qiyin he neirong*, 100–101.

7. Wang Yanan, *Zhongguo banfengjian banzhimindi jingjixingtai yanjiu*.

8. For a thorough review of the debate, see Liu Zhenlan, "Jindai Zhongguo shehui xingzhi shuping."

9. Zhang Dongsun, "You neidi luxing erde zhi you yi jiaoxun." Zhang's other writings on this topic included "Dajia xu qieji Luosu xiansheng gei women de zhonggao"; "Da Gao Jiansi shu"; "Changqi de rennai"; "Zaida Songhua xiong"; "Tamen yu women"; "Zhi Duxiu de xin," and "Xianzai yu jianglai."

10. Zhang Dongsun, "Women weishemo jiang shehuizhuyi."

11. Mao Dun, *Wo zouguo de daolu*, Vol. 1, 116.

12. Zhang Dongsun, "Zaida Songhua xiong."

13. Ibid.

14. For more information about the organizations, see Li Xisuo and Yuan Qing, *Liang Qichao zhuan*, 458–460; Deng Mingyan, *Liang Qichao de shengping ji zhengzhi sixiang*, 93–94.

15. Zhang Dongsun, "Zaida Songhua xiong."

16. Zhang Dongsun, "Xianzai yu jianglai."

17. Liang Qichao, "Fu Zhang Dongsun shu lun shehuizhuyi yundong."

18. Besides his reply to Zhang Dongson, Liang Qichao's writings on that topic also include: "Lishishang Zhonghua guomin shiye zhi chengbai ji jinhou gaijin zhi jiyun" and "Wuqiang jieji dui youqiang jieji." For further discussions, see Meng Xiangcai, *Liang Qichao zhuan*, 277–280; Li Xisuo and Yuan Qing, *Liang Qichao zhuan*, 461–469.

19. Chen Duxiu, "Fu Dongsun xiansheng de xin," 213–214.

20. Li Ji, "Shehuizhuyi yu Zhongguo."

21. Li Da, "Taolun shehuizhuyi bin zhi Liang Rengong."

22. Cai Hesen, "Makesi xueshuo yu Zhongguo wuchanjieji," 75.

23. Cai Hesen, "Makesi xueshuo yu Zhongguo wuchanjieji," 78–79.

24. Li Dazhao, "Zhongguo de shehuizhuyi yu shijie de zibenzhuyi," 603–604. See Jonathen Spence, *The Search for Modern China*, 307–308, for more discussion.

25. Han Jun [Li Hanjun], "Jin le bu le!"

26. Li Rui, *Zaonian Mao Zedong*, 350–351.

27. Mao Zedong, "Letter to Xiao Xudong, Cai Linbin and the Other Members in France," 5–10.

28. Quoted in Robert Marks, *Rural Revolution in Southern China*, 168.

29. Li Chuntao, "Haifeng nongmin yundong jiqi zhidaozhe Peng Pai," 314.

30. *Zhonggong zhongyang wenjian xuanji*, Vol. 1, 3.

31. *Zhonggong zhongyang wenjian xuanji*, Vol. 1, 61–62.

32. Li Dazhao, "Shehuizhuyi xia zhi shiye," 617–618.

33. A brief official evaluation of the debate was offered in *Wusi shiqi qikan jieshao*, Vol. 1, 24. A more recent assessment of the debate was provided by Lei Yi in his "Zhongguo nongcun shehui xingzhi lunzhan yu xinminzhu zhuyi lilun de xingcheng."

34. Li Da, "Taolun shehuizhuyi bin zhi Liang Rengong."

35. Benjamin Schwartz, *Chinese Communism and the Rise of Mao*, 29.

36. The other two issues concerned the development of the Soviet Union itself and the Anglo-Soviet Trade Union Committee, respectively.

37. Joshua Fogel, "The Debates over the Asiatic Mode of Production in Soviet Russia, China, and Japan," 43–44.

38. For more discussions about the Asiatic mode of production in China, see Arif Dirlik, *Revolution and History: The Origins of Marxist Historiography in China 1919–1937*; Joshua Fogel, "The Debates over the Asiatic Mode of Production in Soviet Russia, China, and Japan;" Timothy Brook, ed. *The Asiatic Mode of Production in China*; Sun Chengshu, *Dakai dongfang shehui mimi de yaoshi*.

39. Karl Radek, *Zhongguo geming yundong shi.* Cited in Wang Yichang, "Zhongguo shehuishi lunshi."

40. Leon Trotsky, *Leon Trotsky on China*, 263–264, 303, 324–325.

41. In Mazhaya'er [Madjar], *Zhongguo nongcun jingji yanjiu*, translator's note, 1–22.

42. Joshua Fogel, "The Debates over the Asiatic Mode of Production in Soviet Russia, China, and Japan." 46; see also Karl Wittfogel, *Oriental Despotism, A Comparative Study of Total Power*, 402.

43. Lin Ganquan, Tian Renlong, and Li Zude, *Zhongguo gudaishi fenqi taolun wushinian*, 24.

44. Mazhaya'er [Madjar], *Zhongguo nongcun jingji yanjiu*, 12–13.

45. "Talk with Students of the Sun Yat-sen University" (1927,5,13), 245.

46. For Trotsky's views, see "Trotsky's Second Letter to Preobrazhensky" (late April 1928), in *Leon Trotsky on China*, 281; "Summary and Perspectives of the Chinese Revolution (June 1928)," in Ibid., 303–304; "Manifesto on China of the International Left Opposition" (September 1930), in Ibid., 482.

47. Joshua Fogel, "The Debates over the Asiatic Mode of Production in Soviet Russia, China, and Japan," 43, 60–61.

48. Harold Isaacs expounded the theory in his *The Tradedy of the Chinese Revolution.*

49. For more discussions, see Alexandre Pantsov and Gregor Benton, "Did Leon Trotsky Oppose the CCP Joining the Guomindang 'From the First'?"; Gregor Benton, *China's Urban Revolutionaries*, 9–12.

50. Chen Duxiu, "Women xianzai weishemo zhengdou," 1106–1107.

51. Li Da, *Xiandai shehuixue*, 358, 360–363.

52. Mao Zedong, "Analysis of All the Classes in Chinese Society," 249–262.

53. Mao Zedong, "An Analysis of the Various Classes among the Chinese Peasantry," 303–309.

54. Mao Zedong, "The National Revolution and the Peasant Movement," 387–389.

55. Gan Naiguang, *Zhonguo guomindang jige genben wenti*, 26, 30, 44.

56. Bai Yu, "Chusheng shijia er aixi yumao de Guxiansheng," 16.

57. See Li Shouyong, "Guxiansheng zaonian zai beida de yixie huiyi," 13–14; Tao Xisheng, "Ji Gu Mengyu xiansheng," 29.

58. Gongsun Yuzhi et al., eds., *Zhongguo nongmin ji gengdi wenti*, 14.

59. Ibid., 54.

60. Chen Gongbo, *Kuxiaolu*, 180.

61. For discussions about the differences between *Geming pinglun* and *Qianjin*, see He Hanwen, "Gaizupai huiyilu," 167–168; Fan Yusui, "Wo suo zhidao de gaizupai," 215; Chen Gongbo, *Kuxiaolu*, Vol. 1, 188.

62. Chen Gongbo, "Zhongguo guomindang suo daibiao de shi shemo," 190.

63. Chen Gongbo, "Jinhou de Guomindang."

64. Chen Gongbo, "Jinhou de Guomindang."

65. Qin Yingjun and Zhang Zhanbin, eds., *Dalang taosha*, 437. See also Zhou Fohai, "Shengshuai yuejin hua cangsang," 195.

66. Fang Qiuwei, "Tao Xisheng yu Didiao julebu, Yiwen yanjiuhui," 127.

67. Chen Gongbo, "Wo yu Gongchandang," 84.

68. Tao Xisheng, *Chaoliu yu diandi*, 96.

69. Tao Xisheng, "Bashi zishu," 149.

70. Tao Xisheng, *Chaoliu yu diandi*, 109–110.

71. Tao Xisheng, *Zhongguo shehui zhi shi de fenxi*, 10, 26.

72. Li Ji, "Duiyu Zhongguo shehuishi lunzhan de gongxian yu piping(2)."

73. Jian Bozan, *Lishi zhexue jiaocheng*, 288–289.

74. Tao Xisheng, *Zhongguo shehui zhi shi de fenxi*, 26, 31, 136. For a critical review of Tao's book, see Li Ji, "Duiyu Zhongguo shehuishi lunzhan de gongxian yu piping(2)."

75. Tao Xisheng, *Chaoliu yu diandi*, 145.

76. Tao Xisheng, "Bashi zishu," 149; "Taiwan ban jiaohouji." In *Zhongguo shehui zhi shi de fenxi*.

77. For the Trotskyite criticism of Tao Xisheng, see Li Ji, "Duiyu Zhongguo shehuishi lunzhan de gongxian yu piping(2)." For the Stalinist criticism, see Qiu Xu, "Zhongguo de shehui daodi shi shemo shehui."

78. Gregor Benton, *China's Urban Revolutionaries*, 21–24; Zheng Chaolin, "Chen Duxiu and the Trotskyists," 157.

79. Wang Fan-hsi, *Memoirs of a Chinese Revolutionary*, 77.

80. For controversy over when the group was formed, see Gregor Benton, *China's Urban Revolutionaries*, 29; Pu Qingquan, "Zhongguo tuopai de chansheng he xiaowang," 83–84.

81. There are different stories about how Chen Duxiu received Trotsky's writings. See Pu Qingquan, "Wo suo zhidao de Chen Duxiu"; "Zhongguo tuopai de chansheng he xiaowang." Zheng Chaolin, "Chen Duxiu and the Trotskyists," 146–147.

82. Pu Qingquan, "Wo suo zhidao de Chen Duxiu," 36–37; and "Zhongguo tuopai de chansheng he xiaowang," 84–85; Chen Duxiu, "Women de zhengzhi

yijianshu," 106–137; Zheng Chaolin, *An Oppositionist for Life,* 244; and "Chen Duxiu and the Trotskyists," 146–147.

83. Liu Renjing, "Liu Renjing tan tuoluosijipai zai Zhongguo," 232–233; Pu Qingquan, "Zhongguo tuopai de chansheng he xiaowang," 86–89. Each provides a different date.

84. Wang Fanxi, *Memoirs of a Chinese Revolutionary,* 136–137.

85. Zheng Chaolin, "Chen Duxiu and the Trotskyists," 187–188.

86. Chen Duxiu, "Guanyu Zhongguo geming wenti zhi zhonggong zhong-yang xin," 37–57.

87. Chen Duxiu, "Women de zhengzhi yijianshu," 117.

88. Yan later defected to the Guomindang and moved to Taiwan after 1949.

89. There was much speculation about Ren Shu's identity after his book was published. See Yan Lingfeng, "Guanyu Ren Shu, Zhu Xinfan ji qita"; Dai Zhixian, *Shinian neizhan shiqi de geming wenhua yundong,* 163; Qin Yingjun and Zhang Zhanbin, *Dalang taosha,* 382; Wang Xuewen, "Sanshiniandai Shanghai wenhua zhanxian de yixie douzheng qingkuang,"49; and Zheng Chaolin, "Chen Duxiu and the Trotskyists," 136.

90. Yan Lingfeng, "Guanyu Ren Shu, Zhu Xinfan Ji qita"; Zheng Chaolin, *An Oppositionist for Life,* 213.

91. Quoted in Gregor Benton, *China's Urban Revolutionaries,* 104.

92. *Zhonggong zhongyang wenjian xuanji,* Vol. 4, 298–299.

93. For example, in late 1927, the party still defined the Chinese social-eco-nomic system as the Asiatic mode of production. See *Zhonggong zhongyang wenjian xuanji,* Vol. 3, 487–503.

94. Cai Hesen, "Zhongguo geming de xingzhi jiqi qiantu," 789.

95. In *Jiefangqian de Zhongguo nongcun,* Vol. 1, 40.

96. Li San [Li Lisan], "Zhongguo geming de gengben wenti."

97. Pan Dongzhou was Li Lisan's secretary at that time. He and Xiang Shengwu were later executed by the Nationalists. The other three survived and became prominent theoreticians of the party after 1949.

98. He Ganzhi, *Zhongguo shehui xingzhi wenti lunzhan,* 60.

99. Pan Dongzhou, "Zhongguo jingji de xingzhi."

100. Li Da, *Shehui zhi jichu zhishi,* 558.

101. Suzanne Bernard, "An Interview with Mao Dun."

102. Mao Dun, *Wo zouguo de daolu,* Vol. 2, 83.

103. Mao Dun, "Ziye shi zenyang xiecheng de,"55; "Ziye houji," 553.

104. Mao Dun, "Ziye houji," 553.

105. Suzanne Bernard, "An Interview with Mao Dun."

106. Du Ai, "Daonian weida zuojia Mao Dun xiansheng," 266.

107. See *Tan Pingshan yanjiu ziliao*, 253–254, 271–276; Hua Gang, *Zhongguo dageming shi*, 343–344; Zhou Enlai, "Guanyu dangde liuda de yanjiu," 166.

108. Tao Xisheng, *Chaoliu yu diandi*, 90; and "Guanyu Duxiu de san duan shi," 20–21; Angus W. McDonald, Jr., *The Urban Origins of Rural Revolution*, 290–292.

109. Deng Yanda, "Zhengzhi zhuzhang," 213–219.

110. In *Fujian shibian dangan ziliao*, 36.

111. Wang had also been involved in the peasant movement and once worked for Mao. See Roy Hofheinz, Jr., *The Broken Wave*, 90–91; and *Xiandai shiliao*, Vol. 4, 73–74.

112. Some Chinese Trotskyites claimed that *Dushu zazhi* was the successor of *Dongli* and hence was also a Trotskyite journal (see Chen Bilan, "Huigu wo he Peng Shuzhi de suiyue," 20; and Gregor Benton, *China's Urban Revolutionaries*, 106). Both *Dongli* and *Dushu zazhi* were published by Chen Mingshu's Shenzhou Guoguang Press. The Trotskyite Yan Lingfeng regarded it as the journal of Shengzhou Guoguang Press rather than the Trotskyite organization. See Yan Lingfeng, "Guanyu Ren Shu, Zhu Xinfan ji qita."

113. Wang Lixi and Lu Jingqing, "Disanban juantouyan."

114. Wang Fan-hsi, *Memoirs of a Chinese Revolutionary*, 160.

115. Other journals that also covered the debate included *Feng Tai, Wenshi* [Literature & History], *Sanmin banyuekan* [Three Principles of the People Biweekly], *Chenbao* [Morning News], and *Yishibao* in Beijing, Tianjin, and other places.

116. Zheng Xuejia, *Shehuishi lunzhan de qiyin he neirong*, 19–20; Chen Bilan, "Huigu wo he Peng Shuzhi de suiyue," 20.

117. Wang Xuewen, "Sanshi niandai Shanghai wenhua zhanxian de yixie douzheng qingkuang," 50.

118. *Zhongguo shehuishi de lunzhan*, Vol. 1.

119. Fang Qiuwei, "Tao Xisheng yu didiao julebu, yiwenyanjiuhui," 127–128.

120. Wang Yichang, "Zhongguo shehuishi duanlun."

121. Li Ang, *Hongse wutai*, 5, 98. There is no evidence to prove his claims, but he was a former Communist and a participant in the Nanchang Uprising of 1927. Liu Han, "Nanchang Qiyi canjiazhe," 141.

122. For Zhu Xinfan's background, see Yan Lingfeng, "Guanyu Ren Shu, Zhu Xinfan ji qita."

123. *Xiandai shiliao*, Vol. 1, 278–279; Gao Jun, "Zhongguo shehui xingzhi wenti de lunzhan," 9.

124. Chen's experience with the CCP was well known. For Tao Xisheng's experience with the CCP, see Mao Dun, *Wo zouguo de daolu*, Vol.1, 278; Tao Xisheng, *Chaoliu yu diandi*, 100, 112.

125. See Tao Xisheng, *Chaoliu yu diandi*, 100; Madam Sun Yat-sen, Eugene Chen (Chen Youren), and Deng Yanda, "Dui Zhongguo ji shijie geming minzhong de xuanyan."

126. Angus W. McDonald, *The Urban Origins of Rural Revolution*, 264.

127. Lin Ganquan, Tian Renlong, and Li Zude, *Zhongguo gudaishi fenqi taolun wushinian*, 58–69.

128. Chen Duxiu, "Women de zhengzhi yijianshu," 116.

129. Li Ji, "Duiyu Zhongguo shehuishi lunzhan de gongxian yu piping(2)."

130. Wang Yichang, "Zhongguo shehuishi lunshi."

131. Hu Nai'an, "Haoshouronggui Gu Mengyu," 31.

132. Jing Yuan [Liu Renjing], "Ping liangben lun Zhongguo jingji de zhuzuo."

133. For a recent analysis of the concept of feudalism in twentieth-century China, see Arif Dirlik, "'Feudalism' in twentieth Century Chinese Historiography."

134. See Tao Xisheng, *Chaoliu yu diandi*, 129.

135. He Ganzhi, *Zhongguo shehui xingzhi wenti lunzhan*, 5; Sun Zhuozhang, "Zhongguo jingji de fenxi."

136. According to his recollections, he became interested in the peasant problem after a talk with Cai Hesen in early 1927. See Chen Hansheng, *Sige shidai de wo*, 36.

137. Chen Hansheng, *Sige shidai de wo*, 40.

138. For the activities of the Communist Party in the institute, see Zhang Jiafu, "Genshen yishi (1)."

139. Chen Hansheng, "Zhuiyi wuyou Yang Xingfo," 65; *Sige shidai de wo*, 57–58.

140. Tao Zhifu [Qian Junrui], "Zhongguo nongcun shehui xingzhi yu nongye gaizao wenti," 5–7.

141. Xue Muqiao, "Yanjiu Zhongguo nongcun jingji de fangfa wenti," 36.

142. Yu Lin, "Zhongguo nongcun shehui xingzhi wenda," 5–7.

143. Wang Yichang, "Lun xianjieduan de Zhongguo nongcun jingji yanjiu," 99.

144. *Zhongguo nongcun*, 1(1):103; for more discussion, see Xue Muqiao, "Yanjiu Zhongguo nongcun jingji de fangfa wenti," 41–42.

145. Wang Yichang, "Lun xianjieduan de Zhongguo nongcun jingji yanjiu," 99.

146. For more information about the debate on rent, see Zhang Wentian, "Zhongguo geming jiben wenti," 411; He Ganzhi, *Zhongguo shehui xingzhi wenti lunzhan*, 21–22.

147. Wang Jingbo, "Guanyu Zhongguo nongcun wenti yanjiu zhi shishu," 51.

148. Tao Zhifu [Qian Junrui], "Zhongguo nongcun shehui xingzhi yu nongye gaizao wenti," 17; Zhou Bin, "Zhongguo nongcun jingji xingzhi wenti de taolun," 6.

149. Yu Lin, "Zhongguo nongcun shehui xingzhi wenda," 11; Xue Muqiao, "Zenyang yanjiu Zhongguo nongcun jingji," 31–32; Qian Junrui, "Zhongguo muxia de nongye konghuang," 9.

150. Xue Muqiao, "Zenyang yanjiu Zhongguo nongcun jingji," 28–32; *Zhongguo nongcun*, 1(1):2.

151. Wang Yichang, "Lun xianjieduan de Zhongguo nongcun jingji yanjiu."

152. Wang Jingbo, "Guanyu Zhongguo nongcun wenti de yanjiu zhi shishu."

153. Wang Yichang, "Lun xianjieduan de Zhongguo nongcun jingji yanjiu," 97.

154. Qian Junrui, "Xianjieduan Zhongguo nongcun jingji yanjiu de renwu," 13. The two articles he criticized were Wang Yichang, "Nongcun jingji tongji yingyou de fangxiang zhuanhuan," and Han Dezhang, "Yanjiu nongye jingji suo yudao de jishu wenti." For Qian Junrui' and Wang Yichang's reviews of Buck's and Chen's works, see Qian Junrui, "Ping Pukai jiaoshou suozhu Zhongguo nongchang jingji"; "Ping Chen Hansheng xiansheng zhu xianjin Zhongguo de tudi wenti"; Wang Yichang, "Ping Guangdong nongcun shengchanguanxi yu shengchanli."

155. Qian Mu, *Guoshidagang yinlun*, 18–19.

156. See discussion in Yu Yingshi, *Qian Mu Yu Zhongguo wenhua*, 46–48.

157. Hu Shih & Lin Yu-tang, *China's Own Critics: A Selection of Essays*, 12.

158. Hu Shih, "Historical Foundations for a Democratic China (March 12, 1941)," 57.

159. For examples of such accusation, see Li Da, "Pipan Fei Xiaotong de maiban shehuixue"; Xia Kangnong, "Yizhu ducao de jiepo." The critics argued that although Liang was the representative of the landlords and Fei the representative of the bourgeoisie, their views about the nature of Chinese rural society were the same.

160. Fei Xiaotong, *Lucun nongtian*, 191. Quoted in James P. McGough, *Fei Hsiao-tung*, 110.

161. Zheng Xuejia later remarked that the debate of social history was the "exhibition of the cultural products of the May Fourth Movement." See Zheng Xuejia, *Shehuishi lunzhan de qiyin he neirong*, 1.

NOTES TO CHAPTER FIVE

1. Edgar Snow, *Red Star over China*, 142.

2. Siao Yu [Xiao Yu], *Mao Tse-tung and I Were Beggars*, 6–7.

3. Li Rui, *Zaonian Mao Zedong*, 4, 6–7, 508.

4. Mao Zedong, "Talks at the Yenan Forum on Literature and Art," 73.

5. Mao Zedong, "Letter to Li Jinxi," 135.

6. For reasons and dates of Mao's visit to Shaoshan, see Li Jui, *The Early Revolutionary Activities of Comrade Mao Tse-tung*, 281; Edgar Snow, *Red Star over China*, 159.

7. Zhou Enlai, "Guanyu dang de liuda de yanjiu," 179; "Xuexi Mao Zedong," 333.

8. For Mao's early perceptions and views of the peasant, See Edgar Snow, *Red Star over China*, 133–135; Mao Zedong, "Letter to Li Jinxi," 131; and Li Rui, *Zaonian Mao Zedong*, appendix.

9. Stuart Schram, *The Political Thought of Mao Tse-tung*, 27. See also Stephen Uhalley, *Mao Tse-tung, A Critical Biography*, 27–29, for further discussion.

10. For Mao's views of the peasant in 1922 and 1923, see Zhang Guotao, *The Rise of the Chinese Communist Party*, Vol. 1, 309–310; Li Jui, *The Early Revolutionary Activities of Comrade Mao Tse-tung*, and Schram's introduction.

11. For the rural connections of Lu Xun's family, see Lu Xun, "Eyiben Ah Q zhengzhuan xu ji zhuzhe zixu zhuanlue."

12. Lu Xun, *Diary of a Madman and Other Stories*, 89–100.

13. Fei Xiaotong, "Sunshi chongxi xia de xiangtu," 50.

14. Qin Yingjun and Zhang Dezhan, eds., *Dalang taosha*.

15. Li Rui, *Zaonian Mao Zedong*, 159.

16. Soong Ching Ling, *The Struggle for New China*, 3–4.

17. Chen Zhuofan, "Wo suo zhidao de Deng Yanda," 182.

18. *Tao Xingzhi quanji*, 671.

19. Chen Xinde, "Wei Baqun," 188.

20. *Hunan geming lieshi zhuan*, 111–113; Liu Yuansheng et al., "Shuikoushan shang de hongqi," 303–340.

21. Yuan Bangjian, "Ruan Xiaoxian," 306–307; Zeng Bingrong, "Lijin jianxian weiwu buqu," 63–86.

22. Miao Min, *Fang Zhimin zhandou de yisheng*, 33.

23. Zheng Chaolin, *An Oppositionist for Life*, 205.

24. Zhang Wentao, *Heiqi zhimeng*, 134.

25. Yun Daiying, "Nongcun yundong," 559–561.

26. Ruan Xiaoxian, "Gei tuanzhongyang de liangge baogao,"145.

27. Yuan Bangjian, "Ruan Xiaoxian," 317; Ruan Yingqi, Deng Rongshi, and Yang Jiesheng, "Huang Xuezeng," 205. According to Gong Chu, after Chiang Kai-shek's coup in April 1927, the CCP divided Guangdong into four regions and designated the following four Communists to lead the peasant movement in each region: Peng Pai—eastern region; Huang Xuezeng—southern region; Zhou Qijian—western

region; Gong Chu—northern region. All were natives of the regions in which they were stationed. Gong Chu, *Wo yu hongjun*, 40.

28. Roy Hofheinz, *The Broken Wave*, 181–183.

29. Gong Chu, *Wo yu hongjun*, 22.

30. *Qiongya zongdui shi*, 3.

31. Jiang Jilin and Wang Bingshu, "Liao Mengqiao," 128–129.

32. Chen Qihan, "Xingguo de chuqi geming douzheng," 407.

33. Zhou Chengzhong and Zhang Rixin, "Hu Hai," 122.

34. Xia Daohan, "Gu Bai."

35. Li Tao, "Yi gongnong gemingjun di'ershi diyituan," 107.

36. Li Zhongkai and Xie Zhiqiang, "Liu Shiqi," 97.

37. Gu Zhibiao, "Hongjiaguan juyi," 165.

38. For example, the peasant movement in Hunan was largely initiated by the twenty-nine graduates of the institute who returned to Hunan in August 1925. See Ruan Xiaoxian, "Quanguo nongmin yundong xingshi jiqi zai guomin geming zhong de diwei," 287.

39. Chapman, H. *The Chinese Revolution, 1926–1927*, 11-12. Quoted in Galbiati Fernando, *Peng Pai and the Hai-Lu-Feng Soviet*, 117.

40. Sources: Chen Geng: Shao Shiping, Wang Jinxiang, and Hu Delan, "Min-Zhe-Gan-Wan (Gandongbei) dangshi," 218; Fu Bocui: Lu Xiuqi, "Jiushi laoweng chongrudang—Ji Fu Bocui de kanke daolu"; Hang Gaoren: Xu Binru, "Huiyi Wuxi qiushou baodong"; Li Jiajun: Wang Weizhou, "Chuandong youjijun de douzheng," and Wang Yongqing, "Li Jiajun"; Wang Bolu and Zhang Yanwu: Odoric Y. K. Wou & Wang Quanying, "Rural Mobilization in Time of Political Adversity: The Autumn Harvest Uprising in Southern Henan"; Wang Weizhou, "Wo de Huiyi"; Zhang Shanming: Liu Han et al., "Zhang Shanming"; Zhou Juanzhi: "Zhou Juanzhi," in Li Peng et al., *Anhui lidai mingren*. For all others, see Sun Pufang and Yao Renjuan, "Tudi geming shiqi wuzhuang qiyi de zhuyao lingdaoren jianjie"; *Zhonggong dangshi renwu zhuan*, Vols. 1–60; *Buqu de gongchandangren*, 5 vols.

41. For discussions, see Wang Minzhao, "Yiqie yikao dang he qunzhong"; Nie Rongzhen, "Nanchang qiyi de lishi yiyi he jingyan jiaoxun," 13–14; Ye Jianying, "Dageming shibai yu Guangzhou qiyi," 201.

42. Zhang Yunyi, "Baise qiyi yu hongqijun de jianli," 858.

43. See Keith Schoppa, *Blood Road,* for further discussion about Shen's involvement in national and provincial politics.

44. Deng Zihui and Zhang Dingcheng, "Minxi baodong yu hong ershi jun," 383, 388–389, 395; *Xiandai shiliao*, Vol. 4, 139–140; Lu Xiuqi, "Jiushi laoweng chong rudang."

45. The woman writer Xie Bingying, after paying a visit to Jiaoyang, described Fu as a local despot supported by everyone in the area. See Xie Bingying, *Nubing zizhuan*, 370-375.

46. Wang Shifan, "Xichuan gongzuo baogao," 373.

47. Zhang Xin, "Elite Activism in the Periphery: The Case of Southwest Henan," 78.

48. Yan Yangchu, "Zhi J. A. Jinsboli," 282–283.

49. Yan Yangchu originally planned to start his mass education program in Sichuan—his birthplace—but his superior in the YMCA persuaded him to choose a place near Shanghai. Wu Xiangxiang, *Yan Yangchu zhuan*, 38. During the Anti-Japanese War, Yan moved his base to Sichuan.

50. Sidney D. Gamble, *Ting Hsien, A North China Rural Community*, 147–148.

51. Yan Yangchu, "You wenhua de Zhongguo xin nongmin," 143; "Zhi Ding Shujing," 34. In 1925, Yan was thinking of establishing his base in Wanping of Beijing or Huolu of Hebei. See Yan Yangchu, "Zhi Wang Zhendong deng," 13.

52. Yan Yangchu, "Pingmin jiaoyu yundong de huigu yu qianzhan," 288.

53. Fei Hsiao-tung, *Peasant Life in China*, xiii.

54. Fei Xiaotong, "Chongdu *Jiangcun jingji* xuyan," 6.

55. Yang Mao-chun [Martin Young], *A Chinese Village: Shandong Taitou*. For recent conditions of the village, see Pan Shouyong, "Xunzhao Taitou," 101–107.

56. Lin Yueh-hwa, *The Golden Wing*. For relations between the book and his family and village, see Zhuang Kongshao, "Cong Jinchi tan Lin Yaohua jiaoshou."

57. Daniel Harrison Kulp II: *Country Life in South China, the Sociology of Familism, Volume I, Pheonix Village*. For the production of the book, see Zhou Daming, "Chongfang Fenghuangcun."

58. John Lossing Buck, "The Agricultural Economy of China," 173–174, 186.

59. Liu Shipei, "Nongmin jiku diaochahui zhangcheng," 313.

60. Quoted in Fernando Galbiati, *Peng Pai and the Hai-Lu-Feng Soviet*, 234.

61. In *Zhonggong zhongyang wenjian xuanji*, Vol. 2, 214.

62. Ruan Xiaoxian, "Zhongguo nongmin yundong," 311.

63. Ruan Xiaoxian, "Quanguo nongmin yundong xingshi jiqi zai guomin geming zhong de diwei," 287.

64. Deng Zihui, "Longyan renmin geming douzheng huiyilu," 11, 18; Deng Zihui and Zhang Dingcheng, "Minxi baodong yu hong shi'er jun," 392.

65. He Yulin, "Edongbei tewei He Yulin gei zhongyang de baogao," 50.

66. Yuan Renyuan, "Shimen nanxiang de qiyi," 635.

67. Yang Xiaochu, "Weihua qiyi pianduan," 914–915.

68. Yan Hongyan, "Huiyi Shan-Gan gaoyuan zaoqi de geming wuzhuang douzheng," 489.

69. Mao Zedong, "Xunwu Investigation," 374–376.

70. Fernando Galbiati, *Peng Pai and the Hai-Lu-Feng Soviet*, 138; Yang Hualu and Ke Aizhen, "Fang Zhimin," 2; Kamal Sheel, *Peasant Society and Marxist Intellectuals in China*, 197–198.

71. Shao Shiping, "Fangshengfeng huiyi de shengli," 581.

72. Sidney D. Gamble, *Ting Hsien*, 147; Yan Yangchu, "You wenhua de Zhongguo xin nongmin," 143.

73. Miao Min, *Fang Zhimin zhandou de yisheng*, 51.

74. Xu Xiangqian, *Lishi de huigu*. Vol. 3, 604–605.

75. Sha Ting, "Ji He Long," 74.

76. Chalmers Johnson, *Peasant Nationalism and Communist Power*, 150, 155.

77. Elizabeth Perry, *Rebels and Revolutionaries in North China*, 233.

78. Zhang Lin, "Xu Xiangqian," 64.

79. Xu Xiangqian, *Lishi de huigu*, Vol. 3, 649.

80. Zhuang Tian, *Qiongdao fengyan*, 2.

81. Zhang Dingcheng zhuan bianxiezu, "Zhang Dingcheng," 44, 48.

82. Victor Turner, *The Forest of Symbols, Aspects of Ndembu Ritual*, 94.

83. Quoted in Tao Xiaoguang, "Zhuiqiu zhenli zuo zhenren—Huainian wode fuqin Tao Xingzhi," 199.

84. Lao Xiang [Wang Xiangchen], *Huangtuni*, 9–12.

85. Fang Zhimin, "Ke'ai de Zhongguo."

86. Mao Zedong, "The Orientation of the Youth Movement," 246.

87. Liang Shuming, "Zishu," 31.

88. Peter Burke, *Popular Culture in Early Modern Europe*, 8–9.

89. For the urban origins of Chinese peasant revolutions in Hunan, see Angus McDonald, *The Urban Origins of Rural Revolution: Elites and the Masses in Hunan Province, China, 1911–1927*.

90. Peng Pai, "Haifeng laonongjie baogaoshu," 30.

91. See Fernando Galbiati, *Peng Pai and the Hai-Lu-Feng Soviet*, 56–58, for more discussion.

92. For Yan Yangchu's popular education movement in urban centers, see his "Pingmin jiaoyu xinyundong," 31–46; and "Pingmin jiaoyu yundong," 52–62. Yan's first rural experiment was conducted in Hengshan County of Hunan, after a successful program in Changsha. See Angus McDonald, *The Urban Origins of Rural*

Revolution, 122. In 1924, a mass education program was carried out in the villages of Baoding and the suburbs of Beijing. See Yan Yangchu, "Zhi Tao Xingzhi deng," 8–9.

93. Yan Yangchu, "Pingmin jiaoyu yundong," 60.

94. Li Jinghan, "Shenru minjian de yixie jingyan yu ganxiang," 8.

95. Fei Xiaotong, "Shehui bianqian yanjiu zhong chengshi he xiangcun." See discussions in David Arkush, *Fei Xiaotong and Sociology in Revolutionary China,* 32.

96. Qu Qiubai, "Duoyu de hua," 717.

97. Bingying Nushi [Xie Bingying]. *Congjun riji,* 31.

98. Elizabeth Perry, *Rebels and Revolutionaries in North China,* 217.

99. In *Guangdong nongmin yundong ziliao xuanbian,* 94.

100. James Thomson, *While China Faced West,* 100, 117, 119.

101. Yan Yangchu, "Zhongguo pingmin jiaoyu yundong de zongjie," 207.

102. Pearl Buck, *Tell the People,* 19.

103. Peng Pai, "Laodongzhe tongqinghui de yuanqi," 1.

104. Peng Pai, "Haifeng nongmin yundong," 114. For linguistic difference between Peng Pai and the local peasants, see Hai Feng, *Haifeng wenhua geming gaishu,* 148.

105. Mao Zedong, "Oppose Stereotyped Party Writing," 59.

106. Mao Zedong, "Talks at the Yenan Forum on Literature and Art," 72.

107. Fei Xiaotong, "Chongdu *Jiangcun jingji* xuyan," 10–11.

108. Fei Xiaotong, "Chongdu *Jiangcun jingji* xuyan," 10.

109. Peng Pai, "Haifeng nongmin yundong," 114.

110. Wu Dingbang et al., "Luo Nachuan," 187.

111. Ibid., 330.

112. Yan Yangchu, "Nongcun yundong de shiming," 299.

113. Qu Qiubai, "Duoyu de hua," 701, 719.

114. Peng Pai, "Haifeng nongmin yundong,"109; and "Laodongzhe tongqinghui de yuanqi," 1; Fang Zhimin, "Wo congshi geming douzheng de lueshu," 31.

115. Li Jinghan, "Sheru minjian de yixie jingyan yu ganxiang," 11.

116. Edward Friedman, *Backward toward Revolution,* 120–121, 131.

117. A. S. Mugruzin, *Agrarno-krestianskaia Problema v Kitae v Pervoi Polovine XX veka,* 90.

118. Li Dazhao, "Leting tongxin," 706.

119. Li Yinchun, "Bushi minguo buhao"; Li Yinchun, "Haishi gonghe hao."

120. Arthur Wolf, ed., *Religion and Ritual in Chinese Society*, 9, 39.

121. One such interpretation was offered by Chen Duxiu in 1918. See "Kelinde bei." Lu Xun also discussed the issue in "Geming shidai de wenxue," 422.

122. Li Yiyuan, "Zhongguo wenhua zhong xiaochuantong de zairenshi."

123. Keith Schoppa, *Blood Road*, 222.

124. Peng Pai, "Haifeng nongmin yundong," 114.

125. Peng Pai, "Laodongzhe tongqinghui de yuanqi," 1–2; "Peng Pai gei Li Chuntao," 32.

126. Peng Pai, "Zai diliujie nongmin yundong jiangxisuo de jiangyan," 196–197.

127. Xu Xiangqian, "Benxiang Hailufeng," 215.

128. Yun Daiying, "Nongcun yundong," 560–561.

129. Yu Jinlong, "Paihu douzheng yijiao," 684.

130. Ross Terrill, *Mao, A Biography*, 89, 90.

131. Yang Lisan, "Qiushou qiyi diyituan," 149; Tan Zheng, "Sanwan gaibian," 193.

132. Lai Yi, "Mao weiyuan zai liandui jiandang," 188.

133. Mao Zedong, "Oppose Stereotyped Party Writing," 59–60.

134. Chalmers Johnson, *Peasant Nationalism and Communist Power*, 87.

135. Stephen Uhalley, Jr., *Mao Tse-tung, A Critical Biography*, 74–75.

136. Zhuang Tian, *Qiongdao fengyan*, 8.

137. Liang Shuming, "Zhongguo wenti zhi jiejue," 218.

138. Yan Yangchu, "Zhi M. Fei'erde," 637.

139. Yan Yangchu, "Zhongguo pingmin jiaoyu yundong de zongjie," 207.

140. Yan Yangchu, "Zai Dingxian zhanlanhui shang de yanshuo," 172–173.

141. Shen Shu [Liu Shipei], "Renlei junli shuo," 30. For further discussions, see Peter Zarrow, *Anarchism and Chinese Political Culture*, 83–88; Arif Dirlik, *Anarchism in the Chinese Revolution*, 185–191.

142. Yan Yangchu, "Zai huanying laibin huishang de jianghua," 221.

143. Quoted in Robert Marks, *Rural Revolution in South China*, 225–226.

144. For the cult of Peng Pai, see Robert Marks, *Rural Revolution in South China*, 224–229.

145. Yun Daiying, "Nongcun yundong," 560.

146. Yan Yangchu, "Pingmin jiaoyu yundong de huigu yu qianzhan," 276.

147. Fei Xiaotong, "Maixiang renmin de renleixue," 7–8; Liu Hsiao-hsiao, "Notes on Conversation with Several Chinese Intellectuals," 154.

148. Li Jinghan, "Shenru minjian de yixie jingyan yu ganxiang," 8–9.

149. Deng Zihui and Zhang Dingcheng, "Minxi baodong yu hong shi'er jun," 381, 405.

150. Xie Juezai, "Liuyang yuxian," 145–146.

151. Xu Xiangqian, *Lishi de huigu*, Vol. 2, 312.

152. Zhou Enlai, "Zenyang zuo yige haode lingdaozhe," 132.

153. Liang Shuming initially saw the CCP as a peasant party, not a proletarian organization. After reading an article by Peng Zhen in 1951, however, Liang was convinced that the CCP was indeed a proletarian party. According to Peng, by joining the CCP the peasants would cease to be peasants and become revolutionaries. See Ma Dongyu, *Liang Shuming Zhuan*, 199–200. In fact, Peng's view had been expressed by Liu Shaoqi several years earlier in his famous "How to Be a Good Communist."

154. Li Dazhao, "Qingnian yu nongcun," 179–180; "Zhishi jieji de shengli," 457.

155. Chen Duxiu, "Zhongguo nongmin wenti," 508–515; and "Zhongguo guomin geming yu shehui ge jieji," 557–568.

156. Peng Pai, "Zai Sheng-gang bagong gongren daibiao di sanshiliuci dahui shang de baogao."

157. Peng Pai, "Peng Pai gei Li Chuntao," 39; "yijiu'ersinian shi'eryue wuri Zhonggong Guangdong quwei nongmin yundong weiyuanhui de buchong baogao," 71.

158. Mao Zedong, "Analysis of All the Classes in Chinese Society"; "An Analysis of the Various Classes among the Chinese Peasantry and Their Attitudes toward the Revolution"; "The National Revolution and the Peasant Movement."

159. Yu Dafu, "Xiangcun li de jieji," 41–42.

160. See Philip Huang et al., *Chinese Communists and Rural Society, 1927–1934*, 1978, 22–23, 29–56.

161. Benjamin Schwartz, *Chinese Communism and the Rise of Mao*, 192–196.

162. For discussions, see *Peng Pai Wen Ji*, 17–18; John Isreal,"Reflections on the Modern Chinese Student Movement," 239. The Communists have often been uneasy about the fact that so many Communist leaders were from landlord and rich peasant families, and from time to time they have attempted to conceal the family background of their leaders. For example, immediately after Peng Pai's death in 1929, at least two articles written by his comrades described him as being from a "peasant family." See *Peng Pai yanjiu shiliao*, 266 and 274.

163. Lucien Bianco, "The Peasant Movements," 317. Bianco argued that Peng Pai's family status and his education greatly helped the early development of the Hailufeng peasant movement.

164. Peng Pai, "Haifeng nongmin yundong," 111–112; See also Fernando Galbiati, *Peng Pai and the Hai-Lu-Feng Soviet*, 19.

165. Chen Xinde, "Wei Baqun," 244.

166. Kamal Sheel, *Peasant Society and Marxist Intellectuals in China*, 198.

167. Chen Yun, "Yan Pu tongzhi zhuanlue"; Yan Huaijin, "Yan Pu shengping."

168. Zhou Cantian, "Zeng Tianyu lieshi," 99.

169. Shen Dingyi voluntarily reduced the rent; Fu Bocui also voluntarily gave away some of his rights.

170. Fang Zhimin zhuan bianxiezu, *Fang Zhimin zhuan*, 58–62, 76–77, 134.

171. Tai Yunxing, "Zhou Weijiong," 244.

172. William Hinton, *Fanshen,* 265.

173. William Hinton, *Fanshen*, 267–268.

174. Wang Minzhao, "Yiqie yikao dang he qunzhong—bayi fangwen He Long jiangjun," 124.

175. Peng Pai, "Haifeng nongmin yundong," 147–148.

176. Fang Zhimin, "Wo congshi geming douzheng de lueshu," 15.

177. Zheng Weisan, "Hongse de Huang'an," 731.

178. Li Ting, "Milin xinghuo," 419–420.

179. Pi Shaoyi & Liu Miaoruo, "Hu Yun," 153.

180. Li Rui, *Zaonian Mao Zedong*, 570.

181. James Scott, *The Moral Economy of the Peasant*, 127–130.

182. Kamal Sheel, *Rural Society and Marxist Intellectuals in China*, 229-230.

183Robert Marks, *Rural Revolution in South China*, 174, 191, 227, 282, 285–286.

184. Ralph Thaxton, *China Turned Rightside Up*, xix.

185. Ibid., 27.

186. James Polachek, "The Moral Economy of the Kiangsi Soviet (1928–1934)," 825.

187. Roy Hofheinz, *The Broken Wave*, 110–136, 142, 155, 178, 181, 304–305.

188. Ni Zhongwen, "Huiyi Zheng Weisan tongzhi tan E-Yu-Wan suqu lishi zhong de jige zhongda wenti," 8.

189. Chen Qihan, "Gannan dang de lishi," 1–3; Luo Guibo, "Gannan chuqi geming huodong de diandi huiyi," 22; Xiao Hua, "Xingguo geming douzheng he shaogong guoji shi," 389–390.

190. Gong Chu, *Wo Yu Hongjun*, 27–28.

191. Peng Pai, "Peng Pai gei Li Chuntao," 39.

192. Fang Zhimin, "Wo congshi geming douzheng de lueshu," 43.

193. Mao Zedong, "Report on the Peasant Movement in Hunan," 430.

194. For discussions, see Benjamin Shwartz, *Chinese Communism and the Rise of Mao*, 121–126.

195. For further discussions, see Lucien Bianco, "The Peasant Movements."

196. Barrington Moore, *Social Origins of Dictatorship and Democracy*, 221.

197. Benjamin Shwartz, *Chinese Communism and the Rise of Mao*, 2–3, 198–199, Kung-chuan Hsiao, *Rural China*, 512–514, William Hinton, *Fanshen*, 605–607, Lucien Bianco, "The Peasant Movements"; Eric Wolf, *Peasant Wars of the twentieth Century*, 294; Elizabeth Perry, *Rebels and Revolutionaries in North China*, 246–247, 255–259.

198. Fernando Galbiati, *Peng Pai and the Hai-Lu-Feng Soviet*, 50–53, 101–115.

199. Fernando Galbiati, *Peng Pai and the Hai-Lu-Feng Soviet*, 362–365.

200. Liang Shuming, "Xiangcun jianshe dayi," 666.

201. Liang Shuming, "Xiangcun jianshe dayi," 667.

202. Liang Shuming, "Cunxue xiangxue xuzhi," 459.

203. Liang Shuming, "Shehui benwei de jiaoyu xitong caoan."

204. Liang Shuming, "Wo canjia guogong hetan de jingguo," 891.

205. Qu Junong, "Dingxian jiaoyu gongzuo," 202–204.

206. James Yen [Yan Yangchu], *The Ting Hsien Experiment*, 13–33.

207. Yan was a pious Christian and his wife was the daughter of a Chinese pastor living in New York. After returning to China, Yan realized that he should refrain from propagating his faith because of the existence in China at that time of a strong anti-Christian sentiment.

208. Yan Yangchu, "Pingmin jiaoyu yundongshu," 76.

209. Yan Yangchu, "Pingmin jiaoyu de zhenyi," 112.

210. Yan Yangchu, "Pingmin jiaoyu xinyundong," 31.

211. Zheng Shixing, *Zhongguo xiandai jiaoyu shi*, 116.

212. Tao Xingzhi, "Zhonghua jiaoyu gaizao quanguo xiangcun jiaoyu xuanyan-shu," 646.

213. *Xiangcun jianshe shiyan*, Vol. 3, 31, 32, 40–41.

214. Li Rui, *Zaonian Mao Zedong*, 570.

215. Li Rui, *Zaonian Mao Zedong*, 408–409.

216. Yan Yangchu, "Zai Chengdu xiaoyou huanyinghui shang de jianghua," 480.

217. Zhang Guotao, *The Rise of the Chinese Communist Party*, Vol. 1, 50–51.

218. In 1935, Liang Shuming invited Fei to join his rural reconstruction movement in Shandong. Fei declined. In 1945, Fei was offered a job with the United

Nations Rural Rehabilitation Administration; again he declined. See David Arkush, *Fei Xiaotong and Sociology in Revolutionary China*, 139.

219. Fei Hsiao-tung, *Peasant Life in China : A Field Study of Country Life in the Yangtze Valley*, 5.

220. Fei Xiaotong, *Jiangcun jingji*, 5–6, 12–13.

221. Chen Hansheng, *Sige shidai de wo*, 52–53.

222. Li Jinghan, "Shenru minjian de yixie jingyan yu ganxiang," 8.

223. Mao Zedong, "Guanyu nongcun diaocha," 383.

224. James Thomson, *While China Faced West*, 58.

225. James Thomson, *While China Faced West*, 109.

226. James Thomson, *While China Faced West*, 70–72.

227. For further information, see Zhang Xin, "Elite Activism in the Periphery."

228. Zhao Tongxin, "Wanxi Guaijie Bie Tingfang," 49.

229. See Zhang Xin, "Elite Activism in the Periphery," for more discussion.

230. Yan Yangchu, "Zhi E. Xidengxitelike," 449.

231. For Bie Tingfang's brutal rule, see Bie Guangdian, "Henan neixiang tuhuangdi Bie Tingfang"; Zhang Hexuan, "Wo suo zhidao de Bie Tingfang"; for a favorable treatment of Bie Tingfang, see Zhao Tongxin, "Wanxi Guaijie Bie Tingfang."

232. Fei Xiaotong, *Jiangcun jingji*, 177, 183.

233. Fei Xiaotong, "Dizhu jieceng mianlin kaoyan," 89–98.

NOTES TO CHAPTER SIX

1. James Yen [Yan Yangchu], *The Ting Hsien Experiment*, 9, 39.

2. Fei Xiaotong, *Earthbound China*, foreword; *Xiangtu chongjian yu xiangzhen fazhan*, 2, 8.

3. Eric Hobsbawm, "Some Reflections on the Break-up of Britain," 13.

4. Anthony Smith, ed., *Nationalist Movements*, 24.

5. Eric Wolf, *Peasant Wars of the Twentieth Century*, 154.

6. Eric Wolf, *Peasants*, 109.

7. Chalmers Johnson, *Peasant Nationalism and Communist Power*, ix.

8. Lucien Bianco, "Peasant Movements," 327–328.

9. Benjamin Schwartz, *Chinese Communism and the Rise of Mao*, 3.

10. Hugh Seton-Watson, *The Pattern of Communist Revolution*, 153.

11. Fernando Galbiati, *Peng Pai and the Hai-Lu-Feng Soviet*, vi.

12. Leften Stavrianos, *Global Rift*, 450–456.

13. For more discussion, see Partha Chatterjee, *Nationalist Thought and the Colonial World*, 46–47.

14. Chalmers Johnson, *Peasant Nationalism and Communist Power*, 28–30.

Bibliography

Ai Qing. "Dayanhe" (1933). In *Selected Poems of Ai Qing*. Eugene Chen Eoyang, Peng Wenlan, Marilyn Chin, trans. Bloomington: Indiana University Press, 1982.

———. "Jiubaige" [Nine Hundred Souls] (1937). In *Ai Qing quan ji* [Collected Works of Ai Qing]. Vol. 1. Shijiazhuang: Huashan wenyi, 1994.

Ai Wu. "Lun Ah Q" [On Ah Q]. In *Liushinianlai Lu Xun yanjiu lunwenxuan* [Selected Essays on Lu Xun Studies Published in the Last Six Decades]. Vol. 1, 435–441. Li Zongying and Zhang Mengyang, eds. Beijing: Zhonguo shehui kexue, 1982.

Alter, Peter. *Nationalism*. Stuart McKinnon-Evans, trans. London: Edward Arnold, 1994.

Anderson, Benedict. *Imagined Communities: Reflections on the Origin and Spread of Nationalism*. London and New York: Verso, 1991.

Anonymous. "Yihetuan yougong yü zhongguo shuo" [The Boxers Have Made Contributions to China] (1901). In *Xinhaigeming qian shinianjian shilun Xuanji* [The Current Views During the Decade Prior to the 1911 Revolution], 1(1), 58–62. Zhang Zhan and Wang Renzhi, eds. Beijing: Sanlian, 1960.

———. "Lun Zhongguo yi zuzhi laomin xiehui" [China Should Organize Associations of the Laboring People]. *Hengbao*, nos. 5–6, 1908.

———. "Gao Zhongguo de nongmin" [Declaration to the Chinese Peasant] (1921,4,7). In *Jiefangqian de Zhongguo nongcun* [Rural China Before 1949], Vol. 1, 108. Chen Hansheng, Xue Muqiao and Feng Hefa, eds. Beijing: Zhonguo zhanwang, 1985.

Arkush, David. *Fei Xiaotong and Sociology in Revolutionary China*. Cambridge: Harvard University Press, 1981.

Averill, Stephen C. "Local Elites and Communist Revolution in the Jiangxi Hill Country." In Joseph W. Esherick and Mary Bachus Rankin, eds. *Chinese Local Elites and Patterns of Dominance*. Berkeley and Los Angeles: University of California Press, 1990.

Ba Ren [Wang Renshu]. "Lu Xun de chuangzuo fangfa" [Lu Xun's Artistic Techniques] (1940). In *Liushinianlai Lu Xun yanjiu lunwenxuan*, Vol. 1, 295.

Baihuadaoren [Lin Xie]. "Guomin yijian shu" [A Citizen's Opinions] (1904). In *Xinhaigeming qian shinianjian shilun xuanji*, 1(2), 921.

Bai Yu. "Chushen shijia er aixi yumao de Guxiansheng" [Memories about Gu Mengyu]. *Zhuanji wenxue*, 29(1). Taipei, 1976.

Banhua jicheng: Lu Xun cang Zhonguo xiandai muke quanji [The Journey of the Prints: Lu Xun's Collection of Modern Chinese Wood-engraving Prints]. 5 vols. Nanjing: Jiangsu guji, 1991.

Benton, Gregor. *China's Urban Revolutionaries: Explorations in the History of Chinese Trotskyism, 1921–1952*. Atlantic Highlands, N.J.: Humanities Press, 1996.

Bernard, Suzanne. "An Interview with Mao Dun." *Chinese Literature* (Beijing), 1979(2–3).

Bi Da. "Nongren tong shangren de bijiao" [A Comparison of the Peasant and the Merchant]. *Nongmin*, 2(26), 1926,11,10.

Bianco, Lucien. *Origins of the Chinese Revolution, 1919-1949*. Muriel Bell, trans. Stanford: Stanford University Press, 1971.

———. "The Peasant Movements." In *Cambridge History of China*, Vol. 13. John K. Fairbank and Albert Feuerwerker, eds. Cambridge (England)/New York: Cambridge University Press, 1986.

Bie Guangdian. "Henan neixiang tuhuangdi Bie Tingfang" [Bie Tingfang: the Local Despot of Neixiang, Henan]. *Wenshi ziliao xuanji* [Selected Literary and Historical Materials], No. 38, 176–189. Beijing: Zhongguo wenshi, 1986 (reprint).

Bingying Nushi. *Congjun riji* [Diaries of a Soldier]. Shanghai: Guangming, 1940.

Bolagedatuofu [Blagodatov, A. Vasilevich]. *Zhonguo geming zhaji: 1925–1927* [Notes on the Chinese Revolution: 1925–1927]. Zhang Kai, trans. Beijing: Xinhua, 1985.

Brandt, Loren. *Commercialization and Agricultural Development: Central and Eastern China 1870–1937*. Cambridge: Cambridge University Press, 1989.

Brook, Timothy, ed. *The Asiatic Mode of Production in China*. Armonk, N.Y.: M. E. Sharpe, 1989.

Buck, John Lossing. *Land Utilization in China*. Shanghai: The Commercial Press, 1937.

———. "The Agricultural Economy of China, 1927–1937, as Exemplified by the Work at the University of Nanking." In Paul K. T. Sih, ed., *The Strenuous Decade: China's Nation-building Efforts, 1927–1937*, 171–193. Jamaica, N.Y.: St. John's University, 1970.

Buck, Pearl S. *Tell the People: Mass Education in China*. I.P.R. Pamphlets No. 16. New York: Institute of Pacific Relations, 1945.

Buqu de gongchandangren [Biographies of Communist Martyrs]. 5 vols. Beijing: Renmin, 1980–1988.

Burke, Peter. *Popular Culture in Early Modern Europe*. London: Temple Smith, 1978.

Cai Hesen. "Cai Linbin Gei Mao Zedong" [Cai Linbin's Letter to Mao Zedong] (1920). *Cai Hesen wenji* [Collected Works of Cai Hesen], 49–53. Beijing: Renmin, 1980.

———. "Makesi xueshuo yu Zhongguo wuchanjieji" [Marxist Theory and the Chinese Proletariat] (1921). In *Cai Hesen Wenji*, 74–78.

———. "Zhongguo geming de xingzhi jiqi qiantu" [The Nature and Future of the Chinese Revolution] (1928). In *Cai Hesen wenji*, 783–803.

Chang Yu. "Lun Laiyang minbian shi" [On the Laiyang Peasant Rebellion] (1910). In *Xinhaigeming qian shinianjian shilunxuanji*, Vol. 3, 652–658.

Chatterjee, Partha. *Nationalist Thought and the Colonial World—A Derivative Discourse?* London: Zed Books Ltd., 1986.

Chayanov, A. V. *The Theory of Peasant Economy*. Daniel Thorner, Basile Kerblay, and R. E. F. Smith, eds. Homewood, Ill: Richard D. Irwin 1966.

Chen Bilan. "Huigu wo he Peng Shuzhi de suiyue" [My Life with Peng Shuzhi]. In *Peng Shuzhi xuanji* [Selected Works of Peng Shuzhi], Vol.1. Hong Kong: Shiyue, 1983.

Chen Chunsheng. "Chen Shaobai xiansheng yu Xianggang Zhongguo ribao ji Zhongguo ribao yu Zhongguo geming zhi guanxi" [Chen Shaobai and the China Daily in Hong Kong and the Relations Between the China Daily and the Chinese Revolution." In *Kaiguo wenxian*, Part 1, Vol. 10. Taipei.

Chen Duxiu. "Anhui aiguohui yanshuo" [Speech at the Anhui Patriotic Association] (1905). In *Chen Duxiu zhuzuo xuan* [Selected Works of Chen Duxiu], Vol. 1, 15–16. Ren Jianshu et al., eds. Shanghai: Shanghai renmin, 1993.

———. "Kelinde Bei" [The Von Ketteler Monument] (1918). In Ibid., 415–420.

———. "Fu Dongsun xiansheng de xin" [A Reply to Zhang Dongsun] (1920). In *Chen Duxiu zhuzuo xuan*, Vol. 2, 207–215.

———. "Zhongguo nongmin wenti" [China's Peasant Question] (1923). In Ibid., 508–515.

———. "Zhongguo guomin geming yu shehui ge jieji" [The National Revolution and the Various Social Classes of China] (1923). In Ibid., 557–568.

———. "Women duiyu Yihetuan liangge cuowu de guannian" [Our Two Erroneous Viewpoints About the Boxer Rebellion] (1924). In Ibid., 769–771.

———. "Ershiqi nian yilai guomin yundong zhong suode jiaoxun" [The Lessons of the National Movements in the Last 27 Years] (1924). In Ibid., 812–820.

———. "Hongqianghui yu Zhongguo de nongmin baodong" [The Red Spears and the Chinese Peasant Uprisings] (1926). In Ibid., 1073–1076.

———. "Women xianzai weishemo zhengdou?" [What Do We Struggle for Now?] (1926). In Ibid., 1106–1111.

———. "Geming yu wuli" [Revolution and Violence] (1926)). In Ibid., 1142–1145.

———. "Guanyu Zhongguo geming wenti zhi Zhonggong zhongyang xin" [Letter to the CCP Central Committee about the Problem of the Chinese Revolution] (1929). In *Chen Duxiu zhuzuo xuan*, Vol. 3, 37–57.

———. "Women de zhengzhi yijianshu" [Our Political Views] (1929). In Ibid., 106–137.

Chen Gongbo. "Nongmin yundong zai Zhongguo guomin geming de diwei" [The Role of the Peasant Movement in the Chinese National Revolution]. *Zhongguo nongmin*, nos. 6–7, 1926.

———. "Zhongguo Guomindang suodaibiao de shi shemo" [What Does the Chinese Nationalist Party Represent] (1927). In *Chen Gongbo xiansheng wenji* [Collected Works of Chen Gongbo], Vol.1, 1939. Reprinted by Hong Kong:Yuandong, 1967.

———. "Jinhou de Guomindang" [The Nationalist Party Hereafter] (1928). In Ibid., 1–23.

———. *Kuxiaolu: Chen Gongbo huiyi, 1925 zhi 1936* [Wry Smiles: Memoir of Chen Gongbo, 1925–1936] (1939). 2 vols. Hong Kong: University of Hong Kong Centre of Asian Studies Occasional Papers and Monographs, No. 36, 1979.

———. "Wo yu Gongchandang" [I and the Chinese Communist Party] (1944). In *Chen Gongbo & Zhou Fohai huiyilu hebian* [Memoirs of Chen Gongbo & Zhou Fohai]. Hong Kong: Chunqiu, 1967.

Chen Hansheng [Chen Han-sen]. "Xiandai Zhongguo de tudi wenti" [The Land Problem of Contemporary China] (1933). In *Chen Hansheng wenji* [Collected Works of Chen Hansheng]. Shanghai: Fudan daxue, 1985.

———. "The Good Earth of China's Model Province." *Pacific Affairs*, 1936(9).

——. *Landlord and Peasant in China: A Study of the Agrarian Crisis in South China*. New York: International Publishers, 1936.

——. "Zhuiyi woyou Yang Xingfo" [Memory of My Friend Yang Xingfo]. *Shehui kexue* [Social Sciences] (Shanghai), 1983(9), 65.

——. *Sige shidai de wo* [My Experiences in Four Eras]. Beijing: Zhongguo wenshi,1988.

Chen Qihan. "Xingguo de chuqi geming douzheng" [The Early Revolutionary Struggles in Xingguo]. *Xinghuo liaoyuan*, Vol.1, Part 1. Beijing: Renmin wenxue, 1958.

——. "Gannan dang de lishi" [History of the CCP in Southern Jiangxi]. In *Huiyi Zhongyang suqu* [Remembering the Central Soviet Base Area]. Nanchang: Jiangxi renmin, 1986.

Chen Sanjing. *Huagong yu Ouzhan* [Chinese Laborers and the First World War]. Taipei: Institute of Modern History, Academia Sinica, Manuscript (52), 1986.

Chen Xinde. "Wei Baqun." In *Zhonggong dangshi renwu zhuan* [Biographies of Prominent Figures in the History of the CCP]. Vol. 12, 183–216. Hu Hua, ed. Xian: Shanxi renmin, 1983.

ChenYanqiao. *Lu Xun yu muke* [Lu Xun and Wood-engraving]. Shanghai: Kaiming, 1949.

Chen Yun. "Yan Pu tongzhi zhuanlue" [A Brief Biography of Yan Pu] (1949). In *Zhonggong dangshi renwu zhuan*, Vol. 31, 1–4. Xian: 1987.

Chen Zhuofan. "Wosuo zhidao de Deng Yanda" [Deng Yanda As I Know Him]. *Guangdong wenshi ziliao* (Guangzhou), no. 22. 1978.

Chou Li-po [Zhou Libo]. *The Hurricane*. Peking: Foreign Language Press, 1955.

Cohen, Myron. "Cultural and Political Inventions in Modern China: The Case of the Chinese 'Peasant'." *Daedalus*, Vol. 122, 1993, 151–170.

Cohen, Paul. *History in Three Keys: the Boxers as Event, Experience, and Myth*. New York: Columbia University Press, 1997.

Crook, Isabel and David Crook. *Revolution in a Chinese Village Ten Mile Inn*. London: Routledge & Kegan Paul, 1959.

Dai Zhixian. *Shinian neizhan shiqi de geming wenhua yundong* [The Revolutionary Cultural Movements During the Civil War Decade]. Beijing: Zhongguo renmin daxue, 1988.

Deng Mingyan. *Liang Qichao de shengping jiqi zhengzhi sixiang* [Liang Qichao: His Life and Political Thought]. Taipei: Tianshan, 1981.

Deng Yanda. "Dui Zhongguo ji shijie geming minzhong de xuanyan" [Delaration to the Revolutionary Masses of China and the World] (1927,11). In *Deng Yanda xiansheng yizhu* [Collected Works of Deng Yanda] (1933), 195–202. Hong Kong, 1949 (reprint).

———. "Zhengzhi zhuzhang" [Political Views]. In *Deng Yanda xiansheng yizhu*, 213–219.

———. "Zenyang qu fuxing Zhongguo geming—pingmin geming?" [How to Revive the Chinese Revolution or Mass Revolution?] (1931). In Ibid., 151–187.

———. "Shiliunian shiyiyue dui Zhongguo ji shijie geming minzhong xuanyan" [Declaration to the Revolutionary Masses of China and the World: November 1927]. In *Deng Yanda xiansheng yizhu*, 198–200.

———. "Shijiunian jiuyue shiwuri dui shiju xuanyan" [Declaration About the Current Events: September 15, 1930]. In *Deng Yanda xiansheng yizhu*, 203–207.

Deng Zhongxia. "Lun nongmin yundong" [On Peasant Movement]. *Zhongguo qingnian* [Chinese Youth], no. 11 (1923,11).

———."Zhongguo nongmin zhuangkuang ji women yundong de fangzhen" [The Conditions of the Chinese Peasantry and the Strategy of Our Movement]. *Zhongguo qingnian*, no.13 (1924,1).

Deng Zihui. "Longyan renmin geming douzheng huiyilu" [My Memory of the People's Revolutionary Struggles in Longyan]. In *Fujian dangshi ziliao* (Fuzhou), 1983(2).

Deng Zihui and Zhang Dingcheng. "Minxi baodong yu hong ershi jun" [The Western Fujian Uprising and the Twentieth Red Army]. In *Xinghuo liaoyuan*, 1(1), 1958.

Ding Ling. "Tianjiachong" [The Tianjiachong Village] (1931). In *Ding Ling wenji* [Collected Works of Ding Ling]. Vol. 2, 319–357. Changsha: Hunan renmin, 1983.

———. "Shui" [Flood] (1931). In *Ding Ling wenji*, Vol. 2, 369–406.

———. "Gei Daluxinwen bianzhe de xin" [A Letter to the Editor of the Continental News] (1933). In *Ding Ling yanjiu ziliao* [Materials on Ding Ling]. Yuan Liangjun ed. Tianjin: Tianjin renmin, 1982.

———. *The Sun Shines over the Sangkan River.* Beijing: Foreign Languages Press, 1984.

Dirlik, Arif. *Revolution and History: The Origin of Marxist Historiography in China, 1919–1937.* Berkeley: University of California Press, 1978.

———. *Anarchism in the Chinese Revolution.* Berkeley: University of California Press, 1991.

———. "'Feudalism' in Twentieth Century Chinese Historiography." *China Report*, 33:(1), 1997.

Du Ai. "Daonian weida zuojia Mao Dun xiansheng" [Mourn the Great Writer Mao Dun] (1981). In *Mao Dun zhuanji* [A Special Collection on Mao Dun]. Tang Jinhai et al. eds. Fuzhou: Fujian renmin, 1983, Vol.1.

Du Song. "Tudi geming shiqi Zhongguo nongcun jingji diaochatuan huodong shimo" [Introduction to the Activities of the Chinese Economic Investigation Group during the Land Revolution]. *Zhonggong dangshi ziliao.* No. 45,108–133. Beijing: Zhonggong zhongyang dangxiao, 1993.

Duara, Prasenjit. *Culture, Power, and the State: Rural North China, 1900–1942.* Stanford: Stanford University Press, 1988.

Esherick, Joseph W. "Number Games: A Note on Land Distribution in Prerevolutionary China." *Modern China,* 7(3), 1981, 387–412.

Fan Yusui. "Wo suo zhidao de Gaizupai" [My Knowledge of the Reorganization Group]. In *Wenshi ziliao xuanji,* no. 45, 209–230.

Fang Qiuwei. "Tao Xisheng he Didiao julebu, Yiwen yanjiuhui" [Tao Xisheng, the Low-key Club, and the Society of Art and Literature Studies]. *Minguo dang'an* (Nanjing), 1992(3), 126–132.

Fang Zhimin. "Kusheng" [Cry] (1922). In *Fang Zhimin wenji* [Collected Works of Fang Zhimin], 362–363. Beijing: Renmin, 1985.

———. "Zai Jiangxi diyici quansheng nongmin daibiao dahui shang de kaimuci" [Opening Speech to the First Congress of Peasant Delegates of Jiangxi Province] (1927). In *Fang Zhimin wenji,* 219–220.

———. "Fanyou yundong yu wuren" [The Anti-rightist Campaign and Us] (1927). In *Fang Zhimin wenji,* 238–240.

———. "Ke'ai de Zhongguo" [Beloved China] (1935). In *Fang Zhimin wenji,* 119–143.

———. "Wo congshi geming douzheng de lueshu" [A Brief Account of My Revolutionary Activities] (1935). In *Fang Zhimin wenji,* 4–105.

———. "Gandongbei Suwei'ai chuangli de lishi" [The Creation of the Northeastern Jiangxi Soviet] (1936). In *Fang Zhimin wenji,* 190–208.

Fang Zhimin zhuan bianxiezu [The Compiling Group of The Biography of Fang Zhimin]. *Fang Zhiming zhuan* [A Biography of Fang Zhimin]. Nanchang: Jiangxi renmin, 1982.

Faure, David. *The Rural Economy of Pre-Liberation China: Trade Expansion and Peasant Livelihood in Jiangsu and Guangdong, 1870 to 1937.* Hong Kong/New York: Oxford University Press, 1989.

Fei Xiaotong [Fei Hsiao-tung]. "Shehui bianqian yanjiu zhong dushi he xiangcun" [Cities and Villages in the Study of Social Change]. *Shehui yanjiu,* no. 11. 1933.

———. *Peasant Life in China: A Field Study of Country Life in the Yangtze Valley.* London: G. Routledge & Sons, 1939.

———. *Xiangtu Zhongguo* [From the Soil] (1947). Beijing: Sanlian, 1985 (reprint).

———. "Sunshi chongxi xia de xiangtu" [The Village Under the Impact of Erosion] (1947). In Fei Xiaotong, *Xiangtu chongjian yu xiangzhen fazhan*, 1994.

———. "Dizhu jieceng mianlin kaoyan" [The Landlord Class Is Facing the Test]. In *Xiangtu chongjian* [Rural Reconstruction], 89–98. Shanghai: Guanchashe, 1948.

———. "Ping Yan Yangchu kaifa minli jianshe xiangcun" [Commenting on Yan Yangchu's Idea of Exploiting the Mass Power to Reconstruct the Villages]. *Guancha*, 5(1), 1948.

———. *Wo zhe yinian* [My Last Year]. Beijing: Shenghuo, Dushu, Xinzhi, 1950.

———. "Maixiang renmin de renleixue" [Toward the People's Anthropology] (1980). In Fei Xiaotong, *Xiangtu chongjian yu xiangzhen fazhan*, 1994.

———. *Jiangcun jingji: Zhongguo nongmin de shenghuo* [Peasant Life in China]. Hong Kong: Zhonghua shuju, 1987.

———. *Xiangtu chongjian yu xiangzhen fazhan* [Rural Reconstruction and the Development of Small Towns]. Hong Kong: Oxford University Press, 1994.

———. "Chongdu Jiangcunjingji Xuyan" [Rereading the Preface to Peasant Life in China]. *Beijing daxue xuebao* [Journal of Beijing University], 1996(4).

Fei Hsiao-tung and Chang Chih-i. *Earthbound China: A Study of Rural Economy in Yunnan*. Chicago: University of Chicago Press, 1945.

Feng Xuefeng. "Geming yu zhishijieji" [Revolution and the Intelligentsia] (1928,5). In *Liushinianlai Lu Xun yanjiu lunwenxuan*, Vol. 1.

———. "Lu Xun xiansheng jihua er wei wancheng de zhuzuo—pianduan huiyi" [A Work Planned but not Completed by Lu Xun—Some Fragmentary Memories] (1937,10,15). In *Wo xinzhong de Lu Xun* [Lu Xun in My Heart]. Zhou Jianren, Mao Dun et al., eds. Changsha: Hunan renmin, 1979.

———. "Guanyu zhishifenzi de tanhua—pianduan huiyi" [Lu Xun's Conversation About the Intellectuals] (1946,10,1). In *Wo xinzhong de Lu Xun,* 149–159.

Feuerwerker, Albert. "China's Modern Economic History in Communist Chinese Historiography." In Albert Feuerwerker, ed., *History in Communist China,* 216–246. Cambridge/London: M.I.T. Press, 1968.

———. *The Chinese Economy, ca. 1870–1911*. Ann Arbor: University of Michigan Press, 1969.

Fitzgerald, John. *Awakening China: Politics, Culture, and Class in the Nationalist Revolution*. Stanford: Stanford University Press, 1996.

Fogel, Joshua. "The Debates over the Asiatic Mode of Production in Soviet Russia, China, and Japan." In *The Cultural Dimension of Sino-Japanese Relations: Essays on the Nineteenth and Twentieth Centuries.* Armonk, N.Y.: M. E. Sharpe, 1995.

Friedman, Edward. *Backward Toward Revolution: The Chinese Revolutionary Party.* Berkeley and Los Angeles: University of California Press, 1974.

Friedman, Edward, Paul Pickowicz, and Mark Selden. *Chinese Village, Socialist State.* New Haven and London: Yale University Press, 1991.

Fujian shibian dangan ziliao [The Archival Materials on the Fujian Incident]. Fujian Provincial Bureau of Archives, ed. Fuzhou: Fujian renmin, 1984.

Fujian shibian ziliao xuanbian [Selected Materials on the Fujian Incident]. Xue Moucheng and Zheng Quanbei, eds. Nanchang: Jiangxi renmin, 1983.

Galbiati, Fernando. *Peng Pai and the Hai-Lu-Feng Soviet.* Stanford: Stanford University Press, 1985.

Gamble, Sydney. *Ting Hsien, A North China Rural Community.* New York: Institute of Pacific Relations, 1954.

Gan Naiguang. "Chuangkan de hua" [Introduction] (1926,8,1). *Nongmin yundong,* no. 1 (Guangzhou, 1926, 8).

———. "Shui shi guomingeming de zhulijun" [Who Are the Main Forces of the National Revolution]. *Nongmin yundong,* no. 6 (1926,9,7).

———. *Zhongguo Guomindang jige genben wenti* [Some Fundamental Problems of the Chinese Nationalist Party]. Wuhan: Hubei Sheng dangbu zhixing weiyuanhui Hankou tebieshi dangbu zhixing wei yuan hui. 1926.

Gao Jun. "Zhongguo shehui xingzhi wenti de lunzhan" [The Debate on the Nature of Chinese Society]. In *Zhongguo shehui xingzhi lunzhan ziliao xuanbian* [Selected Materials about the Debate on the Nature of Chinese Society]. Vol. 1. Gao Jun, ed. Beijing: Renmin, 1984.

Gella, Aleksander. "An Introduction to the Sociology of the Intelligentsia." In Gella, Aleksander, ed. *The Intelligentsia and the Intellectuals: Theory, Method, and Case Study.* Beverly Hills, Cal.: Sage, 1976.

Gillin, Donald. *Warlord Yen Hsi-shan in Shanxi Province, 1911–1949.* Princeton, N.J.: Princeton University Press, 1967.

Gong Chu. *Wo yu hongjun* [I and the Red Army]. Hong Kong: Nanfeng, 1954.

Gongsun Yuzhi [Gu Mengyu] et al. *Zhongguo nongmin ji gengdi wenti* [China's Peasant Problem and Land Problem]. Shanghai: Fudan shudian, 1929.

Gottschang, Thomas R. "Incomes in the Chinese Rural Economy, 1885–1935: Comments on the Debate." *Republican China*, 18(1), 1992, 41–62.

Gu Mei. *Zhongguo nongcun jingji wenti* [Problems of Chinese Rural Economy]. Shanghai: Zhonghua shuju, 1931.

Gu Yuanzeng. *"Diguozhuyi yu diguozhuyi guojia de gongrenjieji* yihouji" [Translator's Note About *Imperialism and the Working Class of the Imperialistic Nations].* *Guomin xinbao fukan*, no. 43 (1926,1,24).

Gu Zhibiao. "Hongjiaguan juyi" [The Gathering of Revolutionary Forces in Hongjiaguan]. In *Huiyi He Long* [Remembering He Long]. Zhongguo shehui kexueyuan xiandai gemingshi yanjiushi, ed. Shanghai: Shanghai renmin, 1979.

Guangdong nongmin yundong ziliao xuanbian [Selected Materials about the Peasant Movement in Guangdong]. Beijing: Renmin, 1986.

Guo Dehong. "Jiuzhongguo tudi zhanyou zhuangkuang ji fazhan qushi" [The Conditions and Tendencies of Landholding in Pre-1949 China]. *Zhongguo shehui kexue* (Beijing), 1989(4), 199–212.

———. Zhongguo jinxiandai nongmin tudi wenti yanjiu [A Study of the Land Problem in Modern China]. Qingdao: Qingdao, 1993.

Guominbao. "Da Xijiangsanshi wen" [A Reply to Xijiangsanshi]. In *Guominbao huibian* [The National News: Bound Volume], 208–209. Taipei: Zhongguo guomindang dangshi shiliao bianzuan weiyuanhui. 1968 (Reprint).

Guo Xuyin. "Reconsideration of Chen Duxiu's Attitude Toward the Peasant Movement." *Chinese Law and Government,* Vol. xvii(1–2), 1984, 51–67.

Hai Feng. *Haifeng wenhua geming gaishu* [Introduction to the Cultural Revolution in Haifeng]. Hong Kong: Zhongbao zhoukan, 1969.

Han Dezhang. "Yanjiu nongye jingji suo yudao de jishu wenti" [The Technological Issues in Rural Economic Studies]. *Yishibao*, no. 49. Tianjin, 1935.

Harrison, James. *The Communists and Chinese Peasant Rebellions: A Study in the Rewriting of Chinese History.* New York: Atheneum, 1969.

Hartford, Kathleen. "Will the Real Chinese Peasant Please Stand Up?" *Republican China*, 18(1), 1992, 90–121.

Hayford, Charles W. *To the People: James Yen and Village China*. New York: Columbia University Press, 1990.

———. "The Storm over the Peasant: Rhetoric and Orientalism in Construing China." In Shelton Stromquist, and Jeffrey Cox, eds., *Contesting the Master Narrative.* Iowa City: University of Iowa Press, 1998.

———. "What's So Bad about the Good Earth?" *Education about Asia*, 3(3), 1998.

He Danren. "Guanyu xin de xiaoshuo de dansheng—ping Ding Ling de 'shui'" [About the Birth of the New Novel—On "Flood" by Ding Ling] (1932). In *Ding Ling yanjiu ziliao*.

He Ganzhi. *Zhongguo shehui xingzhi wenti lunzhan* [The Debate on the Nature of Chinese Society]. Shanghai: Shenghuo shudian, 1939.

He Hanwen. "Gaizupai huiyilu" [Memory of the Reorganization Group]. *Wenshi ziliao xuanji*, no.17, 166–184.

He Yulin. "Edongbei tewei He Yulin gei zhongyang de baogao" [Northeastern Hubei Special Committee He Yulin's Report to the Central Committee] (1929,5,7). In *E-Yu-Wan suqu geming lishi wenjian huiji: 1927-1934* [Collected Revolutionary Historical Documents of the Hubei-Henan-Anhui Soviet Area: 1927–1934]. Vol. 5. Wuhan, 1987.

Hinton, William. *Fanshen: A Documentary of Revolution in a Chinese Village*. New York: Vintage Books, 1966.

Ho, Franklin L. "Comments" on Buck and Shen's articles. In Paul K. T. Sih, ed., *The Strenuous Decade: China's Nation-building Efforts, 1927–1937*, 194–204; 233–236. Jamaica, N.Y.: St. John's University, 1970.

Hobsbawm, Eric. "Some Reflections on the Break-up of Britain." *New Left Review*, 105. 1977.

Hofheinz, Roy, Jr. *The Broken Wave: The Chinese Communist Peasant Movement, 1922–1928*. Cambridge: Harvard University Press, 1977.

Hong Shen. "Pinmin canju" [Poverty or Ignorance, Which Is It?] (1916). In *Hong Shen xiju ji* [Plays by Hong Shen]. Shanghai: Xiandai, 1933.

———. "Wukuiqiao" [The Bridge of Five Degree Holders] (1930). In *Hong Shen xuanji* [Selected Works of Hong Shen], 55–124. Beijing: Kaiming, 1951.

———. "Xiangdaomi" [The Fragrant Rice] (1931). In *Hongshen xuanji*.

Hsiao Kung-chuan. *Rural China: Imperial Control in the Nineteenth Century*. Seattle: University of Washington Press, 1960.

Hsu, Leonard. *Sun Yat-sen: His Political and Social Ideals*. Los Angeles: University of Southern California Press, 1933.

Hu Nai'an. "Haoshouronggui Gu Mengyu" [The Senile Gu Mengyu Returned to Taiwan]. *Zhuanji wenxue*, 22(3): 31. Taipei, 1973.

Hu Qiaomu. "Jinian Zhongguo gongchanzhuyi de weida xianqu Li Dazhao" [Commemorating Li Dazhao—The Great Pioneer of the Chinese Communist Movement]. In Zhonggong zhongyang dangshi yanjiushi, ed., *Li Dazhao yanjiu wenji* [Collected Essays on Li Dazhao]. Beijing: Zhonggong dangshi, 1991.

Hu Shi [Hu Shih]. "Historical Foundations for a Democratic China (March 12, 1941)." In *Edmund J. James Lectures on Government*. Second series. Urbana: University of Illinois Press, 1941.

———. "Which Road Are We Going?" (1930). In Hu Shi and Lin Yutang, *China's Own Critics*. Beiping: China United Press, 1931.

Hu Songping. *Hu Shizhi xiansheng nianpu changbian chugao* [A Draft of the Chronology of Hu Shi's Life]. Vol. 3. Taipei: Lianjing chuban, 1984.

Hua Gang. *Zhongguo dageming shi* [History of the Great Revolution of China] (Shanghai, 1931). Reprinted in 1982 by Beijing: Wenshi ziliao.

Huadong shifan daxue jiaoyuxi. *Zhongguo xiandai jiaoyu shi* [History of Modern Chinese Education]. Shanghai: Huadong shifan daxue, 1983.

Huang Kan. "Ai pinmin" [Pity the Poor] (1907). In *Xinhaigeming qian shinianjian shilun xuanji*, 2(2): 786–790.

Huang, Philip C. C. *The Peasant Family and Rural Development in the Yangzi Delta, 1350–1988*. Stanford: Stanford University Press, 1990.

———. "A Reply to Ramon Myers." *Journal of Asian Studies*, 50(3), 1991, 629–633.

———. "The Study of Rural China's Economic History." *Republican China*, 18(1), 1992, 164–176.

Huang, Philip, Lynda Bell, and Kathy Walker. *Chinese Communists and Rural Society, 1927–1934*. Center for Chinese Studies, University of California, Berkeley, 1978.

Hunan geming lieshizhuan [Biographies of the Revolutionary Martyrs of Hunan]. Changsha: Hunan tongsu duwu, 1952.

Hung Chang-tai. *Going to the People: Chinese Intellectuals and Folk Literature 1918–1937*. The Council on East Asian Studies, Harvard University, 1985.

Isreal, John. "Reflections on the Modern Chinese Student Movement." *Daedalus*, Vol. 97, Winter 1968.

Isaacs, Harold R. *The Tragedy of the Chinese Revolution*. First edition published in 1929. Stanford: Stanford University Press, 1961. 2nd rev. edition.

Jian Bozan. *Lishi zhexue jiaocheng* [Lectures on Historical Philosophy]. Changsha, 1938.

———. "Yihetuan yundong" [The Boxer Movement]. In *Yihetuan yundongshi lunwenxuan* [Selected Articles on the Boxer Rebellion], 1–6. Beijing: Zhonghua, 1984.

Jiang Guangci. *Paoxiao le de tudi* [The Roaring Land] (1930). In *Jiang Guangci quanji* [Collected Works of Jiang Guangci]. Vol. 2, 155–423. Shanghai: Shanghai wenyi, 1982.

Jiang Jilin and Wang Bingshu. "Liao Mengqiao." In *Zhonggong dangshi renwu zhuan*, Vol. 56.

Jiang Yongjing. *Baoluoting yu Wuhan Zhengquan* [Mikhail Borodin and the Wuhan Government]. Taipei: Zhongguo xueshuzhuzuo jiangzhu weiyuanhui, 1963.

Jin Chongji and Hu Shengwu. "Yihetuan shiqi de gejieji dongxiang" [The Attitudes of the Various Classes During the Boxer Rebellion]. In *Yihetuan yundongshi Lunwenxuan*, Beijing, 1984.

Jin Yaoji. *Zhongguo xiandaihua yu zhishifenzi* [The Modernization of China and the Intellectuals]. Taipei: Yanxin, 1977.

Jing Yuan. "Ping liangben lun Zhongguo jingji de zhuzuo" [A Review of Two Books about Chinese Economy]. In *Zhongguo shehuishi de lunzhan*, Vol. 1. 1931.

Johnson, Chalmers. *Peasant Nationalism and Communist Power: The Emergence of Revolutionary China, 1937–1945.* Stanford: Stanford University Press, 1962.

Kiernan, V. G. *Imperialism and Its Contradictions.* New York: Routledge, 1995.

Kinkley, Jeffrey C. *The Odyssey of Shen Congwen.* Stanford: Stanford University Press, 1987.

Kohn, Hans. *The Idea of Nationalism: A Study in Its Origins and Background.* New York: Collier Books, 1967.

Kong Fanjian. "Mao Zedong Tongzhi yu banzhimindi banfengjian shehui jingji lilun de xingcheng" [Comrade Mao Zedong and the Formation of the Theory of Semi-colonial and Semi-feudal Social Economy]. *Shehui kexue,* 1983(12), 17–20.

Kovalev, Evgenii Fedorovich. *Arenda i Arendnye Otnosheniia v Kitae: Ocherk* [Rent and Rent Relations in China: A Brief Study]. n.p., 1947.

Kulp, Daniel Harrison II. *Country Life in South China, the Sociology of Familism, Volume I, Pheonix Village.* New York: Columbia University Press, 1925.

Kwok, Daniel. *Scientism in Chinese Thought.* New Haven: Yale University Press, 1965.

———. "Mao Tse-tung and Populism." In Lee Ngok and Leung Chikeung, eds., *China:Development and Challenge, Proceedings of the Fifth Leverhulme Conference.* Hong Kong: Center of Asian Studies, University of Hong Kong, 1979.

Lai Yi. "Mao weiyuan zai liandui jiandang" [Commissiar Mao Built Party Branches at the Batallion Level]. *Xinghuo liaoyuan,* Vol.1, Part 1,1958.

Lao Xiang [Wang Xiangchen]. *Huangtuni* [The Yellow Earth]. Shanghai: Meicheng, 1936.

Lei Xiaocen. *Sanshinian dongluan Zhongguo* [Three Decades of Chaos in China]. Hong Kong: Yazhou, 1955.

Lei Yi . "Zhongguo nongcun shehui xingzhi lunzhan yu xinminzhuzhuyi lilun de xingcheng" [The Debate on the Nature of Chinese Rural Society and the Formation of the Theory of New Democracy]. *Ershiyi shiji* (Hong Kong), 1996(2).

Lenin, V. I. *The Development of Capitalism in Russia.* Moscow: Progress Publishers,1966.

———. *What is to be Done?* Joe Fineberg and George Hanna, trans. London/New York: Penguin Books, 1988.

———. "Democracy and Narodism in China" (1912). In *Lenin: Collected Works*, Vol. 18, 163–169. Moscow: Foreign Languages Press, 1963.

Lewis, Oscar. *Life in a Mexican Village: Tepoztlan Restudied.* Urbana: University of Illinois Press, 1951.

Li Ang [Zhu Xinfan, Zhu Qihua, Zhu Peiwo]. *Hongse wutai* [The Red Stage] (1941). Beiping: Shenli Press, 1946 (reprint).

Li Bo [Zhou Libo]. "Tan Ah Q" [About Ah Q] (1941). In *Liushinianlai Lu Xun yanjiu lunwenxuan*, Vol.1.

Li Chuntao. "Haifeng nongmin yundong jiqi zhidaozhe Peng Pai" [The Peasant Movement in Haifeng and Its Leader Peng Pai] (1924). In *Peng Pai yanjiu shiliao* [Historical Materials on Peng Pai], 280–314. Guangzhou:Guangdong renmin, 1981.

Li Da. "Taolun shehuizhuyi bing zhi Liang Rengong" [Discussions on Socialism and My Criticism of Liang Qichao]. *Xinqingnian*, 9(1), 1921, 5.

———. *Xiandai shehuixue* (1926). In *Li Da wenji* [Collected Works of Li Da], Vol.1. Beijing: Renmin, 1980.

———. *Shehui zhi jichu zhishi* [Basic Knowledge of the Society] (1929,3). In Ibid.

———. "Pipan Fei Xiaotong de maiban shehuixue" [Criticizing the Comprador Sociology of Fei Xiaotong]. *Zhexue yanjiu* (Beijing), 1957(5).

Li Dazhao. "Leting tongxin" [Letters from Leting] (1917). In *Li Dazhao quanji* [Collected Works of Li Dazhao], Vol. 2, 706–708. Shijiazhuang: Hebei jiaoyu, 1999.

———. "Qingnian yu nongcun" [The Youth and the Villages] (1919). In *Li Dazhao quanji*, Vol. 3, 179–183.

———. "Guangming yu hei'an" [Brightness and Darkness] (1919). In Ibid., 186.

———. "Wan'e zhiyuan" [The Sources of All Evils] (1919). In Ibid., 298.

———. "'Shaonian Zhongguo' de 'shaonian xingdong'" [The "Youthful Activities" of the "Young China"] (1919). In *Li Dazhao quanji*, Vol. 3, 318-322.

———. "Dongxi cunluo shenghuo de yidian" [The Differences Between the Village Life in the East and that in the West] (1919). In *Li Dazhao quanji*, Vol. 3, 352.

———. "You jingjishang jieshi Zhongguo jindai sixiang biandong de yuanyin" [The Economic Interpretation of the Changes in Modern Chinese Thought] (1920). In *Li Dazhao quanji*, Vol. 3, 433–441.

———. "Diji laodongzhe" [Lower-class Working People] (1920). In Ibid., 451.

———. "Zhishi jieji de shengli" [The Victory of the Intelligentsia] (1920). In Ibid., 457.

———. "Biange de yuandongli" [The Moving Force for Change] (1920). In Ibid., 534.

———. "Zhongguo de shehuizhuyi yu shijie de zibenzhuyi" [The Chinese Socialism and the International Capitalism] (1921). In *Li Dazhao quanji*, Vol. 3, 603–604.

———. "Shehuizhuyi xia zhi shiye" [The Industry Under Socialism] (1921). In Ibid., 617–618.

———. "Daying diguozhuyi qinlue Zhongguo shi" [History of the British Imperialists' Invasion of China] (1925). In *Li Dazhao quanji*, Vol. 4, 587–594.

———. "Tudi yu nongmin" [The Land and the Peasant] (1925). In Ibid., 616–631.

———. "Sun Zhongshan xiansheng zai Zhongguo minzu gemingshi shang zhi weizhi" [The Role of Mr. Sun Zhongshan in the History of Chinese National Revolution] (1926,3,12). In *Li Dazhao wenji*, Vol. 2.

———. "Makesi de Zhongguo minzu geming guan" [Marx's View of the Chinese National Revolution] (1926,5). In *Li Dazhao wenji*, Vol. 2.

Li Guanyang. "Dui Yan Xishan de pouxi" [An Anatomy of Yan Xishan]. In *Yan Xishan qiren qishi* [Yan Xishan: the Man and His Deeds]. Taiyuan: Shanxi gaoxiao lianhe, 1992.

Li Hanjun. "Jinlebule!" [We Do Make Progress!]. *Xinqingnian*, 9(1), 1921,5.

Li Ji. "Shehuizhuyi yu Zhongguo" [Socialism and China]. *Xinqingnian*, 8(6). 1921.

———. "Duiyu Zhongguo shehuishi lunzhan de gongxian yu piping" [My Contribution to and Criticism of the Debate about Chinese Social History]. In *Zhongguo shehuishi de lunzhan*, Vols. 2–4. Shanghai: Shengzhou guoguang, 1932–1933.

Li Ji. *Li Ji wenji* [Collected Works of Liji]. Vol.1. Shanghai: Shanghai wenyi, 1982.

Li Jinghan. "Shenru minjian de yixie jingyan yu ganxiang" [Some Experiences of and Reflections on Going Deep into the Masses]. *Duli pinglun,* no. 179, 1935,11.

———. *Zhongguo nongcun wenti* [China's Rural Problems]. Shanghai: Shangwu, 1937.

Li Jinming. *Chenying* [Dust Shadow] (1927). Reprinted in *Zhongguo xin-wenxue daxi 1927–1937* [Anthology of Modern Chinese Literature, 1927–1937]. Vol. 6, 65–138. Shanghai: Shanghai wenyi, 1984.

Li Jui [Li Rui]. *The Early Revolutionary Activities of Comrade Mao Tse-tung.* New York: M. E. Sharpe, 1977.

Li Lisan [Li San]. "Zhongguo geming de gengben wenti" [The Fundamental Issues of the Chinese Revolution]. *Buerseweike* [Bulshevik], 3:2–5, 1930.

Li Peng et al. *Anhui lidai mingren* [Prominent Figures in the History of Anhui]. Hefei: Huangshan, 1987.

Li Oufan [Leo Ou-fan Lee]. *Zhongxi wenxue de huixiang* [Rethinking Chinese and Western Literature]. Hong Kong: Sanlian Press, 1986.

Li Rui. *Zaonian Mao Zedong* [The Early Life of Mao Zedong]. Shenyang: Liaoning renmin, 1993.

Li Shouyong. "Guxiansheng zaonian zai Beida de yixie huiyi" [Gu Mengyu's Early Days in Peking University]. *Zhuanji wenxue,* 29(1). Taipei, 1976.

Li Tao. "Yi gongnong gemingjun di'ershi diyituan" [My Memory of the First Regiment of the Second Division of the Workers-Peasants Revolutionary Army]. *Xinghuo liaoyuan,* Vol. 1, Part 1. 1958.

Li Ting. "Milin xinghuo" [Sparks in the Forest]. In *Xinghuo liaoyuan,* Vol.1, Part 1,1958.

Li, V. F., ed. *Intelligentsiia i sotsial'nyi progress v razvivaiushchikhsia stranakh Azii i Afriki* [The Intelligentsia and Social Process in the Developing Countries of Asia and Africa]. Moscow: Nauka, 1981.

Li Xisuo and Yuan Qing. *Liang Qichao zhuan* [A Biography of Liang Qichao]. Beijing: Renmin, 1994.

Li Yiyuan. "Zhongguo wenhua zhong xiaochuantong de zairenshi" [A Re-examination of the Little Tradition in Chinese Culture]. *Xiandai yu chuantong* [Modernity and Tradition] (Guangzhou), 1995(3).

Li Yinchun. "Bushi minguo buhao" [It's not that the Republic is not Good]. In *Nongmin,* 2(14), 1926, 7, 11.

———. "Haishi gonghe hao" [The Republic is Good No Matter What]. In *Nongmin,* 2(17), 1926, 8, 11.

Li Yunjing. *Zhongguo xiandai banhua shi* [A History of Modern Chinese Prints]. Taiyuan: Shanxi renmin, 1996.

Li Zehou. "Lue Lun Lu Xun sixiang de fazhan" [The Evolution of Lu Xun's Thought] (1979). In *Liushinianlai Lu Xun yanjiu lunwen xuan*, Vol. 2, 1982.

———. "Ji Zhongguo xiandai sanci xueshu lunzhan" [Three Academic Debates in Contemporary China]. In Li Zehou, *Zhongguo xiandai sixiang shilun* [Essays on Contemporary Chinese Thought]. Beijing: Dongfang, 1987.

Li Zhongkai and Xie Zhiqiang. "Liu Shiqi." In *Zhonggong dangshi renwu zhuan*, Vol. 57, Xian: Shanxi renmin, 1996.

Li Zixiang. "Laximan baogaoshu zhi nongcun bufen de yantao" [An Examination of the Section on Rural China in the Report of Ludwig Rajchman]. In Qian Jiaju, ed. *Zhongguo nongcun jingji lunwenji* [Collected Essays on the Chinese Rural Economy]. Shanghai: Zhonghua shuju, 1936.

Liang Qichao. "Lishishang Zhonghua guomin shiye zhi chengbai ji jinhou gejin zhi jiyun" [The Fate of the Chinese National Movement in History and the Opportunity for Its Future Development]. *Gaizao*, 3(2), 1920,10.

———. "Fu Zhang Dongsun shu lun shehuizhuyi yundong" [A Reply to Zhang Dongsun: On Socialist Movement]. *Gaizao*, 3(6), 1920,12.

———. "Wuqiangjieji dui youqiangjieji" [The Class with Guns Versus the Class Without Guns] (Speech delivered on 1921,11,12). In Liang Qichao, *Yinbingshi heji*. Beijing: Zhonghua, 1936.

———. "Wuchanjieji yu wuyejieji" [The Class without Properties and the Class without Jobs] (1925,5,1). In *Liang Qichao shiwenxuan* [Selected Poems and Essays of Liang Qichao], 315–316. Guangzhou: Guangdong renmin, 1983.

Liang Shuming [Liang Sou-ming]. "Zhongguo wenti zhi jiejue" [The Solutions of China's Problems] (1930). In *Liang Shuming quanji* [Collected Works of Liang Shuming], Vol. 5. Jinan: Shandong renmin, 1992.

———. "Shandong xiangcun jianshe yanjiuyuan sheli zhiqu ji banfa gaiyao." [The Purpose and Method of the Shandong Academy of Rural Reconstruction] (1930). In *Liang Shuming quanji*, Vol. 5.

———. "Jingyi qingjiao Hu Shizhi xiansheng" [Asking for Advice from Hu Shi] (1930). In *Liang Shuming quanji*, Vol. 5.

———. "Shehui benwei de jiaoyu xitong cao'an" [A Draft about the Society-centered Educational System] (1933). In *Liang Shuming quanji*, Vol. 5.

———. "Zishu" [About Myself] (1934). In *Liang Shuming quanji*, Vol. 2, 1989.

———. "Cunxue xiangxue xuzhi" [Guidelines for Village and Township Schools] (1934). In *Liang Shuming quanji*, Vol. 5, 459.

———. *Xiangcun jianshe dayi* [Essentials of Rural Reconstruction] (1936). In *Liang Shuming quanji*, Vol. 1, 1989.

———. *Xiangcun jianshe lilun* [Theories of Rural Reconstruction] (1937). In *Liang Shuming quanji*, Vol. 2.

———. *Zhongguo wenhua yaoyi* [Essentials of Chinese Culture] (1949). In *Liang Shuming quanji*, Vol. 3, 1990.

———. "Wo canjia guogong hetan de jingguo" [My Participation in the Nationalist- Communist Peace Negotiation] (1950/1951). In *Liang Shuming quanji*, Vol. 6, 1993.

Liao Zhongkai. "Geming jixu de gongfu" [The Art of Carrying on the Revolution] (1919). In *Shuangqing wenji* [Collected Works of Liao Zhongkai and He Xiangning]. Vol. 1. Shang Mingxuan and Yu Yanguang, eds. Beijing: Renmin, 1985.

———. "Zai Guangzhou Zhongguo guomindang zhuidao Liening dahui de yanshuo" [Speech at the Nationalist Party's Ceremony Commemorating Lenin in Guangzhou] (1924,2,24). In *Shuangqing wenji*, Vol.1.

———. "Zai shijing binggongchang qingnian gongren xuexiao de yanshuo" [Speech at the Young Workers' School of the Shijing Arsenal] (1924,3). In *Shuangqing wenji*, Vol. 1.

———."Gemingdang yingyou de jingshen" [The Spirit that a Revolutionary Party Should Possess] (1924,6,24). In *Shuangqing wenji*, Vol. 1.

———. "Nongmin yundong suodang zhuyi zhi yaodian" [Essentials for Making Peasant Movement] (1924,7-8). In *Shuangqing wenji*, Vol. 1, 698–703.

———. "Nongmin jiefang de fangfa" [The Method of Liberating the Peasant] (1924,8). In *Shuangqing wenji*, Vol. 1.

———. "Gemingpai yu fangemingpai" [Revolutionaries and Counter-revolutionaries] (1925,5). In *Shuangqing wenji*, Vol. 1.

Lin Ganquan, Tian Renlong, and Li Zude. *Zhongguo gudaishi fenqi taolun wushinian* [Five Decades of Debate on the Periodization of Ancient Chinese History]. Shanghai: Shanghai renmin, 1982.

Lin Yaohua [Lin, Yueh-hwa]. *The Golden Wing, A Sociological Study of Chinese Familism*. London: Kegan Paul, 1947.

Lin Yutang. *My Country and My People*. New York: John Day, 1935.

Ling Yu. *Cong Biancheng zouxiang shijie: dui zuowei wenxuejia de Shen Congwen de yanjiu* [From the Border Town to the World—A Study on Shen Congwen as a Writer]. Beijing: Sanlian, 1985.

Lippit, Victor. *Land Reform and Economic Development in China: A Study of Institutional Change and Development Finance*. White Plains, N.Y.: International Arts and Sciences, 1974.

Little, Daniel. *Understanding Peasant China: Case Studies in the Philosophy of Social Science.* New Haven/London: Yale University Press, 1989.

———. "New Perspectives on the Chinese Rural Economy, 1885–1935." *Republican China*, 18(1), 1992, 23–40.

Liu Han. "Nanchang Qiyi canjiazhe—zhidao xingming de youduoshao?" [The Participants of the Nanchang Uprising—How Many Names Do We Know?]. *Renwu* [Beijing], 1998(8), 141–142.

Liu Han et al. "Zhang Shanming." In *Nanyue yinglie zhuan* [Biographies of the Martyrs of Guangdong]. Vol. 1. Guangzhou: Guangdong renmin, 1983.

Liu Hsiao-hsiao. "Notes on Converstation with Several Chinese Intellectuals" (1972). In James McGough, ed., *Fei Hsiao-tung: The Dilemma of a Chinese Intellectual.* 1979.

Liu Mengyun [Zhang Wentian]. "Zhongguo jingji zhi xingzhe wenti de yanjiu" [A Study of the Nature of the Chinese Economy]. In *Zhongguo shehuishi de lunzhan*, Vol. 1.

Liu Renjing. "Liu Renjing tan tuoluosijipai zai Zhongguo" [Liu Renjing Talking About the Chinese Trotskyite Group]. *Zhonggong dangshi ziliao*, no. 1. Beijing: Zhonggong Zhongyang dangxiao, 1982.

Liu Shaoqi. *How to be a Good Communist.* Beijing: Foreign Languages Press, 1951.

———. "Guanyu tudi gaige wenti de baogao" [Report on the Land Reform] (1950). In *Liu Shaoqi xuanji* [Selected Works of Liu Shaoqi]. Vol.2. Beijing: Renmin, 1981.

Liu Shipei [Shen Shu]. "Renlei junli shuo" [On the Equalization of Human Strength]. *Tianyi*, Vol. 3:(30), 1907.

———. "Nongmin jiku diaochahui zhangcheng" [Guidelines of the Association for Investigating the Sufferings of the Peasants]. *Tianyi*, Vol. 8–10, 313, 1907.

———. "Hengbao fakanci" [Preface to Hengbao]. *Hengbao*, no. 1, 1908.

———. "Lun Zhongguo tianzhu zhi zui'e" [On the Evils of the Chinese Landlords]. *Hengbao*, no. 7, 1908.

———. "Wuzhengfu geming yu nongmin geming" [The Anarchist Revolution and the Peasant Revolution]. *Hengbao*, no. 7, 1908.

———. "Beidianpian" [Pity the Tenants] (1907). In *Xinhaigeming qian shinianjian shilun xuanji*, 2(2), 744–754.

Liu Yuansheng et al. "Shuikoushan shang de hongqi—Liu Dongxuan lieshi zhuanlue" [The Red Flag on the Shuikou Mountain—A Brief Biography of Martyr Liu Dongxuan]. In *Buqu de gongchandangren.* Vol. 1, 303–340. Beijing: Renmin, 1980.

Liu Zhenlan. "Jindai Zhongguo shehui xingzhi taolun shuping" [A Review of the Discussions on the Nature of Modern Chinese Society]. *Jindaishi yanjiu* (Beijing), 1994(2), 236–263.

Lü Mingzhuo. *Li Dazhao sixiang yanjiu* [A Study of Li Dazhao's Thought]. Shijiazhuang: Hebei renmin, 1983.

Lu Xiuqi. "Jiushi laoweng chong rudang—Ji Fu Bocui de kanke daolu" [A Ninety-year Old Man Re-joins the Party: The Rough Path of Fu Bocui]. *Renwu* (Beijing), 1990(2).

Lu Xun. "Po 'esheng lun" [On Breaking Through the Voices of Evil] (1908). In *Lu Xun Quanji* [Collected Works of Lu Xun]. Vol. 8, 23–38. Beijing: Renmin wenxue, 1981.

———. "Nala zouhou zenyang" [What Will Happen After Nola Leaves?] (1923). In *Lu Xun quanji*. Vol. 1, 162–163.

———. "Lun zhaoxiang zhilei" [On Phototaking and Other Matters] (1925). In *Lu Xun quanji*, Vol. 1,183.

———. "Zailun Leifengta de daodiao" [More on the Collapse of the Leifeng Pagoda] (1925). In *Lu Xun quanji*, Vol. 1, 194.

———. "Eyiben Ah Q zhengzhuan xu ji zhuzhe zixu zhuanlue" [Preface to the Russian Edition of a True Story of Ah Q and a Brief Autobiography of the Writer] (1925). In *Lu Xun quanji*, Vol. 7, 81–82.

———. "Suiganlu sanshiqi" [Random Thought No. 37]. In *Lu Xun quanji*. Vol. 1, 309–310.

———. "Lu Xun zhi Xu Xusheng." [To Xu Xusheng]. In *Lu Xun Quanji*. Vol. 3, 24–25.

———. "Xuejie de sanhun" [The Three Spirits of the Academic Circle] (1926). In *Lu Xun quanji*, Vol. 3.

———. "Ah Q zhengzhuan de chengyin" [The Origins of The True Story of Ah Q] (1926). In *Lu Xun quanji*, Vol. 3.

———. "Geming shidai de wenxue" [The Literature of the Revolutionary Era] (1927). In *Lu Xun quanji*. Vol. 3.

———. "Chenying tici" [Preface to *The Dusty Shadow*] (1927). In *Lu Xun quanji*. Vol. 3, 547.

———. "Yingyiben duanpianxiaoshuo zixu" [Preface to the English Edition of My Short Stories] (1933). In *Lu Xun quanji*, Vol. 7, 389–390.

———. "*Xin E hua xuan xiaoying*" [Preface to *The New Russian Paintings*] (1930). In *Lu Xun quanji*, Vol. 7, 343–348.

———. "Zhi Xiao Jun di wu xin(1934)" [The Fifth Letter to Xiao Jun]. In *Wo Xinzhong de Lu Xun*, 206–240. Changsha: Hunan renmin, 1979.

———. "Zhi Xiao Jun di jiu xin (1934)" [The Nineth Letter to Xiao Jun]. In *Wo xinzhong de Lu Xun*, 206–240.

———. *Diary of a Madman and Other Stories*. William A. Lyell, trans. Honolulu: University of Hawaii Press, 1990.

Luo Baoshan and Sang Bing. "Minzu zichanjieji yu Yihetuan yundong" [The National Bourgeoisie and the Boxer Rebellion]. In *Yihetuan yundongshi lunwenxuan*, 466–491. Beijing: Zhonghua, 1984.

Luo Fu. "Ping 'chuncan'" [My Comment on "The Spring Silkworm"] (1933,7). In *Mao Dun zhuanji*. Vol. 2, Part 2. Fuzhou: Fujian renmin, 1983.

Luo Guibo. "Gannan chuqi geming huodong de diandi huiyi" [Some Memories of the Early Revolutionary Activities in Southern Jiangxi] In *Huiyi Zhongyang suqu*. Nanchang: Jiangxi renmin, 1986.

Luo Shu. "Shengrenqi" [Twice-married Woman](1936). In *Stories from the Thirties*. Vol. 1, 395–415. Gladys Yang, trans. Beijing: Panda Books, 1982.

Ma Dongyu. *Liang Shuming zhuan* [A Biography of Liang Shuming]. Beijing: Dongfang, 1993.

Ma Zha Ya Er [Madjar]. *Zhongguo nongcun jingji yanjiu* [A Study of Chinese Rural Economy]. Chen Daiqing and Peng Guiqiu, trans. Shanghai: Shenzhou guoguang, 1934. 3rd ed.

Mao Dun. "Mud" (1929). In Helen Siu, ed. *Furrows*, 33–39.

———. "Du Ni Huanzhi" [My Reading of Ni Huanzhi] (1929). In *Mao Dun quanji* [Collected Works of Mao Dun], Vol. 19, 197–217. Beijing: Renmin wenxue, 1991.

———. "Dazexiang" [The Daze Village] (1930). In *Mao Dun quanji*, Vol. 8, 208–216. Beijing: Renmin wenxue, 1985.

———. "Chuncan" [The Spring Silkworm] (1932). In *Mao Dun quanji*, Vol. 8, 312–337.

———. "Ziye houji" [Postscript to the Twilight] (1932). In *Mao Dun quanji*, Vol. 3, 553–554.

———. "Ziye shi zenyang xiecheng de" [How Did I Write the Twilight]. (1939). In *Mao Dun quanji*. Vol. 22, 52–56. Beijing, 1993.

———. "Diquan duhougan" [My Comments on *The Underground Spring*] (1932). In *Mao Dun quanji*. Vol. 19, 331–335. Beijing, 1991.

———. "Qiushou" [The Autumn Harvest] (1933). In *Mao Dun quanji*. Vol. 8, 338–368.

———. "Candong" [The Last Days of Winter] (1933). *In Mao Dun wenji*, Vol. 8, 369–389.

———. "Wang Tongzhao de Shanyu" [The Mountain Rain by Wang Tongzhao] (1933). In *Mao Dun quanji*,Vol. 19, 557–569.

———. "Zhongguo xinwenxue daxi—xiaoshuo yiji daoyan" [Introduction to *The Anthology of Modern Chinese Literature*, Vol. 1] (1935). In *Mao Dun quanji*, Vol. 20, 485–492. Beijing, 1990.

———."Lun Lu Xun de xiaoshuo" [On Lu Xun's Stories] (1948). In *Mao Dun quanji*, Vol. 23, 430-438.

———. *Wo zouguo de daolu* [My Life]. 3 vols. Hong Kong: Sanlian, 1981.

Mao Zedong. "Letter to Li Jinxi" (1917,8,23). In *Mao's Road to Power*, Vol. 1, 130–136. Stuart Schram, ed. New York: M. E. Sharpe, 1992.

———. "Letter to Xiao Xudong, Cai Linbin, and the Other Members in France" (1920,12,1). In *Mao's Road to Power*, Vol. 2, 5–14, 1994.

———. "Analysis of All the Classes in Chinese Society" (1925,12). In *Mao's Road to Power*, Vol. 2, 249–262, 1994.

———. "An Analysis of the Various Classes among the Chinese Peasantry and Their Attitudes toward the Revolution] (1926,1). In *Mao's Road to Power*, Vol. 2, 303–309, 1994.

———. "The National Revolution and the Peasant Movement" (1926,9). In *Mao's Road to Power*, Vol. 2, 387–392, 1994.

———. "Report on the Peasant Movement in Hunan" (1927,2). In *Mao's Road to Power*, Vol. 2, 429–464, 1994.

———. "Xunwu Investigation" (1930). In *Mao's Road to Power*, Vol. 3, 296–418, 1995.

———. "Lun Lu Xun" [On Lu Xun] (1937, 10). In *Mao Zedong ji* [Collected Works of Mao Zedong]. Vol. 5, 379–382. Hong Kong: Jindai shiliao gongyingshe, 1975.

———. "Chinese Revolution and Chinese Communist Party" (1939). In *Selected Works of Mao Tse-tung*, Vol. 2. Beijing: Foreign Languages Press, 1965.

———. "The Orientation of the Youth Movement" (1939,5,4). In *Selected Works of Mao Tse-tung*, Vol. 2, 1965.

———. "Guanyu nongcun diaocha" [About Rural Investigation] (1941). In *Mao Zedong nongcun diaocha wenji*, 21–27. Beijing: Renmin, 1982.

———. "Oppose Stereotyped Party Writing" (1942). In *Selected Works of Mao Tse-tung*, Vol. 3, 1965.

———. "Talks at the Yenan Forum on Literature and Art" (1942,5). In *Selected Works of Mao Tse-tung*, Vol. 3, 1965.

———. "On the People's Democratic Dictatorship." In *Selected Works of Mao Tse-tung*, Vol. 4.

Marks, Robert. *Rural Revolution in South China: Peasants and the Making of History in Haifeng County, 1570–1930*. Madison: University of Wisconsin Press, 1984.

Marx, Karl. *The 18th Brumaire of Louis Bonaparte* [1852]. New York: International Publishers, 1991.

———. *Karl Marx on Colonialism and Modernization: His Dispatches and Other Writings on China, India, Mexico, the Middle East and North America*. Edited with an introduction by Shlomo Avineri. New York: Doubleday, 1968.

McDonald, Angus, W. Jr. *The Urban Origins of Rural Revolution, Elites and the Masses in Hunan, China, 1911–1927.* Berkeley and Los Angeles: University of California Press, 1978.

McGough, James P., ed. and trans. *Fei Hsiao-tung: The Dilemma of a Chinese Intellectual.* New York: M. E. Sharpe, 1979.

Meisner, Maurice. *Li Ta-chao and the Origins of Chinese Marxism.* Cambridge: Harvard University Press, 1967.

Meng Xiangcai. *Liang Qichao zhuan* [A Biography of Liang Qichao]. Beijing: Beijing, 1980.

Miao Min. *Fang Zhimin zhandou de yisheng* [Fang Zhiming's Life as a Fighter]. Beijing: Gongren, 1958.

Moore, Barrington, Jr. *Social Origins of Dictatorship and Democracy.* Boston: Beacon Press, 1966.

Moulder, Frances. *Japan, China, and the Modern World Economy: Toward a Reinterpretation of East Asian Development ca. 1600 to ca. 1918.* London/New York/Melbourne: Cambridge University Press, 1977.

Mugruzin, A. S. *Agrarnye Otnosheniia v Kitae v 20–40-kh Godakh xx v.* [Agrarian Relations in China between the 1920s and 1940s]. Moscow: Nauka, 1970.

———. *Agrarno-krestianskaia Problema v Kitae v Pervoi Polovine XX veka* [The Peasant and Agrarian Problem in China in the First Half of the 20th Century]. Moscow: Nauka, 1994.

Myers, Ramon H. *The Chinese Peasant Economy: Agricultural Development in Hopei and Shantung, 1890–1949.* Cambridge: Harvard University Press, 1970.

———. "How Did the Modern Chinese Economy Develop?—A Review Article." *Journal of Asian Studies*, 50(3), 1991, 604–628.

Nairn, Tom. *The Break-up of Britain: Crisis and Neo-nationalism.* London: NLB, 1981.

Ni Zhongwen. "Huiyi Zheng Weisan tongzhi tan E-Yu-Wan suqu lishizhong de jige zhongda wenti" [Memory of Comrade Zheng Weisan's Discussions about some Important Issues in the History of the Hubei-Henan-Anhui Soviet Area]. *Wuhan daxue xuebao* [*Journal of Wuhan University*], 1983(3).

Nie Rongzheng. "Nanchang qiyi de lishi yiyi he jingyan jiaoxun" [The Historical Significance, Experience and Lessons of the Nanchang Uprising]. In *Xinghuo liaoyuan*, Vol. 1, part 1. Beijing, 1958.

North, Robert and Xenia Eudin. *M. N. Roy's Mission to China: The Communist–Kuomintang Split of 1927.* Berkeley: University of California Press, 1963.

Ouyang Fanhai. "Lun Ah Q zhengzhuan" [On the True Story of Ah Q] (1942). In *Liushinianlai Lu Xun yanjiu lunwenxuan*, Vol. 1, 514–544.

Paauw, Douglas S. "The Kuomintang and Economic Stagnation, 1928–1937." *Journal of Asian Studies*, Vol. 16, 1957, 213–220.

Pan Dongzhou. "Zhongguo jingji de xingzhi" [The Nature of the Chinese Economy]. *Xinsichao*, no. 5. Shanghai, 1930,4.

Pan Shouyong. "Xunzhao Taitou" [Looking for Taitou]. *Dushu* [Beijing], 1999(2):101–107.

Pantsov, Alexander, and Gregor Benton. "Did Trotsky Oppose Entering the Guomindang 'From the First'." *Republican China*, 19(2), 1994, 52–66.

Peng Pai. "Laodongzhe tongqinghui de yuanqi" [The Origin of the Associaition of the Laborers Sympathizers] (1921,7). In *Peng Pai wenji* [Collected Works of Peng Pai], 1–2. Beijing: Renmin, 1981.

———. "Peng Pai gei Li Chuntao" [Peng Pai's Letter to Li Chuntao] (1922,11,18). In *Peng Pai wenji*, 10–12.

———. "Haifeng zongnonghui dui shiju xuanyan" [Declaration of the Haifeng General Peasant Association About the Current Events] (1923). In *Peng Pai wenji*, 25–26.

———. "Haifeng laonongjie baogaoshu" [Report on the Peasant Festival of Haifeng] (1923,5). In *Peng Pai wenji*, 30–31.

———. "Peng Pai gei Li Chuntao" [Peng Pai's Letter to Li Chuntao] (1923,6,5). In *Peng Pai wenji*, 32.

———. "Peng Pai gei Li Chuntao" [Peng Pai's Letter to Li Chuntao] (1923,7,19). In *Peng Pai wenji*, 39.

———. "Peng Pai gei Li Chuntao" [Peng Pai's Letter to Li Chuntao] (1923,7,30). In *Peng Pai wenji*, 40.

———. "Haifeng nongmin qigao tongbao shu" [A Letter to Our Compatriots from the Peasants of Haifeng] (1923,8). In *Peng Pai wenji*, 43–45.

———. "Peng Pai gei Liu Renjing [Peng Pai's Letter to Liu Renjing] (1924,1,20). In *Peng Pai wenji*, 53–55.

———. "Guanyu Haifeng nongmin yundong de yifengxin" [A Letter About the Haifeng Peasant Movement] (1924,5,11). In *Peng Pai wenji*, 57–62.

———. "Yijiu'ersinian shi'eryue wuri gei Zhonggong Guangdong quwei nongmin yundong weiyuanhui de buchong baogao" [Supplementary Report to the Committee for Peasant Movement of the CCP Guangdong Regional Committee Made on December 5, 1924]. In *Peng Pai wenji*, 68–69.

———. "Zai shenggang bagong gongren daibiao di sanshiliu ci dahui shang de baogao" [Report to the 36th Congress of the Delegates of the Striking Workers of Hong Kong and Guangzhou] (1925,10,18). In *Peng Pai Wenji*, 94–100.

———. "Haifeng nongmin yundong" [The Peasant Movement of Haifeng] (1926). In *Peng Pai wenji*, 101–186.

———. "Zai diliujie nongminyundong jiangxisuo de jiangyan" [Speech to the Sixth Class of the Peasant Movement Institute] (1926,6,2). In *Peng Pai Wenji*, 194–197.

Perkins, Dwight. *Agricultural Development in China*. Chicago: Aldine Publishing, 1969.

———. "Growth and Changing Structure of China's Twentieth Century Economy." In *China's Modern Economy in Historical Perspective*. D. Perkins, ed. Stanford: Stanford University Press, 1975

Perry, Elizabeth. *Rebels and Revolutionaries in North China: 1845-1945*. Stanford: Stanford University Press, 1980.

Pi Shaoyi and Liu Miaoruo. "Hu Yun." In *Zhonggong dangshi renwu zhuan*, Vol. 18, 146–166. Xian, 1984.

Pisarev, A. A. *Gomindan i agrarno-krest'yanski vopros v Kitae v 20-30 gody XX v.* [The Nationalist Party and the Agrarian/Peasant Question in China in the 1920s and 1930s]. Moscow: Nauka, 1986.

Polachek, James. "The Moral Economy of the Kiangsi Soviet (1928–1934)." *The Journal of Asian Studies*, 42(4), 1983.

Polanyi, Karl. *Primitive, Archaic and Modern Economies: Essays of Karl Polanyi*. George Dalton, ed. Boston: Beacon Press, 1968.

Pu Qingquan. "Zhongguo Tuopai de chansheng he miewang" [The Birth and Death of the Chinese Trotskyism]. *Wenshi ziliao xuanji*, No. 71, 27–78.

———. "Wosuo zhidao de Chen Duxiu" [Chen Duxiu as I Know Him]. *Wenshi ziliao xuanji*, no. 71, 79–101.

Qi Shufen. *Jingji qinlue xia zhi Zhongguo* [China under Economic Invasion]. Shanghai: Guanghua, 1925.

Qian Jiaju. "Dingxian de shiyan yundong neng jiejue Zhongguo nongcun wenti ma?" [Can the Dingxian Experimental Movement Solve China's Rural Problem?] (1934). Qian Jiaju, ed. *Zhongguo nongcun jingji lunwenji*, 23–36.

———, ed. *Zhongguo nongcun jingji lunwenji* [Collected Essays on Chinese Rural Economy]. Shanghai: Zhonghua shuju, 1936.

Qian Jiaju and Li Zixiang, eds. *Zhongguo xiangcun jianshe pipan* [Criticizing the Rural Reconstruction Movement of China]. Shanghai: Xinzhi, 1936.

Qian Junrui. "Ping Bokai jiaoshou suozhu Zhongguo nongchang jingji" [About *The Chinese Farm Economy* by Professor John Buck]. *Zhongguo nongcun*, 1(1), 1934.

———. "Zhongguo muxia de nongye konghuang" [The Current Agricultural Depression in China]. *Zhongguo nongcun*, 1(3), 1934.

————. "Ping Chen Hansheng xiansheng zhu *Xianjin Zhongguo de tudi wenti*-jianping Chen xiansheng jinzhu *Guangdong nongcun shengchanguanxi yu shengchanli*" [My Comments on *The Current Agrarian Problem in China* by Chen Hansheng—Also on His Recent Work *The Production Relations and Production Forces in Rural Guangdong*]. *Zhongguo nongcun*, 1(5).

————. "Xianjieduan Zhongguo nongcun yanjiu de renwu—Jianlun Wang Yichang, Han Dezhang liangxiansheng nongcun jingji yanjiu de zhuanxiang" [The Current Tasks of Chinese Rural Economic Studies—With Discussions on Wang Yichang and Han Dezhang's Shift of Rural Economic Studies]. *Zhongguo nongcun*,1(6), 1935.

Qian Moxiang and Shen Jichang. "Hong Shen de nongcun sanbuqu" [Hong Shen's Village Trilogy]. In *Hong Shen yanjiu zhuanji* [A Special Collection on Hong Shen]. Sun Qingwen, ed. Hangzhou: Zhejiang wenyi,1986.

Qian Mu. *Guoshi dagang* [An Outline of the National History] (1929). Taipei: Lianjing, 1998 (reprint).

Qian Xingtun [A Ying]. "Siqule de Ah Q shidai" [The Dead Ah Q Era] (1928,3). In *Liushinianlai Lu Xun yanjiu lunwenxuan*, Vol. 1.

Qiao Xuwu. "Ji Bai Lang Shi" [An Account of the Bailang Rebellion]. In Du Chunhe, ed., *Bai Lang qiyi* [The Bailang Rebellion]. Beijing: Zhongguo shehui kexue, 1980.

Qin Yingjun and Zhang Zhanbin eds. *Dalangtaosha—Zhonggong yida renwu zhuan* [Biographies of the Delegates to the First National Congress of the Chinese Communist Party]. Beijing: Hongqi, 1991.

Qing Jian. "Ah Q shidai meiyou si" [The Ah Q Era Has not Ended] (1928,6). In *Liushinianlai Lu Xun yanjiu lunwenxuan*, Vol. 1, 92–93.

Qiongya zongdui shi [A History of the Hainan Column]. Qiongya wuzhuangdouzhengshi bangongshi, ed. Guangzhou: Guangdong renmin, 1986.

Qiu Xu. "Zhongguo de shehui daodi shi shemo shehui—Tao Xisheng cuowu yijian zhi piping" [What is the Nature of the Chinese Society: A Criticism of Tao Xisheng's Erroneous Views]. *Xinsichao*, no. 4, 1930, 2.

Qu Junong. "Dingxian jiaoyu gongzuo" [The Educational Work in Dingxian] (1936). First published in Qu Junong, *Dingxian jiaoyu wenlu* [Collected Works on the Education in Dingxian]. Beiping: Minjianshe, 1937. Reprinted in Lu Hongji, *Zhongguo jinshi de jiaoyu fazhan: 1800–1949* [The Development of Education in Modern China: 1800–1949]. Hong Kong: Huafeng, 1983.

Qu Qiubai. "Yihetuan yundong zhi yiyi yu wusa yundong zhi qiantu" [The Significance of the Boxer Movement and the Future of the May

Thirtieth Movement] (1925). In *Qu Qiubai wenji* [Collected Works of Qu Qiubai]. Vol. 3, 340–353. Beijing: Renmin, 1989.

———. "Guomin geming zhong zhi nongmin wenti" [The Peasant Question in the National Revolution] (1926). In *Qu Qiubai wenji*, Vol. 4, 381–395, 1993.

———. "Duoyu de hua" [Superfluous Words] (1935). In *Qu Qiubai wenji*, Vol. 7, 693–725, 1991.

Ransome, Paul. *Antonio Gramsci: A New Introduction*. London: Harvester Wheatsheaf, 1992.

Rawski, Thomas. *Economic Growth in Prewar China*. Berkeley: University of California Press, 1989.

———. "Ideas About Studying China's Rural Economy: A Comment in the Commentaries." *Republican China*, 18(1), 1992, 146–163.

Redfield, Robert. *Tepoztlan, A Mexican Village: A Study of Folk Life*. Chicago: University of Chicago Press, 1930.

Ren Shu. "Zenyang qieshi yanjiu Zhongguo jingji wenti de shangque" [My Views About How to Study the Problem of Chinese Economy]. In *Zhongguo shehuishi de lunzhan*, Vol. 3.

Rong Mengyuan. "Yihetuan fandi yundong" [The Anti-imperialistic Boxer Movement]. *Lishi jiaoxue*, 1980(11).

Ruan Xiaoxian. "Gei tuanzhongyang de liangge baogao" [Two Reports to the Central Committee of the Communist Youth League]. In *Ruan Xiaoxian wenji* [Collected Works of Ruan Xiaoxian]. Guangzhou: Guangdong renmin, 1984.

———. "Zhongguo nongmin yundong" [The Peasant Movement of China] (1926). In *Ruan Xiaoxian wenji*.

———. "Quanguo nongmin yundong xingshi jiqi zai guomin geming zhong de diwei" [The Situation of the National Peasant Movement and Its Role in the National Revolution] (1926). In *Ruan Xiaoxian wenji*.

Ruan Yingqi, Deng Rongshi, and Yang Jiesheng. "Huang Xuezeng." In *Zhonggong dangshi renwuzhuan*, Vol. 14, 193–219. Xian, 1984.

Schoppa, Keith R. *Blood Road: The Mystery of Shen Dingyi in Revolutionary China*. Berkeley and Los Angeles: University of California Press, 1995.

Schram, Stuart R. *The Political Thought of Mao Tse-tung*. New York: Praeger, 1963.

Schwarcz, Vera. *The Chinese Enlightenment, Intellectuals and the Legacy of the May Fourth Movement of 1919*. Berkeley and Los Angeles: University of California Press, 1986.

Schwartz, Benjamin. "The Intelligentsia in Communist China, A Tentative Comparison." In Richard Pipes, ed., *The Russian intelligentsia*, 164–181. New York: Columbia University Press, 1961.

————. *Chinese Communism and the Rise of Mao*. Cambridge: Harvard University Press, 1961.

————. ed. *Reflections on the May Fourth Movement: A Symposium*. Harvard East Asian Monographs. Cambridge, Mass.: East Asian Research Center, Harvard University, 1973.

Scott, James. *The Moral Economy of the Peasant*. New Haven/London: Yale University Press, 1976.

Selden, Mark. *The Yenan Way in Revolutionary China*. Cambridge: Harvard University Press, 1971.

Seton-Watson, Hugh. *The Pattern of Communist Revolution: A Historical Analysis*. London: Methuen, 1953.

Sha Ting. "Ji He Long" [About He Long]. In *He Long*. Hong Kong: Guangjiaojing, 1977.

Shao Shiping. "Fangshengfeng huiyi de shengli" [The Victory of the Fang Shengfeng Meeting]. *Xinghuo liaoyuan*, Vol. 1, Part 2. Beijing, 1958.

Shao Shiping, Wang Jinxiang, and Hu Delan. "Min-Zhe-Wan-Gan (Gandongbei) dangshi" [History of the CCP in Fujian-Zhejiang-Anhui-Jiangxi (Northeast Jiangxi)]. In *Fujian dangshi ziliao*, no. 1, 1983.

Sheel, Kamal. *Peasant Society and Marxist Intellectuals in China: Fang Zhimin and the Origin of a Revolutionary Movement in the Xinjiang Region*. Princeton: Princeton University Press, 1989.

Shen Congwen. "Zhangfu" [The Husband] (1930). In *Shen Congwen xuanji* [Selected Works of Shen Congwen], Vol. 2, 313–333. Chengdu: Sichuan renmin, 1983.

————. "Biancheng tiji" [Preface to the Border Town] (1934). In *Shen Congwen wenchi* [Collected Works of Shen Congwen], Vol. 6, 70–72. Shao Huaqiang and Ling Yu, eds. Guangzhou: Huacheng/Hong Kong: Sanlian, 1983.

————. "Changhe tiji" [Preface to the *Long River*] (1943). In *Shen Congwen wenchi*, Vol. 7, 2–8.

Sheng Yueh. *Sun Yat-sen University in Moscow and the Chinese Revolution: A Personal Account*. Lawrence: Center for East Asian Studies, University of Kansas, 1971.

Siao Yu. *Mao Tse-tung and I Were Beggars*. New York: Syracuse University Press, 1959.

Siu, Helen ed. *Furrows, Peasants, Intellectuals, and the State: Stories and Histories from Modern China*. Stanford: Stanford University Press, 1990.

Smedley, Agnes. *The Great Road: The Life and Times of Chu Teh*. New York: Monthly Review Press, 1956.

Smith, Anthony. *Nationalist Movements*. New York: St. Martin's Press, 1976.

Snow, Edgar. *Red Star over China* (1936). New York: Grove Press, 1968 (reprint).

Song Qingling [Song Ching-ling]. *The Struggle for New China*. Beijing: Foreign Languages Press, 1953.

Spence, Jonathan. *The Search for Modern China*. New York and London: W.W. Norton, 1990.

Stalin, J. V. "Talk with Students of the Sun Yat-sen University" (1927,5,13). In *J. V. Stalin: Works*, Vol. 9. Moscow: Foreign Languages Press, 1952–.

———. *Marxism and the National and Colonial Question*. New York: International Publishers, n.d.

———. *On the Opposition (1921–1927)*. Beijing: Foreign Languages Press, 1974.

Stavrianos, Leften S. *Global Rift: The Third World Comes of Age*. New York: Morrow, 1981.

Su Xuelin. *Ersanshi niandai zuojia zuopin* [The Writers of the 1920s and 1930s and Their Works]. Taipei: Guangdong, 1979.

Sun Chengshu. *Dakai dongfang shehui mimi de yaoshi: Yaxiya shengchanfangshi yu dangdai shehuizhuyi* [The Key to Understanding the Oriental Society: The Asiatic Mode of Production and Contemporary Socialism]. Shanghai: Dongfang, 2000.

Sun Pufang and Yao Renjuan. "Tudi geming shiqi zhuming wuzhuang qiyi de zhuyao lingdaoren jianjie" [A Brief Introduction to the Important Leaders of the Well-known Uprisings during the Period of Land Revolution]. *Renwu*, 1985 (4) and (6).

Sun Zhongshan [Sun Yat-sen]. "Zhina baoquan fenge helun" [On the Preservation and Partition of China] (1903). In *Guofu Quanji* [Collected Works of Sun Zhongshan], Vol. 2. Taipei: Zhongguo guomindang zhongyang weiyuanhui, 1988.

———. "Zhongguo wenti de zhen jiejue" [The True Solution to China's Problem] (1904). In *Guofu Quanji*, Vol. 2, 67–74.

———. "Minsheng zhuyi sidagang: minguo yuannian shi'eryue jiuri zai Hangzhou guomin gonghuisuo huanyinghui yanjiang" [The Four Principles of the People's Livelihood: Speech at the Welcome Meeting at the Hangzhou Citizens' Assembly Place on December 9, 1912]. In *Guofu quanji*, Vol. 2, 318–319.

———. "Zai Riben Rihua xueshengtuan huanyinghui de yanshuo" [Speech at the Welcome Meeting of the Japanese–Chinese Student Delegation in Japan] (1913,2.22). In *Sun Zhongshan quanji* [Collected Works of Sun Zhonshan], Vol. 3, 20. Beijing: Zhonghua shuju, 1981–1986.

———. "Zhi Beijing canyiyuan zhongyiyuan dian" [Telegram to the Two Houses of the Parliament in Beijing] (1917,3.9). In *Sun Zhongshan quanji*, Vol. 4, 18.

———. "Nongmin dalianhe" [The Great Alliance of the Peasants] (1924, 8). In *Guofu quanji*, Vol. 2.

———. "Genzhe yao you qi tian" [The Tillers Should Have Land] (1924,8,21). In *Guofu quanji*, Vol. 2, 719–723.

Sun Zhuozhang. "Zhongguo jingji de fenxi" [An Analysis of the Chinese Economy]. In *Zhongguo shehuishi de lunzhan*, Vol. 1.

———. "Zhongguo tudi wenti" [China's Land Problem]. In *Dushu zazhi*, 2(1).

Tai Hsuan-chih. *The Red Spears, 1916–1949*. Ronald Suleski, trans. Ann Arbor: Center for Chinese Studies, University of Michigan,1985.

Tai Yunxing. "Zhou Weijiong." In *Zhonggong dangshi renwu zhuan*, Vol. 6, 234–249, 1982.

Tan Pingshan yanjiu shiliao [Collected Materials on Tan Pingshan]. Guangzhou: Guangdong renmin, 1989.

Tan Yankai. "Guomin zhengfu xianzhuang baogao" [Report About the Current Situation of the National Government], *Zhongguo nongmin* [The Chinese Peasant], nos. 6–7, 1926.

Tan Zheng. "Sanwan gaibian" [The Sanwan Reform]. In *Xinghuo liaoyuan*, Vol. 1, Part 1, 1958.

Tang Jinhai. "Lun Mao Dun wenxue piping de meixue jiazhi" [On the Aesthetic Value of Mao Dun's Literary Critics]. In *Mao Dun zhuanji*, Vol. 2, Part 1.

Tang Yingwei. *Zhongguo xiandai muke shi* [History of Modern Chinese Wood-engraving]. Chongan (Fujian): Zhongguo muke yongping hezuo gongchang, 1944.

Tao Xiaoguang. "Zhuiqiu zhenli zuo zhenren—huainian wode fuqin Tao Xingzhi" [Search for the Truth, Be the Truthful Man: Remembering My Father Tao Xingzhi]. *Wenshi ziliao xuanji*, No. 72, 195–218.

Tao Xingzhi. "Zhonghua jiaoyu gaizao quanguo xiangcun jiaoyu xuanyan-shu" [Declaration of China National Education Reform Society on Rural Education of China] (1926,12,3). In *Tao Xingzhi quanji* [Collected Works of Tao Xingzhi], Vol.1. Changsha: Hunan jiaoyu, 1984.

Tao Xisheng. "Zhongguo shehui zhi shi de fenxi" [A Historical Analysis of the Chinese Society] (1929, Shanghai). Taipei: Quanmin, 1954 (reprint).

———. *Chaoliu yu diandi* [Currents and Drops]. Taipei: Zhuanji wenxue, 1964.

———. "Ji Gu Mengyu xiansheng" [About Gu Mengyu]. *Zhuanji wenxue*, 21(2). 1972.

———. "Guanyu Duxiu de sanduanshi" [Three Stories about Chen Duxiu]. *Zhuanji wenxue*, 30(5). 1977.

———. "Bashi zishu" [My Eighty Years of Life]. *Zhuanji wenxue*, 33(6). 1978.

Tao Zhifu [Qian Junrui]. "Zhongguo nongcun shehui xingzhi yu nongye gaizao wenti" [The Nature of Chinese Rural Society and the Issue of Agricultural Reform]. In *Zhongguo nongcun*, 1(11). 1935,8.

Tawney, R. H. *Land and Labor in China* (1932). Boston: Beacon Press, 1966 (reprint).

Terrill, Ross. *Mao, A Biography*. Stanford: Stanford University Press, 1999.

Thaxton, Ralph. *China Turned Rightside Up: Revolutionary Legitimacy in the Peasant World*. New Haven/London: Yale University Press, 1983.

Thomson, James C. Jr. *While China Faced West: American Reformers in Nationalist China, 1928-1937*. Cambridge: Harvard University Press, 1969.

Trotsky, Leon. *Leon Trotsky on China*. Les Evens and Russel Block, eds. New York: Monad Press, 1976.

Turner, Victor. *The Forest of Symbols, Aspects of Ndembu Ritual*. Ithaca: Cornell University Press, 1967.

Uhalley, Stephen Jr. *Mao Tse-tung, A Critical Biography*. New York: New Viewpoints, 1975.

Wakeman, Frederic, Jr. *The Fall of Imperial China*. New York: The Free Press, 1975.

Wang Chengren and Bai Shengxiang. "Shilun xinhaigeming shiqi zichanjieji gemingpai dui nongmin de fadong he lingdao" [On Bourgois Revolutionaries' Mobilizing and Leading the Peasants during the 1911 Revolution]. *Wuhan daxue xuebao*, 1981(5): 35–44.

Wang Fan-hsi [Wang Fanxi]. *Memoirs of a Chinese Revolutionary*. Gregor Benton,trans. New York: Columbia University Press, 1991.

Wang Jingbo. "Guanyu Zhongguo nongcun wenti yanjiu zhi shishu" [An Experimental Interpretation of the Research on China's Rural Problems]. *Zhongguo nongcun*, 1(10). 1935.

Wang Jingwei. "The Difference Between Communism and Sun Yat-senism." *The China Weekly Review*, 1927, 12, 17.

Wang Lixi. "Zhongguo shehuishi lunzhan xumu" [The Prelude to the Debate on Chinese Social History]. In *Zhongguo shehuishi de lunzhan*, Vol. 1.

Wang Lixi and Lu Jingqing. "Disanban juantouyan" [Preface to the Third Edition] (1931,11,12). In *Zhongguo shehuishi de lunzhan*, Vol. 1, 3rd ed., 1931.

Wang Minzhao. "Yiqie yikao dang he qunzhong—Bayi fangwen He Long jiangjun" [All Depends on the Party and the Masses—An Interview with General He Long on August 1] (1951). In *Huiyi He Long*. Shanghai, 1979.

Wang Shifan. "Xichuan gongzuo baogao" [A Report on Our Work in Xichuan]. In *Xiangcun jianshe shiyan*, Vol. 3. Guangzhou, 1937.

Wang Tongzhao. "Chenchuan" [The Sunken Boat] (1927). In *Wang Tongzhao duanpian xiaoshuo xuan* [Selected Short Stories of Wang Tongzhao]. Beijing: Renmin wenxue, 1957.

———. *Shanyu* [The Mountain Rain] (1933). In *Wang Tongzhao wenji* [Collected Works of Wang Tongzhao]. Vol. 3. Jinan: Shandong renmin, 1980.

Wang Weizhou. "Chuandong youjijun de douzheng" [The Struggle of the Eastern Sichuan Guerrilla Forces]. *Xinghuo liaoyuan*, Vol. 1, Part 2, 933–940.

———. *Wo de huiyi* [My Memoir]. In *Zhonggong dangshi ziliao*, 1982(1).

Wang Xuewen. "Sanshiniandai Shanghai wenhua zhanxian de yixie douzheng qingkuang" [The Struggles within the Cultural Circle in Shanghai in the 1930s]. *Dangshi ziliao congkan* [Materials about the History of the CCP], no. 3. Shanghai: Shanghai renmin, 1980.

Wang Yanan. "Fengjian shehui lun" [On Feudal Society]. In *Zhongguo shehuishi de Lunzhan*, Vol. 1. Shanghai, 1932.

———. Zhongguo banfengjian banzhimindi jingji xingtai yanjiu [A Study of the Semi-feudal and Semi-colonial Economic Formation of China]. Beijing: Renmin, 1957.

Wang Yao. *Lu Xun zuopin lunji* [Colleted Essays about Lu Xun's Works]. Beijing: Renmin wenxue, 1984.

Wang Yichang. "Zhongguo shehuishi duanlun" [A Brief Discussion of Chinese Social History]. In *Zhongguo shehuishi de lunzhan*, Vol. 1.

———. "Zhongguo shehuishi lunshi" [History of the Debate on Chinese Social History]. In *Zhongguo shehuishi de lunzhan*, Vol. 2.

———. "Lun xianjieduan de Zhongguo nongcun jingji yanjiu" [On Current Studies of Chinese Rural Economy]. *Zhongguo nongcun*, 1(7). 1935.

———. "Nongcun jingji tongji yingyou de fangxiang zhuanhuan" [A Necessary Change of Direction in Rural Economic Statistics]. *Yishibao* [Tianjin], no. 48. 1935.

———. "Ping *Guangdong nongcun shengchanguanxi yu shengchanli*" [About *The Production Relations and Production Forces in Rural Guangdong*]. *Zhongguo nongcun*, 1(10). 1935.

———."Guanyu Zhongguo nongcun shengchanli yu shengchanguanxi" [On the Production Forces and Production Relations in Rural China]. *Zhongguo nongcun*, 1(2).

Wang Yilin. "Chen Duxiu and the Trotskyites." *Chinese Law and Government*, Vol. xvii, nos. 1–2 (1984), 68–80.

Wang Yongqing. "Li Jiajun" [Li Jiajun]. In *Sichuan jinxiandai renwu zhuan* [Biographies of Prominent Figures in Modern Sichuan]. Ren Yimin, ed. Chengdu: Sichuansheng shehuikexueyuan, 1985.

Wei Zhen. "'Mari shibian' qinli ji" [My Experience of the May 21, 1927, Incident of Changsha]. In *Wenshi ziliao xuanji*, no. 45, 16–35. Beijing, 1986 (reprint).

Wen Shan. *Xiangcun de huoyan* [The Flame in the Village]. Shanghai: Guanghua, 1930.

Wiens, Thomas B. "Trends in the Late Qing and Republican Rural Economy: Reality or Illusion?" *Republican China*, 18(1), 1992, 63–76.

Wittfogel, Karl. *Oriental Despotism, A Comparative Study of Total Power*. New Haven: Yale University Press, 1957.

Wolf, Arthur, ed. *Religion and Ritual in Chinese Society*. Stanford: Stanford University Press, 1974.

Wolf, Eric. *Peasants*. Englewood Cliffs, N.J.: Prentice-Hall, 1966.

———. *Peasant Wars of the Twentieth Century*. New York: Harper & Row, 1968.

Wong, R. Bin. "Studying Republican China's Economy: What's New and What's Needed." *Republican China*, 18(1), 1992, 77–89.

———. "Chinese Economic History and Development: A Note on the Myers-Huang Exchange." *Journal of Asian Studies*, 51(3), 1992, 600–611.

Wou, Odoric Y. K. and Wang Quanying. "Rural Mobilization in Time of Political Adversity: The Autumn Harvest Uprising in Southern Henan." *Republican China*, 20(1), 1994, 83–126.

Wright, Mary, ed. *China in Revolution: The First Phase 1900–1913*. New Haven and London: Yale University Press, 1968.

Wu Bannong. "Lun 'Dingxian zhuyi'" [On Dingxian-ism] (1934). In Qian Jiaju, ed., *Zhongguo nongcun jingji lunwenji*, 15–22.

Wu Dingbang et al. "Luo Nachuan." In *Zhonggong dangshi renwu zhuan*, Vol. 8, 185–199, 1983.

Wu Tien-wei. "A Review of the Wuhan Debacle: The Kuomintang-Communist Split of 1927." *Journal of Asian Studies*, 29(1), 1969.

Wu Xiangxiang. *Yan Yangchu zhuan* [A Biography of Yan Yangchu]. Taipei: Shibao, 1981.

Wu Zuxiang. "Young Master Gets His Tonics." (1932). Cyril Birch trans. In *Modern Chinese Stories and Novellas 1919–1949*. Joseph S. M. Lau, C. T. Hsia, and Leo Ou-Fan Lee, eds. New York: Columbia University Press, 1981

———. "Yiqianbabai dan" [1800 Piculs] (1933). In *Wu Zuxiang xiaoshuo sanwen xuan* [Selected Stories and Proses of Wu Zuxiang], 74–116. Beijing: Renmin wenxue, 1954.

———. "Tianxia taiping" [The Great Peace Under the Heaven] (1934). In *Wu Zuxiang xiaoshuo sanwen ji,* 117–142. Beijing, 1954.

Wusi shiqi qikan jieshao [Introduction to the Periodicals of the May Fourth Period]. 3 vols. Beijing: Renmin, 1958.

Xia Daohan. "Gu Bai." In *Zhonggong dangshi renwu zhuan*, Vol. 12, 273–292, 1983.

Xia Kangnong. "Yizhu ducao de jiepo" [An Anatomy of a Poisonous Blade of Grass]. *Xinguancha* [Beijing], no.166. 1957,8,1.

Xiandai shiliao [Modern Historical Materials]. Vol.1; 4. Shanghai: Haitian, 1933.

Xiang Peiliang. "Lun Guduzhe" [On the Loner]. In *Liushinianlai Lu Xun yanjiu lunwenxuan*, Vol.1.

Xiangcun jianshe shiyan [Experiments of Rural Reconstruction]. 3 vols. Zhang Yuanshan and Xu Shilian, eds. Shanghai: Zhonghua, 1936.

Xiao Hua. "Xingguo geming douzheng he shaogong guoji shi" [The Revolutionary Struggles in Xingguo and the Division of the Young Communist International]. In *Huiyi Zhongyang suqu,* 1986.

Xie Bingying. *Nubing zizhuan* [An Autobiography of a Female Soldier] (1936). Shanghai: Chenguang, 1949 (reprint).

Xie Juezai. "Liuyang yuxian" [Coming Across Danger in Liuyang]. In *Xinghuo liaoyuan*, Vol. 1, Part 1. Beijing, 1958.

Xu Binru. "Huiyi Wuxi qiushou baodong" [My Memory of the Autumn Harvest Uprising in Wuxi]. *Zhonggong dangshi ziliao*, 1980(6):140–146. Beijing: Zhonggong dangshi ziliao.

Xu Xiangqian. "Benxiang Hailufeng" [Marching toward Hailufeng]. *Xinghuo liaoyuan*, Vol.1, Part 1. Beijing, 1958.

———. *Lishi de huigu* [Historical Retrospections]. 3 vols. Beijing: Jiefangjun, 1985.

Xuan Lu [Shen Dingyi]. "Nongjia" [The Peasant Household]. *Xingqi pinglun*, 1920,1,18.

———. "Duanping" [A Brief Comment]. *Xingqi pinglun*, 1920,1,18.

Xue Muqiao. "Zenyang yanjiu Zhongguo nongcun jingji" [How Do We Study the Rural Economy of China]. *Zhongguo nongcun*, 1(1). 1934.

———. "Yanjiu Zhongguo nongcun jingji de fangfa wenti—dafu Wang Yichang, Wang Yuquan, Zhang Zhicheng zhuxiansheng" [The Method of Studying Chinese Rural Economy: My Reply to Wang Yichang, Wang Yuquan and Zhang Zhicheng]. *Zhongguo nongcun*, 1(11). 1935.

Xu Zhiying and Ni Tingting. "Zhongguo nongcun de mianying: Ershi niandai xiangtu wenxue guankui" [The Face and Shadow of the Chinese Village: Some Observations about the Regional Literature of the 1920s]. *Wenxue pinglun* [Beijing], 1984(5): 72–90.

Yan Huaijin. "Yan Pu shengping" [The Life of Yan Pu]. In *Zhonggong dangshi renwu zhuan,* Vol. 31, 5–24. Xian, 1987.

Yan Hongyan. "Huiyi Shan-Gan gaoyuan zaoqi de geming wuzhuang douzheng" [Early Revolutionary Military Struggles of the Shanxi-Gansu Plateau]. *Xinghuo liaoyuan,* Vol. 2.

Yan Lingfeng. "Zai 'zhanchang' shang suo fajian de 'xingshizourou'" [A "Walking Corpse" Found in the "Battlefield"]. In *Zhongguo shehuishi de lunzhan,* Vol. 1.

———. "Guanyu Ren Shu, Zhu Xinfan ji qita" [About Ren Shu, Zhu Xinfan and other Matters]. In *Zhongguo shehuishi de lunzhan,* Vol. 3.

———. *Zhongguo jingji wenti yanjiu* [A Study of the Chinese Economy]. Shanghai: Xinshengming, 1931.

Yan Yangchu [James, Yen]. "Pingmin jiaoyu xin yundong" [The New Mass Education Movement] (1922,12). In *Yan Yangchu quanji* [Collected Works of Yan Yangchu], Vol.1, 31-46. Changsha: Hunan jiaoyu, 1989.

———. "Pingmin jiaoyu" [Mass Education] (1923). In *Yan Yangchu quanji,* Vol. 1, 47–51.

———. "Pingmin jiaoyu yundong" [The Mass Education Movement] (1924,9). In *Yan Yangchu quanji,* Vol. 1, 52–62.

———. "Zhi Tao Xingzhi deng" [Letter to Tao Xingzhi and Others] (1924). In *Yan Yangchu quanji,* Vol. 3, 8–9, 1992.

———. "Zhi Wang Zhendong deng" [Letter to Wang Zhendong and Others](1925,1,30). In *Yan Yangchu quanji,* Vol. 3,13.

———. "Zhi Ding Shujing" [Letter to Ding Shujing] (1926,7,12). In *Yan Yangchu quanji,* Vol. 3.

———. "Pingmin jiaoyu yundongshu" [Techniques of Mass Education Movement] (1926,9,14). In *Yan Yangchu quanji,* Vol. 1, 75–80.

———. "Guanyu pingmin jiaoyu jingshen de jianghua" (1926,11,31). In *Yan Yangchu quanji,* Vol. 1, 81–89.

———. "Zhi Cai Tinggan" [Letter To Cai Tinggan] (1926,12,24). In *Yan Yangchu quanji,* Vol. 3.

———. "Pingmin jiaoyu de zhenyi" [The True Meaning of Mass Education] (1927). In *Yan Yangchu quanji,* Vol. 1, 104–113.

———. "Pingmin jiaoyu gailun" [Introduction to Mass Education] (1928,4). In *Yan Yangchu quanji,* Vol. 1, 121–133.

———. "You wenhua de Zhongguo xin nongmin" [China's New Educated Peasants] (1929). In *Yan Yangchu quanji*, Vol. 1, 141–160.

———. "Zai Dingxian zhanlanhui shang de yanshuo" [Speech at the Dingxian Exhibition] (1930). In *Yan Yangchu quanji*, Vol. 1, 172–173.

———. "Zhi Cao Yanshen" [To Cao Yanshen] (1931,5,19). In *Yan Yangchu quanji*, Vol. 3.

———. "Zai zhouhui shang de jianghua" [Speech to the Weekly Meeting] (1931,12). In *Yan Yangchu quanji*, Vol. 1, 181–182.

———. "Zai huanying laibin huishang de jianghua" [Speech at the Welcome Meeting for Our Guests] (1932,4,16). In *Yan Yangchu quanji*, Vol. 1, 219–223.

———. "Zhi J. A. Jinsboli" [Letter to John Kingsbury] (1932,5,20). In *Yan Yangchu quanji*, Vol. 3, 282–283.

———. "Zhonghua pingmin jiaoyu cujinhui Dingxian gongzuo dagai" [A Summary of the Work of the Chinese Association for Promoting Mass Education in Dingxian] (1933,7). In *Yan Yangchu quanji*, Vol. 1, 245–249.

———. "Nongcun yundong de shiming" [The Mission of the Rural Movement] (1934,10). In *Yan Yangchu quanji*, Vol. 1, 293–304.

———. "Zhonghua pingmin jiaoyu cujinhui Dingxian shiyan gongzuo baogao" [Report on the Work of the Chinese Association for Promoting Mass Education in Dingxian] (1934,10). In *Yan Yangchu quanji*, Vol. 1, 307–347.

———. "Zhi E. Xidengxitelike" [Letter to Edgar Sydenstricker] (1934,11,23). In *Yan Yangchu quanji*, Vol. 3.

———. "Nongcun jianshe yaoyi" [Main Ideas of Rural Reconstruction] (1938,4). In *Yan Yangchu quanji*, Vol. 2, 38–47.

———. "Zhongguo pingmin jiaoyu yundong de zongjie" [A Summary of the Mass Education Movement of China] (1945). In *Yan Yangchu quanji*, Vol. 2.

———. "Zhi M. Fei'erde" [Letter to Marshall Field] (1945,4,28). In *Yan Yangchu quanji*, Vol. 3.

———. "Pingmin jiaoyu yundong de huigu yu qianzhan" [Retrospects and Prospects of the Mass Education Movement] (1946). In *Yan Yangchu quanji*, Vol. 2.

———. "Zai Chengdu xiaoyou huanyinghui shang de jianghua" [Speech at the Welcome Meeting of My Former Schoolmates in Chengdu] (1985,9,18). In *Yan Yangchu quanji*, Vol. 2.

Yang Hualu and Ke Aizhen. "Fang Zhimin." In *Zhonggong dangshi renwu zhuan*, Vol. 39.

Yang Lisan. "Qiushou qiyi diyituan" [The First Regiment in The Autumn Harvest Uprising]. In *Xinghuo liaoyuan*, Vol. 1, Part 1. Beijing, 1958.

Yang, Martin. *A Chinese Village: Taitou, Shantung Province*. New York: Columbia University Press, 1945.

Yang Xiaochu. "Weihua qiyi pianduan" [Some Episodes of the Weihua Rebellion]. *Xinghuo liaoyuan*, Vol. 1, Part 2.

Yang Zhijie and Peng Yunqian. "Lun Zhao Shuli chuangzuo de fanfengjian zhuti" [The Anti-feudal Themes in Zhao Shuli's Writings]. *Wenxue pinglun*, 1981(3): 20–30.

Ye Fu. *Muke shouce* [A Handbook of Wood-engraving]. Shanghai: Wenhua gongyingshe, 1948.

Ye Jianying. "Dageming shibai yu Guangzhou qiyi" [The Failure of the Great Revolution and the Guangzhou Uprising]. In *Xinghuo liaoyuan*, Vol. 1, Part 1. Beijing, 1958.

Ye Shengtao. "Bei'ai de zhongzai" [The Sorrowful Heavy Burden]. In *Ye Shengtao Wenji* [Collected Works of Ye Shengtao], Vol.1. Beijing, Renmin wenxue, 1958.

———. "Chizhe de jiao" [The Bare Foot] (1927). In *Ye Shengtao wenji*, Vol. 2.

———. "Duoshoule sanwudou" [A Year of Good Harvest] (1933). In *Ye Shengtao wenji*, Vol. 2.

Ye Zi. "Fengshou" [The Harvest] (1933). In *Ye Zi xuanji* [Selected Works of Ye Zi], 1–46. Beijing: Renmin wenxue, 1959.

———. "Xiangdao" [Guide] (1933). In *Ye Zi xuanji*.

———. "*Fengshou* zixu" [Preface to *The Harvest*]. In *Ye Zi yanjiu ziliao* [Materials about Ye Zi]. Ye Xuefen, ed. Changsha: Hunan renmin, 1985.

———. "*Fengshou* Xu" [Preface to *The Harvest*] (1935,1,16). In *Ye Zi xuanji*.

Yen, James, Y. C [Yan Yangchu]. *The Ting Hsien Experiment* (1934). Reissued in 1972 by the International Institute of Rural Reconstruction, Silang, Cavite, Philippines.

Yi Sheng. "Disanyang shijie de chuangzao—women suo yingdang huanying de Lu Xun" [The Creation of the Third Kind of World—The Lu Xun We Should Welcome] (1927,2). In *Liushinianlai Lu Xun yanjiu lunwenxuan*, Vol. 1.

Yip Ka-che. "Nationalism and Revolution: The Nature and Causes of Student Activism in the 1920s." In F. Gilbert Chan and Thomas H. Etzold, eds., *China in the 1920s: Nationalism and Revolution*, 94–107. New York: New Viewpoints, 1976.

Young Arthur N. *China's Nation-building Effort, 1927–1937, The Financial and Economic Record*. Stanford: Hoover Institution Press, 1971.

Yu Bida. "Nongren de changchu he duanchu" [The Strong and Weak Points of the Peasants]. *Nongmin*, 2(21), 1926, 10, 20.

Yu Dafu. "Xiangcun li de jieji" [The Classes in the Villages] (1927,9,14). In *Yu Dafu Wenji* [Collected Works of Yu Dafu], Vol. 8, 41–42. Hong Kong: Salian/Guangzhou:Huacheng, 1982.

———. "Nongmin wenyi de tichang" [My Advocation of the Peasant Literature]. In *Yu Dafu Wenji*, Vol. 5, 280–282.

———. "Nongmin wenyi de shizhi" [The Nature of the Peasant Literature]. In *Yu Dafu wenji*,Vol. 5, 283–290.

Yu Jinlong. "Paihu douzheng yijiao" [An Episode of the Struggle in Honghu Area]. *Xinghuo liaoyuan*, Vol. 1, Part 2. Beijing, 1958.

Yu Lin. "Zhongguo nongcun shehui xingzhi wenda" [Questions and Answers about the Nature of Chinese Rural Society]. *Zhongguo nongcun*, 1(12). 1935.

Yu Yingshi. *Qian Mu yu Zhongguo wenhua* [Qian Mu and the Chinese Culture]. Shanghai: Shanghai yuandong, 1994.

Yuan Bangjian. "Ruan Xiaoxian." In *Zhonggong dangshi renwu zhuan*, Vol. 1, 290–346. Xian, 1980.

Yuan Liangjun. *Lu Xun yanjiushi* [A History of Lu Xun Studies]. 2 vols. Xian: Shanxi renmin, 1986.

Yuan Renyuan. "Shimen nanxiang de qiyi" [The Rebellion of Nanxiang of Shimen]. *Xinghuo liaoyuan*, Vol. 1, Part 2.

Yun Daiying. "Nongcun yundong" [Rural Movements] (1924,6). In *Yun Daiying wenji* [Collected Works of Yun Daiying]. Vol. 1, 559–561. Beijing: Renmin, 1984.

Zarrow, Peter. *Anarchism and Chinese Political Culture*. New York: Columbia University Press, 1990.

Zeng Bingrong. "Lijin jianxian weiwu buqu—Zhou Qijian zhuanlue" [Biography of Zhou Qijian]. In *Buqu de gongchandangren*, Vol. 2, 63–86. Beijing, 1981.

Zhang Dingcheng. "Zhongguo gongchandang chuangjian Minxi geming genjudi" [The CCP's Creation of the Western Fujian Revolutionary Base Area]. In *Fujian dangshi ziliao*, no.1. 1983.

Zhang Dingcheng, Deng Zihui, and Tan Zhenlin. "Minxi sannian youji zhanzheng" [The Three-year Guerilla War in Western Fujian]. In *Xinghuo liaoyuan*, Vol. 4.

Zhang Dingcheng zhuan bianxiezu [Group for Compiling Zhang Dingcheng's Biography]. "Zhang Dingcheng." In *Zhonggong dangshi renwu zhuan*, Vol. 36, 1–61. Xian, 1988.

Zhang Dongsun. "Women weishemo jiang shehuizhuyi" [Why Do We Speak for Socialism]. *Jiefang yu gaizao*, 1(7). 1919,12,1.

———. "You neidi luxing er de zhi you yi jiaoxun" [One more Lesson Learned from my Trip to the Interior]. *Shishi xinbao* [The China Times], 1920,11,6.

———. "Xianzai yu jianglai" [The Present and the Future]. *Gaizao*, 3(4), 1920,11.

———. "Dajia xu qieji Luosu xiansheng gei women de zhonggao" [We Should Firmly Remember Mr. Russell's Sincere Advice]. *Xinqingnian*, 8(4), 1920,12.

———. "Da Gao Jiansi shu" [My Reply to Gao Jiansi]. *Xinqingnian*, 8(4), 1920,12.

———. "Changqi de rennai" [Long-term Endurance]. *Xinqingnian*, 8(4), 1920,12.

———. "Zai da Songhua xiong" [One more Reply to Songhua]. *Xinqingnian*, 8(4), 1920,12.

———. "Tamen yu women" [They and We]. *Xinqingnian*, 8(4), 1920,12.

———. "Zhi Duxiu de xin" [A Letter to Chen Duxiu]. *Xinqingnian*, 8(4), 1920,12.

Zhang Guotao. "Zhishi jieji zai zhengzhi shang de diwei ji zeren" [The Political Role and Responsibilities of the Intellectuals]. *Xiangdao zhoubao*, no. 12. 1922,12,6.

———. *The Rise of the Chinese Communist Party: 1921–1927*. Vol. 1. Lawrence: University Press of Kansas, 1971.

Zhang Hexuan. "Wo suo zhidao de Bie Tingfang" [Bie Tingfang As I Know Him]. *Wenshi ziliao xuanji*, no. 47, 31–65. Beijing, 1986 (reprint).

Zhang Ji. "Zhang Ji jun you Lundun laihan" [A Letter from Zhang Ji in London]. *Hengbao*, no. 4.

Zhang Jiafu. "Genshen yishi (1)" [Memoir (1)]. *Zhonggong dangshi ziliao*, 1980(6), 74–139. Beijing: Zhonggong dangshi ziliao.

Zhang Lin. "Xu Xiangqian." In *Zhanggong dangshi renwu zhuan*, Vol. 56, Xian, 1996.

Zhang Pengyuan [Chang Peng-yuan]. "Qingmo minchu de zhishifenzi (1898–1921)" [The Intellectuals of the Late Qing and Early Republic Period (1898–1921)]. In Li Enhan, Zhang Pengyuan et al, *Jindai Zhongguo—zhishifenzi yu ziqiang yundong* [Modern China: The Intellectuals and the Self-strengthening Movement]. Taipei: Shihuo, 1972.

Zhang Tiezheng. "Hebei Sanhexian nongcun shehui gaikuang" [The General Situation of the Rural Society of Sanhe County, Hebei Province] (1934). In Qian Jiaju, ed., *Zhongguo nongcun jingji lunwenji*, 475–487.

Zhang Wentao. *Heiqi zhi meng: Wuzhengfu zhuyi zai Zhongguo* [The Dream of the Black Flag: Anarchism in China]. Nanchang: Jiangxi renmin, 1987.

Zhang Wentian. *Zhongguo geming jiben wenti* [The Fundamental Problems of the Chinese Revolution] (1933). Part was reprinted as an appendix to his *Zhongguo xiandai geming yundong shi* [A History of Modern Chinese Revolutionary Movement]. Shanghai: Shenghuo Press, 1938; Beijing: Zhongguo renmin daxue, 1987 (reprint).

Zhang Xin. "Elite Activism in the Periphery: The Case of Southwest Henan." *Republican China,* 19(2), 1994, 67–103.

Zhang Yunyi. "Baise qiyi yu hongqijun de jianli" [The Baise Uprising and the Creation of the Seventh Red Army]. In *Xinghuo liaoyuan,* Vol. 1, Part 2.

Zhao Tongxin. "Wanxi guaijie Bie Tingfang" [The Weird Hero of Wanxi: Bie Tingfang]. *Zhongwai zazhi,* Vol. 28, no. 5, 1980.

Zheng Chaolin. *An Oppositionist for Life: Memoirs of the Chinese Revolutionary Zheng Chaolin.* Gregor Benton, trans. Atlantic Highlands, N.J.: Humanities Press, 1997.

———. "Chen Duxiu and the Trotskyists." In Gregor Benton, *China's Urban Revolutionaries, Explorations in the History of Chinese Trotskyism, 1921–1952.*

Zheng Dahua. *Liang Shuming yu xiandai xinruxue* [Liang Shuming and Modern New-Confucianism]. Taipei: Wenjin Press, 1993.

Zheng Shixing [Cheng Shih-hsing]. *Zhongguo xiandai jiaoyu shi* [A History of Modern Chinese Education]. Taipei: Sanmin shuju, 1981.

Zheng Tianting. "Zhuiji 1928 nian Liang xiansheng zuo xiangzhi shijiang" [Memory of Liang Shuming's 10 Lectures on Village Government in 1928]. In *Liang Shuming xiansheng jinian wenji* [Commemorating Liang Shuming: Collected Essays], 24–26. Beijing: Zhongguo gongren, 1993.

Zheng Weisan. "Hongse de Huang'an" [The Red Huang'an]. In *Xinghuo liaoyuan,* Vol. 1, Part 2.

Zheng Xuejia. *Shehuishi lunzhan de qiyin he neirong* [The Origins and Content of the Debate on Social History]. Taipei: Zhonghua zazhishe, 1965.

Zhonggong dangshi renwu zhuan [Biographies of Prominent Figures in the History of the CCP]. Vol. 1-60. Hu Hua, ed. Xian: Shaanxi renmin, 1980–1996.

Zhonggong zhongyang wenjian xuanji [Selected Documents of the CCP Central Committee]. 15 vols. Beijing: Zhongyang dangxiao, 1990–.

Zhongguo jindaishi zhengminglu [Controversies About Modern Chinese History]. Nanjing: Jiangsu jiaoyu, 1987.

Zhongguo nongcun jingji ziliao [Collected Materials on Chinese Rural Economy]. 2 vols. Feng Hefa, ed. First published in 1933. Taipei: Huashi, 1978 (reprint).

Zhongguo nongcun jingji ziliao xubian [Supplement to Collected Materials on Chinese Rural Economy]. 2 vols. Feng Hefa, ed. First published in 1935. Taipei: Huashi, 1978 (reprint).

Zhongguo nongcun shehui xingzhi lunzhan [The Debate on the Nature of Chinese Rural Society]. Zhongguo nongcun jingji yanjiuhui [Association of Chinese Rural Economy Studies], ed. Shanghai: Xinzhi, 1936.

Zhongguo shehuishi de lunzhan [The Debate on the Social History of China]. Wang Lixi and Lu Jingqing, eds. 4 vols. Shanghai: Shengzhou guoguang, 1931–1933.

Zhongguo xinxing banhua wushinian xuanji [Selected Modern Chinese Prints of the Last Five Decades]. Vol.1: 1931–1949. Shanghai: Shanghai renmin meishu, 1981.

Zhongguo xunbao [China News]. "Zhongguo qingzhong lun" [On the Urgent and Non-urgent Issues of China], no. 30,1900,11, 26.

Zhou Bin. "Zhongguo nongcun jingji xingzhi wenti de taolun—yige laowenti de quanshi" [Discussions on the Issue of the Nature of Chinese Rural Economy—The Interpretation of an Old Question]. *Zhongguo nongcun*, 1(11). 1935.

Zhou Cantian. "Zeng Tianyu lieshi—Ji lieshi Zeng Tianyu tongzhi de shenghuo pianduan" [The Martyr Zeng Tianyu—Some Episodes in his Life]. In *Hongse fengbao* [The Red Tempest]. Vol. 2. Nanchang: Jiangxi renmin, 1958.

Zhou Chengzhong and Zhang Rixin. "Hu Hai." In *Zhonggong dangshi renwuzhuan*, Vol. 19, 122–141. Xian, 1985.

Zhou Daming. "Chongfang Fenghuangcun" [Revisiting the Fenghuang Village]. *Dushu*, 1998(9), 68–70.

Zhou Enlai. "Jianjue suqing dangnei yiqie fei wuchanjieji de yishi" [Resolutely Eliminating the Non-proletarian Consciousness Within Our Party] (1928,11,11). In *Zhou Enlai xuanji* [Selected Works of Zhou Enlai], Vol.1, 8–9. Beijing: Renmin, 1980.

———. "Zhonggong zhongyang gei Hongsijun qianwei de zhishi" [A Directive to the Front Committee of the Fourth Red Army from the Central Committee of the Communist Party] (1929,9,28). In *Zhou Enlai xuanji*, Vol. 1.

———. "Wo yao shuo de hua" [What I Want to Say] (1941,1,16). In *Liushinianlai Lu Xun yanjiu lunwen xuan*, Vol. 1.

———. "Guanyu yijiuersi zhi yijiuerliu nian dang dui Guomindang de guanxi" [On our Relations with the Nationalist Party from 1924 to 1926] (1943). In *Zhou Enlai xuanji*, 1980.

————. "Zenyang zuo yige haode lingdaozhe" [How to be a Good Leader] (1943,4,22). In *Zhou Enlai xuanji*, Vol. 1.

————. "Guanyu dang de liuda de yanjiu" [A Study of the Sixth National Congress of the CCP] (1944,3). In *Zhou Enlai xuanji*, Vol. 1.

————. "Xuexi Mao Zedong" [Learn from Mao Zedong] (1949,5,7). In *Zhou Enlai xuanji*, Vol. 1.

————. "Zai Zhonghua quanguo wenyi gongzuozhe daibiao dahui shang de zhengzhi baogao" [Political Report to the National Conference of the Delegates of Literary and Art Workers of China] (1949,7,6). In *Zhou Enlai xuanji*, Vol. 1.

Zhou Fohai. "Shengshuai yuejin hua cangsang" [Memoir] (1942). In *Chen Gongbo & Zhou Fohai huiyilu hebian* [Memoirs of Chen Gongbo & Zhou Fohai]. Hong Kong: Chunqiu, 1967.

Zhou Shizhao. "Xiangjiang de nuhou" [The Roar of the Xiang River]. In *Guanghui de wusi* [The Glorious May Fourth Movement]. Beijing: Zhongguo qingnian, 1959.

Zhu Xinfan. "Guanyu Zhongguo shehui zhi fengjianxing de taolun" [Discussions About the Feudal Nature of the Chinese Society]. In *Zhongguo shehuishi de lunzhan*, Vol. 1.

Zhuang Kongshao. "Cong Jinyi tan Lin Yaohua jiaoshou" [*The Golden Wing* and Professor Lin Yaohua]. *Dushu*, 1984(1),123–131.

Zhuang Tian. *Qiongdao fengyan* [Warfare on Hainan Island]. Guangzhou: Guangdong renmin, 1979.

Zou Rong. *Gemingjun* [The Revolutionary Army] (1903). In *Xinhaigeming qian shinianjian shilun xuanji*, 1(2), 649–677.

Index

www.ingramcontent.com/pod-product-compliance
Lightning Source LLC
Chambersburg PA
CBHW020342270326
41926CB00007B/284